T0344245

MODAL LOGIC FOR OPEN MINDS

CSLI Lecture Notes Number 199

MODAL LOGIC
——FOR——
OPEN MINDS

JOHAN VAN BENTHEM

CSLI
PUBLICATIONS
Center for the Study of
Language and Information
Stanford, California

Copyright © 2010
CSLI Publications
Center for the Study of Language and Information
Leland Stanford Junior University
Printed in the United States
14 13 12 11 10   1 2 3 4 5

Library of Congress Cataloging-in-Publication Data
Benthem, J. F. A. K. van, 1949–
 Modal logic for open minds / written by Johan van Benthem.

 p. cm. – (CSLI studies in computational linguistics)

 Includes bibliographical references and index (p.).

 ISBN 978-1-57586-599-7 (cloth : alk. paper)
 ISBN 978-1-57586-598-X (pbk. : alk. paper)

 1. Modality (Logic)   I. Title. II. Series.

 BC199.M6B465 2010
 160–dc22

                                                  2009044686
                        CIP

∞ The acid-free paper used in this book meets the minimum requirements
of the American National Standard for Information Sciences—Permanence
 of Paper for Printed Library Materials, ANSI Z39.48-1984.

CSLI was founded in 1983 by researchers from Stanford University, SRI
 International, and Xerox PARC to further the research and development of
integrated theories of language, information, and computation. CSLI headquarters
 and CSLI Publications are located on the campus of Stanford University.

CSLI Publications reports new developments in the study of language,
information, and computation. Please visit our web site at
http://cslipublications.stanford.edu/
for comments on this and other titles, as well as for changes
and corrections by the author and publisher.

Contents

Preface

Modal logic was born in the early part of the 20th century as a branch of logic applied to the analysis of philosophical notions and issues. While it still retains a bit of this grandeur, today, modal logic sits at a cross-roads of many academic disciplines, and thus, it provides a unique vantage point for students with broad interdisciplinary interests. These notes are the accumulated material for a course taught for many years at Stanford to students in philosophy, symbolic systems, linguistics, computer science, and other fields. The purpose is to give them a modern introduction to modal logic, beyond lingering conceptions dating back to the distant past – and topics include both technical perspectives, and a wide range of applications showing the current range of the field. To check if the picture in these notes is representative, the reader may consult the 2006 *Handbook of Modal Logic*, Elsevier, Amsterdam, co-edited with my colleagues Patrick Blackburn and Frank Wolter, Elsevier Science Publications, Amsterdam. For philosophers, it may also be of interest to check with my 1988 lecture notes *Manual of Intensional Logic*, CSLI Publications, Stanford, which then represented my ideal of a modern introduction to the field. Some topics have panned out, but others have proved remarkably wide off the mark.

Part I is about basic techniques, Part II gives a first round of theory consolidating these. Part III then tells the story of a wide spectrum of modern applications, many of them about the study of agency, and Part IV is about theoretical issues again, arising out of these. Finally, there is a coda on modal perspectives in the heartland of classical logic itself. Working through this material will give you a modern view that enables you to understand many strands in current research, and maybe even participate in the enterprise, given the (Heaven knows) many open problems in the field today, far beyond the old "capitalism" of studying a zoo of modal logics like "K", "T", "$S4$", "$S5$" that once ruled.

There are excellent introductions to modal logic today, of which P. Blackburn, M. de Rijke & Y. Venema, 2000, *Modal Logic*, Cambridge University Press, Cambridge, will often be cited in this book. In addition, there are web resources like `http://www.aiml.net/`, as well as many relevant entries in the Stanford Encyclopedia of Philosophy (`http://plato.stanford.edu/`).

Still, I felt there was room for something new: a less technical, but still substantial broad text at an earlier level, that initiates a larger student audience to the intellectual excitement of the field of modal logic as a whole, while training them in basic modern techniques that should allow them to see further than the generations before them.

How to use these notes: theme selection

This book is intended as an advanced undergraduate/beginning graduate course on Modal Logic. Each short chapter in these notes corresponds roughly to 1 $^1/_2$ hour class meeting, supported by a section. A typical course of mine would cover, after the introduction, most of the "mechanics" of the field: basic themes and theory (some 8 topics from Parts I and II), followed by a selection of some 6 current applications from Part III (knowledge and dynamics, but also time and space, were the usual favorites, for their concreteness). With some recap sessions, this came to 9 weeks in a typical Stanford spring quarter.

But as I kept on writing, more and more things crept in. Therefore the book can be used in other ways as well. For instance, after a brief recap of Part I, Part III could be excellent primary reading material for a graduate course on Philosophical Logic, especially, since many of its chapters are largely self-contained. Parts II and IV would also make good secondary material for a course on Metatheory of Logic. And finally, the whole text again could be used by researchers in areas where modal logic is applied these days (such as agent systems, artificial intelligence, or game theory) to learn more of what makes it tick.

Finally, it is a pleasure to acknowledge all the help that I have had. Eric Pacuit wrote extensive reader's notes that transformed the text. Audrey Yap and Tomohiro Hoshi went through the text with their students, and provided valuable feedback and suggestions. I also received occasional comments from many others, including Fenrong Liu, Darko Sarenac, and Urszula Wybraniec-Skardowska. Then there was the proof-reading team of Viktoria Denisova, Nina Gierasimczuk, Lena Kurzen, Fenrong Liu, Minghui Ma, Ştefan Minică and Junhua Yu.

Throughout the stages of the production process, Fernando Velázquez-Quesada was responsible for making this book happen at all. With all this said, it remains to thank my Stanford students in this course for all the good times we have had over the years.

Johan van Benthem, Amsterdam & Stanford.

1

A whirlwind history, and changes in perspective

Some truths seem merely "contingent", such as the fact what clothes you are wearing today: this could easily have been otherwise. But other truths seem "necessary", such as the fact that, like it or not, you are not someone else. Modal notions of necessity, possibility, and contingency were standard fare in traditional logic up to the 19th century, and reasoning with them was considered a core part of the discipline. All these notions went out the door in the work of the founding fathers of modern logic, like Boole and Frege. In particular, in his famous little book *Begriffsschrift* from 1879, often taken to be the founding document of modern logic, Frege has a mysterious passage where he seems to be ticking off a list of things that are irrelevant to logic, and one of them is modality. According to that passage, saying that some proposition is necessarily true just means that it is true, plus some autobiographical information about how strongly you believe in it. That list was Kant's Table of Categories[1], and what happened was that modern logic just kept "extensional" notions like negation and quantification, while dropping "intensional" ones like modality. The result are the familiar logical systems like propositional and predicate logic, which describe properties and relations of objects in fixed situations, represented by models. This historical restriction of the agenda and core tools has proved immensely beneficial, especially in the analysis of the foundations of mathematics, whose Golden Age was in the 1930s with classical results on provability, completeness, computability, and definability by Hilbert, Post, Gödel, Tarski, Turing, and many others. The millennium issue *TIME 2000* placed Gödel, Turing, and Wittgenstein among the twenty most influ-

---

[1] Frege does not bother to say this. The habit of citing sources and crediting other authors is much more recent than you might think!

1

ential intellectuals of the 20th century, an incredible harvest for a small discipline like logic. This book presupposes that readers know the attractions and power of this approach, including the notions of logical syntax, semantics, proof, and meta-theory of formal systems.

Even so, while extensional logics might be adequate for analyzing mathematical proof and truth in an eternal realm of abstraction, modality made a fast come-back. Soon philosophers started using modern logic to deal with patterns of reasoning as used by real agents, expressed in natural language: the noisy, diverse, and fascinating medium which is the trademark of mankind on this planet. And then, one finds that there is a host of notions of a "modal" character going far beyond mere truth: necessity, knowledge, belief, obligation, temporal change, action, and so on. Indeed, it is hard to think of any use of language which is purely informative: every sentence we utter resonates in a web of communication, expectations, goals, and emotions. Modal logic as we know it today tries to analyze this structure with techniques taken from the mathematical turn in modern logic. Incidentally, Frege had nothing against this move per se. In a famous analogy, he compared a formal language to a *microscope*: very precise, but limited in its realm of application, while natural language was more like the human *eye*: less precise, but universal in its perceptive sweep.[2]

What follows here is a lightning history. For details and bibliographical references, we refer the reader to four sources. On the philosophy connection, see Roberta Ballarin's entry on modal logic in the *Stanford Encyclopedia of Philosophy* (Ballarin, 2008) plus the chapter "Logic in Philosophy" by J. van Benthem in Jacquette (2007). Van Benthem's *Manual of Intensional Logic* (van Benthem, 1988a) extends the canvas to linguistics and computer science, while the editorial introduction to the 2006 *Handbook of Modal Logic* (Blackburn et al., 2006) includes interfaces with all fields in play today.

For a start, soon after Frege and Russell, modal logic made its come-back through a study of the notion of *strict implication* $A \Rightarrow B$ (C. I. Lewis). This strengthens the usual propositional implication $A \to B$, which amounts to a mere truth-functional link $\neg(A \wedge \neg B)$ between the antecedent and the consequent, to the stronger modal connection $\neg\Diamond(A \wedge \neg B)$: it is *impossible* for A to be true, and yet have B false. Modalities per se were then studied by Carnap, Kanger, Kripke, and

---

[2]Steltzner (1996) explains how the major employer in Frege's Jena was Zeiss Optics, with its visionary leader Carl Zeiss and Ernst Abbe, and how Frege was supported all of his life through anonymous donations from this source. Modern logic owes a lot to enlightened industrialists who wanted to give back to society.

many subsequent authors, explaining a necessity statement $\Box\varphi$ as saying that φ holds throughout some relevant range of situations. This *multiple reference* view takes a modal necessity operator $\Box$ as a universal quantifier $\forall$, and the possibility operator $\Diamond\varphi$ as an existential quantifier $\exists$, both ranging over the relevant "worlds", points in time, situations, or whatever relevant semantic entity, where φ is true. But there are alternatives. As early as the 1930s, Gödel interpreted necessity $\Box\varphi$ as "mathematical provability" of φ (an $\exists$-type account!), while Tarski interpreted modal formulas as describing subsets in topological spaces, with $\Box\varphi$ standing for the topological interior of the set defined by φ.[3] These lecture notes will mainly take the now dominant universal range view, but we will briefly discuss alternatives in the appropriate places. Maintaining some bio-diversity of approaches is a good survival strategy for a field. But whatever view we take, it will be clear that modal logic thrives on co-existence with standard logical systems.

Another source of diversity are the many different technical approaches in the field. These lecture notes will cover both the traditional deductive (proof-theoretic) and semantic (model-theoretic) styles, with one excursion to algebraic methods, an important topic that we had to forego. But on the whole, we will take the viewpoint of "possible worlds semantics", though resolutely cleansed from its outdated metaphysical interpretations. We will also introduce some new themes beyond the standard catechism, however: in particular, some awareness of expressive power and invariance, and of the computational complexity of modal languages. These further perspectives greatly enrich one's view of what a modal logic – and indeed any logical system – actually is.

In terms of its natural habitat, modal logic was the main technical vehicle for philosophical logic since the 1950s, and its practitioners like Prior, Kripke, Hintikka, Lewis, or Stalnaker produced a series of beautiful systems, and associated notions and issues that became influential in philosophy, setting the agenda for debates in metaphysics, epistemology, and other fields. This is the period when labels like "modal logic", "epistemic logic", "doxastic logic", "deontic logic", "temporal logic", etcetera, were coined, which still form a geography that is widely used, witness many chapters in the *Handbook of Philosophical Logic* (Gabbay and Günthner, 1983-1989). In the 1970s, this philosophical phase was consolidated into a beautiful mathematical theory by authors like Blok, Fine, Gabbay, Goldblatt, Segerberg, and Thomason. But simultaneously, modal logic crossed over to linguistics, when "Montague seman-

---

[3] As we shall see later, this is a more complex semantic $\exists\forall$-type account.

tics" gave the study of intensional expressions in natural language pride of place, using mixes of modal logic with type theory and other tools from mathematical logic. In the same decade and especially through the 1980s, modal notions found their way into computer science in the study of programs and computation (Pratt, 1976), and into economics in the study of knowledge of players in games (Aumann, 1976). And this migration across the university is still continuing: in the 1990s, modal languages have turned up in the study of grammars, data-base languages, and more recently, in web design, and the structure of vector spaces used in mathematical image processing. The present lecture notes reflect these realities, including ups and downs in specific fields – and understanding modal logic today means seeing a total picture, just like reading your worldwide investment portfolio.

In these twists and turns, something strange has happened, which confuses many people. Many logicians still see modal logic as an *enrichment* of classical logic. The modalities increase expressive power, and may lead to intricate issues of the interplay between, say, quantification over objects and modal reference to worlds. But there is another, and perhaps by now the more widespread, perspective which views things the other way around. Modal operators are themselves a sort of quantifiers, but special "local" ones referring only to objects "accessible" from the current one. Viewed in this way, modal languages are not extensions, but rather *fragments* of classical ones, with restricted forms of quantification – and this weakness is at the same time a clear strength. Compared to classical systems, modal logics *lower complexity* (they tend to be decidable; and their validities can be described in transparent variable-free notations), and moreover, modal logics make us aware of the *expressive fine-structure* of the richer languages they are part of. One theme throughout these notes is the resulting "balance" between expressive power and computational complexity: gains in one will be losses in the other. Such a balance is not peculiar to modal logic: higher up, first-order logic itself is an elegant compromise between expressive power and axiomatizability (note how second-order logic gains in the first, and loses the second). Indeed, awareness of this fundamental trade-off is essential to understanding the whole point of using logical languages to formalize an area of reasoning.

Of course, this does not mean that the "extension" view of modal logics has become invalid. But consider an extended system like "modal predicate logic", which many people consider "obvious". From a modern point of view, such a system is a potentially explosive combination of diverse ideas: standard quantifiers over the object domain, restricted local quantifiers over worlds, and also some (insidiously) hidden assumptions about how these two realms of objects and worlds are related. No wonder that the semantics of modal predicate logic has been under debate with both philosophers and mathematicians right up until today. We will bring the reader up-to-date in one of our chapters, showing how old debates between Kripke and Lewis on "trans-world identity" have returned in mathematics in the 1980s.

A related feature of research today is that tribal labels like "philosophical", "mathematical" or "computational" logic mean less than they used to. Many topics in these lectures on modal logic cannot be classified as just one or the other, and this reflects intellectual realities. For instance, the modern study of rational agency and games combines fundamental insights from all these sources, without any particular pecking order. In our view, this is typical of logic: its themes migrate between academic fields, and in doing so, modify their initial agenda. But there is no reason to be pessimistic, the way some philosophers have the gloomy view that, once logic becomes technical, it leaves for good. Prodigal sons tend to return from their travels – though on the whole, a bit wiser than when they left. Some signs of such homecomings may be seen in current areas like formal epistemology and philosophy of action, and a number of illustrations will be found in these notes, when discussing logics of knowledge, interaction, and games.

The same is true for the popular division between "pure" versus "applied" logic, often misused as a label. Like any healthy discipline, logic generates theory in a process of reflection on applications, and this can go through many cycles. Indeed, in modal logic, *fundamental theory* has always a unifying force counteracting expansion. This shows at two places in these notes. Part II describes theory that arose out of reflection on basic developments in Part I. In Part III, we go on to describe a wide range of applications from the last decades, with a new round of modern theory in Part IV. And so it goes on and on.

Part I

Core Concepts

In this first Part, we discuss the major technical notions in modal logic, all stated for the basic language, but with a broader thrust for logic in general that will become clear as we proceed. Our emphasis is on propositional modal logic, and that for two reasons: (a) this is by now the dominant practice in the area, and (b) essential features of the modalities come out best on a weaker base. We may think of propositional modal logic as a system in between propositional logic and first-order predicate logic, core topics that the reader has probably studied in a first introductory course. But taking the modal view also throws new light on first-order quantification in the end – as will be explained in detail in the next part of these lectures.

Most chapters in this first part represent major logical themes by themselves – and they require at least one extended classroom session: expressive power, axiomatic deduction, completeness, and computational complexity. The latter topic is rather new in introductions to modal logic, and it might be skipped – though I personally feel that this material belongs to "what every educated student should know" these days. I have hesitated about also including correspondence theory as a core topic, but placed it in the next part eventually.

2

Basic language and semantics

2.1 Syntax of modal propositional logic

A logical formalism starts with a language, a system of *patterns* behind some practice of communication and reasoning. These patterns are formal and austere, but that is precisely why they highlight basic features of the phenomenon described, while also suggesting analogies across different situations. Our basic language has the following syntax:

Definition 2.1.1 (Basic modal language). Formulas are defined as follows. We first chose a basic set of unanalyzed propositions:

$$AT := p, q, r \ldots \text{plus} \top (\text{"always true"}) \text{ and } \bot (\text{"always false"})$$

Next, we define inductively how to construct further expressions, using the format:

$$\varphi ::= AT \mid \neg\varphi \mid (\varphi \wedge \psi) \mid (\varphi \vee \psi) \mid (\varphi \rightarrow \psi) \mid \Diamond\varphi \mid \Box\varphi$$

Here is how one reads items on the last line: "all atoms are formulas", "if φ is a formula, then so is $\neg\varphi$", "if φ, ψ are formulas, then so is $(\varphi \wedge \psi)$", etcetera. The understanding is that formulas are all and only the syntactic strings arising from this recursive process in a finite number of steps. While this format, originally invented for defining programming languages, is more terse than the usual formulations in most logic textbooks, it is very perspicuous – and its brevity in ink and paper also helps save the tropical rainforest.

Remark (Notation). In many passages in these lectures, I will denote arbitrary propositions by proposition letters $p, q, \ldots$ but sometimes also by capital letters $A, B, \ldots$ or Greek symbols $\varphi, \psi, \ldots$. This practice is not very consistent, but most readers should agree that it is nice to have different clothes to wear, depending on one's mood.

There are many possible readings for the modality $\Box$ (pronounced "box"), as we have hinted at in our Introduction: necessary truth, knowledge, obligation, ... ◇ is the dual modality, called "diamond". Getting ahead of our formal presentation, we can think of this second notion as defined, since there are two intuitive "dualities" between the two modalities – like those between the universal quantifier ∀ and existential quantifier ∃ of first-order logic:

Fact. The following two principles are intuitively valid:

$$(a)\ \Diamond\varphi \leftrightarrow \neg\Box\neg\varphi \qquad\qquad (b)\ \Box\varphi \leftrightarrow \neg\Diamond\neg\varphi$$

Interestingly, many notions in natural language come in dual pairs: the universal and existential quantifiers, "always" and "sometimes", obligation and permission, "already" and "not yet", etcetera. The phenomenon is so pervasive that it has been proposed to use it in broadcasting our presence and communicating with other civilizations in the cosmos.[4] So, one could take either modality as primitive, and some people have strong preferences.[5]

Here is a formalization of a philosophical claim with both modalities:

Example (Deep philosophy?). A student in Amsterdam in the 1970s once challenged me to formalize his profound conviction that "nothing is absolutely relative". Here is what I came up with:

$$\neg\Box(\Diamond\varphi \wedge \Diamond\neg\varphi)$$

which is equivalent, using some negation-pushing, to the implication $\Box\Diamond\varphi \rightarrow \Diamond\Box\varphi$. This principle has been studied in modal logic as the "McKinsey Axiom", and we will see later what it means. Does this capture the student's wisdom? I leave that for you to judge.

Patterns should highlight important issues at a glance. Our discussion of duality was a good example. Here are some further useful distinctions that can be made with modal formulas:

Illustration (Important modal patterns).

1. *Distinguishing scopes of modal operators.* The assertion

"If you do p, you must also do q"

has two non-equivalent readings, expressed by the two formulas

$p \rightarrow \Box q$ ("narrow scope" for $\Box$ over $\rightarrow$)
$\Box(p \rightarrow q)$ ("wide scope" for $\Box$ over $\rightarrow$)

This is a very popular confusion, from the Middle Ages right until the current literature. The two scopes come together in a principle

---

[4]Cf. the highly original monograph Freudenthal (1960) – written by a famous Dutch mathematician.

[5]I myself tend to be a box-man in axiomatic proof settings, and a diamond-man in semantic settings, depending on what works best.

that is called *Modal Distribution*:

$$\Box(p \rightarrow q) \rightarrow (\Box p \rightarrow \Box q)$$

whose validity, and controversial epistemic interpretation, will occupy us in later chapters.

Less confusing, but equally important, is the following modality-quantifier interchange:

"I know that someone appreciates me"

It has two possible readings, expressible as follows (with $\Box$ now standing for knowledge):

$\Box \exists x A(x, m)$ "*de dicto*" reading: modal qualification of a proposition
$\exists x \Box A(x, m)$ "*de re*" reading: assigning modal properties to objects

The two are not equivalent: though in this particular example, you might agree that the de re version implies the de dicto one. But I might know that I have at least one fan, even though, sadly, I will never find out in my entire life who that fan was.

2. *Iterations of modal operators.* Modal operators in natural language do not often occur stacked, except for American date lines like "I thought that we could, like, maybe, go out for a drink, sort of". It may be important for you to reduce this to its true logical form! More serious stacked versions occur with the epistemic interpretation of modality, where the following principles of "positive" and "negative" introspection have been hotly debated:

If I know, do I know that I know? $\Box \varphi \rightarrow \Box \Box \varphi$
And if I don't know? $\neg \Box \varphi \rightarrow \Box \neg \Box \varphi$

More generally, a logical formalism removes ambiguity from natural language, which has no brackets to disambiguate expressions, and no perspicuous recursion of operators.

Example (Disambiguation). The un-bracketed flat symbol string $\neg \Box p \rightarrow q$ has three different modal readings:

$$\neg(\Box p \rightarrow q) \qquad \neg \Box(p \rightarrow q) \qquad (\neg \Box p \rightarrow q)$$

One can picture these readings more concretely as different syntax trees:

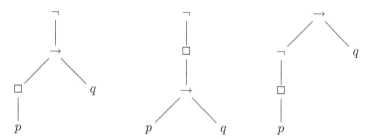

Logical syntax comes with some useful notions that measure expressive complexity. In particular, it is not the total number of modal operators that counts, but scoping:

Definition 2.1.2 (Modal depth). The *modal depth* $md(\varphi)$ of a formula φ is the maximal length of a nested sequence of modal operators. This can be defined by the following recursion on our syntax rules:

1. $md(p) = 0$,　　2. $md(\neg\varphi) = md(\varphi)$,
3. $md(\varphi \wedge \psi) = md(\varphi \vee \psi) = md(\varphi \to \psi) = \max(md(\varphi), md(\psi))$,
4. $md(\Diamond\varphi) = md(\Box\varphi) = md(\varphi) + 1$.

For instance, this works out to $md(\neg(\Box p \wedge \Diamond((p \wedge q) \wedge \neg\Diamond r))) = 2$.

As with logical systems in general, the mapping between intensional expressions in natural language and the formulas of modal logic is not unique – but we will not pursue this topic here. In any case, it is good to realize that modal expressions occur seldom as sentence operators – except in pompous phrases like "it is necessary that" – but rather in other linguistic categories such as adverbs ("maybe"), verbs ("can"), and adjectives ("possible"). Finally, the patterns discussed here serve two main purposes. Just like natural language, any logical language has several main uses, and at least two are crucial in logical theory: *describing situations, and formulating inferences*. The former perspective will soon take us to issues of modal definability and expressive power, the latter to axiomatic principles that can be employed in modal reasoning, a topic which we have not much emphasized yet.

Principles of modal reasoning are easily formulated in this notation. Most interpretations agree on basic modal laws like

$$\neg\Diamond\varphi \leftrightarrow \Box\neg\varphi \qquad \text{or} \qquad \Diamond(\varphi \vee \psi) \leftrightarrow \Diamond\varphi \vee \Diamond\psi$$

These resemble laws for quantifiers – on the analogy

$$\Diamond : \exists \qquad\qquad \Box : \forall$$

But some modal laws change colours across different interpretations of $\Box$. The simple principle

$$\Box\varphi \to \varphi \qquad\qquad (\text{``Veridicality''})$$

is valid for knowledge, but it is invalid for modalities expressing an obligation (what ought to be the case need not be true), or the result of an action (what will be made the case need not be true now). A modal formalism allows us to play on with this. For instance, the iterated principle $\Box(\Box\varphi \to \varphi)$ might well be considered valid on the obligation interpretation – though, true to form, it will not imply $\Box\varphi \to \varphi$.

2.2 Semantics of modal propositional logic

Our language will be interpreted over simple graph-like structures:

Definition 2.2.1 (Possible worlds models). [6] A *possible worlds model* is a triple $M = (W, R, V)$ of a non-empty set of *possible worlds* W, a binary *accessibility relation* R between worlds, and a *valuation map* V assigning truth values $V(p, s)$ in $\{0, 1\}$ to proposition letters p at worlds s.[7] Often, one works with *pointed models* (M, s) having one distinguished "current world" s serving as the "vantage point".

There are many interpretations for "possible worlds" s, ranging from metaphysical worlds[8] to worlds in science-fiction, states of a computer, board positions in chess, or deals in a card game. With such interpretations, the accessibility relation R can be universal (every world is accessible to every other), or constrained to game states reachable by later play, epistemic states constrained by what agents can see, points in space with their neighbours, etcetera. A particularly helpful geometrical interpretation is in machine diagrams or *process graphs*, where modal formulas describe possible evolutions starting from the current state of the process, with accessibility arrows for possible transitions.

Remark (Poly-modal languages). Transitions in process graphs are often *labeled* with action types or events, so that we can have different accessibility relations R_a, and corresponding *labeled modalities* $\langle a \rangle, [a], \langle b \rangle, [b]$, etc. We will be using the latter "poly-modal languages" throughout these notes, but for now, we just continue with the unlabeled case, which is a pilot for all the rest.

Next, we make precise sense of the earlier-mentioned analogy between modal operators and quantifiers:

---

[6] By now, this is mainly a nostalgic name – but we stick to it like to any academic ritual. We will also use other common terms for these structures occasionally, like "relational models", or "Kripke models".

[7] Sometimes, we also write "$s \in V(p)$" for "$V(p, s) = 1$". This reflects a widely used identification of propositions with sets of worlds.

[8] Ridiculed in Voltaire's novel *Candide*, where survivors of the Lisbon Earthquake of 1755 are told by philosophers that they live in "the best of all possible worlds".

Definition 2.2.2 (Truth definition for the modal language). A modal formula φ is *true* at world s in model $M = (W, R, V)$ written $M, s \models \varphi$, in virtue of this inductive clauses, following their syntax:[9]

$$
\begin{array}{lll}
M, s \models p & \text{iff} & V(p, s) = 1 \\
M, s \models \neg\varphi & \text{iff} & not\ M, s \models \varphi \\
M, s \models \varphi \wedge \psi & \text{iff} & M, s \models \varphi\ and\ M, s \models \psi \\
M, s \models \Box\varphi & \text{iff} & for\ all\ t\ with\ Rst\colon M, t \models \varphi \\
M, s \models \Diamond\varphi & \text{iff} & for\ some\ t\ with\ Rst\colon M, t \models \varphi
\end{array}
$$

Example (Computing truth values of formulas in a model). In the following process graph, some states have a unique outgoing arrow (the process is "deterministic" there), in others, there are several (the process is then "non-deterministic"), while there is also a "dead-lock" state without any outgoing arrows at all:

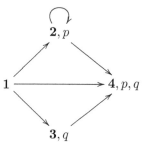

The valuation is written into the diagram in an obvious manner, by marking worlds. Here are some facts – for later reference, please note your own informal "model-checking procedure" here:

$$
\begin{array}{lll}
\Diamond\Box p & \text{is true precisely in worlds} & \mathbf{1, 2, 3} \\
\Box(q \to p) & \text{is true precisely in worlds} & \mathbf{2, 3, 4}
\end{array}
$$

Next, strip this model of its valuation for p, q:

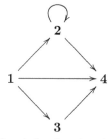

All four worlds can still be defined uniquely then by modal formulas true only at them:

---

[9]We only display clauses for two Boolean operators, but the remaining ones for disjunction and implication are similar.

4 is the only world satisfying	$\Box\bot$	("end point", "dead-lock")
3 is the only world with	$\Diamond\Box\bot \wedge \Box\Box\bot$	
1 is the only world with	$\Diamond(\Diamond\Box\bot \wedge \Box\Box\bot)$	
2 is the only world with	$\Diamond\Diamond\top \wedge \neg\Diamond(\Diamond\Box\bot \wedge \Box\Box\bot)$ [10]	

If we drop the loop, however, states 2 and 3 become modally indistinguishable – as you might try to prove informally:

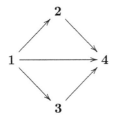

Truth definitions are often considered somewhat boring, with clauses that seem trivial ("not" means *not*, etcetera). But there are interesting features to the process of evaluation sketched here. For a start, systematically, for any given modal formula, you can tabulate for all sub-formulas in which worlds they are true, working upwards in the construction tree of the formula. Thus, in the first model above:

p	is true precisely in worlds	**2, 4**
$\Box p$	is true precisely in worlds	**2, 3, 4**
$\Diamond\Box p$	is true precisely in worlds	**1, 2, 3**

This method may be turned into an *efficient algorithm* for model-checking given modal formulas in given finite models, and we will compare this with the more complex case of first-order logic in a later chapter. We will give one more dynamic take on evaluation soon, but for now, we return to the reasoning side of modal logic.

2.3 Valid modal reasoning, a sneak preview

Universally valid principles are defined as usual:

Definition 2.3.1 (Modal validity). A modal formula φ is *valid*, written as $\models \varphi$, if $M, s \models \varphi$ for all models and worlds.

This is the sense in which the earlier two duality principles $\Diamond\varphi \leftrightarrow \neg\Box\neg\varphi$, $\Box\varphi \leftrightarrow \neg\Diamond\neg\varphi$ were valid, or the mentioned modal distribution laws $\Diamond(\varphi \vee \psi) \leftrightarrow (\Diamond\varphi \vee \Diamond\psi)$.

---

[10]There is often more than one natural choice for the world-defining formulas. For instance, we can define point **2** uniquely without cleverness, using the conjunction of the negated definitions for all the other points. More generally, in finite models, "the last world always comes for free".

One thing leads to another. As in propositional and predicate logic, there are strong dualities between the two modalities and disjunction/conjunction, resulting in automatic further laws for $\Diamond, \Box, \wedge, \vee$. Thus, switching operators, the obvious valid counterpart to $\Diamond(\varphi \vee \psi) \leftrightarrow \Diamond\varphi \vee \Diamond\psi$ is the principle $\Box(\varphi \wedge \psi) \leftrightarrow \Box\varphi \wedge \Box\psi$. On the same pattern of standing and falling together, invalid principles are:

$$\Diamond(\varphi \wedge \psi) \leftrightarrow \Diamond\varphi \wedge \Diamond\psi \qquad \Box(\varphi \vee \psi) \leftrightarrow \Box\varphi \vee \Box\psi \quad {}^{11}$$

Invalidity of a formula is demonstrated concretely by displaying *counter-examples*, i.e., concrete models M with a world s where the invalid formula is not true:

Example (Counter-example to "$\Diamond$ over $\wedge$"). In the black dot in the following model M, $\Diamond p$ and $\Diamond q$ are true, but $\Diamond(p \wedge q)$ is not:

We will talk later about algorithmic methods for finding such counter-examples to invalid principles more systematically, turning an "art" of finding counter-examples into a "science".

Additional validities arise as axioms for modal logics with special interpretations, in the form of special constraints on the accessibility relation R. For instance, imposing the earlier Veridicality as a valid principle in our models (in Chapter 9, we will make it precise what this means) has the following effect:

$$\Box\varphi \to \varphi \qquad \text{says that the relation } R \text{ is } \textit{reflexive}: \forall x Rxx$$

Another well-know example makes accessibility work in one step:

$$\Diamond\Diamond\varphi \to \Diamond\varphi \qquad \text{says } R \text{ is } \textit{transitive}: \forall x \forall y(Rxy \to \forall z(Ryz \to Rxz))$$

Observations like these lead to the famous "landscape of modal logics", with axioms of different strengths on top of the universal validities, and ubiquitous names like "T", "$S4$", "$S5$", whose botanical exploration has been a hallmark of modal logic in its earlier phases. We, too, will study possible modal axioms in more detail in Chapters 8 and 9.

---

[11] Actually, in both cases, one implication is valid: which one? This is the so-called *monotonicity* of $\Diamond$ and $\Box$.

2.4 Semantics as dynamic procedure: modal evaluation games

But there is still more to our "simple" truth definition! Evaluating a modal formula φ may be viewed as a dynamic procedure, which is of interest by itself. One particularly lively way of doing this is by means of a *game*, a technique of growing importance in logic today.

Definition 2.4.1 (Modal evaluation game). Let M, s be a model, and φ a modal formula. We define a two-person game $game(M, s, \varphi)$ between a player *Verifier* (V), claiming that φ is true, and *Falsifier* (F) claiming φ is false. The game starts at the world s. Each move is dictated by the main operator of the formula φ and we move to its sub-formulas: the total length is bounded by the operator depth:

atom p	*test p at s*: if true, then V wins, if false, then F wins,
$\varphi \vee \psi$	V *chooses* a disjunct and play continues with that,
$\varphi \wedge \psi$	F *chooses* a conjunct and play continues with that,
$\Diamond\varphi$	V *picks* an R-*successor* t of the current world, play continues with φ at t,
$\Box\varphi$	F *picks* an R-*successor* t of the current world, play continues with φ at t,
$\neg\varphi$	players switch roles in the φ game.

A player also loses when (s)he must pick a successor, but cannot do so.

Example (A complete game tree). Here is the complete game tree for the modal formula $\Box(\Diamond p \vee \Box\Diamond p)$ played starting at state **1** in the following modal model (you may want to check beforehand if it is true):

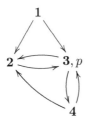

In Figure 1, we draw the game nodes, plus the player that is to move next, plus the relevant formula. Bottom leaves have "win" if Verifier wins (the atom is true there), "lose" otherwise.

In this game, both players have winning runs. But even though Verifier has fewer winning runs than Falsifier, in the response dynamics of this game tree, the advantage is still clearly for her. The important game-theoretic concept here is that of a *strategy*, a rule which tells a player what to do at each of her turns. For, Verifier has a *"winning*

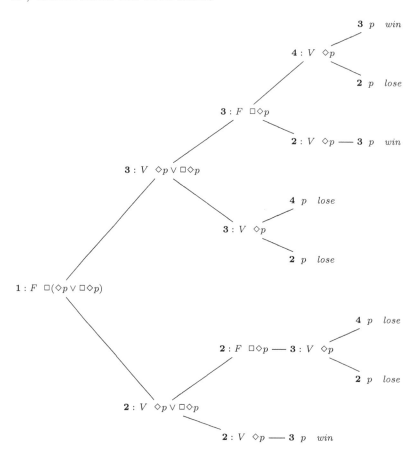

FIGURE 1   A complete game tree for the example on page 19.

strategy" in this game, a rule for playing that ensures a win for her whatever Falsifier does. The moves prescribed by this strategy are indicated by the double lines in the following picture:

Example (A winning strategy in a modal game tree). Figure 2 shows how Verifier should responde to Falsifier's moves.

Note that a strategy can encode subtle interactive behaviour. For instance, Verifier has to hand the initiative to Falsifier at state 3 on the right in the game tree if she is to win! Moreover, the full picture of interaction in this game would look at all possible strategies; for instance, note that Verifier also has a *losing strategy*, ensuring that she loses whatever Falsifier does.

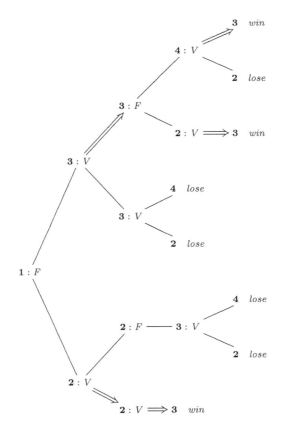

FIGURE 2   Winning strategy for Verifier in the example on page 20.

The remaining operation of negation as role switch involves the same tree structures. For instance, the game for the formula $\neg\Box(\Diamond p \vee \Box\Diamond p)$ looks exactly like the game tree that we drew for $\Box(\Diamond p \vee \Box\Diamond p)$, but with (a) all V, F turn markings interchanged at intermediate nodes, and (b) all "win", "lose" markings switched at end nodes.

Note also that these game trees are *themselves* modal models as we defined them here, with nodes as worlds, and moves as accessibility relations. This gives a foothold for applications of modal logic to *game theory*. We pursue this in Chapter 17 of our lectures. For the moment, games are just a didactic tool in our presentation of modal logic.[12]

---

[12]In fact, evaluation games in the style explained here work just as well for first-order logic, and many other logical systems.

Finally, the reason for Verifier's advantage in the above game is intuitively clear: after all, she is defending a *true statement* in the model M at the initial state s. As a simple challenge to the reader, we state the general fact behind this observation:

Key Lemma. The following two assertions are equivalent for all modal formulas and pointed models:

1. φ is true in M at s,
2. V has a winning strategy in $game(M, s, \varphi)$.

Proof. The proof is a simple induction on the syntactic construction of the formula φ and going through its successive cases will make you appreciate the very strong connection between the logical operators in our basic modal language and game moves. $\square$

If the formula is false, then Falsifier has a winning strategy, and hence modal evaluation games are *"determined"*: one of the two players has a winning strategy. We will prove in Chapter 17 why determinacy must always hold for logical games of the present kind.

Exercises Chapter 2

1. (a) For each point s in the following model, give a modal formula that is only true at s:

Use modal formulas involving only "true" ($\top$) and "false" ($\bot$).

(b) Try the same in the following model. Explain your difficulty.

2. (a) Determine in which states of the following model the modal formula $\Diamond\Box\Diamond p$ is true:

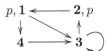

(b) Give a complete game tree for the evaluation game for $\Diamond\Box\Diamond p$ in this model starting in state **1**.

(c) Indicate the winning strategies for the player who has them.

3. ("Treasure Island") Consider the following model with 9 states, and an accessibility relation allowing one step east or south (insofar as possible) from each point. State **9** has a treasure, marked by the proposition letter t, pirates are standing at **3**, **6**, and **7**, marked by the proposition letter p:

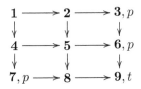

(a) In which states are the following modal formulas true?
$$\Diamond t, \quad \Diamond\Box t, \quad \Diamond p, \quad \Box\Diamond p$$

(b) For each state, find a modal formula true only there.

3

Expressive power and invariance

3.1   Invariance and expressive power

The expressive power of any language can be measured through its power of distinction – or equivalently, by the situations it considers indistinguishable. A language with just the expressions "Yes" and "No" lumps all situations in the universe together into two giant classes. Richer languages make more distinctions. So, to capture the expressive power of a language, we need to find some appropriate structural *invariance* between models. This idea has a long history in mathematics and the natural and cognitive sciences, dating back to Helmholtz's analysis of perception in the 19th century, and it also applies to logic.

For first-order logic, the basic invariance is mathematical *isomorphism*, i.e., a structure-preserving bijection between models that leaves all basic properties and relations of objects the same. It is easy to see that first-order logic does not distinguish between objects **a** in one model M, and their images $f(\mathbf{a})$ in models N related to M via an isomorphism f. This fit is perfect for *finite models*, where two models are isomorphic if and only if they satisfy the same first-order sentences. For infinite models, the implication from isomorphism to satisfying the same sentences still holds, but the converse is trickier.[13] We will not go into details here, as our concern is with modal logic.

As we will explain in Chapters 6 and 7, the "Golden Rule" of logic says that the balance of expressive power of a language and the computational complexity of reasoning with it is constant! In particular, first-order logic is indeed more expressive than modal logic, but then, its validities are *undecidable* – whereas basic modal logic, as we shall see in Chapters 4 and 6, is decidable.

---

[13] A better invariance for first-order logic, though still no perfect fit, is "potential isomorphism" – a notion that is explained in Appendix A.

3.2   Bisimulation as process equivalence

The right semantic equivalence for the basic modal language is as follows, and it is best motivated by viewing our models as pictures of processes that need to be in "harmony":

Definition 3.2.1 (Modal bisimulation). A *bisimulation* is a binary relation E between the worlds of two pointed models M, s and N, t such that sEt and also, for any worlds x, y, whenever xEy, then

  1. x, y verify the same proposition letters
  2. (a) if xRz in M, then there exists u in N with yRu and zEu
     (b) if yRu in N, then there exists z in M with xRz and zEu.

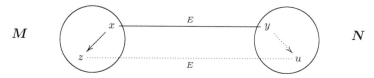

14

Clause 1 expresses "local harmony", the zigzag or "back-and-forth" clauses 2 the dynamics of simulation.[15] An obvious example of a bisimulation between two models is the earlier-mentioned case of a one-world cycle versus a 2-cycle. Just connect all points via the dotted lines:

Example (Existence and non-existence of bisimulations). The dashed lines in the following picture describe a bisimulation:

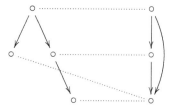

But no bisimulation connects the top worlds of the following two models – as may be seen by supposing there is one, and then chasing further links down the two diagrams:

---

[14]Setting things up this way makes bisimulations automatically non-empty.

[15]To keep the accessibility relations in the two models under consideration distinct, we sometimes write R^M versus R^N.

Bisimulations have two major uses, involving model transformations going in opposite directions:

Definition 3.2.2 (Tree unraveling). Every model M, s has a bisimulation with a rooted tree-like model constructed as follows. The worlds in the *tree unraveling* are all finite paths of worlds in M starting with s and passing to R-successors at each step. One path has another path accessible if the second is one step longer than the first. The valuation on paths is copied from that on their last nodes.

Trees are easy to visualize, as a "normal form" for modal models.

Example ("Model expansion" from a finite graph to an infinite tree).

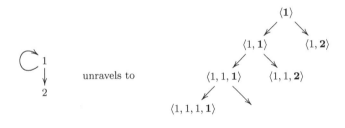

But bisimulation can also be used to simplify given models to smaller equivalent ones. The following construction of "model contraction" has a few technical details that we omit here, but we trust the student will get the idea from our hints plus a concrete illustration.

Definition Sketch ("Model contraction"). First observe that any model M has bisimulations with respect to itself, for instance, the identity relation. Also, given any family of bisimulations $\{E_i\}_{i \in I}$ between two models M, N, it is easy to see that their set-theoretic union $\bigcup_{i \in I} E_i$ is again a bisimulation: the latter is called the *largest bisimulation*. Now, it is easy to define a "quotient" of any model M with respect to the largest bisimulation on that model, where the new worlds are the equivalence classes of bisimilar old worlds – and the resulting *bisimulation contraction* is a minimal representation of the modally relevant structure of the original model M.

We will not give further formal detail for bisimulation contraction, but here is an example that gives the idea:

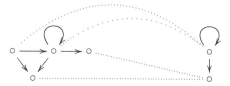

In the model to the left, there are two kinds of worlds. One kind of world are end points without successors, the other kind are worlds that can reach both an endpoint and a world "of their own kind". The model to the right is a smallest representation of the two types.

Digression While process equivalence is the most vivid intuition behind bisimulation, the latter invariance has also been proposed in set theory (e.g., by Aczel). For instance, reading arrows as pointing at elements, the following two trees depict intuitively "the same set":

as is seen by tagging nodes, starting from the empty set at endpoints:

But this is also a typical example of bisimulation, connecting points with the same tags.[16]

3.3   Modal Invariance

Now we connect up our structural comparison of models with the modal language. Here is the key result for bisimulation (which led to the latter's discovery, speaking historically):

Lemma (Invariance Lemma). For any bisimulation E between models M and N and any two worlds x, y with xEy,

$$M, x \models \varphi \text{ iff } N, y \models \varphi \text{ for all modal formulas } \varphi.$$

---

[16] Barwise and Moss (1996) is an extensive exploration of set theory in this style, involving modal languages, be it "infinitary" ones allowing the use of arbitrary conjunctions and disjunctions over (finite or *infinite*) sets of formulas.

Proof. By induction on formulas. First reformulate the assertion to

Every modal formula φ is invariant across all bisimulation links. (*)

Base case φ is a proposition letter p. This follows from Clause 1 for a bisimulation.[17] *Boolean cases* usually consist of what logicians call "abstract nonsense", but nonsense pleasing in its lightness nevertheless. Here is the sub-routine for negation. The inductive hypothesis says that (*) already holds for φ, and we now want to show it for $\neg\varphi$:

> Let xEy, and $\boldsymbol{M}, x \models \neg\varphi$. Then *not* $\boldsymbol{M}, x \models \varphi$ by the truth definition. Then *not* $\boldsymbol{N}, y \models \varphi$ by the inductive hypothesis for φ. So $\boldsymbol{N}, y \models \neg\varphi$, again by the truth definition,

and the same for the opposite direction. The argument for a disjunction is very similar. So, the action must be in the clause for the modality: as this is the only place left where something of interest can happen. This makes sense, since we are doing modal logic. Also, we can predict that for this modal step, the remaining condition on bisimulations, namely the zigzag clause 2 must be essential. Enough by way of preliminaries:

> Let xEy, and assume that $\boldsymbol{M}, x \models \Diamond\varphi$. By the truth definition, there is a world z with $R^M xz$ and $\boldsymbol{M}, z \models \varphi$. Then the *zigzag condition* on a bisimulation E gives a state u with $R^N yu$ and zEu. The inductive hypothesis for φ applied (not to xEy, but) to the link zEu, gives that $\boldsymbol{N}, u \models \varphi$. Then by the truth definition once more, $\boldsymbol{N}, y \models \Diamond\varphi$.

The argument with more relations, and corresponding filled poly-modalities $\langle a \rangle$ is exactly the same. □

As an immediate application, one can now show that certain properties of worlds are *undefinable* in the modal language. It suffices to give one model $\boldsymbol{M}, s$ where the property holds at world s, and then provide a bisimulation E with another model $\boldsymbol{N}, t$ where the property does not hold at the E-connected world t. For instance, the earlier-mentioned bisimulation between the 2-point cycle and the 1-point cycle shows that *irreflexivity* ($\neg Rxx$) is not a modally definable property of states. Also we can show failures of bisimulation:

Example (Bisimulation and non-bisimulation between process graphs). The two black worlds in the models $\boldsymbol{M}, \boldsymbol{N}$ are connected by the bisimulation given by the dotted lines – but no bisimulation includes a match between the black worlds in $\boldsymbol{N}$ and $\boldsymbol{K}$:

---

[17]Base cases of an induction are usually hardwired into the relevant definitions.

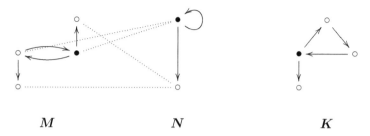

$$M \qquad\qquad N \qquad\qquad K$$

We can show this failure of bisimulation by noting that the model in the middle satisfies the modal formula $\Diamond\Diamond\Box\bot$ in its black world, while the one on the right does not.

A more positive application of invariance is "transfer". In particular, all modal properties of worlds are preserved under our basic model constructions of Unraveling and Contraction.

3.4   A tiny bit of modal model theory

There is a large literature on the above notions, but here we just direct your attention to one obvious issue. We can *convert* the Invariance Lemma in special cases, making the fit between the modal language and our structural invariance precise:

Proposition 3.4.1. Let worlds s, t satisfy the same modal formulas in two *finite* models M, N. Then there exists a bisimulation between M, N connecting s to t.

Proof. For the bisimulation E, take "modal equivalence" itself, i.e., satisfaction of the same modal formulas! This relation clearly connects s to t, while it also preserves proposition letters. Next, suppose that sEt, and Rsu in M. Suppose that there is no v in N with Rtv and uEv. That is, for all of the finitely many successors v of t in N, there is a modal formula α_v true at u in M, but false in N at v.[18] Let α be the conjunction of all these formulas. Then we have α true at u in M, and hence the formula $\Diamond\alpha$ true at s in M. Therefore, by the definition of the relation E, $N, t \models \Diamond\alpha$. Thus, by the truth definition, t has an R-successor v where α holds, and this contradicts the construction of α, which had one falsified conjunct at each such R-successor.[19]   □

---

[18] We can state things in this single direction without loss of generality, perhaps by adding one negation.

[19] Technically, this is not an inductive argument – but rather the latest fashion in the field: a "co-inductive" argument.

For infinite models, this converse implication from modal equivalence to bisimilarity does not hold, and you may want to try your hand at a counter-example. We conclude by stating a truly general equivalence, without proof. This match made in heaven requires a leap of the imagination, extending our modal language to an "infinitary" version allowing arbitrary *infinite conjunctions and disjunctions* of formulas:

Theorem 1. The following are equivalent for any two modal models M, s and N, t:

1. s and t satisfy the same infinitary modal formulas,
2. there is a bisimulation between M and N connecting s with t.

Infinite modal formulas may look daunting, and they go beyond received ideas of "syntax" – but infinite logical languages work well in modal logic, model theory, and set theory.[20]

3.5 Bisimulation games

As we saw already with semantic evaluation, we can bring out the dynamics and the fine structure of logical notions further by means of suitable *games*. Invariance is no exception. The fine-structure of bisimulation suggests the following notion:

Definition 3.5.1 (Bisimulation games). Player S ("Spoiler") claims that two models M, s and N, t are different, while player D ("Duplicator") says they are similar. They play over k rounds, starting from the match $s - t$. If objects matched in a round differ in any atomic property, S wins. In each round, starting with $m - n$, Spoiler chooses either model M, and an R-successor x of m, or model N, and an R-successor x of n. Next, Duplicator must respond with a successor y in the other model, and the world match after the round is $x - y$. If a player cannot choose a successor when it is her turn in a round, she loses.[21]

Of course, all this is easily formulated with many labeled relations, instead of a single one. Again, as with modal evaluation games, it can be seen from general game-theoretic results that either Duplicator or Spoiler has a winning strategy in any game like this (see Chapter 17).

The preceding game matches up bisimulation very precisely with the basic modal language. Here is how, again using an earlier fundamental game-theoretic notion:[22]

---

[20] For instance, each model M, s is *defined up to bisimulation* by one infinitary modal formula, true only at M, s and all N, t bisimilar to it.

[21] There is also a natural infinite version of this game, where no finite length k is chosen beforehand, and Duplicator must keep responding forever to win.

[22] In what follows, we fix a modal language with a *finite set* of proposition letters.

Theorem 2 (Adequacy for bisimulation games). The following are equivalent for any two models M, s, N, t, finite or infinite:

1. M, s and N, t satisfy the same formulas up to modal depth k,
2. Duplicator has a *winning strategy* in the k-round game starting from M, s, N, t.

Proof. The proof from 2 to 1 is by induction on the depth k of modal formulas. *Base case $k = 0$.* The game is over at the start, and since Duplicator wins, all proposition letters have the same truth values in s and t. Hence, all purely Boolean formulas without modal operators also have the same truth values, and these are the formulas of modal depth 0. *Induction step k to $k + 1$.* Let φ be a modal formula of depth $k + 1$ true at s. Any such φ is equivalent to a Boolean combination of (i) proposition letters, and (ii) formulas of the form $\Diamond\psi$, with ψ a modal formula of depth $\leq k$. It clearly suffices to consider the latter case. Suppose that $M, s \models \Diamond\psi$. Then there is an R-successor u of s with $M, u \models \psi$. Now imagine that the $k + 1$-round bisimulation game starts with Spoiler choosing model M, and going to this successor u – as he is allowed to do. The assumed winning strategy for Duplicator then yields a response for her, i.e., a successor v for t in N, such that Duplicator still has a winning strategy in the remaining k-round game starting from the match $u - v$. By the inductive hypothesis, the latter implies that $N, v \models \psi$. But then $N, t \models \Diamond\psi$.

From 1 to 2, we need an additional crucial fact about modal logic that we have not stated before:

Lemma (Finiteness Lemma). Given any finite set of proposition letters, and a fixed natural number k, up to logical equivalence, there are only *finitely many modal formulas* of modal depth $\leq k$.[23]

Given this fact, here is the winning strategy for Duplicator:

"At round i of the game, make sure that you have a link $u - v$ with M, u and N, v satisfying the same formulas up to modal depth $k - i$"

At the start of the bisimulation game, the initial worlds s, t satisfy the condition. At any stage, the condition implies as a special case that, at any link, all proposition letters get the same value: so Duplicator can never lose that way. Next, suppose the condition is satisfied at some stage i with link $u - v$, and Spoiler makes his move, say, picking a world x with Rux in M. Now, look at the set Σ of all modal formulas of depth $k - i - 1$ that are true at x – a set that we can take to be finite by the

---

[23] We will not prove the Finiteness Lemma, but it is an easy induction on the natural number k, using well-known Boolean equivalences and normal forms.

Finiteness Lemma, without loss of generality. Hence, the conjunction $\bigwedge \Sigma$ holds at x and so $\boldsymbol{M}, u \models \Diamond \bigwedge \Sigma$. Now $\Diamond \bigwedge \Sigma$ is a formula of modal depth $k - i$, and hence, by our assumption about Duplicator's strategy, $\boldsymbol{N}, v \models \Diamond \bigwedge \Sigma$. But then, there must be a successor world y of v in $\boldsymbol{N}$ satisfying $\Diamond \bigwedge \Sigma$, and this is the response which Duplicator needs to maintain her "invariant" – since x and y will now satisfy the same modal formulas up to modal depth $k - i - 1$. □

Let us illustrate how tight this fit with the modal language really is.

Example (Structural differences and modal formulas). Consider the following models in their roots, marked in black. Duplicator has a (trivial) winning strategy in the 1-round game, but Spoiler can win in two rounds – first going down in $\boldsymbol{M}$, and then taking a b or c arrow to trap Duplicator at her middle node in $\boldsymbol{N}$. In an obvious sense, this strategy exploits the modal "difference formula" $\langle a \rangle (\langle b \rangle \top \wedge \langle c \rangle \top)$ of depth 2, which is true at the root of the model $\boldsymbol{M}$, but not at that of $\boldsymbol{N}$:

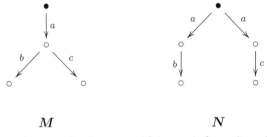

$$\boldsymbol{M} \qquad\qquad \boldsymbol{N}$$

Spoiler can make sure he keeps verifying sub-formulas of this initial formula, while forcing Duplicator into matched worlds in the other model where that sub-formula is false.

Next, take the non-bisimulation pair $\boldsymbol{N}, \boldsymbol{K}$ of this earlier example:

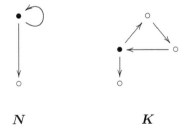

$$\boldsymbol{N} \qquad\qquad \boldsymbol{K}$$

Starting from a match between the two black dots, Spoiler needs 3 rounds to win: forcing Duplicator in two rounds into a matched pair where one world has no successor, while the other does. One strategy for this exploits the earlier modal difference formula $\Diamond \Diamond \Box \bot$.

But the analogy between the modal language and games is even tighter than all this. Note that, in the first example above, the modal difference formula $\langle a \rangle (\langle b \rangle \top \wedge \langle c \rangle \top)$ has three modalities, while only its modal depth 2 was needed. Can we do better? Here is a modal difference formula for the roots of the two models which uses only two modalities:

to the left, we have the truth of $[a]\langle b \rangle \top$, but not to the right.

What does this tell us about the bisimulation game? This formula defines *another winning strategy* for Spoiler (players can have many different winning strategies in a game!), where he first starts in model M, goes down the a-arrow, and then makes his next choice in the model N. Thus, the syntactic feature of alternation of box and diamond modalities indicates a game move of *switching* models, whereas the earlier "uniform" difference formula let Spoiler stay inside one model with his choices. On the basis of these observations, one can strengthen the Adequacy Lemma to a more informative explicit version:

Theorem 3 (Strong adequacy for bisimulation games). Spoiler's winning strategies in a k-round game between models M, s, N, t explicitly match the modal formulas of *operator depth k* on which s, t disagree.

Finally, here is a question you should have asked yourself by now. What is a *bisimulation itself* in this game perspective? This is a strategy for Duplicator! In each round, she can appeal to the zigzag clause to plot her next move. And there is no bound to this, that clause is always available (like an idealized doctor or mother, taking care of you forever):

Fact. Duplicator's winning strategies in an *infinite* game between M, s, N, t match the bisimulations between them linking s to t.

Infinite never-ending games may seem like an extravaganza – but in reality, many useful games produce infinite histories, and there are even logical languages whose evaluation games on models are infinite: see our Chapter 22 on "modal fixed-point languages".

Exercises Chapter 3

1. (a) Draw a bisimulation between the following two models, connecting the black points. Check that it satisfies the two necessary properties of Harmony and Zigzag:

   (b) Show that no bisimulation exists between the black points in the next two models, by giving a modal formula true in only one of them:

   (c) Show how Spoiler can use your "difference formula" of the previous case to win the bisimulation game between the two models, starting from the match between the black points.

2. The earlier "Treasure Island" has now changed. Find its bisimulation contraction, starting from the initial states on the upper left. Draw the bisimulation:

    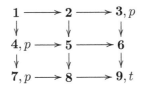

3. Give an inductive proof of Theorem 3 for bisimulation games.

4

Validity and decidability

4.1 Validity and deciding the minimal modal logic

A modal formula was *valid* if it is true at all worlds in all models. The valid formulas form the *minimal modal logic*, true solely in virtue of local quantification in any graph. It often takes little effort to recognize modal formulas as valid or not. What is the general situation? Logicians think here in terms of "decision procedures", algorithmic "mechanical" methods that test whether a given formula is valid, or follows logically from others. Indeed, the idea that logical deduction is essentially linked to computation goes back to the Middle Ages. Two landmark facts dominate the history here. Validity in *propositional logic* can indeed be tested by an algorithmic decision procedure, viz. the truth table method, and computers can do this, too. But the dream that all logical validity might be computable was shattered by the discovery in the 1930s that validity for *predicate logic* has no mechanical testing method at all. Or, put more succinctly: "first-order logic is undecidable". Of course, this is not all. In between propositional and predicate logic, many logics are still decidable – with *monadic predicate logic*, first-order logic with unary predicates only, as a prime example.[24]

This leads to the "Balance" mentioned earlier in this course. Modal logic sits in between propositional logic and predicate logic qua expressive power over its models. But, what about the computational complexity of its validity problem? Does it side with propositional logic (where that problem is decidable), or with predicate logic (where it is undecidable)? There is no obvious truth table method for modal logic, since there are infinitely many models (both finite and infinite ones) to be searched in principle. But here is the truth:

---

[24]Indeed, existing methods for proof search in predicate logic (which you may have been taught in your first logic course) often do decide validity in special cases, though there is no guarantee that must do so.

Theorem 4. The minimal modal logic is decidable.

There are many proofs of this result, backed up by concrete decision procedures. Methods include "semantic tableaux", and others that you may know from standard logic courses. In this chapter, we will prove decidability in a number of different ways. Each pass will tell us something more about what makes modal logic tick, showing some interesting difference with first-order logic as a whole.

4.2   The finite model property

Basic modal logic has the *finite model property* (*FMP*):

Theorem 5. Every satisfiable modal formula (that is, true in some M, s) has a finite model.

By contrast, first-order logic has no *FMP*. Let the formula λ say that $<$ is *an irreflexive transitive order where every point has a successor.* The natural numbers with "smaller than" are a model. λ has only infinite models: any finite transitive model in which each point has a successor must have loops, which are forbidden by the irreflexivity.

The *FMP* does not give decidability per se. We still might have to check all finite models: infinitely many. But it does when we can find an *effective bound* on the size of a verifying model in terms of the given formula φ. This strengthened version of the *FMP* is called the *effective finite model property*. Our first analysis works by a method of *selection*:

Theorem 6. Modal logic has the effective finite model property.

Proof. Consider any formula φ satisfied in a model M, w. For convenience, unravel M via a bisimulation to a tree, so φ holds at the root. The essential point is that evaluation of φ only needs *finite path depth* into the tree, and *finite branching width*. Here is the idea. Consider φ as a Boolean combination taken from a finite set of propositional atoms and modal formulas $\Diamond\alpha$ (this is always possible, looking at φ from the outside).[25] For atoms, it is enough to know the valuation at the current world. For each true diamond formula in this set, we choose a verifying successor world in the model. The total number needed is bounded by the number of sub-formulas of φ, which is at most the size $length(\varphi)$ of φ itself. For false diamonds, we need not choose any worlds at all, as these only constrain what should hold at successors we need for other reasons. Going down the tree in this fashion, we lose one level of modal

---

[25] We made this same point earlier in Chapter 3, in our proof of the Adequacy Lemma for bisimulation games. For instance, the formula $\neg(p \wedge \Diamond(q \vee \Box p) \wedge \Box s)$ is equivalent to the Boolean combination $\neg(\boldsymbol{p} \wedge \Diamond(\boldsymbol{q \vee \Box p}) \wedge \Box \boldsymbol{s})$, where we consider the bold-face sub-formulas temporarily as "units".

operator depth in each round: the process stops at $md(\varphi)$. Moreover, the width of the process is also clearly bounded by the size of the formula. We can make this precise by induction on finite sets of formulas (counting their total number of operators): if such a set consists of true formulas at a node s, then there is a finite sub-tree starting at s which still verifies the whole set. We put together the finite sub-models for the α's (which exist by the inductive hypothesis) to get the total model for the set one node higher up.

We can compute an effective upper bound on the size of the models constructed in this proof, viz. $length(\varphi)^{md(\varphi)+1}$. This gives an algorithm for deciding validity. Enumerate all modal models up to this size – using the fact that, modulo isomorphism of models, there are only finitely many of these. Check if the given formula φ holds in any one of these models. If so, φ is of course satisfiable – and if not, it is not satisfiable at all. This decides SAT (the satisfiability problem) for modal formulas. And then we can decide validity of any formula φ by deciding satisfiability of $\neg\varphi$. □

Remark (Finite depth property). Implicit in this proof is a feature of modal formulas called their "Finite Depth Property". For any model M, s and modal formula φ, $M, s \models \varphi$ iff $M|k, s \models \varphi$, where $M|k, s$ is the sub-model of M whose domain consists of s plus all worlds reachable from it in at most k successor steps, with k the modal depth of φ. Modal formulas can only "see" the current model locally via successor paths up to their own modal depth.

Related to this argument is the general method of *filtration*, which we only sketch here. It proceeds by contracting all worlds that agree on each sub-formula of the φ at issue, and it is also somewhat reminiscent of our earlier bisimulation contractions.

Definition 4.2.1 (Filtrated model). Consider any model M, and take any modal formula φ. The *filtrated model* $M|\varphi$ arises as follows. Set $w \sim v$ if worlds w, v agree on the truth value of each sub-formula of φ. Take the equivalence classes $w^{\sim}$ of this relation as the new worlds. For accessibility, set $w^{\sim} R v^{\sim}$ iff there are worlds $s \sim w$, $t \sim v$ with sRt. Finally, for the valuation, set $w^{\sim} \models p$ iff $w \models p$.

Clearly, filtrated models are finite, and also, relevant formulas do not change truth values, as seen by a simple induction on their construction:

Fact. For each sub-formula α of φ, we have this equivalence:

$$M, s \models \alpha \text{ iff } \alpha \text{ holds at } s^{\sim} \text{ in the filtrated model } M|\varphi.^{26}$$

---

[26] The method works much more generally, but it needs further twists to preserve

4.3 Inductive analysis of valid sequents

Next, we look into the concrete syntactic structure of valid inferences.

Definition 4.3.1 (Modal sequents). A *modal sequent* consists of two sequences of modal formulas separated by a double arrow: $\varphi_1 \ldots \varphi_k \Rightarrow \psi_1, \ldots \psi_m$. Such a sequence is valid if in every world in every model, the *conjunction* of the φ's implies the disjunction of the ψ's.[27]

This implies that a sequent is valid whenever some formula appears on both sides. This convention makes for better combinatorial reduction laws than the stipulation $\& \Rightarrow \&$. Here, order and multiplicity of formulas on either side of the arrow is immaterial: just think of them as sets. We use letters $A, B, \ldots$ for finite sets of formulas. Now, we give a set of principles that decompose questions of validity into ever-simpler equivalent ones, so that the associated procedure terminates. The first of these are purely propositional:

Fact (Valid propositional reduction laws).

1. A sequent with only atoms is valid iff some formula occurs on both sides.
2. $A, \neg\varphi \Rightarrow B$ iff $A \Rightarrow B, \varphi$
3. $A \Rightarrow B, \neg\varphi$ iff $A, \varphi \Rightarrow B$
4. $A, \varphi \wedge \psi \Rightarrow B$ iff $A, \varphi, \psi \Rightarrow B$
5. $A \Rightarrow B, \varphi \wedge \psi$ iff both $A \Rightarrow B, \varphi$ and $A \Rightarrow B, \psi$

Proof. This is a routine exercise in propositional logic.[28] □

Reducing sequents by these rules leads to ever simpler ones in terms of logical operators, until you hit atomic ones that you can decide "on sight". So, this is a decision procedure for propositional logic. Now for the modal operators. Starting from the outside of formulas in a sequent, we can reduce sequents until all outer Boolean connectives have disappeared. We are left with (using only diamonds here as primitive modalities) irreducible sequents

$$\boldsymbol{p}, \Diamond\varphi_1, \ldots, \Diamond\varphi_k \Rightarrow \Diamond\psi_1, \ldots, \Diamond\psi_m, \boldsymbol{q} \qquad (4.1)$$

with $\boldsymbol{p}, \boldsymbol{q}$ sequences of proposition letters. Now, we reduce these sequents by means of the following observation, which is again a highly typical modal style of argument:

---

special relational features of the original model, such as transitivity.

[27] It also makes sense to speak of global *truth* of a sequent in a whole model, but we will not use this here.

[28] You can easily find similar decomposition rules for the other connectives.

Fact (Modal Decomposition Fact). A modal sequent of the form $p, \Diamond\varphi_1, \ldots, \Diamond\varphi_k \Rightarrow \Diamond\psi_1, \ldots, \Diamond\psi_m, q$ is valid iff either

1. p, q overlap, or
2. for some i $(1 \leq i \leq k)$, the sequent $\varphi_i \Rightarrow \psi_1, \ldots, \psi_m$ is valid.

Proof. From right to left. If either 1 or 2 holds, a simple argument shows that 4.1 is valid. This involves just the modal truth definition and the definition of sequent validity. Next, *from left to right*, argue by contraposition. Suppose that neither 1 nor 2 holds. Then, as none of the 2-type sequents are valid, there exist k models M_i, w_i in which φ_i is true while all the right-hand formulas ψ_j are false. Now put all these models together *under one new root v* – and stipulate an extended valuation at v that makes the p true, but not the q:

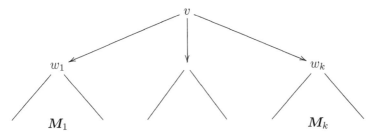

Then the new root v satisfies the whole left-hand side of 4.1, but none of the formulas on its right-hand side hold:[29] and so we have shown that 4.1 is not valid. □

Comment: proof calculi Sequents are normally used in *proof theory*. We then read the above rules bottom up, as introducing new logical operators into inferences already proved. For instance, if we have $\varphi_i \Rightarrow \psi_1, \ldots, \psi_m$, then we conclude $\Diamond\varphi_i \Rightarrow \Diamond\psi_1, \ldots, \Diamond\psi_m$. Reading the rules that way gives a complete proof system for the minimal modal logic.

For modal logic, this reveals a delightful subtlety, which connects up with so-called "substructural logics". Our sequents had *sets* of formulas. This validates *structural rules* of inference on sequents, allowing us to contract two instances of the same formula into one, or permute occurrences of formulas on the same side of the $\Rightarrow$. One structural manipulation seems particularly harmless, viz. suppression of multiple occurrences of the same formula:

---

[29] Here, we really need to prove that our formulas do not change truth values in passing from the separate models into the new "rooted" one – something that can be done by choosing an appropriate *bisimulation*: which one?

Structural rules of *Contraction*

(a) if $\mathcal{A}, \varphi, \varphi \Rightarrow \mathcal{B}$, then $\mathcal{A}, \varphi, \Rightarrow \mathcal{B}$

(b) if $\mathcal{A} \Rightarrow \mathcal{B}, \varphi, \varphi$, then $\mathcal{A} \Rightarrow \mathcal{B}, \varphi$

But this may be fatal to decidable proof search: if we use Contraction backwards, searching for possible proofs of the current sequent, this rule *increases the size* of the sequents that are potential candidates for derivation. In general, this is inevitable. For first-order logic, Contraction is indispensable, since it is involved when we appeal more than once to the same quantifier, for instance, taking different instances of a universal formula $\forall x \varphi$. And this can explode proof search spaces – as first-order logic is undecidable. But for modal logic, this does not happen. The above semantic argument shows that the rule of Contraction is not needed for deriving modal validities: we only need Permutation of formulas, and Monotonicity: insertion of additional formulas right and left.[30] The latter rules, read backwards, do not increase the complexity of our search space. Thus, we have one more, proof-theoretic explanation of the decidability of the basic modal logic.

4.4 Semantic tableaux

Here is one final re-interpretation of our inductive analysis. Reading things in the opposite direction, we can think of the preceding reduction rules as analyzing what it would take to produce a *counter-example* for an initial sequent $\varphi_1 \ldots \varphi_k \Rightarrow \psi_1, \ldots \psi_m$. In a stepwise manner, the rules analyze the nature of some possible model M, s where all antecedent formulas are true and all consequent formulas are false. The result of such an analysis is a finite tree of sequents in which each logical operator gets analyzed, whose branches either "close" (when some formula occurs in both antecedent and consequent set), or stay "open". Such trees are called *semantic tableaux*. If all branches close, there is no counter-example, and the initial sequent was valid. If at least one branch remains open, even when all rules have been applied, a counter-example may be read off from that branch.

We do not explain this method in technical detail here, but we do give one heuristic illustration:

Example (Modal semantic tableaux). Consider the modal formula $\square(p \to q) \to (\square p \to \square q)$. Can we find a counter-example? We put it on top of a tree to be constructed, with a marker for the world:

$$\bullet \; \square(p \to q) \to (\square p \to \square q) \; 1$$

---

[30] Proof systems without a contraction rule are crucial to *categorial grammar* and *linear logic*, two logical approaches to language and computation.

Things to the left of a dot have to be true, things to the right, false. Analyzing this in propositional logic, there is only one way in which a counter-example might be obtained:

$$\Box(p \to q) \bullet \Box p \to \Box q \ 1$$

Repeating this step, we get:

$$\Box(p \to q), \Box p \bullet \Box q \ 1$$

Now we need to deal with the modal boxes. The ones to the left do not make any existential requirement, but the one on the right asks for a successor 2 of the current world 1 where q is false, while at the same time, all formulas that are boxed to the left must be true:

$$p \to q, p \bullet q \ 2$$

Analyzing this in propositional logic again, there are two ways to make the implication to the left true, written as the following "splitting":

$$q, p \bullet q \ 2 \qquad\qquad p \bullet q, p \ 2$$

Now both of these nodes close, since there are formulas occurring on both sides, making it impossible to give a counter-example. Thus, the initial sequent was valid, and indeed, we have shown, once more, that the modal distribution axiom is valid.[31]

We display the complete resulting *closed tableau* in full:

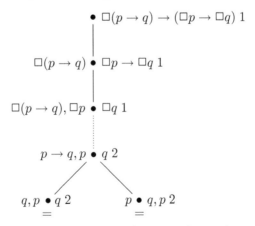

Next, consider the converse implication $(\Box p \to \Box q) \to \Box(p \to q)$. Here is the initial node of its tableau:

$$\bullet \ (\Box p \to \Box q) \to \Box(p \to q) \ 1$$

---

[31]To make all this precise, semantic tableaux need a lot of syntactic "book-keeping", which detracts a bit from the elegance of the idea behind this method.

We go through the rules a bit more quickly:

$$\Box p \to \Box q \;\bullet\; \Box(p \to q)\; 1$$

We first make a propositional split:

$$\Box q \;\bullet\; \Box(p \to q)\; 1 \qquad\qquad \bullet\; \Box(p \to q), \Box p\; 1$$

To the left, we create a successor 2 of 1, and write in the requirements:

$$q \;\bullet\; p \to q\; 2$$

Applying an implication rule again, this yields:

$$q, p \;\bullet\; q\; 2$$

and this closes. But we can also investigate the remaining case to the right, attaching two successor worlds 3, 4 to 1, one for each box (there is absolutely no reason to assume that both boxed formulas need to be falsified in one single successor world):

$$\bullet\; p \to q\; 3 \qquad\qquad \bullet\; p\; 4$$

Applying an implication rule again, this yields:

$$p \;\bullet\; q\; 3 \qquad\qquad \bullet\; p\; 4$$

Both nodes remain open, and no more decomposition rules apply.
The total semantic tableau is then as follows:

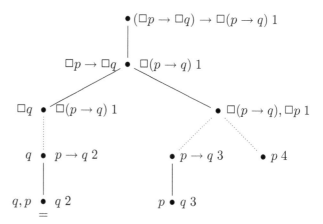

From the markings on the right branch of this tree, it is immediate to read off a concrete counter-example M for the initial sequent. The set of worlds of the model M is $\{1, 3, 4\}$, the accessibility relation is

$\{(1, 3), (1, 4)\}$, and the valuation makes p true at 3, and q nowhere:

It is easy to see that $(\Box p \rightarrow \Box q) \rightarrow \Box(p \rightarrow q)$ is false at world 1 in this model: the tableau steps themselves show how.[32]

Tableau rules These two examples show general tableau rules in action. For instance, a "conditional $\alpha \rightarrow \beta$ to the right" (i.e., to be made false) gets its antecedent α on the left in a node marked with the same world (to be made true there), leaving the consequent β on the right. The modal rule is a bit more ambitious. A box formula $\Box\varphi$ to the right leads to a new node marked for a fresh successor world of the current one, where φ is put on the right (representing some successor world where φ is to be made false). This is an "active" onetime construction rule. Modal formulas $\Box\varphi$ to the left in a node, however, marked for some world w, say, are "passive" but may have to be applied many times. Every time we construct a tableau node for a successor world v of w, we must place φ on its left.

Semantic tableaux were first proposed for first-order logic in the 1950s, but they also turned out very appropriate to modal logic, and they are widely used today in automated deduction.

4.5   Decidability via translation

We conclude with a fourth, short, and chique proof of decidability, which points toward yet another view of modal logic, viz. as a member of a much larger family of logics. We will see soon in these lectures how all basic modal formulas can be *translated* into first-order formulas. In fact, they can be translated into a fragment of first-order logic using only *two variables* over worlds, free or bound. Now, it was shown in the 1970s that this "two-variable fragment" FO_2 of first-order logic is decidable! Therefore, since the translation of modal formulas to two-variable formulas is effective, modal validity can be decided, too.

But beware with such easy reductions. The computational complexity of deciding FO_2 is in fact higher than that for modal logic, so in that respect, we are explaining "obscurum per obscurius". Moreover, this path seems a dead-end as far as generalizations are concerned.

---

[32]On its open branch, the tableau leaves the propositional valuation underdetermined, thus in effect creating a family of counter-examples.

Already the three-variable fragment FO_3 of first-order logic is undecidable (it contains all of relational algebra), so we cannot reduce validity for modal logics with additional typically 3-variable frame conditions like transitivity, even though these are known to be decidable.

Indeed, validity is also decidable for many stronger modal logics than the minimal one, working only on special model classes – which we will discuss in more detail later. Proofs for this are often adaptations of the ones presented here. For the modal logic $S5$, where accessibility is an *equivalence relation*, or the *universal relation* which holds between all worlds, perhaps the simplest proof is again by translation. In $S5$ models, a modal $\Box$ is just a universal quantifier $\forall$, and a $\Diamond$ an existential $\exists$. Then, all modal formulas translate into equivalent formulas of *monadic first-order logic*, a system which is obviously decidable.

Something to think about Here is a sweeping statement about the landscape of all modal logics. There are countably many decision procedures (algorithms are finite sets of instructions, which can be enumerated), and there are uncountably many modal logics: essentially, modulo some closure conditions, they are all subsets of the countable set of all formulas. Therefore, most modal logics must be undecidable. But, all logics found until the early 1970s were in fact decidable! Only then people constructed finitely axiomatized undecidable modal logics, borrowing ideas from standard logic. We will give an example of an undecidable modal logic much later in Chapter 24.

Finally, just to jog your mind, here is an outrageous result from the 1980s. It is *undecidable* whether a given modal logic is decidable! And maybe that fact is not so strange after all. As all academic researchers know, it can be extremely hard to see that something is easy.

Exercises Chapter 4

1. (a) Derive the correct sequent rules for implication from those stated for negation and conjunction, given the standard propositional definition of $\rightarrow$ in terms of $\wedge$ and $\neg$.

   (b) Which of the following two implications is valid? Give an informal argument, and also an outline of a sequent proof in the minimal logic:

   $$\Box(p \rightarrow q) \rightarrow (\Diamond p \rightarrow \Diamond q)$$
   $$(\Diamond p \rightarrow \Diamond q) \rightarrow \Box(p \rightarrow q)$$

   (c) As for the invalid formula, draw a counter-example.

2. (a) Supply all missing steps in the proof of the Modal Decomposition Fact. In particular, identify the precise place where you need a bisimulation.

   (b) What is the formulation of that Fact when stated in terms of $\Box$ rather than $\Diamond$?

   (c) Using semantic tableau rules, prove the following formula:

   $$\Box(p \wedge q) \rightarrow (\Diamond p \vee \Box q)$$

3. Prove the key Lemma justifying the Filtration method by induction on modal formulas.

4. Make the statement precise that modal $S5$ is translatable into monadic first-order logic. Is there also a converse translation?

5

Axioms, proofs, and completeness

5.1 Describing validities by proofs

Universal validity of a formula φ was defined somewhat abstractly as truth of φ at each world in each model. How can we describe the form of these validities more concretely? After all, logic is also about valid arguments, and premises $\varphi_1, \ldots \varphi_k$ imply conclusion ψ iff the implication $(\varphi_1 \wedge \cdots \wedge \varphi_k) \to \psi$ is a valid formula. One concrete method in logic is this: give a *proof system*, that is, a concrete set of initial principles and derivation rules that produce only valid principles (this property is called *soundness*) - and hopefully also, all of the valid principles (the famous property of *completeness*). Logical proof systems exist in many different formats: our "sequent calculus" in Chapter 4 was an example. Not all logics have complete proof systems, but there is no reason not to try in the case of modal logic.

5.2 A short-cut through first-order logic?

But perhaps we do not have to try at all? One quick, but sneaky route is as follows. Using the method of Chapter 7 (but in your heart, you already know how to do this) *translate* modal formulas into first-order ones, and then use any complete proof system that you have learnt for the latter system to derive the (translated) modal validities.

Example (Modal distribution law). Instead of proving the semantically valid modal distribution law $\Box(p \to q) \to (\Box p \to \Box q)$, one can easily derive its first-order translation (note how modal boxes become successive bounded universal quantifiers here) $\forall x (\forall y (Rxy \to (Py \to Qy)) \to (\forall y (Rxy \to Py) \to \forall y (Rxy \to Qy)))$ – using only standard axioms and rules of first-order logic.

But this does not give much insight into the peculiarities of modal reasoning, which is, amongst other things, done in *variable-free no-*

tation. Moreover, a first-order proof for a translated modal formula might contain "junk": intermediate formulas that have no modal counterparts, which offends our sense of purity.[33] Therefore, we also want to find more intrinsically modal proof systems. Nevertheless, a comparison with, say, axioms for *FOL* is useful. We shall appreciate better what we need, and what not. For concreteness, Herbert Enderton's famous textbook *A Mathematical Introduction to Logic* (Enderton, 1971), used by many generations of Stanford students, has the following set:

(a) all tautologies of classical logic,
(b) distribution: $\forall x(\varphi \to \psi) \to (\forall x\varphi \to \forall x\psi)$,
(c) universal instantiation: $\forall x\varphi \to [t/x]\varphi$, provided that t is freely substitutable for x in φ,
(d) vacuous universal generalization: $\varphi \to \forall x\varphi$, provided that x is not free in φ,
(e) a definition of $\exists x\varphi$ as $\neg\forall x\neg\varphi$,[34] and
(f) the rule of Modus Ponens: "from φ and $\varphi \to \psi$, conclude ψ.

Here, each axiom can come with any finite prefix of universal quantifiers. This special feature provides the effect of the rule of

(g) Universal Generalization: "if φ is provable, then so is $\forall x\varphi$".

The syntactic provisos on Axioms (c) and (d) are a common source of errors, and they reflect the fact that the first-order language is all about variable dependency and variable handling.

Theorem 7. A first-order formula is valid iff it is provable using the Enderton axioms.

We will present a variable-free proof system for the modally valid formulas. Even so, many systems for *automated deduction* do use translation into first-order logic, since computational techniques have been highly optimized for the latter widely used system – and a user need not care so much what happens "under the hood" of the computer.

5.3 The minimal modal logic

Our basic modal proof system is like part of Enderton's complete set, but without syntax worries:

Definition 5.3.1 (Minimal modal logic). The minimal modal logic K is the proof system with the following principles:

(a) all tautologies from propositional logic,

---

[33] In fact, this junk is almost bound to occur in a proof for modal distribution.
[34] Or one can make both quantifiers primitive, with an axiom $\exists x\varphi \leftrightarrow \neg\forall x\neg\varphi$.

(b) modal distribution $\Box(\varphi \to \psi) \to (\Box\varphi \to \Box\psi)$,

(c) a definition of $\Diamond\varphi$ as $\neg\Box\neg\varphi$,

(d) the rule of Modus Ponens,

(e) and a rule of Necessitation: "if φ is provable, then so is $\Box\varphi$".

Proofs are finite sequences of formulas, each of them either (i) an instance of an axiom, or (ii) the result of applying a derivation rule to preceding formulas. A formula φ is provable: written as $\vdash \varphi$, if there is a proof ending in φ. If we want to indicate the specific modal logic we are using, we write it as a subscript: for instance, $\vdash_K \varphi$.

Our variable-free modal notation has no laws like the above first-order (c) and (d). These do appear, in a sense, in stronger systems. If you wish, the axiom $\Box\varphi \to \varphi$ of the stronger modal logic T is an instance of universal instantiation.[35] Likewise, an $S5$-axiom like $\Diamond p \to \Box\Diamond p$, valid on models where the accessibility relation holds between all worlds, is really the vacuous generalization $\exists x P x \to \forall x \exists x P x$.

5.4 The art of formal proof

Finding formal proofs is a skill that can be drilled into students, and though it has few practical applications, it has a certain unworldly beauty. We will not emphasize this drill here, but the student will do well to study a few derivations in detail, and see the bag of useful tricks that goes into them. Roughly speaking, proofs in the minimal modal logic often have a propositional core, which is then "lifted" to the modal setting. Many textbooks provide examples: say, the *Manual of Intensional Logic* (van Benthem, 1988a) has a few annotated ones.

Learning formal proof is a matter of practice. You build up a library of useful sub-routines, you learn to recognize formal patterns (in fact, logic courses have been used as a laboratory for a variety of cognitive psychology experiments) and soon you are airborne.[36]

Example (Distribution rules).

(a) If $\varphi \to \psi$ is provable, then so is $\Box\varphi \to \Box\psi$:

1)	$\varphi \to \psi$	provable by assumption
2)	$\Box(\varphi \to \psi)$	Necessitation rule on 1
3)	$\Box(\varphi \to \psi) \to (\Box\varphi \to \Box\psi)$	modal distribution axiom
4)	$\Box\varphi \to \Box\psi$	Modus Ponens on 2, 3

---

[35] But this often-cited analogy is not quite right, if you think it through: why?

[36] If all else fails, you can opportunistically seek an informal semantic argument for inspiration, and hide the idea in formal steps later.

(b) If $\varphi \to \psi$ is provable, then so is $\Diamond\varphi \to \Diamond\psi$:

1)	$\varphi \to \psi$	provable by assumption
2)	$\neg\psi \to \neg\varphi$	propositional logic, 1
3)	$\Box\neg\psi \to \Box\neg\varphi$	by the subroutine (a)
4)	$\neg\Box\neg\varphi \to \neg\Box\neg\psi$	propositional logic, 3
5)	$\Diamond\varphi \to \Diamond\psi$	definition of $\Diamond$

Related useful observations about modal provability include the widely used principle of

Replacement by Provable Equivalents:
if $\vdash \alpha \leftrightarrow \beta$ then $\vdash \varphi[\alpha] \leftrightarrow \varphi[\beta]$.[37]

Next, as for proving real theorems, it often helps to start at the end, and first reformulate what we are after. This is of course, standard heuristics: reformulate the result to be proved in a *top-down manner*, until you see *bottom-up* which available principles will yield it:

Example (An actual theorem of K). Using these observations, we show that $\vdash_K (\Diamond\varphi \wedge \Box(\varphi \to \psi)) \to \Diamond\psi$:

1) by propositional logic, it suffices to prove the equivalent $\Box(\varphi \to \psi) \to (\Diamond\varphi \to \Diamond\psi)$, which is again equivalent to

2) $\Box(\varphi \to \psi) \to (\neg\Box\neg\varphi \to \neg\Box\neg\psi)$, which is equivalent to

3) $\Box(\varphi \to \psi) \to (\Box\neg\psi \to \Box\neg\varphi)$

4) Now we recognize a propositional core tautology that we can use: $(\varphi \to \psi) \to (\neg\psi \to \neg\varphi)$, and apply our distribution rule to it:

5) $\Box(\varphi \to \psi) \to \Box(\neg\psi \to \neg\varphi)$, and combining this with a distribution axiom to obtain:

6) $\Box(\varphi \to \psi) \to (\Box\neg\psi \to \Box\neg\varphi)$, we get the desired conclusion.

The very typographical cut-and-pastes that you will do in typing up these proofs show the workings of (i) proof structure, (ii) pattern recognition, (iii) modularity, and (iv) sub-routines!

Other well-known theorems of the minimal logic K are principles such as the distribution of $\Box$ over $\wedge$:

$$\Box(\varphi \wedge \psi) \to (\Box\varphi \wedge \Box\psi)$$

and its diamond counterpart $\Diamond(\varphi \vee \psi) \to (\Diamond\varphi \vee \Diamond\psi)$. The latter can also be derived from the former by a more general system property of *Duality*, just as in classical logic. Finally, another simple way of "seeing" K-theorems is through analogies with first-order logic.

---

[37]Here $\varphi[\alpha]$ is a formula containing one of more occurrences of the sub-formula α, and $\varphi[\beta]$ results from $\varphi[\alpha]$ by replacing all of these by occurrences of β.

5.5   Proofs in other modal logics

Stronger modal logics increase deductive power by adding further axiom schemata to the minimal logic K. Then the flavour of finding derivations may change, as you develop a feeling for what the additional syntactic power gives you. Here are some well-known examples:

Example (T, $S4$ and $S5$). The modal logic T arises from K by adding the axiom schema of Veridicality $\Box\varphi \to \varphi$. The logic $S4$ adds the schema $\Box\varphi \to \Box\Box\varphi$ to T, which for knowledge is called Positive Introspection. Finally, the logic $S5$ adds the schema $\Diamond\varphi \to \Box\Diamond\varphi$ to $S4$.

We will discuss these logics later on, but here is one illustration:

Fact. The following principle is provable in $S4$: $\Box\Diamond\Box\Diamond\varphi \leftrightarrow \Box\Diamond\varphi$

Proof. The main steps are these. *From left to right.* (a) First, prove that the formula $\Box\alpha \to \Diamond\alpha$ is provable for all formulas α (this is easy to do even in the modal logic T), so that we have $\Box\Diamond\varphi \to \Diamond\Diamond\varphi$. Next (b) apply earlier sub-routines to get $\Box\Diamond\Box\Diamond\varphi \to \Box\Diamond\Diamond\Diamond\varphi$. Then (c) derive $\Diamond\Diamond\Diamond\varphi \to \Diamond\varphi$ in $S4$, and apply an earlier sub-routine to get $\Box\Diamond\Box\Diamond\varphi \to \Box\Diamond\varphi$. *From right to left.* "Blow up" the initial box in $\Box\Diamond\varphi$ to three boxes, using the $S4$-axiom. Then replace the second of these by a diamond, using the same principles as before. $\Box$

You can see more concretely what is going on by a "picturesque" *semantic argument* for the validity of $\Box\Diamond\Box\Diamond\varphi \leftrightarrow \Box\Diamond\varphi$ on reflexive and transitive models for $S4$. There is even a kind of heuristic translation between the semantic argument and a syntactic proof. But a semantic argument may give you more. If you analyse things well in your pictures, you will see that reflexivity is not needed.

Perhaps you can also find shorter, or otherwise different proofs for the above semantic validities. Theorems in a logical system may well have more than one non-equivalent proof!

5.6   The science of proof

On the practical side, computers can search for proofs in much faster, mechanical ways. Existing theorem provers for modal logic use various techniques.[38] Usually, these are not in the above axiomatic style, but they use a variety of other methods: (a) translation into first-order logic plus "resolution" methods, (b) the above "semantic tableaux", which are formal versions of semantic decision procedures, or (c) specially optimized modal calculi. On the theoretical side, there is a field of

---

[38]You can look up information on the web page `http://www.aiml.net`.

logic called *Proof Theory* that deals with the structure of formal proofs, transformations between equivalent proofs, and the like. Deep results in Proof Theory include "cut-elimination theorems" telling us that – for appropriate logics – theorems derived in axiomatic format can also be derived in a "sequent calculus" (cf. Chapter 4) with only introduction rules for logical operators. The latter format is very perspicuous for theoretical purposes. Another proof-theoretic theme concerns the surplus of proofs, as finite combinatorial objects establishing validity. A proof often has "algorithmic content", which allows us to extract more concrete information about valid formulas, and perhaps even extract programs whose execution provably meets given specifications.

5.7   The completeness theorem

Perhaps the most important result for the minimal modal logic is this:[39] what K derives is the whole truth (*completeness*), and nothing but the truth (*soundness*).

Theorem 8. For all modal formulas φ, $\vdash_K \varphi$ iff $\models \varphi$

Completeness theorems were first proved by Emil Post for propositional logic in the 1920s, and – much deeper – by Kurt Gödel in 1929 for first-order logic. Surprisingly, they connect the very general notion of validity ($\models$) with a very concrete one of provability ($\vdash$).

Soundness. This is usually easy to prove, by induction on the length of proofs. One first checks that all axioms of the stated forms are valid, and next, that all the derivation rules preserve validity. For the minimal logic K, this is easy to see by inspection.[40]

Completeness. This involves a more complicated argument. It is like the completeness proofs for first-order logic that you may have seen already – but with some simplifications due to the simple structure of the modal language. The emphasis in this book will not be on proving completeness theorems, even though these are a large "industrial" part of the field. But we will tell you about the main proof steps here.

The cover argument. We argue by contraposition. Suppose a modal formula φ is not derivable in K. We reformulate this assumption using the following notion, that is important in its own right.

Definition 5.7.1 (Consistency). A set Σ of formulas is *consistent* if for no finite conjunction σ of formulas from Σ, the negation $\neg\sigma$ is provable in the logic K.

---

[39]The result goes back essentially to Stig Kanger and Saul Kripke in the 1950s.

[40]Soundness is not always trivial: logics for program correctness have tricky proof rules for structured data and recursion, whose soundness can be in doubt.

Consistent sets have simple useful properties that we do not prove here. One is that, if φ is not derivable, then the set $\{\neg\varphi\}$ is consistent. Now we show that in general, any consistent set of formulas Σ has a satisfying model, which provides a semantic counter-example for the non-derivable formula φ, whence the latter is not semantically valid.

Maximally consistent sets. Any consistent set of formulas is contained in a *maximally consistent set of formulas*, i.e., a consistent set which has no consistent proper extensions. This may be proved by general set-theoretic principles ("Zorn's Lemma"). More popular is an explicit "Lindenbaum construction" enumerating all (countably many) formulas of the modal language: $\psi_1, \psi_2, \ldots$ and then, starting from Σ, working stage by stage, adding the currently scheduled formula if it is still consistent with those already chosen. In the countable limit, the result of this is still consistent, since by our definition, an inconsistency can only involve finitely many formulas, and hence it would already have shown up at some finite stage. It is easy to see that the preceding construction yields a maximally consistent set.

Maximally consistent sets have pleasant decomposition properties, making them behave like complete records of possible worlds:

Fact. Let Σ be a maximally consistent set. Then the following equivalences hold, for all modal formulas:

    (i) $\neg\varphi \in \Sigma$ iff   not $\varphi \in \Sigma$

    (ii) $\varphi \wedge \psi \in \Sigma$ iff $\varphi \in \Sigma$ and $\psi \in \Sigma$

This may be shown by simple propositional reasoning (K contains all Boolean tautologies). It also follows easily that maximally consistent sets are closed under K-derivable formulas.

Now we unpack modalities. First we say that $\Sigma R \Delta$ if for every formula α in the maximally consistent set Δ, we have $\Diamond\alpha$ in Σ. Soon, this R will become the accessibility relation in a model that we are going to create. Now we have the following further decomposition:

Fact. (iii) $\Diamond\varphi \in \Sigma$ iff   there is some Δ with $\Sigma R \Delta$ and $\varphi \in \Delta$

The proof is trivial from right to left. From left to right, it is the only place in the whole completeness proof where we use the typically modal principles of K.[41] Consider the set of formulas $\Gamma = \{\varphi\} \cup \{\alpha \mid \Box\alpha \in \Sigma\}$: by the earlier definition of accessibility, any maximally consistent set containing this will be a R-successor of Σ.

Claim. The set Γ is consistent.

---

[41] In fact, here is where you could have *discovered* these key axioms!

Proof. Suppose it were not: then by the definition of consistency, there is a conjunction α of some finite set of formulas with $\Box\alpha$ in Σ such that K proves $\neg(\alpha \wedge \varphi)$, hence also $\alpha \to \neg\varphi$. By Necessitation, K then also proves $\Box(\alpha \to \neg\varphi)$, and by modal distribution, it proves $\Box\alpha \to \Box\neg\varphi$. Now we assumed $\Box\alpha \in \Sigma$ for all separate $\alpha \in \alpha$. But by our earlier observations about derivability, together, these formulas imply that $\Box\alpha \in \Sigma$, and since maximally consistent sets are closed under provable consequence, we have $\Box\neg\varphi \in \Sigma$. Now, given K's definition of $\Diamond$ in terms of $\Box$, this contradicts the fact that $\Diamond\varphi \in \Sigma$. □

The Henkin model. Now we define a model $M = (W, R, V)$ as follows.

Definition 5.7.2 (Canonical model). The worlds W are all maximally consistent sets, the accessibility relation is the above defined relation R, and for the propositional valuation V, we set $\Sigma \in V(p)$ iff $p \in \Sigma$.

Then we have everything in place for the final argument:

Lemma (Truth Lemma). For each maximally consistent set Σ, and each modal formula φ,

$$M, \Sigma \models \varphi \quad \text{iff} \quad \varphi \in \Sigma$$

Proof. The proof is a straightforward induction on formulas φ, using all the ready-made ingredients provided in the decomposition facts for maximally consistent sets. A typical feature of the Truth Lemma, and one of its conceptual delights for logicians, is the harmony between a formula just *belonging* to Σ as a syntactic object, and that same formula being *true* at Σ, now viewed as one world in a universe of worlds where modal evaluation can take place. □

Actually, this proof establishes something more than we stated. "*Weak completeness*" is the property that every valid formula is derivable – or equivalently, that every consistent formula has a model. But we have really proved "*strong completeness*": all consistent sets have a model. Equivalently, this says that each valid consequence φ from a set of formulas Σ, finite or infinite, has a proof using only assumptions from that set: $\Sigma \models \varphi$ iff $\Sigma \vdash \varphi$.

There is something magical about this completeness argument, since we conjured up a counter-model out of our hat, using just the syntax of the modal language plus some simple combinatorial facts about provability in the minimal modal logic. Even so, the Henkin model *is* a concrete semantic object when we disregard the syntactic origins of its worlds, and as such it even has a remarkable property. All consistent sets can be made true in one and the same model! While we could also have seen this differently,[42] it is a characteristic fact about the modal language, that makes the Henkin model "largest" or "universal" among all models. By contrast, first-order logic has no such universal model, since its maximally consistent theories hate each other so much that they cannot live consistently in the same model.

Modern finite versions The following observation has become standard in the literature. One further remarkable feature of the completeness proof is that it can also be carried out in a *finite universe of formulas*. Just consider the initially given consistent formula and all its sub-formulas as your total language. Everything we have defined and proved also applies when relativized to that setting, with some notions and results even getting simpler. As a result, we get finite models for consistent formulas whose size is a function of the number of sub-formulas. This is one more way of seeing that modal logic is decidable.

5.8 Applications of completeness

You need to understand how completeness theorems are used. Note that $\models$ is defined with a universal quantifier over models, and $\vdash$ with an existential quantifier over proofs. This highlights one basic feature. If we want to show that some formula is non-derivable, this is a hard task proof-theoretically, as we need to see that *every* proof fails. But on the equivalent semantic side, this says there *exists* some model for the negation of the formula. So, one counter-example suffices. Note that this application involves only *soundness*.[43] Here is a more theoretical application of *completeness*. We show that some derivation rules beyond those stated are "admissible" for modal reasoning:

Fact. If $\vdash_K \Box\psi$, then $\vdash_K \psi$.

In other words, provability in K also satisfies a converse rule of "De-Necessitation". This rule is trivial in modal logics upward from T: but for K, it is by no means obvious.

Proof. Suppose that ψ is not provable. Then by completeness, there is a counter-model M with a world w where $\neg\psi$ holds. Now here is a semantic trick that is used a lot in modal logic. Take any *new* world v,

---

[42]For instance, here is an alternative construction. For each satisfiable set of formulas in the language, take one verifying model, and then form the so-called "*disjoint union*" of all these models: this also works.

[43]It is a tragic feature of many deep logical results that their easy side makes for the most concrete applications, whereas the deeper converse side is only there for theoretical enlightenment. Or stated more positively, the most important insights in logic are free from any base motive of practical gain.

add it to M and put just one extra R-link, from v to w:

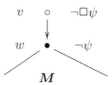

The atomic valuation at v does not matter. In the new model M^+, $\Box\psi$ is clearly false at v – hence it is not universally valid, and so by soundness, $\Box\psi$ is not derivable in K. $\qquad\Box$

In addition to axioms, modal rules of inference are a fascinating subject of study by themselves. A nice general result is "Rybakov's Theorem" from the 1980s, stating that it is *decidable* if a given rule of inference is admissible for the widely used modal logic *S4*.

Finally, having a complete axiom system does not make a logic decidable, witness the case of first-order logic. Given any formula φ, enumerating all possible proofs for it must indeed produce a proof if it is valid. But if φ is not valid, we have to sit through the entire infinite process, to make sure that it was not derivable. As it happens, we have seen already that modal validity was decidable – but this feature of modal logic was for additional reasons.

5.9   Coda: modal logic via proof intuitions

Purely proof-theoretic modal intuitions may run deep. See the passage on H.B. Smith in the *Manual of Intensional Logic* (van Benthem, 1988a). This early pioneer of modal logic in the 1930s took the view that the heart of modal reasoning was not in specific axioms or rules, but rather in two major principles which had to be respected by any modal system. Smith considered finite sequences of modalities as the core notions that a modal logic is trying to capture:

$$-, \Diamond, \Box, \Diamond\Diamond, \Diamond\Box, \Box\Diamond, \Box\Box, \ldots$$

He then formulated two intuitive desiderata on any concrete modal proof system:

(a) *Distinction*: no two distinct sequences are provably equivalent,

(b) *Comparison*: of any two sequences, one implies the other.

The two requirements are at odds, since (a) wants the logic to be weak, while (b) wants it to prove a lot. Indeed, these requirements cannot be met in "normal modal logics" extending K.[44] But even so,

---

[44]The reader may want to try her hand at the simple but clever argument.

Smith's intuitions are fascinating, and they have been modeled in suitably generalized logics over variants of our possible worlds semantics.

This excursion is also interesting because it reminds you how, through no fault of theirs, interesting ideas that do not "fit" may drop by the wayside as a science progresses.

Exercises Chapter 5

1. Prove the following formula in K: $\Box(\varphi \wedge \psi) \leftrightarrow (\Box\varphi \wedge \Box\psi)$.

2. Prove the formula $\Box\Diamond\Box\Diamond\varphi \leftrightarrow \Box\Diamond\varphi$ in the logic $K4$: $S4$ minus Veridicality.

3. Show that the following rule is admissible in K: if $\vdash \Box\alpha \vee \Box\beta$, then $\vdash \alpha$ or $\vdash \beta$.

4. Prove the Boolean decomposition facts about maximally consistent sets stated in our completeness argument.

5. Prove that no "normal modal logic", i.e., a set of modal formulas extending the set of theorems of K and closed under Modus Ponens, Necessitation, and Substitution of formulas for proposition letters, satisfies both requirements stated by H. B. Smith.

6

Computation and complexity

We have seen that validity in the minimal modal logic is not only axiomatizable, but even decidable. But that still does not give us a good sense of the true computational complexity of deciding whether given formulas or arguments are valid. Logics may be decidable, yet wildly infeasible in practice. For instance, though propositional logic and modal logic are both "decidable", are they really in the same league? To answer such questions, and many others about actual performance of algorithms, computer scientists developed Complexity Theory. One can measure the complexity of a task in terms of *time* (number of steps taken) and *space* (size of the memory employed).[45] Measures for time and space involve some task-dependent variable: often the length of the input formula, or the size of some given finite model. Thus, we are measuring *rates of growth*, rather than specific numbers – just as in discussions of economic growth or pollution, where exponential growth is a threatening sign that things are getting out of hand. Computationally, exponential growth is seen as a boundary of infeasible computability – while beyond that, undecidability: the absence of any algorithm solving the given task, is just "thunder in the distance".

6.1 Complexity: the merest sketch

Complexity theory measures the computation time or memory space needed for performing some task as a function of input size (an excellent text is Papadimitriou (1994)). In particular, among all decidable problems, it distinguishes "feasible" rates of growth such as linear, quadratic, or more generally polynomial (the complexity class called P), versus "infeasible" ones like non-deterministic polynomial time problems in NP, and then beyond to polynomial space ($PSPACE$),

---

[45]This can depend on one's units, but there is a calibration on *Turing machines*.

exponential time ($EXPTIME$), and ever higher up:

$$P \quad NP \quad PSPACE \quad EXPTIME \quad \cdots \quad Undecidable$$

To get some feeling for natural tasks calibrated in this way:

(a) sorting numbers by magnitude, or finding a path from some node of a graph to another "goal node", takes quadratic time,

(b) parsing a sentence grammatically takes cubic time,

(c) solving a Traveling Salesman problem is in NP, while

(d) finding a winning strategy in many parlour games is in $PSPACE$.

Some of these classes become clearer through their connections with logical tasks you already understand. There are many further classes in the dotted area. For instance, the large decidable "Guarded Fragment" of first-order logic to be discussed later in Chapter 7 has doubly exponential complexity $2EXPTIME$: it may take on the order of $2^{2^{|\varphi|}}$ steps to decide whether a guarded formula φ has a model.[46]

Making these notions precise is a bit tedious, and often puts people off by its accidental details of the workings of Turing machines or other devices. We will stick with this basic outline here, and rely on the reader's intuitive understanding in the discussion to follow.

Here are a few quick theoretical observations. One reason why time-measures interleave with space-measures is this. In P-time steps, you can only visit polynomially many memory locations: and so P (and even NP) is contained in polynomial space. Conversely, with polynomially many memory locations, you can still revisit them, using essentially more time-steps. But there is an exponential upper limit, as repeating exactly the same trajectories makes no sense. This explains the inclusion of $PSPACE$ in $EXPTIME$. A less obvious result is Savitch's Theorem stating that $PSPACE = NPSPACE$, where "N" refers to the action of a non-deterministic algorithm that is allowed guesses. The most famous open problem in the field is whether $P = NP$, or in later terms: whether model-checking and satisfiability for propositional logic have the same complexity. Most people expect the answer to be negative, but "$P = NP$" has resisted solution since the 1970s.

Finally, inside complexity classes such as P, $PSPACE$, there may be further fine-structure. Some problems sit at the upper end, and are *complete for the class*. That is, every other problem in the class is polynomial-time reducible to them. For instance, the satisfiability problem for propositional logic is *NP-complete*: it is the universally

---

[46]Here, $|\cdot|$ is a widespread notation for input size. E.g., $|\varphi| = length(\varphi)$, $|M|$ is the size of the model M, etc.

hardest task of its kind, and likewise, model-checking for propositional formulas is complete for the class P.

6.2 Complexity profile of a logic

To really understand how a logical system works, it helps to check the complexity for all the basic tasks that it tends to be used for:

Definition 6.2.1 (Satisfiability). Determining validity, or equivalently, *testing for satisfiability* of given formulas, is answering the question: "Given a formula φ, determine whether φ has a model".

But there are other, equally important tasks for a logic. Here is one:

Definition 6.2.2 (Model-checking). Model-checking, or *testing for truth* of formulas in given models, is answering the question: "Given a formula φ and a finite model M, s, check whether $M, s \models \varphi$".[47]

Often the working of a semantic truth definition seems "obvious", and students have no problems determining truth values in simple diagrams. The model-checking issue shows the interesting issues of "speed of understanding" behind this apparently simple practice.

Here is a third key task for a logical system, related to our discussion of invariance and expressive power:

Definition 6.2.3 (Model equivalence). Model comparison, or *testing for equivalence* of given models, is answering the question: "Given two finite models M, s, N, t, check if they satisfy the same formulas."

Consider the "complexity profiles" for two well-known classical logics around modal logic. Again we suppress some details to keep you alert. The entries in the following list mean that the problems have a solution algorithm inside the indicated class (an *upper bound*), and there is no solution method in a lower class (the given class is also a *lower bound*):

Theorem 9. The complexity profiles of propositional and first-order logic are as listed in the following table:

	Model-Checking	Satisfiability	Model Comparison
Propositional logic	*linear time (P)*	NP	*linear time (P)*
First-order logic	*PSPACE*	*undecidable*	NP

Proof. We merely give a few hints why all this is the case – in particular, without worrying about lower bounds backing up our upper bounds. First consider the profile of *propositional logic.* (a) *Model-checking is in P.* Given a fixed valuation, and an arbitrary formula φ, the task

---

[47]Model-checking also makes sense in suitably well-behaved infinite models.

of finding the truth value takes time polynomial in the size of φ. Just compute truth values for sub-formulas, working upwards in the syntactic construction tree of φ, and note that the number of sub-formulas is the length of φ (disregarding brackets). So the task just takes *linear time*, no higher polynomial degree is needed. (b) *Satisfiability is in NP*. Given any propositional formula φ, testing if it has a model takes non-deterministic polynomial time: we first guess some valuation (this is one non-deterministic step for the "N"), then compute a truth value **t** in polynomial time, as indicated before. This may require running through all lines of a truth table, so being in *NP* has a vague odour of exponential time, even though *NP* is lower in the complexity hierarchy.[48] (c) *Model equivalence is in linear time* (and hence in *P*) since two valuations satisfy the same formulas if they are the same, and this can be checked just running along the values for each proposition letter.

For the full *first-order language* these tasks work out as follows. *Model-checking* is in *P* if we fix the formula, and let the model size $|M| = n$ vary. Then we can write an obvious evaluation program whose iteration loops correspond to quantifiers: say, two nested loops in a checker for $\forall x \exists y Rxy$. We just measure the running time, which is n^2 for $\forall x \exists y Rxy$. If we also give the formula as an argument, however, we need a program which analyzes both the formula of quantifier depth k and the model of size n, and the above measure would give *EXPTIME*: n^k steps. But we can do better by being more careful about memory use, and show that this verification only requires *PSPACE* in $n + k$. *Satisfiability* is undecidable, of course: this is the well-known "undecidability of first-order logic" – though things are sometimes much better with fragments of the full language, as we will see in Chapter 7. Finally, as we have stated in Chapter 3, *model equivalence* in first-order logic amounts to the existence of an *isomorphism* between the given finite models. This "graph isomorphism problem" is at most in *NP*, but its precise complexity has not yet been determined.[49] □

6.3 The complexity profile of basic modal logic

Where does the basic modal language fit? Its model-checking problem, i.e., our best performance using the truth definition of Chapter 2, turns out to be efficient, and fast. While first-order model-checking requires a complete search through the whole model, repeated with every quantifier iteration and hence generating exponential growth, there are much faster modal algorithms. Also, close-reading the above decidability ar-

---

[48] Incidentally, validity is then in *co-NP*: the complement of this complexity class.

[49] For details of all these assertions, read Börger et al. (1997).

gument tells us where to locate satisfiability. Finally, the third basic task, testing for modal equivalence, or equivalently, for the existence of a bisimulation, has turned out relatively efficient, too:

Fact. The complexity profile for the minimal modal logic is as follows:

Model-Checking	Satisfiability	Model Comparison
P	$PSPACE$	P

Proof. (a) *Model-checking.* The best modal model-checking algorithm takes time steps of order $length(\varphi) \cdot size(\boldsymbol{M})^2$. Consider any modal formula φ of length m and finite model $\boldsymbol{M}$ of size n. Compute the truth values of all φ's sub-formulas, bottom-up, in all worlds of the model. Note that there are at most m sub-formulas, each uniquely marked by operators or proposition letters occurring in φ. For each sub-formula, this takes one pass through the model: n steps to compute its truth value, and then record it – in all the worlds of $\boldsymbol{M}$. Moreover, the number of steps at each world is bounded: we compute a truth value for

(a) atoms (1-step look-up), (b) a Boolean operator (fixed step size), or
(c) $\Diamond\psi$ with ψ_j truth values already available in each world.

The latter subroutine takes at worst n steps, searching through all successors of the current world. Adding up the number of rounds and their maximal cost, we get the stated bound:

$$m \cdot (n \cdot n)$$

The reader may find it of interest to see just how this argument differs from model-checking for first-order logic, and why a similar algorithm does not work there.[50] [51]

(b) For *satisfiability*, the crux (due to Fisher & Ladner in the 1970s) is that our proof of the finite model property need not *display* a model for the given formula. One can check for the existence of such a model branch by branch, erasing "work space", so that we can make do with polynomial space. Our first "model selection argument" in Chapter 4

---

[50]Vardi proved this relevant result: *finite variable fragments* of first-order logic with a fixed number of variables have a *PTIME* model-checking problem.

[51]A more precise look at our argument reveals an extra time requirement. To feed the model $\boldsymbol{M}$ to the algorithm, we think of it as a list of worlds (objects) *plus* the accessibility relation, which may contain at most n^2 items. Searching for successors of a given world requires inspection of this list, which would drive up the above estimate to n^2 steps, but not the polynomial-time outcome. Thus, these estimates depend on how we represent the computation and the data. But details of this do not matter up to constant factors in the polynomial. Of course, in practice, this is *essential* – and there is often a long way to efficient programs that work.

gives a prima facie *EXPTIME* bound: the model produced was exponential in the size of the given formula φ: "length-to-the-power-of-depth". In general this is unavoidable. There are modal formulas whose smallest models are exponential in just this sense. But we do not need to construct the whole model to check if one exists. One runs an algorithm that checks depth-first if the right branchings can be constructed, keeping track of all sub-formulas to be made true at each point (as in programming, say, with *Prolog*). This takes only polynomial space.

A way of seeing this is in terms of our earlier *semantic tableaux*, finite syntactic trees whose nodes record requirements to be met by a verifying model. These requirements are sets of sub-formulas of φ, with truth values indicated: of the order of $|\varphi|$. As we go down the tree, the modal depth of these sets decreases steadily, and so the maximal length of a branch is also of order $|\varphi|$. Thus, *on each branch* the maximum storage required is of size $|\varphi| \cdot |\varphi|$.[52] Now, we need no more. Say, after we checked the left-most branch, making sure its final requirements (depth 0) are consistent (a simple test), we backtrack, free the space below the backtracking point, go down the next branch, etcetera.

(c) *Model comparison*. We saw in Chapter 3 that finite models M, s and N, t satisfy the same modal formulas iff there is a bisimulation between them. Now, finding a bisimulation is a simple process of starting "from above", first putting all links between all worlds in the two models, and then successively eliminating all links that could never make it into any bisimulation.[53] We just sketch the algorithmic procedure, which is easy to visualize. Start with the universal relation that holds between any two points in the two models. This has at most n^2 pairs, where n is the maximum of the sizes of M and N:

- In step 1, remove all pairs that disagree on atomic propositions.
- In step $k + 1$ of the procedure, the previous stage has left us with a relation E_k. Now, remove all pairs (x, y) from the latter where x has some successor z in M such that for no successor u of y in N, the pair (z, u) belongs to E_k, and vice versa for some successor of y without an E_k-counterpart in M.

This procedure must stabilize at some stage: that is, $E_{k+1} = E_k$. If this happens with the initial link $s - t$ still in, then we have the required

---

[52]We do need some space for *pointers* keeping track of where we are in the recursion, so that we know where to backtrack, once some branch has been checked. But all this takes just linear space.

[53]For the cognoscenti, this is the computation of a bisimulation as a *greatest fixed-point* of some monotone operator on relations between finite models M, s and N, t. Cf. the lucid textbook Huth and Ryan (2000), or also our Chapter 22.

bisimulation. Otherwise, there is none. Both assertions are easy to see: throughout, we have only thrown away pairs which would be winning for the player Spoiler in some k-round bisimulation game, as in Chapter 3. The amount of time in this procedure is polynomial.[54] $\qquad\Box$

Some clarification behind all this: once again, analysis of given algorithms finds an *upper bound* on the complexity of the logical task. To show a *lower bound*, one must prove that *all* algorithms solving the task have at least this complexity. This may be much harder. One common method is this. There exists a set of "calibration problems" whose precise complexity has been determined. One can now *reduce* some such known problem, say in *NP* or *PSPACE*, to satisfiability in modal logic, with a reduction in polynomial time, and get a lower bound. This reduction method works for many problems with many logics.

6.4 Stronger modal logics and richer languages

We can also take these same issues to deductively stronger modal logics, such as *S4* or *S5*. Satisfiability in *S4* sides with *K*: it is in *PSPACE*-complete – but *S5* sides with propositional logic:

Fact. The satisfiability problem for *S5* is *NP*-complete.

Proof. We just state some relevant facts:

(a) Every model for *S5* has a bisimulation with a model where accessibility is the universal relation $W \times W$ on the worlds W,

(b) A formula satisfiable on *S5*-models, has a model of size *linear* in its length: much smaller than for basic modal logic. $\qquad\Box$

Here is a well-known example of a subtlety in complexity for modal logics. What about the system "2-*S5*" with two modalities, and two accessibility relations? This occurs in epistemic logic with two agents (see Chapter 12). Models now involve two equivalence relations, and satisfiability jumps back to *PSPACE*: social life is more complicated than being alone! With 3 or more agents, complexity remains the same.

Another main point is that complexity results are affected by the *expressive power* of the language. In Chapters 7 and 10, we define richer modal systems, and this move may drive up complexity even of the minimal modal logic of the new languages. For instance, adding a *universal modality* (with universal access to each world in a model) can make *PSPACE* logics *EXPTIME*, and sometimes even undecidable, by

---

[54] Alberto Policriti has given a very fast implementation in time $n \cdot \log(n)$.

giving encodings for undecidable benchmark problems, such as simulating computation of Turing machines, or geometrical "Tiling Problems" (cf. Chapter 24). For our purposes, we end with one general lesson:

"The Balance": expressive power versus computational effort In logic just as in physics, there is a "Golden Rule" of design: what you gain in one desirable dimension, you lose in another. In particular, high expressive power of a system means high complexity in terms of the three basic logical tasks hat we have outlined. And weakness may be strength. Thus, first-order logic itself is expressively weaker than second-order logic, the natural medium for defining many mathematical notions. But its poverty has a striking reward, viz. the recursive enumerability of valid consequence, and hence the Completeness Theorem, as well as powerful model-theoretic existence properties such as the Compactness Theorem.[55] A major methodological issue in logic is then to strike a *Balance* between expressive power and computational complexity. Many modal logics are good compromises on this road.

A final practical comment. Complexity in the sense of this chapter is a *worst-case measure*. It does not predict average behaviour. Many tasks that are exponential in principle run happily in real time. Practical groups worldwide (for some examples, see http://www.aiml.net and http://www.hylo.loria.fr) work with a mix of computational experimentation plus theoretical analysis to see how given modal logics actually behave on large classes of input problems.

---

[55]All these good properties fail for the much more expressive second-order logic.

Exercises Chapter 6

1. Evaluate modal formulas φ as follows. Start in a finite model M, s, and find all subformulas $\Box\psi$ of φ whose truth value needs to be determined. For these, run through all R-successors of s, and repeat the process for ψ.
   (a) Explain how this process may take exponential time in the size of M and φ.
   (b) Analyze how this algorithm differs from the one described in our text.
   (c) Why does the algorithm in our text not work for arbitrary first-order formulas?

2. The details of computing bisimulation:
   (a) Give an example of how the algorithm for testing bisimulation works. Take two concrete models and show how successive cross-links between worlds disappear.
   (b) Analyze in detail how much (P-)time is required by the given bisimulation algorithm as a function of the sizes of the given finite models M and N (i.e., their number of worlds).

3. A *celebrity* is someone who does not know anyone else in a group, and who is known by everyone else. Give a procedure that checks whether a given a group of n persons contains a celebrity. What is the complexity of this problem, in terms of n?

Part II

Basic Theory

After the introduction of the basic modal notions in Part I, we now continue with the theoretical study of a number of phenomena behind the behaviour that we have observed. Many of these have to do with understanding the systematic connections between modal logic and classical logics, mainly first-order, but also higher-order. In the next chapters, we strike out from the basic modal logic in a number of ways. First, there is a dimension of *expressive power*, i.e., what our formalism can say about the graph models that have been our exclusive semantic interest so far. We show in Chapter 7 how the modal language sits in a larger hierarchy of classical languages, viewing it as a way of providing "fine-structure" to classical model theory. Independently, there is a dimension of *deductive power*, and in Chapter 8 we look at the landscape of "modal logics" that extend the minimal modal logic while staying within its language. This landscape has been the usual focus in modal logic, but by now, other themes have become just as prominent – and thus our hike will be short. These logical systems may be viewed as special theories of restricted classes of models, and in Chapter 9, we focus on this connection per se using "correspondence" techniques. Beyond expressive and deductive power, there is a less well-defined, but real third dimension in current research, of changing the models one is dealing with, and this *descriptive power* is the topic of Chapter 10. Finally, Chapter 11 is about modal predicate logic mixing modality with object predicates and quantifiers: the grand old lady of a field which has largely "gone propositional" in recent decades.

7

Translation and varieties of expressive power

7.1 The classical standard translation

The clear analogy between the modal box $\Box$ and the universal quantifier $\forall$, and the modal diamond $\Diamond$ and the existential quantifier $\exists$ can be made precise via an effective translation from modal formulas into first-order ones, which formalizes the modal truth conditions:

Definition 7.1.1 (Standard translation). Consider a first-order language over our graph models $M = (W, R, V)$ with one binary predicate letter R for the accessibility relation, and unary predicate letters $P, Q, \ldots$ matching proposition letters $p, q, \ldots$. Let variables $x, y, z, \ldots$ range over worlds. The *standard translation* $ST(\varphi)$ of a modal formula φ is a first-order formula with one free variable x defined inductively:

$$
\begin{aligned}
ST(p) &= Px \\
ST(\neg\varphi) &= \neg ST(\varphi) \\
ST(\varphi \wedge \psi) &= ST(\varphi) \wedge ST(\psi) \\
ST(\Diamond\varphi) &= \exists y(Rxy \wedge [y/x]ST(\varphi)) \text{ [56]} \quad \text{where } y \text{ is a new variable} \\
ST(\Box\varphi) &= \forall y(Rxy \rightarrow [y/x]ST(\varphi)) \quad \text{where } y \text{ is a new variable}
\end{aligned}
$$

For instance,

(a) $\Diamond p$ says that $\exists y(Rxy \wedge Py)$: there exists a successor world of x where p holds,

(b) $\Box\Diamond(p \vee q)$ says that $\forall y(Rxy \rightarrow \exists z(Ryz \wedge (Pz \vee Qz)))$.

What should be obvious from this definition is the following equivalence, viewing possible worlds models as semantic structures that serve

---

[56] Here $[y/x]\varphi$ is the result of substituting y for all free occurrences of variable x in the formula φ. By choosing a new variable, y is "freely substitutable" in this way without clashes of bound variables. For a more sophisticated form of variable management, see the 2-variable analysis presented below.

both languages, modal and first-order, with the obvious assignment function "$x := w$" mapping the variable x to the world w:

Lemma (Switch Lemma).

$$\boldsymbol{M}, w \models \varphi \quad \text{iff} \quad \boldsymbol{M} \models ST(\varphi)[x := w], \quad \text{for all modal formulas } \varphi.$$

The assertion on the right is read according to the truth definition for first-order logic. In the early days, this Lemma was ritually proved by induction on φ – but all you really need is an ability to perform a Gestalt Switch between modal formulas and first-order formalizations of their semantic truth conditions on the same model $\boldsymbol{M}$.

Of course, the same translation, and its accompanying perspective switch, works for other modal languages. For instance, we can just as well have many binary accessibility relations R_i for a language with indexed modalities $[i]$, $\langle i \rangle$. More examples will come later.

7.2 The modal fragment

The standard translation takes the modal language into a part of a full first-order language:

Definition 7.2.1 (Modal fragment). The modal fragment of first-order logic is the set $\{ ST(\varphi) \mid \varphi$ is a basic modal formula$\}$. We will call formulas in the modal fragment "modal formulas" when usage is clear from the context. Sometimes this even extends to first-order formulas that are logically equivalent to formulas of the form $ST(\varphi)$.

Here is the more general picture:[57]

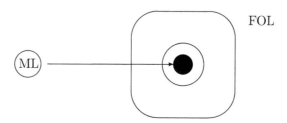

The embedding provided by the translation ST is proper. For instance, viewed as a property of a world x, the following analogous first-order formula is not in the modal fragment, and more strongly, it is not even semantically equivalent to any formula in this fragment:

---

[57]The shaded circle is the "modal fragment" in our narrower sense, as just the set of translations of modal formulas. The wider circle indicates the first-order formulas that are equivalent to such translations.

$\exists y(Rxy \wedge \neg Ryx \wedge Py)$ there exists a proper successor world of x where p holds.

Fact. Proper succession is modally undefinable.

Proof. It suffices to observe that this property of graph models is not invariant for the semantic *bisimulations* of Chapter 3. The dark world to the left in the 2-world model below has the above succession property, but it fails in its bisimulation contraction to a reflexive 1-loop:

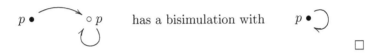

The modal fragment is characterized completely by this invariance:

Theorem 10 (Modal Invariance Theorem). The following assertions are equivalent for first-order formulas $\varphi = \varphi(x)$ with one free variable:

(a) φ is equivalent to a modal formula,

(b) φ is invariant for bisimulation.

A proof can be found in Chapter 25. But what you see already is that the modal language may be viewed in a natural manner as the bisimulation-invariant fragment of first-order logic, defining special properties of models that satisfy a much stricter semantic "transfer" criterion than just invariance under isomorphism.

7.3   Discussion: what good is a translation?

Translations between logical languages raise some general issues of reduction between formal systems, and modal logic provides a nice concrete focus. Of course, in some circles, "reducibility" via translation is a dreaded "*R*-word", but let's discuss things without drama.

Balance of expressive power and complexity Recall an earlier theme. The modal language "strikes a good balance". It is reasonably expressive: it can formulate natural properties of graph models, and valid reasoning patterns with these – and yet, it is so much weaker than full first-order logic that it escapes "Church's Curse": validity in basic modal logic is *decidable*, as we have seen. This combination of features is a role model for other fragments of first-order logic.

Uses and non-uses of a translation ST may be used directly to show that modal logic inherits the following fundamental properties of full first-order logic – even though these things were proved separately in earlier days when people's eyes were still clouded:

Theorem 11 (Compactness Theorem). Every finitely satisfiable set of modal formulas has a model itself.

Theorem 12 (Löwenheim-Skolem Theorem). Every satisfiable modal formula has a countable model.

But we already proved something much stronger than the latter theorem, namely, the Finite Model Property of modal logic, which has no counterpart for first-order logic. Its proof was not automatic, involving a deeper analysis of what makes the modal language special.

Moreover, more complicated properties of first-order logic need not transfer in the same easy manner. Despite a popular prejudice, fragments do not inherit all good properties of the bigger language automatically! Consider the following important first-order result:

Theorem 13 (Craig's Interpolation Theorem). If $\varphi \models \psi$, then there exists an "interpolant" α with $\varphi \models \alpha \models \psi$ such that every non-logical symbol in α occurs in both φ and ψ.

In particular, if φ, ψ are modal formulas, Craig's theorem says that they must have a first-order interpolant α. But what guarantees that this α itself is modal? This is not clear at all.[58] As it happens, the modal fragment has interpolation, and in fact, it inherits all nice properties of first-order logic that you get in a first advanced course. But this requires honest work via modal arguments.[59]

Tandem approach Does the translation ST mean that we can forget the modal language, and just do first-order logic? Several arguments plead against this:

- The translation encodes just one semantics for modalities (for instance, the proof-theoretic account of modality in Chapter 21 is quite different). So, the modal language still has an independent status.

- Thinking in the opposite direction: finding useful fragments of a larger language with a nice (variable-free) notation is a valuable art.

Therefore, we advocate using both viewpoints *in tandem*. Indeed, being able to look at the same topic in different ways is a typical abstract skill that one learns in academic life, transcending petty quarrels.

---

[58] You might want to reflect on what it is about the *form* of, say, the Löwenheim-Skolem Theorem versus the Craig's Interpolation theorem that makes the one, but not the other, transfer easily to modal logic.

[59] This harmony is still not understood precisely, though bisimulation seems an important clue. In fact, many natural-looking fragments of first-order logic lack interpolation, and this scarcity has been analyzed and explained in Balder ten Cate's dissertation *Model Theory for Extended Modal Languages* (ten Cate, 2005).

7.4 Extended modal languages

The first-order setting suggests a move to richer modal languages. In many applications, the basic modal language has the annoying feature of "being just a bit off for the job", and additional expressive power would make our life a lot easier. While some logicians feel this is "cheating", since one should only walk in the wooden shoes of our modal forefathers, the reality of modal logic today is "language design". Here are three examples of first-order definable additions.

Definition 7.4.1 (Universal modality). The *universal modality* reads as follows: $M, s \models U\varphi$ iff $M, t \models \varphi$ *for all worlds* t in the model, accessible or not. The dual *existential modality* $E\varphi$ is defined as $\neg U \neg \varphi$.

Universal and existential modalities are often used when we want to define global notions, not tied to any specific world. An example is global entailment between modal propositions φ, ψ in our model, in the form $U(\varphi \to \psi)$.[60] One immediate question is now if such additions disrupt the properties that we have so carefully investigated for the basic modal language. Here are a few facts about "*MLU*", basic modal logic extended with the universal modality. You may be able to figure out a few, just by looking at the following statements:

(a) The ST-translation extends, with a clause $ST(U\varphi) = \forall x ST(\varphi)$.

(b) There is a characteristic notion of bisimulation for MLU, where we either add zigzag clauses for going to arbitrary new worlds, or equivalently, we add the requirement that the domain and range of an MLU-bisimulation between two models M and N be the whole universes of these models.

(c) Validity in MLU is decidable, though the computational complexity goes up from the $PSPACE$-completeness of basic modal logic to $EXPTIME$-completeness.

(d) There is a simple axiomatization for MLU which has the minimal modal logic for $\Box, \Diamond$, modal $S5$ for U, E, plus connection axioms $U\varphi \to \Box\varphi$.[61]

Many further new operators exist, like this "other-worldly" one:

Definition 7.4.2 (Modal difference logic). "Difference logic" is a slightly more ambitious extension of the basic modal language, which has been proposed in temporal logics for specifying process behaviour:

$$M, w \models D\varphi \text{ iff } \textit{there exists at least one } v \neq w \text{ with } M, v \models \varphi.$$

---

[60]It may look as if this addition takes us all the way up to first-order logic – but our modal language still lacks lots of expressive first-order features.

[61]The axioms for the modal logic $S5$ are presented and discussed in Chapter 8.

The existential modality is now definable as $E\varphi := D\varphi \vee \varphi$, and then the following formula expresses φ's truth "in a unique world": $E(\varphi \wedge \neg D\varphi)$.[62] This extended language has a simple extended notion of bisimulation whose formulation we leave to the reader. Also, the validities of the system can be axiomatized completely on top of the minimal modal logic K. For instance, the symmetry of the inequality relation $\neq$ shows up in the axiom

$$D\neg D\neg\varphi \to \varphi.$$

Validity is still decidable, but the complexity goes up!

Other kinds of extension of the basic modal language occur in temporal logic. In this setting, we read "worlds" as points in time, ordered by an accessibility relation of "earlier than":

Definition 7.4.3 (Temporal "Until" or "Since"). $M, t \models UNTIL\ \varphi\psi$ holds iff $\exists t' > t : M, t' \models \varphi \wedge \forall t''((t < t'' \wedge t'' < t') \to M, t'' \models \psi)$:

Such expressive extensions are a good test for the viability of our modal theory (and your understanding of it): they all generalize bisimulation, completeness, and other earlier themes.

Hybrid logic A systematic program of extending the basic modal language as required by specific applications has been long in the making. In retrospect, expressive extensions occur with Arthur Prior in the 1950s, who added what are now called *nominals*, that is, proposition letters a that denote one particular time-point, or world in a model, instead of the usual p that can denote any set of worlds.[63] Nominals, and the above universal modality U inspired the extended modal logic program of the "Sophia School", an innovative group of Bulgarian logicians in the 1980s. In the 1990s, this approach led to so-called *hybrid logic*, a family of first-order extensions of the basic modal language.[64]

Basic hybrid languages have nominals, the universal modality, and *"reset modalities"* $@_a\varphi$ saying that φ is true at the world denoted by a.

---

[62] *Alternative viewpoint*: difference logic may be viewed as a "bi-modal logic" of one new relation $\neq$, in addition to R, which has some special frame properties.

[63] In temporal logic, stronger and stronger modalities were added in the 1970s – up to a point where the "modal" notation had become as expressive as first-order logic itself. This was achieved by "hiding variables" in ways that ultimately went back to a famous paper by Quine: "Variables Explained Away", in Quine (1966).

[64] The chapter on "Hybrid Logic" by Areces and ten Cate in Blackburn et al. (2006) surveys this lively area in depth.

Stronger expressive resources occur as well, in particular the *"binder"* $\downarrow x \cdot \varphi$ saying that φ holds when we let the propositional variable x denote the current world. Thus, the formula $\downarrow x \cdot \Diamond x$ says that the current world w is accessible to itself: Rww.[65] The full hybrid language sketched so far has the following inductive syntax:

$$p \mid a \mid x \mid \neg\varphi \mid \varphi \wedge \psi \mid \Diamond\varphi \mid @_a\varphi \mid @_x\varphi \mid \downarrow x \cdot \varphi$$

The semantics involves modal models M as usual, plus an assignment function g mapping propositional variables x to worlds $g(x)$. One then defines when a hybrid formula is true at a world given an assignment. We display a few truth conditions that give the idea:

$$
\begin{array}{lll}
M, g, w \models a & \text{iff} & V(a) = \{w\} \\
M, g, w \models x & \text{iff} & w = g(x) \\
M, g, w \models \Diamond\varphi & \text{iff} & \text{there is a } v \text{ with } Rwv \text{ and } M, g, v \models \varphi \\
M, g, w \models @_a\varphi & \text{iff} & M, g, v \models \varphi \text{ where } V(a) = \{v\} \\
M, g, w \models @_x\varphi & \text{iff} & M, g, g(x) \models \varphi \\
M, g, w \models \downarrow x \cdot \varphi & \text{iff} & M, g[x := w], w \models \varphi
\end{array}
$$

This widely used modal language can still be translated into first-order logic. The extended translation takes any hybrid formula φ and variable x, and writes an equivalent first-order formula $ST_x(\varphi)$ with free variable x. The reader will find it instructive to look for the right inductive clauses – but to set you on your path, here are two:

$$
\begin{aligned}
ST_x(@_y\varphi) &= ST_y(\varphi) \\
ST_x(\downarrow y \cdot \varphi) &= [y/x]ST_x(\varphi)
\end{aligned}
$$

The fragment of first-order logic obtained in this way is clearly stronger than the basic modal one. Which precise language is it? We will return to that question in Section 7.6.

7.5 Fine-structure of first-order logic: counting variables, and guards

Given this plethora of extended modal languages, what is the general situation? The preceding examples were fragments of first-order logic under suitable extensions of the standard translation ST. What sort of fragment are "modal" languages? One line runs as follows, using the *number of variables* needed as a measure of *fine-structure*:

Fact. Each basic modal formula can be translated into an equivalent first-order formula using only two variables, free or bound.

---

[65]Simple as it is, this first-order property is not definable in the modal base language: just unravel a reflexive point to a bisimilar infinite irreflexive tree.

Proof. The following example will show the general trick. To translate the modal formula $\square\lozenge p$, ST might take a first-order formula with fresh bound variables for each modality:

$$\forall y(Rxy \rightarrow \exists z(Ryz \wedge Pz))$$

but you can also say this equivalently by "recycling" the two variables x, y as follows:

$$\forall y(Rxy \rightarrow \exists \boldsymbol{x}(R\boldsymbol{x}z \wedge P\boldsymbol{x}))$$

It is easy to generalize this to a systematic 2-variable translation that works for any modal formula. □

More systematically, there is a fine-structure hierarchy of finite-variable fragments *FO1*, *FO2*, *FO3*, ... of the full first-order language. The basic modal language uses only 2 variables, a temporal language with *UNTIL* uses 3 variables, as is easy to check in the same style as above by recycling variables.[66] It has indeed been proposed that the right way of thinking about modal languages is as variable-free notations for finite-variable fragments. But this fine-structure hierarchy does not explain the *decidability* of modal languages.

Fact. The 3-variable fragment *FO3* is undecidable.

Proof. The reason is that the complete algebra of binary relations can be formulated in this language, including the Boolean operations in a format like this (with just 2 variables):

$$(R \cup S)(x, y) \leftrightarrow Rxz \vee Szy$$

but the crucial operation of *composition* essentially involves 3 variables, since we need to explicitly state the existence of an intermediate point between the two arguments:

$$(R; S)(x, y) \leftrightarrow \exists x(Rxz \wedge Szy).$$

In logic, this relational algebra is known to be undecidable.[67] □

So, here is another line of analysis. Consider what is clearly the typical clause in the ST translation:

$\lozenge p$ goes to the bounded or "guarded" quantifier $\exists y(Rxy \wedge Py)$.

These "guards" turn out to be a more revealing form of fine-structure, regulating which local part of the model the "modal" quantifiers range over – and this gives the following orthogonal fine-structure for the full language of first-order logic:

---

[66] Still more complex notions, like suprema in orderings, use 4 variables.

[67] For more details, you can consult, e.g., Monk (1976).

variable levels   quantifier bounds

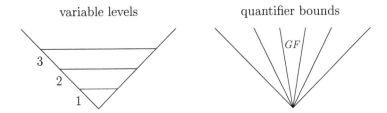

Generalizing this observation, here is a very strong fragment of first-order logic, far beyond the basic modal language, which still behaves in our general modal style (Andréka et al., 1998). It balances right at the edge between good expressive power and undecidability.

Definition 7.5.1 (Guarded Fragment). The *Guarded Fragment* consists of all formulas generated by the following syntax rule:

atoms $P\boldsymbol{x}$ with $\boldsymbol{x}$ a tuple of variables $|\ \neg\varphi\ |\ (\varphi\vee\psi)\ |\ \exists\boldsymbol{y}(G(\boldsymbol{x},\boldsymbol{y})\wedge\varphi(\boldsymbol{x},\boldsymbol{y}))$

where $G(\boldsymbol{x},\boldsymbol{y})$ is an atom with variables from the sequences $\boldsymbol{x},\boldsymbol{y}$ occurring in any order and multiplicity.

Note how we generalize the idea that modal evaluation needs to take place at single worlds, while we also allow cumulative reference to sets of objects $\boldsymbol{x},\boldsymbol{y}$ provided they are guarded. Note also that we do *not* allow new variables $\boldsymbol{z}$ to occur in the final guarded formula $\varphi(\boldsymbol{x},\boldsymbol{y})$.

This fragment still has a characteristic notion of "guarded bisimulation", and moreover, its complexity stays low:

Theorem 14. The Guarded Fragment is decidable.

The proof generalizes the modal filtration method of Chapter 4 to first-order formulas, and while not too hard, it is beyond the scope of this introductory course. It can be shown that many extended modal languages end up inside the Guarded Fragment under translation.

The above logics with universal and difference modalities involve slight additions to guarded syntax. More importantly, so does the temporal logic of *UNTIL*, which requires an slight extension, still decidable, to the so-called *Loosely Guarded Fragment*. The essential feature in "loose guarding" is this: in *UNTIL*-statements of the form

$$\exists y(x < y \wedge Ay \wedge \forall z((x < z \wedge z < y) \rightarrow Bz)),$$

each pair of variables from $\{x, y, z\}$ occurs under some guard predicate.

By contrast, the definition of relational composition was not loosely guarded. In the crucial formula $\exists z(Rxz \wedge Szy)$, the variables x, y do not occur together under a guard.

7.6 The cliffs of undecidability

So, where is the danger zone: what expressive power makes first-order logic drop down the cliff? Syntactically, allowing *arbitrary* conjunctions of guard atoms instead of single ones makes first-order fragments undecidable. For instance, one can effectively reduce the satisfiability problem for the undecidable 3-variable fragment $FO3$ to satisfiability for a conjunctively guarded language. More generally, we will explain in Section 7.8 below that undecidability tends to strike as soon as a first-order language can encode *"grid structure"*. And the basic "convergence property" needed for the basic "cells" of this structure is typically one step beyond the guarded fragment, requiring a quantification

$$\forall y(Rxy \to \forall z(Rxz \to \exists u(Ryu \land Rzu)))$$

that lacks guard atoms for object combinations like x, u or y, z. In fact, this convergence formula is not even loosely guarded.

Finally, here is another non-guarded statement, viz. *transitivity* of the accessibility order:

$$\forall x \forall y(Rxy \to \forall z(Ryz \to Rxz)).$$

This may seem strange, as modal logicians believe that this ubiquitous property only makes life easier. But it is known that the complete first-order theory of a transitive relation is undecidable. The fact that many modal logics over transitive models are decidable must have a special explanation, and we will mention one below.

Bounded Fragment The transition from decidable to undecidable fragments is also nicely illustrated by the earlier full hybrid language. It can be shown that its translations are precisely equivalent to all first-order formulas in the so-called *Bounded Fragment* (*BF*), where all quantifiers occur relativized to accessibility atoms:

$$\exists y(Rxy \land \varphi), \qquad \forall y(Rxy \to \varphi).$$

The special quantification pattern of *BF* has come up in set theory, arithmetic, and other areas of logic.[68] This differs from the Guarded Fragment in that the formula φ behind the quantifier prefix may contain other free variables than the x, y occurring in the atom. And this difference is significant. The Bounded Fragment is undecidable!

---

[68] *BF* can be characterized semantically as consisting, up to logical equivalence, of the first-order formulas invariant under taking *generated submodels* (i.e., sub-models closed under R-successors). This is a special case of bisimulation invariance.

7.7 Moving up and sideways: higher-order and fixed-point languages

Classical first-order logic can be extended in many ways. Adding quantification over sets or predicates leads to *second-order logic*. We will encounter this much more expressive logic in our study of "frame correspondences" for modal axioms in Chapter 9. Another important extension for mathematical and computational reasons adds *fixed-point operators* that form, e.g., the transitive closure of an accessibility relation, or define other important notions inductively. We will see examples in many later chapters, and we will study modal logics with fixed-point operators in Chapter 22. The point to make here is this:

The behaviour of a logic is often best seen when it is put in a richer environment – just as a good test of people's character is to see what happens when they suddenly get wealthy:

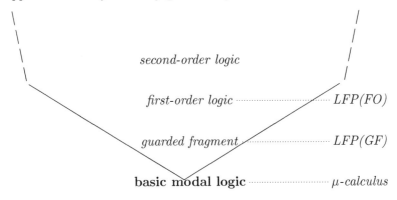

For instance, first-order logic with added smallest and greatest fixed-point operators (*"LFP(FO)"*) makes a huge jump in complexity, since it can define the natural numbers up to isomorphism, and hence encode True Arithmetic. By contrast, modal fixed-point logics (an example is the modal μ-calculus (cf. the chapter by Bradfield & Stirling in Blackburn et al. (2006), cf. also Chapter 22) remain decidable![69]

7.8 Another source of complexity: combination of modal logics

In addition to increasing expressive power by strengthening the basic modalities, one other striking modern direction is *combination of basic modalities*. This happens in modal logics for modality and time, or for

---

[69] Even the complete Guarded Fragment with added fixed-point operators (*"LFP(GF)"*) remains decidable, as has been shown by Erich Graedel.

knowledge and action of agents in Part III of these lectures. Here we only note a few issues, as background to our discussion of decidability. Technical details will be found in Chapter 24 in Part IV.

When both components of a combined logic are simple, a "Divide-and-Conquer" strategy might say that the whole system will be simple, too. But this crucially depends on a third "argument": the manner of composition. A telling discovery in the 1990s has been that modal system combination can lead to high complexity, depending on how we let the separate modalities "interact". Here is a typical illustration:

Theorem 15. The minimal modal logic of two modalities [1], [2] satisfying the axiom $[1][2]\varphi \to [2][1]\varphi$, in a language with the added universal modality U, is undecidable.

Instead of a proof, we sketch the background. What the axiom says is easily seen by frame correspondence (see Chapter 9 for definitions). It forces frames (W, R) for the logic to look like a *grid structure* satisfying a first-order convergence property, similar to one we already mentioned:

$$\forall xyz : (xR_1y \land yR_2z) \to \exists u : (xR_2u \land uR_1z).$$

The most typical example for this is the structure $\mathbb{N} \times \mathbb{N}$, where we take two relations: $NORTH$ moving one step from (i, j) to $(i, j+1)$ and $EAST$ moving from (i, j) to $(i + 1, j)$:

$$\vdots$$

$$(0, 1) \dashrightarrow (1, 1)$$
$$\uparrow \qquad \qquad \wedge$$
$$(0, 0) \longrightarrow (1, 0) \qquad \cdots$$

Now, as we will show in Chapter 24, on such grid models, our simple bi-modal language can express geometrical *Tiling Problems* that are undecidable, sometimes even of very high second-order complexity.

Perhaps the simplest way of understanding this is by noting that successive horizontal rows of an infinite grid can encode successive tape configurations of Turing machines on any input, while vertical moves mimic computation steps. And as it turns out, the bi-modal language is strong enough to express these two directions.[70]

---

[70]Grid patterns also occur naturally with logics of agency (see Chapters 14, 17). We will see that the interchange axiom $K[a]\varphi \to [a]K\varphi$ for knowledge and action, which expresses a seemingly natural harmless feature of "Perfect Recall", can lead to systems with very high complexity. In fact, the combined modal logic of agents with perfect memory is as rich as some standard mathematical theories.

Trees versus grids This analysis gives us an appealing general view-point on the "danger zone" described in Section 7.6, which is often cited in the modal literature.

Modal logics of *trees* are harmless, modal logics of *grids* are dangerous!

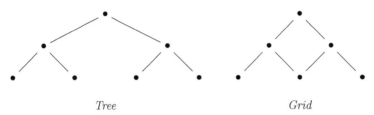

Tree   Grid

Once again, this shows how the Guarded Fragment manages to stay decidable. Its formulas define tree structure, but they typically cannot express grid structure. In line with this syntactic fact, unlike trees, grid structure is typically not invariant under *bisimulations* – as can be seen by unraveling a grid to a tree by the methods of Chapter 3.

7.9 Conclusions

Given this lush landscape of possible logics, including a great variety of "modal languages", the reader may well want to step back, and ask what made the original modal base logic so special, given that something must "give" in its system properties when we move to all these extensions. Topics like this are studied in Abstract Model Theory, and in Chapter 25, we will present a few general results, including a proof of the Modal Invariance Theorem, as well as a *Lindström Theorem* explaining what makes the basic modal logic so unique.

Exercises Chapter 7

1. Here are some questions about translations:
   (a) Translate the following modal formula into a first-order one with 2 variables x, y only (free or bound): $\langle b \rangle(\langle a \rangle p \wedge [b] \langle a \rangle q)$.
   (b) Show that this first-order formula is not modally definable:

   $$UNTIL\ pq \quad \exists y((x < y \wedge Py \wedge \forall z((x < z \wedge z < y) \rightarrow Qz))$$

   (c) Interpret the modal language in the original Leibniz models, saying that $\Box \varphi$ is true if φ is true at every world. Based on this, give a simpler translation of the basic modal language into a first-order language. In which fragment do you end up? Conclude that this version of modal logic is decidable.
   (d) Let first-order models have a family of relations $Dx, \boldsymbol{y}$ (with $\boldsymbol{y}$ a finite sequence of variables) saying that x is independent from the sequence of variables $\boldsymbol{y}$. Interpret first-order formulas $\exists x \varphi(x, \boldsymbol{y})$ (with $x, \boldsymbol{y}$ all the free variables of φ) as saying there is some x independent from $\boldsymbol{y}$ such that φ holds. Show that this first-order logic is decidable.

2. Consider the modal logic of $\Diamond, \Box$ extended with the modality E: "at some world".
   (a) Show that all formulas of this extended modal language can be translated into the 2-variable fragment of first-order logic.
   (b) Show that Ep is not invariant for basic modal bisimulation.
   (c) Define the appropriate *strengthened bisimulation* for this language precisely.
   (d) What is the complexity of model-checking?
   (e) Show that we still cannot define the "difference modality" in this language.

3. In temporal logic, $SINCE\ pq$ is true at a point if p holds at some earlier point, while q holds at all points in between.
   (a) Translate the modal statement $SINCE\ pq$ into a first-order formula, using a binary predicate "<" for "later than".
   (b) Show that 3 variables suffice for translating any formula in a temporal language with proposition letters, Booleans, and the $UNTIL$ and $SINCE$ operators into first-order logic.

4. Consider hybrid languages extending basic modal logic:
   (a) Give the first-order translation for the full hybrid language, and show its semantic correctness by an inductive argument.

(b) Give a converse translation from the Bounded Fragment into the full hybrid language, and prove its completeness as well.

5. Recall the Guarded Fragment:
   (a) Explain the basic idea of guarded formulas, and find some examples beyond those in the text.
   (b) The formula $Ex\neg Px$ is not definable by a guarded formula. How would you try to prove this?

6. Using two binary relation symbols *East* and *North*, define as much as you can of the complete first-order theory of the grid model $\mathbb{N} \times \mathbb{N}$. Which formulas are guarded, which ones are not?

8

Increasing deductive power: the landscape of modal logics

In this chapter, we look at another dimension of modal logic. We do not increase the expressive strength of our basic language – but we now extend its deductive strength, by means of further axioms on top of the minimal logic. This is a difference with first-order logic, where just one system of validities emerged.[71] Various "modal logics" represent natural clusters of axioms that people have found plausible for certain readings of the modalities $\Box, \Diamond$. And of course, there is also the joy of pure exploration of a landscape. Our presentation is discursive, as we just want to extend your erudition a little bit.[72]

8.1 Some old favourites

The minimal modal logic has been explored already in Chapter 5.[73] Here are some ubiquitous further systems, following Lewis' original nomenclature for systems of "strict implication". We start by recalling our preliminary discussion of famous modal systems:

Definition 8.1.1 (*T*, *S4*, and *S5*). The system T adds the axiom schema $\Box\varphi \to \varphi$ to K, or equivalently, $\varphi \to \Diamond\varphi$. Next, *S4* adds the *4* axiom $\Box\varphi \to \Box\Box\varphi$ to T, or equivalently $\Diamond\Diamond\varphi \to \Diamond\varphi$. Finally, *S5* adds the following axiom to *S4*: $\Diamond\Box\varphi \to \varphi$, or equivalently, $\varphi \to \Box\Diamond\varphi$.

These logics have very different validities, and hence different repertoires of modal assertions. To see this, define a *modality* as a finite sequence of modal operators:

---

[71]That is, if one disregards competitors like intuitionistic or linear logic.

[72]Some students find it preferable to first study Chapter 9 on frame correspondence, to have a better semantic grasp of what the axioms in this chapter say.

[73]Aside: "minimal" is a relative term, and we will see even weaker systems later.

Fact. K and T have infinitely many non-equivalent modalities, $S4$ has only 7, $S5$ just 3.

Proof. One can easily give models consisting of finite intransitive chains that show how K and T can distinguish infinitely many modalities. The "collapse" in $S4$ involves the fact that all modalities become provably equivalent to one of the following:

$$p \quad \Box p \quad \Diamond p \quad \Box \Diamond p \quad \Diamond \Box p \quad \Diamond \Box \Diamond p \quad \Box \Diamond \Box p$$

Clearly, $S4$ collapses repeated cases $\Box\Box$ and $\Diamond\Diamond$ to single ones, and as for alternations of length 4, recall an earlier-mentioned fact that the following principle is provable as well:

$$\Box \Diamond \Box \Diamond \varphi \leftrightarrow \Box \Diamond \varphi$$

Finally, $S5$ is so strong as to make every modality equivalent to one of three: $-, \Diamond, \Box$. Here is a typical example of a relevant derivation:

$$\vdash_{S5} \Box\Diamond\varphi \leftrightarrow \Diamond\varphi$$

1)	$\Box\Diamond\varphi \to \Diamond\varphi$	T axiom
2)	$\Diamond\varphi \to \Box\Diamond\Diamond\varphi$	$S5$ axiom
3)	$\Diamond\Diamond\varphi \to \Diamond\varphi$	$S4$ axiom
4)	$\Box\Diamond\Diamond\varphi \to \Box\Diamond\varphi$	from line 3 in K
5)	$\Diamond\varphi \to \Box\Diamond\varphi$	from lines 2 and 4

$\Box$

Here is something even stronger, showing how $S5$ is still close to propositional logic, making it a popular system in many applications:

Fact. In $S5$, every formula is equivalent to one of modal depth ≤ 1.

Proof. It is easy to find an algorithm that works inside out. Using principles of Boolean algebra and the modal distribution laws of K, place outermost modalities in front of either purely propositional formulas (then the job is done), or of conjunctions or disjunctions containing at least one modalized conjunct or disjunct. Next, identify "reduction principles" for modalities over conjunctions and disjunctions that still contain modalities inside, which are provable in $S5$ (no such principles hold even in $S4$). Here is one example:

$$\Box(\varphi \vee \Box\psi) \leftrightarrow (\Box\varphi \vee \Box\psi) \qquad [74]$$

$\Box$

---

[74]You will be asked to find the complete list in the Exercises to this chapter.

Other modal logics In addition to these well-known modal logics, there are many others. For instance, the logic *K4* is *S4* minus the *T*-axiom, which only requires transitivity of accessibility relations. This works for temporal order with an accessibility relation "later than" that is not necessarily reflexive. One more axiom that makes sense in such a temporal setting is the following *right-linearity axiom*, which added to *K4* gives the logic *K4.3*:

$$(\Diamond \varphi \wedge \Diamond \psi) \to (\Diamond(\varphi \wedge \psi) \vee \Diamond(\varphi \wedge \Diamond \psi) \vee \Diamond(\psi \wedge \Diamond \varphi))$$

But modal axioms have many shapes and motivations – see Section 8.3 below on "Löb's Axiom" in provability logic (cf. also Chapter 21) that gives rise to a famous axiomatic system *GL*.

Much of the field has been about taxonomy of such axiomatic systems. In these lectures, we present a modern view largely ignoring this traditional perspective, so you will get only a minimum of these codes, which included tongue-breakers like *S4.3Grz*... Our reason is that these systems are not "different modal logics", but different special theories of particular kinds of accessibility relation. We do not speak of "different first-order logics" when we vary the underlying model class. There is no good reason for that here, either.[75]

8.2 The lattice of modal logics: two highways

There are many other modal logics, in fact: *uncountably many*. Here is how you count:

(a) There are countably many formulas: all finite strings from a finite alphabet,

(b) Modal logics are essentially the $2^{\aleph_0}$ possible subsets of these.[76]

In this vast ocean of possibilities, only few specific modal logics have been explored. Moreover, some forms of good system behaviour are necessarily less abundant:

(c) There are only countably many *decidable* modal logics, because there are only countably many decision procedures.

Now, starting from the minimal modal logic *K*, two main "highways" lead into the realm of modal logic. One leads to the system *"Id"*: the

---

[75] I have hesitated about giving a catalogue of modal logics with their usual names, since my aim is to do away with botany of formal systems. Still, I cannot deny its powerful hold over practitioners, maybe even my readers. Even today you will often hear, to my mind, weird statements like "belief is *KD45*": again a code name – as if reciting some formal system amounts to understanding a phenomenon.

[76] Modal logics are sets of formulas satisfying deductive closure conditions, but this does not affect the count essentially.

logic of reflexive isolated points, axiomatized by

$$\Box\varphi \leftrightarrow \varphi$$

the other toward the system *"Un"* (the logic of irreflexive isolated end-points), axiomatized by

$$\Box\bot$$

In an obvious manner, both make every modal formula equivalent to a purely propositional one. Here is partial map of the resulting landscape of modal logic, with some more names:

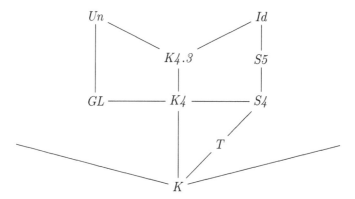

Theorem 16. Every modal logic in the base language that extends the minimal K is contained in one of the two systems Id or Un.

Think of the first road as leading to Heaven, and the other going to Hell. Indeed, the latter route contains exciting and seductive spots.

Proof. We give a sketch, as the main idea is within your reach by now. Take any consistent modal logic L. Consider any frame $F = (W, R)$ [77] where all axioms of L hold for all valuations V. *Case 1*: Frame F has some end point. Then L also holds for all valuations in the generated sub-frame consisting of just that end point (modal formulas "do not look back"), and $L \subseteq Un$. *Case 2*: Frame F has no end-points. Then the map sending every point in F to one single reflexive point is a functional bisimulation (also called a "p-morphism"), a construction that preserves truth of modal theories. Hence $L \subseteq Id$.[78]   □

---

[77] We will study this natural purely relational notion underlying our models in Chapter 9. You may want to return to this passage later.

[78] This proof skates over some difficulties, and it also uses technical notions from modal model theory. Still, our case distinction is the heart of the matter!

The lattice of modal logics nurtures fascinating mathematical phenomena. For instance, there are interesting "intervals" between logics, and a famous one is that between $S5$ and Id. "Bull's Theorem" tells us that it contains only countably many logics, each of which is the complete logic of some specific finite frame! We will analyze possible axioms in this landscape systematically in Chapter 9, by semantic correspondences with special conditions on the accessibility relation.

The Id-route contains most major modal logics, including the main ones used for modeling knowledge, read as the box modality $\Box\varphi$ that "φ is true in all epistemically accessible alternatives". Our further chapters will have many examples. But the other road contains intriguing logics, too, and we will discuss one to show the surprising power of modal logic.

8.3 Modal logic of provability and proofs

We saw earlier that the modal box can also be read as provability: the existence of a proof, or more general, "evidence" for an assertion. Note that we now take an "existential quantifier" view of knowledge, rather than the above "universal quantifier" one – while still staying inside modal semantics. Here is an illustration of this "provability logic". The modal distribution axiom gets a new meaning, as the formula

$$\Box(\varphi \rightarrow \psi) \rightarrow (\Box\varphi \rightarrow \Box\psi):$$

if $\varphi \rightarrow \psi$ is provable and also φ, then ψ is provable. In a picture:

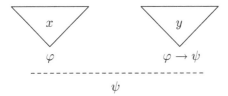

In terms of proofs, this modal law says that, if x is a proof of φ, and y a proof of $\varphi \rightarrow \psi$, then juxtaposition of the trees x, y joined by an application of Modus Ponens at the bottom is a proof for ψ: so, the modal axiom is a constructive form of Modus Ponens.[79]

Remark: Co-existence The provability interpretation sees necessity as having compelling reasons for an assertion. There is no contradiction with the earlier semantic account of basic modal logic. In the completeness theorem for first-order logic, you see just these two faces. Validity

---

[79]Modal logics can also be enriched with explicit *proof terms*, to formalize this richer interpretation. Chapter 21 elaborates this, and has further references.

quantifies universally over models, and the equivalent notion of provability is existential quantification, but over a *different domain*, viz. that of syntactic proofs.

In particular, we can study provability logics for specific mathematical theories, and then plain modal formulas come to express deep assertions in the foundations of mathematics. The highway toward *Un* contains the following important modal system:

Definition 8.3.1 (Gödel-Löb provability logic). The Gödel-Löb logic *GL* extends the minimal modal logic *K* with the following axiom:

$$\Box(\Box\varphi \to \varphi) \to \Box\varphi$$

To understand this system, the modal box $\Box\varphi$ now says that the formula φ is provable in some specific mathematical theory crucial to the foundations of mathematics, viz. "Peano Arithmetic". The axiom looks strange from an *Id*-route perspective, since it seems to say that the formerly harmless principle of modal Veridicality can only hold for provable formulas. But what it really reflects is a deep result about formal arithmetic called "Löb's Theorem".

We will study this system in more detail in Chapter 21 – but right here, it serves as a useful reminder that there are very natural modal logics which are utterly unlike the usual systems of *T*, *S4* or *S5* that have tended to dominate the philosophical literature.

8.4   Completeness theorems

There are many completeness theorems for axiomatic systems in the landscape that we have just discussed. A typical example is that for the modal logic *S4* when we restrict validity to models whose accessibility relation is both *reflexive* and *transitive*:

Theorem 17. For all modal formulas φ, $\vdash_{S4} \varphi$ iff $\models_{refl \& trans} \varphi$.

For all logics mentioned so far, the outcome turns out to be similar. Provability in the logic amounts to validity of formulas in models whose underlying frame satisfies a semantic condition *corresponding* to the axioms for the logic – in a sense made precise in Chapter 9. Proofs of completeness are sometimes just like for the minimal modal logic. For instance, working with maximally consistent sets in *S4*, the defined accessibility relation in the Henkin model (cf. Chapter 5) is automatically reflexive and transitive. But for other logics, things can be much more complicated, and there is a whole industry of techniques, such as "bull-dozing", or more refined forms of model surgery.[80]

---

[80]See the earlier-mentioned textbook Blackburn et al. (2001) for a detailed expo-

Remark: Two Directions There are really two directions in modal completeness research. One direction starts from a given proof system (usually, a set of axioms and rules), and asks for a natural class of models over which universal validity coincides with provability in the system. This corresponds with tasks of *semantic modelling*, where we start from a linguistic practice of speaking and reasoning, and construct some semantic account for that. The other direction starts from some independently given class of models, and asks for a complete axiomatization of the modal validities over it: its "modal axiomatic theory". The latter direction has been dominant in temporal logics (cf. Chapter 18), where we think of Time as independent from language. This can lead to very interesting new modal axioms.

Example (Modal logic of Minkowski space-time). In relativistic space-time, the universe consists of tuples (x, y, z, t) of three spatial coordinates plus a temporal one. Simplifying, consider a one-dimensional space with pairs (x, t). Crucial to physics is the "future light-cone", i.e., the set of all pairs "reachable" from the current one by some signal at most as fast as the speed of light. In a picture, rotated for convenience, this gives us the following "causal accessibility relation":

$$(x, t)R(x', t') \quad \text{iff} \quad x \leq x' \text{ and } t \leq t'$$

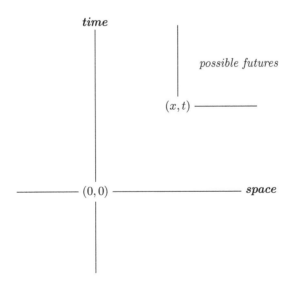

The modal logic of this spatio-temporal structure extends $S4$ with the following so-called "Geach Axiom", whose precise semantic meaning will be determined in the next chapter:

$$\Diamond \Box \varphi \to \Box \Diamond \varphi$$

The resulting modal logic $S4.2$ is indeed the complete logic of Minkowski space-time.[81] The proof (due to Shehtman, Goldblatt in the 1970s) is complex, and it involves transforming counter-examples on abstract possible worlds models into concrete physical spaces.

In either direction, success is not assured when seeking completeness theorems! There are simple modal proof systems for which no complete semantics exists at all (this "modal incompleteness" was discovered in the early 70s; cf. Chapter 26), and there are frames whose complete modal theory is not effectively axiomatizable (compare Gödel's earlier incompleteness theorem about the first-order theory of arithmetic). So far, the hunt for completeness has been remarkably successful, but later in these notes (cf. Chapter 24), we will also see settings where the modal theories of natural models are not axiomatizable at all.

---

[81]The converse McKinsey Axiom $\Box \Diamond \varphi \to \Diamond \Box \varphi$ added to $S4$ gives the logic of *atomic pre-orders*, in which every world "sees" a reflexive end-point.

Exercises Chapter 8

1. Prove the Modal-Depth-One Lemma for *S5*, and give the corresponding algorithm.

2. Show that the following holds in all transitive reflexive models:

$$\Box\Diamond\Box\Diamond\varphi \rightarrow \Box\Diamond\varphi$$

3. Supply the missing steps in the formal derivations of this chapter.

4. Consider a "hedgehog" model with a root • and ever longer finite sequences of any length going out (take the "transitive closure" of the arrows shown):

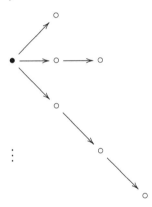

Show that Löb's Axiom holds in every point of this model, whatever valuation you take.

5. Prove that the accessibility relation in the Henkin model, defined as in Chapter 5, for the modal logic *S4* is reflexive and transitive.

6. Is the modal logic *S4* also complete for finite trees?

9

What axioms say: frame correspondence

9.1 Basic examples and frame truth

What made Kanger-Kripke semantics so attractive in the 1950s? It shed new light on old modal axiom systems via *systematic correspondences* between modal axioms and simple intuitive properties of the modal accessibility relation R. Here are some famous examples:

$$T\text{-axiom} \quad \Box p \to p \quad \text{and} \quad \text{reflexivity}$$

$$K4\text{-axiom} \quad \Box p \to \Box\Box p \quad \text{and} \quad \text{transitivity}$$

$$S5\text{-axiom} \quad \Diamond\Box p \to p \quad \text{and} \quad \text{symmetry}$$

To formulate this precisely, we tighten up some definitions:

Definition 9.1.1 (Frames and frame truth). A *frame* $\boldsymbol{F} = (W, R)$ is a directed graph. A modal model $\boldsymbol{M}$ in our earlier sense can be viewed as a frame plus a valuation: $(\boldsymbol{F}, V)$. We say that $\boldsymbol{F}, x \models \varphi$ ("frame truth at a world") if $(\boldsymbol{F}, V), x \models \varphi$ for *all valuations* V. We write $\boldsymbol{F} \models \varphi$ iff φ is true at all worlds x in $\boldsymbol{F}$.

Fact. $\boldsymbol{F}, x \models \Box p \to \Box\Box p$ iff the relation R is transitive at x: i.e., $\forall y(Rxy \to \forall z(Ryz \to Rxz))$.

Truth in models is not appropriate for bringing out such correspondences, as special valuations may validate axioms even though the underlying frame has no nice behaviour at all. E.g., the $K4$-axiom is valid in a model over any frame if the valuation value $V(p) = W$.

9.2 A correspondence proof

Here is how we prove frame correspondences at a high precision level. Consider the preceding Fact:

From right to left. Let the valuation V be totally arbitrary. Assume that $\Box p$ holds at x. We show that $\Box\Box p$ holds at x, too. So, let Rxy and Ryz. By transitivity, Rxz: and so p holds at z, using our assumption.

From left to right. There are two useful ways of going about this.

(1) Contraposition. Suppose transitivity fails: there are x, y, z with Rxy, Ryz, but not Rxz. Define a valuation V by setting $V(p) = W - \{\, z\,\}$. This gives a model where at x, $\Box p$ is true but $\Box\Box p$ is false. So $\Box p \to \Box\Box p$ does not hold on our frame $\boldsymbol{F}$ at x for all valuations, and we refuted the left-hand side.

(2) Direct route. Assume that the left-hand side holds, and use an "inspired valuation". Namely: set $V(p) = \{u \mid Rxu\}$. This makes $\Box p$ true at x, and because the axiom holds at x for all valuations, it also holds for this one: whence $\Box\Box p$ must be true at x for this particular valuation. But that can only be (check your truth definition!) because $\forall y(Rxy \to \forall z(Ryz \to Rxz))$.

How would you find such an "inspired valuation"? By a powerful heuristics of "minimal verification" for axioms, to be explained below.

9.3 Second-order translation and modal correspondence theory

Correspondences may also be essentially second-order. The key example is Löb's Axiom in provability logic. Here we just state the result for frames globally, with truth *in all worlds*:

Theorem 18. $\boldsymbol{F} \models \Box(\Box\varphi \to \varphi) \to \Box\varphi$ iff

(1) R is transitive, and

(2) R is reverse well-founded: there are no chains $x_1 R x_2 R \cdots$.[82]

The proof of this correspondence is a bit more complicated than the above one. We postpone it to Chapter 21. Here is a striking difference: transitivity was simply definable in first-order logic, but well-foundedness cannot be defined in first-order logic at all.[83]

The general fact here is that frame truth is a *second-order* notion: we quantify over all valuations, i.e., over functions. Indeed, for modal formulas φ with proposition letters $p_1, \ldots, p_k$, the definition of frame truth works out to the following second-order translation:

Fact. $\boldsymbol{F}, x \models \varphi$ iff $\boldsymbol{F}, x \models \forall P_1 \cdots \forall P_k ST(\varphi)$,

---

[82] In particular, (2) implies the absence of any cycles, including reflexive ones.

[83] This requires a compactness argument as in your first meta-logic course.

where ST is the "standard translation" of Chapter 7. Second-order logic is very complex: its validities are non-axiomatizable to a high degree, and many other familiar properties of first-order logic disappear. Against the background of these storm clouds, natural questions emerge that are studied in *Modal Correspondence Theory*.[84] This theory contains – amongst other things – complete characterizations of

(a) When a given modal axiom has a first-order frame correspondent (it must be preserved under "ultrapowers" of frames),

(b) When a first-order frame property has a modal definition (it must be preserved under "generated subframes", "disjoint unions", "*p*-morphic images", and "reverse ultrafilter extensions").

All these notions are well-explained in Blackburn et al. (2001).

Many axioms in modal logic have first-order correspondents, so we are essentially doing a bit of second-order logic, but still so close to the border with first-order logic that we get pleasant results. In addition to these mathematical results for connoisseurs, the theory also provides algorithmic information on computing frame correspondents. This theme is more practical, and we will demonstrate how it works.

9.4   The substitution algorithm

We start with a heuristic example: analyzing the *K4*-axiom, now with all its boxes marked:

$$[1]p \rightarrow [2][3]p$$

Which modal box here matched which universal quantifier in the corresponding first-order transitivity formula

$$\forall y(Rxy \rightarrow \forall z(Ryz \rightarrow Rxz))?$$

Intuitively, it makes sense to match up the nested sequences of operators in these formulas: [2] is then the first universal quantifier $\forall y(Rxy \rightarrow$, [3] the second the $\forall z(Ryz \rightarrow$ while ("subtracting equals from equals"), the modality [1] must then have something to do with the remainder, i.e., the final atom Rxz. This will be amplified in what follows.

As we shall see, the antecedent of the modal axiom sets up a *minimal valuation*, which is then *substituted* in the skeleton provided by the consequent. For a precise statement of the following algorithm and its correctness, we refer to the literature (again, Blackburn et al. (2001) is a good source). Hopefully, you can learn by doing. The heuristics in what follows is easy to understand. An implication is like a *promise*:

---

[84]Check the "Correspondence Theory" chapter in the *Handbook of Philosophical Logic* (Gabbay and Günthner, 1983-1989) vol. II, or van Benthem (1985).

"give me the antecedent, and I will give you the consequent". And obviously, you get the maximal advantage of a promise by satisfying the antecedent in some minimal way, and then reaping the full benefits of the consequent.[85]

Example ($\Box p \to \Box\Box p$ ($K4$ axiom)). We look at an arbitrary world x. This will give us a local condition that must hold there, and we get the total frame correspondent by prefixing one universal quantifier $\forall x$.

Phase 1: Analyze the antecedent. The minimal way of making the antecedent true is by having the proposition p true *only at the R-successors of x*: we must do at least this much to make $\Box p$ true anyway, but no more is needed. Define a minimal valuation as follows:

$$Pu := Rxu$$

What this says semantically is that, in the given frame, we take the proposition letter p to denote just the set of R-successors of the world x. The "u" is then a syntactic free variable here, which can be used at various places in a formula for different syntactic substitutions.

Phase 2: Read the consequent. What $\Box\Box p$ says is

$$\forall y(Rxy \to \forall z(Ryz \to Pz)).$$

Phase 3: Plug in the description of the minimal valuation. In our case, Pz becomes Rxz. The result is precisely transitivity:

$$\forall y(Rxy \to \forall z(Ryz \to \boldsymbol{Rxz}))! \quad [86]$$

Example ($\Box p \to p$ (T-axiom)). The same method works. This time, we plug in the minimal valuation for p in the consequent Px. The result is Rxx, that is, precisely reflexivity.

Example ($p \to \Box\Diamond p$ ($S5$-axiom)). *Phase 1: Analyze the antecedent.* This is even easier than the preceding. The minimal way of making this antecedent true has p true *only at x*: with a minimal valuation

$$Pu := x = u$$

Phase 2: Read the consequent. What $\Box\Diamond p$ says is evidently that $\forall y(Rxy \to \exists z(Ryz \land Pz))$.

Phase 3: Plug in the description of the minimal valuation. In our case, for Pz we get $x = z$. The result is $\forall y(Rxy \to \exists z(Ryz \land \boldsymbol{x = z}))$, which is a somewhat pompous way of saying[87] just $\forall y(Rxy \to Ryx)$,

---

[85] If an indigent professor offers you a high grade "if you pay", give one cent, and demand the A^+.

[86] We get the outermost universal quantifier $\forall x$ "for free" in our analysis.

[87] We might distinguish a fourth phase of *Simplification* by logical equivalences. This simplifies things and cuts through complications. Logic also has the inverse use of making simple things look impressively complicated.

indeed the definition of *symmetry*.

Thus, for the *S5* axioms, their famous relational properties come out *automatically* of this algorithm!

Some obvious refinements of the substitution method deal with antecedents that involve diamonds, conjunctions and disjunctions. Here is an illustration from Chapter 8:

Example (The *Geach Axiom* $\Diamond\Box p \to \Box\Diamond p$). A minimal way of making the antecedent true proceeds as follows. First, pick any R-successor y of x. Then make $\Box p$ minimally true there in the earlier fashion:

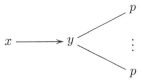

In the corresponding property, this step prefixes a universal quantifier

$$\forall y(Rxy \to -$$

so diamonds in the antecedent become universal. You may find this strange, but it makes sense. By our standard translation, the modal diamond in the Geach axiom $\Diamond\Box p \to \Box\Diamond p$ is an existential $\exists y(Rxy \wedge \cdots$ in the antecedent of an implication. Now quantifiers in antecedents can be "pulled outside" modulo logical equivalence, but in doing so, they "flip": and in particular, an existential quantifier becomes a universal one, with a fresh variable.[88]

After that, the minimal valuation for the antecedent is as before:

$$Pu := Ryu$$

This is substituted in the antecedent (taking care to avoid bound variable clashes), to get the following "convergence" property:

$$\forall y(Rxy \to \forall s(Rxs \to \exists t(Rst \wedge Ryt)))$$

This relational condition occurred in the Minkowski space of Chapter 8. In computation (Chapter 14) it is called confluence, or "Church-Rosser". It is often pictured as a "diamond diagram", which you can find in the picture below for the "poly-modal Geach Axiom".

9.5   Correctness of the algorithm, and variations

A general result on frame correspondence covering many cases was found in 1973 by Henrik Sahlqvist, then an Oslo master's student, who

---

[88]Here is a concrete example in first-order logic: the formula $\exists y(Rxy \wedge Py) \to Q$ (where the variable x does not occur free in Q) is logically equivalent with the formula $\forall y((Rxy \wedge Py) \to Q)$, or with $\forall y(Rxy \to (Py \to Q))$.

observed a recurrent syntactic form:

Theorem 19. There exists an effective algorithm that translates all modal axioms of the special form $A \to B$ into corresponding first-order properties, where

- A is constructed from basic formulas $\Box \cdots \Box p$ using only $\wedge, \vee, \Diamond$;
- B is "positive": constructed from proposition letters with only the logical operations $\wedge, \vee, \Diamond, \Box$.

Sketch.

(a) One direction of the correspondence is easy, since our construction algorithm only involved taking logical equivalents and first-order substitution instances for second-order quantifiers. For, a true modal formula in a frame, viewed as a universal second-order sentence as in Section 9.3, implies all its syntactic substitution instances (even whether these instances are "minimal" or not).

(b) Conversely, let the antecedent A hold in a frame under any valuation V. Then, by our syntactic analysis of the above special A-shapes, there is also a minimal valuation V^- that still makes the antecedent true, which can be described by a first-order formula.[89] Given the truth of the computed correspondent, the consequent then also holds for that minimal V^-. But now, since the consequent B is syntactically positive, it is easily seen to have the following semantic *monotonicity* property: its truth is not affected by going to any larger valuation V on the frame. In particular, B is still true under the original valuation V. Thus, we see that $A \to B$ is true in the given frame.

$\Box$

The result is not easily improved. Allowing $\Box$ to scope over $\Diamond$ in the antecedent is fatal: unlike the Geach Axiom, its converse, the

$$\text{McKinsey Axiom} \qquad \Box \Diamond p \to \Diamond \Box p$$

has no first-order correspondent at all. We did note in Chapter 8 that the latter principle is often added to the axioms of $S4$, to define the *atomic pre-orders*, a first-order definable notion. However, it can be shown in a precise sense that the latter result is not provable using the substitution method of this chapter.[90] Likewise, Löb's Axiom falls outside our methods – but see Chapter 22 for a recent take.

---

[89] Here we skim over the earlier extraction of diamonds to become universal prefix quantifiers. But that step does not essentially change the analysis.

[90] These results are in van Benthem (1985).

From a practical viewpoint, most modal axioms proposed in the literature have first-order computable form. Of course, one has to find their correspondents, even when the axioms are wrapped in syntax that can be more complex than our modal languages so far.

A good test for the method are extended languages:

Example (Poly-modal Geach Axiom $\langle a \rangle [b]p \rightarrow [a]\langle b \rangle p$). Using the same method as above, one can show that this defines the confluence property

$$\forall y (R_a xy \rightarrow \forall z (R_b xz \rightarrow \exists u (R_b yu \wedge R_a zu))):$$

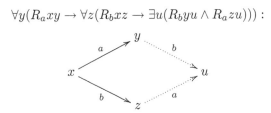

Correspondence methods also work for our earlier extended modal languages with universal modalities, temporal operators, and the like.

Example (Universal relation). The formula $Ep \rightarrow \Diamond p$ holds in a frame iff the relation R is universal. From right to left, this is obvious. From left to right, starting from world x, take any y and set $V(p) = \{y\}$. Then Ep holds at x, and so $\Diamond p$ holds, and then by definition, Rxy.

There are some technical issues about comparison with the earlier modal translation ST on models in Chapter 7, but we leave matters here.[91] We will see further examples of our techniques in Part III.

Recent extensions of the substitution algorithm even work for non-first-order languages with fixed-points (cf. Chapters 7, 14), and they show, in particular, how Löb's Axiom yields to our style of analysis after all. We will indicate how this works in Chapter 22. The methods of this chapter also extend to higher-order languages, as has been shown in the computational literature on automated deduction. One powerful methodology is this: one takes the given axioms for some modal logic L, computes their correspondents in a classical logical language using some built-in translation algorithm, and then performs modal deduction in L via translated forms in a theorem prover for classical logic.

---

[91] For instance, the relational properties in correspondence analysis need *not* be preserved under *bisimulation*! Even transitivity is not. Bisimulation is an uninvariance concerning truth on models, not on frames.

Exercises Chapter 9

1. Compute a frame correspondent for the modal formulas
$$\Diamond p \to \Diamond \Box p \quad \text{and} \quad [a][b]p \to [b][a]p$$
via our algorithm – and show that they are correct.

2. Compute the frame correspondences for two axioms relating past and future in temporal logic: $q \to HFq$ and $q \to GPq$. Here, assume that F (and G) and P (and H) refer to different accessibility relations R_F, R_P. How must the two then be related?

3. Show in more detail that the Sahlqvist substitution algorithm is semantically correct.

4. Prove that the combination of $S4$ plus the McKinsey Axiom $\Box\Diamond p \to \Diamond\Box p$ defines the first-order class of atomic pre-orders.

10

Descriptive power: extended modal languages

Applications of modal logic often require more *expressive power* than our base system here – while at the same time, we would like to preserve its simplicity and nice properties. Such extensions come in different forms, and we have already seen how one can say more about semantic graph models using stronger modalities in Chapter 8. Another line of extension rather changes the type of structures that the relevant modal language is concerned with, a direction of investigation that we will call extension of *descriptive power*. We discuss a few examples in this chapter, without any pretense at completeness. Here the check-list of "nice things" to retain includes earlier topics like bisimulation, first-order translation, frame correspondence, axiomatic minimal logic, interesting special-purpose axioms, decidability, and games. We will discuss some of these issues in a light impressionistic manner.[92]

10.1 Poly-modal languages

We have already encountered the widely used family of poly-modal languages whose syntax has indexed modalities $\langle a \rangle, \langle b \rangle, [a], [b], \ldots$ where $a, b, \ldots$ denote different accessibility relations. Motivation is found in two major types of interpretation:

Knowledge $[i]$: "in every world that is indistinguishable for agent i"

(cf. the epistemic logic of Chapter 12)

Action $[a]$: "after every successful completion of action a"

(cf. the dynamic logic of Chapter 14)

---

[92]In my own course, I use this chapter not for additional facts, but as a source of examples to check if you have understood the material about basic modal logic. You should be able to find good generalizations by yourself.

But other systems, too, involve several accessibility relations, such as temporal logic (Chapter 18) with its modalities $[<]$: "always in the future", $[>]$: "always in the past".[93]

The truth definition for all these cases runs as follows:

$$M, x \models \langle a \rangle \varphi \text{ iff there exists a world } y \text{ with } R_a xy \text{ and } M, y \models \varphi$$

This is pretty much like our basic modal logic, and indeed, generalizations of all our earlier notions and results are a straightforward, and largely typographical, exercise.

Things become more interesting when we require special connections between the different accessibility relations. In temporal logic, the "before" relation is the *converse* of the "after" relation, and we will see many further examples in what follows – for instance, with combined epistemic-dynamic logics in Chapter 15. Such connections often validate additional axioms beyond the minimal poly-modal logic, and we will show how this may drive up complexity of the logic considerably, even toward undecidability, in Chapter 24.

10.2 Polyadic modal languages

Polyadic modal languages change the argument type of syntactic modalities from unary to binary, or even higher, and the corresponding semantic move is to have models with at least ternary accessibility relations. The intended interpretation works as follows:

Definition 10.2.1 (Ternary modal semantics)**.** For models with a ternary accessibility relation, we define truth as follows:

$$M, x \models \Diamond \varphi \psi \text{ iff } \exists yz : R^3 x, yz \ \& \ M, y \models \varphi \ \& \ M, z \models \psi$$

The motivation for ternary relations often has to do with "composition" or "construction":

"string x is the *concatenation* of strings y and z (in that order)",

"transition arrow x is the *composition* of y and z (in that order)",

"information piece x is the *sum* of y and z", etcetera.

---

[93]Many systems have special-purpose notations. For instance, in temporal logic, $[<]$ is written as "G" and $[>]$ as "H" – while epistemic logic uses K_i for $[i]$.

While this move seems to go beyond standard modal logic, a first-order translation for the key modality is straightforward (note again the guarded quantifier bound):

$$\exists yz(Rxyz \wedge \varphi(y) \wedge \psi(z))$$

One usually defines the universal dyadic modality $\Box\varphi\psi$ dually as

$$\neg\Diamond\neg\varphi\neg\psi \quad {}^{94}$$

Spelling out what this means, $\Box\varphi\psi$ gets a disjunction in its consequent:

$$\forall yz(Rxyz \rightarrow (\varphi(y) \vee \psi(z)))$$

You may find this surprising, preferring a conjunctive $\forall yz(Rxyz \rightarrow (\varphi(y) \wedge \psi(z)))$. But the latter can be defined in our language. For instance, the conjunct $\forall yz(Rxyz \rightarrow \varphi(y))$ is

$$\Box\varphi\bot$$

In general, this is a genuine extension of our earlier framework. Ternary relations do not reduce to binary ones: think of the primitive relation of "betweenness" Bx,yz in geometry ("x lies on the line segment with end-points y,z"). Likewise, dyadic modalities do not reduce to combinations of unary ones! In particular, $\Diamond\varphi\psi$ is not equivalent to $\Diamond\varphi \wedge \Diamond\psi$ for binary accessibility relations.[95]

We can also generalize the notion of *bisimulation*, keeping in mind an Invariance Lemma – and the reader may find it useful to experiment with formulating the right back- and forth- clauses for a ternary relation. Also, watch out how you formulate tree unraveling! This takes care in marking the right paths through a tree-like model.[96]

The minimal logic is like the base logic K, with distribution of $\Diamond$ over $\vee$ in both arguments:

$$\Diamond(\varphi_1 \vee \varphi_2)\psi \leftrightarrow \Diamond\varphi_1\psi \vee \Diamond\varphi_1\psi,$$ and likewise for the ψ-argument.

Decidability follows from our techniques of Chapter 4. There is even a Decomposition Lemma yielding a complete sequent calculus. Substitution-based frame *correspondence* also goes through.

Fact. Associativity $\Diamond p\Diamond qr$ corresponds to a first-order principle of "re-composition": $\forall yzuv : ((Rx,yz \wedge Rz,uv) \rightarrow \exists s(Rs,yu \wedge Rx,sv))$.

---

[94] One can argue as to the most appropriate "dual" reflecting the former $\neg\Diamond\neg$.

[95] Still, there exist non-meaning-preserving *validity-preserving* reductions between dyadic modal languages and "bimodal" ones, that we do not formulate here. These replace one ternary relation Rx,yz in a model by a combination of two new binary relations R_1, R_2.

[96] The point is that we must mark the difference between going from world x to y in the context of one ternary "triangle" x,yz_1 and in another x,yz_2.

Proof. Find a "minimal valuation" for the antecedent, as before.[97] □

But the *landscape* of important modal logics is quite different here. In dyadic modal logic, there is no *S4* or *S5*: many important landmarks in this new area do not even *have* resounding names ...

10.3 Geometry and Arrow Logic

Dyadic modal systems speak more in concrete settings. In Chapter 19, we will look briefly at modal logics of affine geometry, where the ternary relation is spatial *betweenness*, while $\Diamond pq$ says that the current point lies on a line segment whose end-points satisfy φ and ψ.[98] In this setting, models suddenly become very concrete spatial arrangements:

Example (Triangle models). In the following "annotated triangle", the worlds are the vertices, while the lines just help to indicate betweenness, proposition letters are true at points are marked.

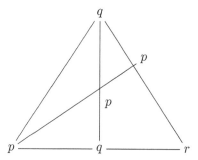

The right-most vertex is uniquely defined by r, the one in the middle by $p \wedge \Diamond qq$, the right-most p-point is defined uniquely by $p \wedge \Diamond qr$ – and continuing in this way, each vertex has a unique modal definition.

Another concrete interpretation is in terms of *Arrow Logic*. This system was invented as a generalization of Relational Algebra, the first-order theory of Boolean operations on binary relations – viewed as sets of ordered pairs (x, y) – as well as the operations of *composition* and *converse*: in particular, to remedy the latter's undecidability. We will discuss Relational Algebra in more detail in Chapters 14, 22 – but for now, it suffices to state the semantics of Arrow Logic. Worlds are "arrows", that is, transitions between states viewed as primitive objects, i.e., as first-class citizens of our semantics. Formulas are expressions

---

[97]*Caveat.* In antecedent positions, a universal modality □pq in front of proposition letters now no longer guarantees the existence of unique minimal valuations, because of its disjunctive character.

[98]Note that a special property of *symmetry* holds here for the ternary relation: Rx, yz iff Rx, zy.

that denote binary relations, now viewed as, not sets of ordered pairs, but sets of arrows. The Boolean operations retain their usual interpretation. Converse then becomes a unary modality, composition a binary one, involving two natural accessibility relations between arrows:

Definition 10.3.1 (Semantics of Arrow Logic). *Arrow models* $M = (W, C, R, V)$ consist of a set of objects W with a valuation V plus a ternary relation C of composition, and a binary one R of conversion:

• Arrow a verifies $\varphi \bullet \psi$ [99] iff a is *C-composed* out of two arrows b, c verifying φ, ψ, respectively.
• Arrow a verifies $\varphi^\cup$ iff a has an *R-converse* arrow that verifies φ.

The arrow language has a decidable minimal logic, which contains the most widely used laws of Relational Algebra. Modal correspondence techniques determine what principles of this system really say:

Fact. $\neg\varphi^\cup \leftrightarrow (\neg\varphi)^\cup$ holds in a frame iff the relation R is a *function* r.

In terms of this "reversal" function r, further correspondences become more perspicuous, witness the following complex axiom:

Fact. The principle $\varphi\bullet\neg(\varphi^\cup\bullet\psi) \to \neg\psi$ holds in a frame iff the following first-order Triangle Law holds: $\forall xyz : Cx, yz \to Cz, r(y)x$.

Proofs are via standard substitution arguments of our earlier kind.

On top of this minimal logic, Arrow Logic views the further valid principles of Relational Algebra as a penumbra of optional extras, reflecting mathematical facts about the set theory of ordered pairs – whose sum total is responsible for the undecidability of the full system.

10.4   Below "minimal": neighbourhood models

Sometimes even the minimal system K with our semantics on directed graphs is too strong, and we wish to reject, e.g., its Distribution of $\square$ over $\to$ or of $\Diamond$ over $\vee$. Here is some motivation:

(a) "Logical omniscience" in epistemic logic (Chapter 12): the knowledge of realistic agents might not be closed under taking all its logical consequences.

---

[99] In terms of our earlier notation, this would be the standard $M, a \models \varphi \bullet \psi$.

(b) Non-distribution of outcomes in game logics (Chapter 17) when we read the modal $\langle G, i\rangle\varphi$ as "player i has a strategy forcing the outcomes of game G to satisfy φ, whatever others do".

A generalized semantics blocking distribution was proposed in the 1960s by Scott and Montague. We move from a world-to-world relation Rst to a world-to-set relation RsX, which says that "X is a neighbourhood of s", in some free-wheeling topological sense:

Definition 10.4.1 (Neighbourhood semantics). The basic truth clause is as follows (some neighbourhood of the current world is "all φ"):

$$\boldsymbol{M}, s \models \Box\varphi \quad \text{iff} \quad \exists X (RsX \ \wedge \ \forall x \in X : \boldsymbol{M}, x \models \varphi)$$

A more concrete motivation are *modal logics of topology* that we will study in Chapter 19. Note that our original graph models are still the special case with $R^{old}xy$ iff $R^{new}x\{y\}$.

The complete logic of these models is the minimal K dropping distribution in general, for either disjunction or conjunction. Still, one retains the valid *upward monotonicity* of $\Box$:

$$\Box\varphi \rightarrow \Box(\varphi \vee \psi) \quad \text{[100]}$$

Neighbourhood semantics is an obvious generalization of our earlier basic modal logic – and the reader may wish to generalize earlier notions and results for herself. As for semantic invariance and expressive power of the new system, here is the *zigzag* clause for the characteristic invariance notion of *bisimulation* between models $\boldsymbol{M}, \boldsymbol{N}$:[101]

If sZt and $R^{M}sX$, then there is a set Y with $R^{N}tY$ such that $\forall y \in Y \exists x \in X : xZy$ – and *vice versa* starting from sZt and $R^{N}tY$.

The point of this two-quantifier clause becomes clear when checking how modal invariance holds under just this stipulation for the zigzag clause.[102] Indeed, our truth definition in neighbourhood models treats one single modal operator $\Box$ as a two-quantifier combination $\exists\forall$ – and

---

[100] Weaker systems without even this monotonicity modify modal truth to the variant clause $\boldsymbol{M}, s \models \Box\varphi$ iff $Rs\{x \in W \mid \boldsymbol{M}, x \models \varphi\}$.

[101] Finding this notion in real-time has been a favourite exercise in Stanford classrooms since the mid 1990s.

[102] There is a *prima facie* attractive stronger equivalence clause, too: viz., if sZt and $R^{M}sX$, then there exists a set Y with $R^{N}tY$ such that $\forall y \in Y \exists x \in X : xZy$

this observation has driven validity reductions of neighbourhood semantics to *bi-modal* standard models.

The same point comes out under, again, *translation*. One can view the neighbourhood truth definition as translating modal formulas into a *two-sorted first-order language* with "points" (variables $x, y, \ldots$) and "neighbourhoods" $(n, m, \ldots)$, where the latter correspond to some, but not necessarily all sets of points. We then use two hard-wired primitive relations N ("neighbourhood of") and E ("element of"):

$$\Box p \qquad \text{translates as} \qquad \exists n(Nxn \land \forall y(Eyn \to Py))$$

This is actually a guarded formula in the sense of Chapter 7, and so neighbourhood semantics stays well within *decidable* modal fragments of full first-order logic.

That the minimal modal logic over neighbourhood models is decidable may in fact be seen through various techniques. A particularly simple argument uses the following version of our earlier Decomposition Lemma in Chapter 4:[103]

Fact. A modal sequent of the form $p, \Box\varphi_1, \ldots, \Box\varphi_k \Rightarrow \Box\psi_1, \ldots, \Box\psi_m, q$ is valid iff either

(a) p, q overlap, or
(b) for some i $(1 \geq i \geq k)$, j $(1 \geq j \geq m)$, the sequent $\varphi_i \to \psi_j$ holds.

A proof is left to the exercises: but it is highly recommended, because it demonstrates the "looser" character of neighbourhood models over our standard directed graphs so far.

Analyzing this argument in detail even yields the *computational complexity* of satisfiability (cf. Chapter 6) in the minimal neighbourhood logic: this system side with propositional logic, which is much simpler than the *PSPACE*-complete as for the minimal modal logic K:

Fact. Satisfiability in neighbourhood semantics is *NP*-complete.[104]

Finally, we mention our earlier *frame correspondences* for additional modal axioms in the "landscape" of possible modal neighbourhood logics. For instance, modal distributivity over disjunctions, though not minimally valid, expresses the special frame condition that

(a) The neighbourhood relation is monotonic: if RsX and $X \subseteq Y$, then RsY, and

---

and $\forall x \in X \exists y \in Y : xZy$. But you will find no need for such an added clause in an inductive proof for the Invariance Lemma.

[103] Note the small but telling difference with the original, more complex reduction.
[104] This outcome is sensitive to assumptions on the neighbourhood relation.

(b) The neighbourhood relation is intersective: if RsX and RsY, then $Rs(X \cap Y)$.

Together, these conditions make RsY behave much like a world-to-world relation, as we can – at least in finite models – now define a standard accessibility relation

$R^{\#}xy$ as "y belongs to the intersection of all neighbourhoods of x".

Also, in this generalized setting, old correspondences for modal logics acquire a new thrust. For instance, the neighbourhood frame condition for the $K4$ axiom $\Box p \to \Box\Box p$, our starting point in Chapter 9, is now a natural *cut property* extending ordinary transitivity.[105]

In this chapter, we have lightly discussed a few extensions of basic modal logic to semantic structures of a more complex "similarity type". We have mostly just suggested how all our earlier themes still make sense, though it can be fun to look more closely at actual details.

---

[105]There are even *Sahlqvist Theorems*: though not all issues have been cleared up.

Exercises Chapter 10

1. Consider translations again:
   (a) Give a first-order translation for a dyadic modal language with binary modalities $\Diamond\varphi\psi$ over ternary relational models. How many variables do you need to use?
   (b) Prove the Invariance Lemma for the appropriate notion of bisimulation.
   (c) Prove the frame correspondence for the associativity axiom $\Diamond(\Diamond pq)r \rightarrow \Diamond p(\Diamond qr)$.

2. Consider the following two "annotated triangles". The worlds are the vertices: the lines just help to indicate betweenness, and proposition letters true at points are marked.

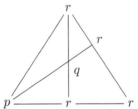 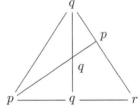

   One can be contracted under bisimulation to a smaller figure. How? Which triangle has all its points uniquely definable? How?

3. Some properties of neighbourhood semantics:
   (a) Explain with concrete examples why the principles of distribution over both $\wedge$ and $\vee$ fail for the modal operator $\Box$ in general neighbourhood semantics.
   (b) Prove the Invariance Lemma for the appropriate bisimulation of this language. Prove that, if two *finite* models M, s and N, t verify the same modal formulas, then there exists a neighbourhood bisimulation between M, N linking s to t.
   (c) "The complexity of neighbourhood modal logic can never exceed that of the minimal K over directed graphs, since we have only added more models". Explain why this is a fallacy. Must weaker logics be less complex than stronger ones?
   (d) Prove the reduction for neighbourhood validity stated in the chapter text. (Hint: it may help to draw some of the "lolly pictures" from our main text.) Show how this fact implies the stated NP-completeness of satisfiability.

11

Modal predicate logic

Most research in modal logic today is about propositional languages, as will be clear from a quick look at the *Handbook of Modal Logic*. To a large extent this is a historical accident: the research community has been held up on the way because there were already so many natural wonders in this restricted territory. Even so, in this chapter, we briefly look at what happens when we mix modal operators with first-order predicate logic. There is no pretense at completeness: you should just read this material to get sensitized to what lies ahead.

11.1 Modal predication and objects

Much of the history of modal logic in philosophy is tied up with modal assertions about individuals and their properties. Aristotle already asserted that objects have some properties necessarily, and others only accidentally. Thus, Marilyn Monroe was essentially identical to Norma Jeane Baker, but only accidentally blonde. Quine raised some famous worries about the consistency of this type of discourse, in his example of the "Rational Cyclist":

> Cyclists are necessarily two-legged, but not necessarily rational. Mathematicians are necessarily rational, but not necessarily two-legged. Consider a cycling mathematician. Is he both necessarily rational and not necessarily rational, with the same contradiction in his legs?

With a little reflection, one can see that this conundrum does not make a modal predicate logic impossible. It rather makes it imperative! If you formalize Quine's prose, you see the hidden options. Saying that cyclists are necessarily two-legged means either of two things:

$$\forall x(Cx \to \Box Tx) \qquad \text{or} \qquad \Box\forall x(Cx \to Tx)$$

119

Negating this assertion gives options as well. Saying that cyclists are not necessarily rational might mean any of the following:

$$\neg\forall x(Cx \to \Box Rx), \qquad \forall x(Cx \to \neg\Box Rx) \quad \text{or} \quad \neg\Box\forall x(Cx \to Rx)$$

I am not even going to dignify Quine's "paradoxette" with an extensive analysis, but it should be clear that once you sort all this out in the right formal system, there is no difficulty whatsoever in saying in which senses the given assertions are jointly consistent, or not.

11.2 Language, models, semantics

But what is the correct formal system? At the level of a *formal language*, this seems easy to say. We just take the syntax rules of first-order predicate logic, and add the modalities $\Box, \Diamond$ as unary operators on formulas φ. In case these formulas have free variables ($\varphi = \varphi(x, y, \ldots)$), we can then automatically express modal predication. This formalism at once expresses well-known philosophical distinctions, such as that between "de re" predications

$\exists x \Box Px$ some objects necessarily have the property P,

and "de dicto" predications like

$\Box \exists x Px$ it is necessarily true that some objects have the property P.

While this may sound like somewhat stilted philosopher's jargon, the "de re" versus "de dicto" distinction is crucial to many expressions in natural language, as pointed out by Richard Montague. I might know "de dicto" that the ideal partner for me exists somewhere in this city – but the tragedy of urban life is that I might walk these streets through all my years, without knowing "de re" of any particular person that (s)he is that ideal partner. Failure to convert de dicto into de re may mean no progeny, and Darwinian disaster!

The more tricky issue is the semantics for this language. There have been many proposals, and much controversy concerning the interpretation of what it means for an object to occur across different worlds. For concreteness, we state one version that has been widely used.

Definition 11.2.1. *Models* for modal predicate logic are structures $M = (W, R, D, V)$ with W a set of possible worlds, R an accessibility relation, and D a domain map assigning sets of objects to each possible world. Finally, V is a valuation function interpreting each predicate letter P at each world w as a predicate $V(P, w)$ of the right arity.[106]

---

[106] One can think of a family of first-order models ordered by accessibility, but the framework is richer, since the same model can occur at different worlds with different local accessibility patterns. Also, one could think of the objects as forming

Now we must combine the semantics of predicate logic, which has *assignments* taking variables to objects with the earlier one for modal propositional logic. The following stipulation explains when a formula φ is true at world w under assignment a, where we assume that the values $a(x)$ for the free variables x in φ are in the domain D_w:

$\boldsymbol{M}, w, a \models Px$	iff	the tuple of objects $a(\boldsymbol{x})$ belongs to the predicate $V(P, w)$
$\boldsymbol{M}, w, a \models \neg\varphi$	iff	*not* $\boldsymbol{M}, w, a \models \varphi$
$\boldsymbol{M}, w, a \models \varphi \vee \psi$	iff	$\boldsymbol{M}, w, a \models \varphi$ *or* $\boldsymbol{M}, w, a \models \psi$
$\boldsymbol{M}, w, a \models \exists x\varphi$	iff	*for some* $d \in D_w$, $\boldsymbol{M}, w, a[x := d] \models \varphi$
$\boldsymbol{M}, w, a \models \Diamond\varphi$	iff	*for some* v *with* Rwv where $a(x) \in D_v$ for all free variables x in φ, $D, \boldsymbol{M}, v, a \models \varphi$

Here individual quantifiers range over the local domain of objects existing at the current world. The clause for the modality makes sure that all objects used by a to evaluate $\Diamond\varphi$ in w are also available for evaluating φ in v. On the basis of this truth definition, Boolean conjunction $\wedge$, modal box $\Box$ and universal quantifiers $\forall$ are defined as usual.

Remark (Cumulation). Often, the modal clause of the preceding semantics is simplified by making a further structural assumption, viz. that object domains grow along accessibility:

> For all w, v, $Rwv \rightarrow D_w \subseteq D_v$ Domain Cumulation

Now we can just stipulate that

$$\boldsymbol{M}, w, a \models \Diamond\varphi \quad \text{iff} \quad \text{\textit{for some} } v \text{ \textit{with} } Rwv, \boldsymbol{M}, v, a \models \varphi$$

We keep this condition as an optional extra. Our preference is to see what proposed axioms mean in terms of frame correspondence (see below) – and the weaker the base used then, the better.

Example (Refuting a de dicto to de re conversion). The following model has worlds w, v, $R = \{(w, w), (w, v)\}$, $D(w) = \{1\}$, $D(v) = \{1, 2\}$, $V(P, w) = \{1\}$, $V(P, v) = \{2\}$. This makes the modal formula $\Box\exists xPx \rightarrow \exists x\Box Px$ false at w:[107]

---

one universal set that is "available" in some sense, but our modal predicate-logical language only looks at what is available inside worlds.

[107] We leave it to the reader to give a counter-example with one constant domain.

When interpreting formulas $\Box Px$, this semantics takes it for granted that recognizing the same object across worlds is unproblematic. This crucial aspect of Kripke's views on modality was challenged by Lewis, who proposed a "counterpart theory" where objects can only have *counterparts* more or less like them in other worlds, with modality accessing these counterparts rather than the very same objects. Philosophically, Kripke's views in his 1972 book *Naming and Necessity* have won the day – and possible worlds are mostly viewed as different states of affairs draped around the familiar objects in our actual world. But Chapter 26 will sound a new round in the debate with Lewis.

11.3 Minimal logic and correspondence for axioms

Our models with Domain Cumulation validate a *minimal modal predicate logic* merging standard predicate logic with just the minimal propositional modal logic K, where Cumulation ensures validity of the modal distribution axiom.[108] This combination proves some interesting combined principles, such as the following de re to de dicto implication:

$$\exists x \Box Px \to \Box \exists x Px$$

This can be seen semantically, or via a simple deduction combining well-know principles:

$$Px \to \exists x Px, \quad \Box Px \to \Box \exists x Px, \quad \exists x \Box Px \to \Box \exists x Px$$

On top of this minimal logic, as in Chapter 9, further axioms impose additional constraints on suitably defined frames, via systematic *correspondence arguments*:

Definition 11.3.1. A formula φ of modal predicate logic holds in a *frame* $\mathbf{F} = (W, R, D)$ (i.e., a model stripped of its valuation for predicates) iff φ is true at $\mathbf{F}$ under all valuation functions V.

For instance, the following famous modal predicate-logical principle

$$\forall x \Box Px \to \Box \forall x Px \qquad \text{Barcan Axiom}$$

holds in frame if and only if we have a converse to Domain Cumulation:

$$Rwv \to D_v \subseteq D_w \qquad \text{No Object Growth}$$

Together with Domain Cumulation, this principle is sometimes also called the "constant domain assumption". In that case, modal variation only concerns the fixed set of objects. We mention a few more cases in the exercises to this chapter. Behind these observations lies a generalization of the *Sahlqvist Theorem* of Chapter 9, whose proof extends here.

---

[108] *Caveat*: This merge is more than just the union of valid formulas. For, axiom *schemata* formerly valid in just one component logic are now allowed with arbitrary substitution instances in the combined language.

[109] But also, like in propositional modal logic, some principles remain more complex. For instance, it can be shown (we give some hints in an Exercise) that our earlier de dicto de re principle $\Box\exists x Px \to \exists x \Box Px$ has no first-order frame correspondent on our general models.

11.4 Some model theory of modal predicate logic

Expressive power can be analyzed with the techniques of Chapters 3 and 7. The first-order correspondence language L_{corr} has two sorts of "worlds" and "objects", binary relations Rwv for world accessibility and Ewx for object x being in the domain of world w, and $(k+1)$-ary predicates Pwx for each k-ary predicate Px of objects.

Definition 11.4.1. The *standard translation* $trans(\varphi)$ takes formulas φ of modal predicate logic to L_{corr}-formulas with the same free object variables as φ plus one free world variable w:

$$trans(Px) = Pwx$$
$$trans(\neg\varphi) = \neg trans(\varphi)$$
$$trans(\varphi \vee \psi) = trans(\varphi) \vee trans(\psi)$$
$$trans(\exists x\varphi) = \exists x(Ewx \wedge trans(\varphi))$$
$$trans(\Diamond\varphi) = \exists v(Rwv \wedge \bigwedge_i Evx_i(x_i \text{ free in } \varphi) \wedge [v/w]trans(\varphi))$$

Any model M for modal predicate logic is at the same time one for L_{corr}, and indeed the following equivalence relates the above modal semantics with standard first-order evaluation:

Theorem 20 (Translation Theorem). For each model M and formula φ of modal predicate logic, $M, w, a \models \varphi$ iff $M, a^+ \models trans(\varphi)$, where the assignment a^+ sends object variables to their a-values, while the free world variable of $trans(\varphi)$ goes to the world w.

Thus, syntactically, modal predicate logic becomes a fragment of the full two-sorted first-order language L_{corr}. In this setting, its special characteristic semantic invariance is then a mixture of two structural relations: *modal bisimulation* plus the notion matching it for a full first-order language, namely, *potential isomorphism* (cf. Chapter 7):

Definition 11.4.2. A *world-object bisimulation* between two models M, N for modal predicate logic is a relation Z between tuples wd in M and ve in N of the same length (here, bold face letters denote finite sequences, and objects in matched tuples belong to the specified initial world) that satisfies: (a) each match between corresponding objects in

---

[109]More precisely, there is an effective translation into first-order frame properties for all modal predicate-logical formulas $\alpha \to \beta$, where α has the inductive syntax rule $\exists \mid \wedge \mid \vee \mid \Diamond \mid \gamma$ with γ having syntax $Px \mid \forall \mid \Box$, while β is a wholly positive formula with syntax rule $Px \mid \forall \mid \exists \mid \wedge \mid \vee \mid \Diamond \mid \Box$.

matched tuples induces a partial isomorphism for predicate logic, (b) if wRw' in M, then there is a world v' in N with vRv' and $w'dZv'e$, and vice versa in the other direction, and (c) if d in M, then there is an object e in N with the pair wdd, vee in Z – and again vice versa.

Here is an analogue for modal predicate logic of the Modal Invariance Theorem of Chapter 7, just as an illustration:

Theorem 21 (Invariance Theorem). The following are equivalent for formulas φ in L_{corr}:

1. φ is invariant for world-object bisimulations,
2. φ is definable by a formula of modal predicate logic.

11.5 Tricky phenomena

Our results so far suggest smooth generalization. But over the last decades, it has emerged that modal predicate logic can behave quite differently from its propositional counterpart. A striking instance is *incompleteness*: often, there is no complete axiomatization for model classes that caused no problems in the propositional case. In addition, there are failures of model-theoretic results such as interpolation theorems. Thus, choosing the right semantics for modal predicate logic is not an easy matter. We will discuss these issues in Chapter 26.

Here we conclude with a modern diagnosis in terms of "combining modal logics", mentioned briefly toward the end of Chapter 7. We are really trying to merge two different logical systems, each with its own semantics: the propositional modal realm of worlds and accessibility, and first-order predicate logic over domains of individual objects. Now, Chapter 27 shows how first-order logic *itself* is a modal logic, interpreted over spaces of variable assignments, with accessibility relations R_x for moving from one assignment to another differing from it only in the value for the variable x. Modal predicate logic, then, is what is technically called a *product* of two modal logics, and we will see in Chapter 24 that product logics can be very unlike their components.

More conceptually, the underlying issue here is what are to be the *"objects"* in a modal predicate logic. Recent proposals tend to make them a family of functions across worlds, turning models into mathematical categories. But whichever way we construe them, it is important to perform this extension also from a practical point of view. Knowing objects like persons, telephone numbers, or even rules and methods is crucial to natural language and human agency.[110]

---

[110]I am gradually becoming more uneasy about this omission, and these pangs of conscience may show in a second edition of this book.

Exercises Chapter 11

1. Show that the modal distribution law is not valid in a modal predicate logic allowing arbitrary changes between world domains.

2. Prove that, using our most general semantics without Domain Cumulation, the axiom $\exists x \Box Px \rightarrow \Box \exists x Px$ corresponds, in the technical sense, to $\forall w : \forall v (Rwv \rightarrow \forall x (Exw \rightarrow Exv))$.

3. Give a detailed frame correspondence argument that the Barcan Axiom defines reverse domain inclusion along accessibility.

4. *(Difficult)* Prove that, on frames with Domain Cumulation, the modal predicate-logical axiom $\Box \exists x Px \rightarrow \exists x \Box Px$ is first-order definable by the conjunction of the two first-order properties (a) No Object Growth, (b) each world whose domain has more than one object has at most one world successor.

5. *(Very difficult)* Prove that, on general models, the same modal axiom $\Box \exists x Px \rightarrow \exists x \Box Px$ is not first-order definable.

6. Prove the Translation Theorem stated in Section 11.4.

Part III
Selected Applications

Modal logic is in use today across a wide range of disciplines, and no introductory course can do justice to its whole range. The following chapters reflect the major illustrations from which I have chosen over the years, loosely grouped under two headings.

The first group (Chapters 12–17) is about a basic interest unifying the diverse systems of *philosophical logic*, viz. information, rational agency, and interaction. I present traditional labels like "epistemic" or "doxastic" logic in one coherent story, mixing in dynamic logic from computer science, and ending in modern logics of games played by agents with preferences and goals. But modal structures arise equally well in the heartland of *mathematical logic*, and Chapters 18–21 give examples ranging from the study of time and space to the foundations of mathematics. I have not added a separate group of chapters on the area with perhaps the bulk of logic research today, viz. *computational logic*, but its themes play throughout these notes, in particular, dynamic and temporal logic, but also our concern with complexity.[111]

Even so, I had to make choices, and some important topics are missing from this survey, especially on the mathematical side. The reader will have to check with the *Handbook of Modal Logic* (Blackburn et al., 2006) to find chapters dealing with such topics as the widespread *algebraic approaches* to the field (nowadays also including "co-algebra"), *infinitary modal languages*, and modal *set theory*.

These chapters are light, and they merely serve to introduce students to their areas. Even so, there is a lot of material, and in a typical course, I just choose a three-week line of special topics, depending on student interest. In particular, the chapters on epistemic, doxastic and dynamic logics are favourites for their appealing intuitions and links across disciplines, while temporal and spatial logics are popular for the way they throw new light on "standard" structures in mathematics.

The main notions and techniques from Parts I and II will return throughout the chapters to come. Relational graph models are central, from knowledge to time, space, and provability, even when notations differ. Thus, hopefully, you will see the unity of modal logic precisely in this diversity. Even so, the style in what follows differs from the "instruction manual" in Parts I and II, as we are introducing new areas relying on these earlier results. One final difference with standard logic texts is worth noting. While introductions to propositional or predicate

---

[111]Personally, I find all these standard terms misleading and useless, and if the reader finds it hard to classify the content of these lectures as philosophical, mathematical, or computational, then all the better!

logic (or modal logic in the preceding parts) usually train students with abstract technical examples, modal logic in the areas discussed here requires a real *Art of Modeling*. It is not trivial to find good models for information states, processes, or games, and a certain creativity is required. Unlike drill in formal deductions or truth definitions, modeling is not a skill that can be taught in some algorithmic fashion. But we hope that the student will also pick up some significant abilities in tying logic to meaningful real scenarios.

Introducing chapters 12 through 17: Modal logics of agency

While philosophical logic has been a diverse collection of topics, there is a more systematic view that ties many of these together. Logic has been traditionally considered the study of reasoning, or even more specialized: deductive proof. But in recent decades, a much broader view has emerged where logic is about a wide spectrum of common sense reasoning activities, often intertwined with natural language. But one can go still one step further. Reasoning, after all, is just one form of information handling by rational agents. Agents can also make observations, ask questions, and thus direct information flow from many sources, either alone or in interaction with others. Think of a scientific experiment, where observation occurs entangled with deduction, a match made immortal by Sherlock Holmes. Or think of a debate, the original paradigm for logic historically, where several agents interact, and where a natural mixture occurs of deductive moves, questions, and perhaps even observation of new relevant facts. In recent years, there has been a move toward bringing this full reality into the scope of logic, including the informational events that drive it. Here is a glimpse of what a logic of full-blooded agency involves.

Rational agents are endowed with a number of powers and can perform many cognitive tasks. You can think of them as a next stage after classical Turing machines, that are still simple robot-like agents for basic computational tasks. Here are some core features of agency that have turned out amenable to logical investigation. First of all, agents exercise informational powers, through external acts of observation, or internal acts of inference, introspection, or memory retrieval. In doing so, they change their knowledge, but also other attitudes that guide behaviour, such as their beliefs. But this information gathering is not a blind process: it has a direction, given by an agenda of current "issues", and the agenda items are steered by agents' questions, and other acts. In a stronger sense, these directions are tied up with genuine goals, having to do with agents' preferences and evaluation of situations, another crucial aspect of rational agency. Without the latter, there is just logical "kinematics", but no deeper explanatory "dynamics" of behaviour. And finally, human agency is crucially interactive, largely taking place in social settings. As in physics, where "many-body interaction" is the key, strategic "many-mind interactions" drive logical behaviour, including conversation, argumentation, or more general games.

Thus, we get a picture of individual agents endowed with a set of core capacities, involved in dynamic transitions of various kinds from one state to another, and in the process, creating long-term practices over time, with larger groups of participants. Now you can see what the following chapters are trying to do. They give you the logical apparatus to talk about agents' attitudes like knowledge or belief, and they study dynamic informational events that change these attitudes, such as observation or communication. Next, they consider how agents evaluate the world, as expressed in their preferences, and ways these may change, too. And finally, they bring it all together in the study of games, where agents display all these abilities in one setting, with strategic interactive behaviour over time. By the time you have mastered these chapters, you will be in an excellent position to join in the modern study of agency, which opens up exciting new horizons for logic.

12

Epistemic logic

Modal logics have been typically used to model what philosophers call *propositional attitudes* such as "x knows that φ", "x believes that φ", etcetera. Natural language is very rich in these, which probably says something about human cognition, but philosophers and logicians have mainly concentrated on a few. In this chapter, we consider *knowledge*.

12.1 Epistemic notions across disciplines

Epistemic notions have been discussed in philosophy ever since Plato, who analyzed knowledge as "justified true belief". True belief alone is not enough for knowledge: I might believe that the Earth is round because my Palo Alto psychic told me it is shaped like her glass bowl, but is this knowledge? That is why Plato added a demand for "justification".[112] In this century, the "Gettier Paradox" is taken by many to show that Plato's Formula is not enough – and there has been a rich tradition of finding further ingredients. Another area where epistemic attitudes come up is theology. Religious people believe, they do not necessarily know that their beliefs are correct. That is why there is a genuine "act of faith", that we do not experience when entrusting ourselves to the known truth that $2 + 3 = 5$.[113]

Natural language has a vast array of epistemic phrases, such as "know, believe, be convinced, doubt". And even without such *explicit* expressions, there may be implicit epistemic attitudes. "Oedipus saw his father on the road, quarreled with him, and then killed him." In the sense of bare perception, he just saw a man who happened to be his father. In the sense of epistemic seeing, he saw the man and recognized him. We would call him guilty of parricide in the second case, not the

---

[112]In view of later multi-agent concerns, you might ask: *whose* justification?

[113]Logic-minded theologians have tried to give proofs for God's existence, often with a modal flavour. A good reference is Plantinga (1978).

first – though the Greek tragedy did not acknowledge this distinction. Virtually everything we say has this potential ambiguity. In Koestler's *Darkness at Noon* a communist prisoner is shown the statement that "in 1947, I had discussions with American spy so-and-so". His jailers tell him this is just the literal truth, so why not sign? But, at the time of meeting, the statement was only true in the bare sense (he did not know that the American was a spy), while signing it now will be interpreted epistemically as an admission of guilt.[114]

Issues of knowledge have also come up in computer science. Though computational agents are not humans, it is convenient to reason about them as if they were.[115] By now, multi-agent systems are the reality of computing with the Internet, or the Grid, and border-lines with other disciplines get blurred. In particular, in economics, the paradigm for "multi-agent systems" are *games*, and epistemic notions were introduced in the foundations of game theory in the 1970s, to provide an underpinning for standard solution concepts like Nash equilibrium. Epistemic issues also come up in the foundations of mathematics - and we will touch upon "intuitionistic logic" in Chapter 20, which sees mathematics as epistemic travel through a universe of information states.

If you find this host of subjects bewildering, please realize that disciplinary boundaries are artificial if you focus on issues of information, agency and cognition – the broader area we are entering now. That is why (some) logicians have no difficulty in making such mental leaps.

12.2 Epistemic logic: basic language and semantics

We start with the simplest language, where knowledge of agents refers to their current *information range*, being the set of all possible worlds they consider compatible with the actual world. While epistemic logic was initially developed as an account of the knowledge of single agents in some philosophical sense, perhaps its most interesting uses have to do with information in ordinary life and human interaction. Here is a typical intuitive situation of this sort.

Example (Questions and Answers). I approach you in Amsterdam, and ask "Is this building the Rijksmuseum?". As a well-informed and helpful Dutch citizen, you answer truly: "Yes". This is the sort of thing we all do competently all the time. But subtle information flows. By asking the question, I convey to you that I do not know the answer, and also, that I think it is possible that you do know. This information

---

[114]Note again the multi-agent "control": *whose* description is being used?
[115]Another logic-laden epistemic topic is *security* in electronic communication.

flows before you have said anything at all.[116] After that, by answering, you do not just convey the topographical fact to me that this building is the Rijksmuseum. You also make me know that you know, and that you know that I know you know, etc. This knowledge up to every finite depth of iteration is called *common knowledge*. It mixes "factual" information with "social" information about the information of others.

In particular, epistemic *overtones* concerning mutual information of agents are not mere side-effects of communication. They steer concrete actions. If I know that you do not know that I know your pin code and account number, I may well try to empty your bank account. But if I know that you know that I know these data, I will not. Here is a basic epistemic language that captures the essentials of our example.

Definition 12.2.1 (Basic epistemic language). The *basic epistemic language EL* extends propositional logic with modal operators $K_i \varphi$ ("*i* knows that φ"), for each $i \in I$, as well as $C_G \varphi$: "φ is common knowledge in the group G". The inductive syntax rule is as follows, where "p" stands for any choice of proposition letters:

$$p \mid \neg\varphi \mid \varphi \vee \psi \mid K_i \varphi \mid C_G \varphi$$

We write $\langle i \rangle \varphi$ for the existential modality $\neg K_i \neg \varphi$: which says intuitively that "agent *i* considers φ possible". The existential dual modality of $C_G \varphi$ is written as $\langle C_G \rangle \varphi$.[117]

These agent modalities can deal with the preceding scenario:

Example (Questions and Answers, continued). Let $\boldsymbol{Q}$ ask a factual question "φ?", to which $\boldsymbol{A}$ answers truly: "Yes". The presupposition for a normal truthful answer is that $\boldsymbol{A}$ knows that φ: which may be written as $K_{\boldsymbol{A}} \varphi$. The question itself, if it is a normal co-operative one, conveys at least the presuppositions

(i) $\neg K_{\boldsymbol{Q}} \varphi \wedge \neg K_{\boldsymbol{Q}} \neg \varphi$ ("$\boldsymbol{Q}$ does not know whether φ"),

(ii) $\langle \boldsymbol{Q} \rangle (K_{\boldsymbol{A}} \varphi \vee K_{\boldsymbol{A}} \neg \varphi)$ ("$\boldsymbol{Q}$ thinks that $\boldsymbol{A}$ may know the answer").

After the whole two-step communication episode, φ is known to both agents: $K_{\boldsymbol{A}} \varphi \wedge K_{\boldsymbol{Q}} \varphi$, while they also know this about each other: $K_{\boldsymbol{Q}} K_{\boldsymbol{A}} \varphi \wedge K_{\boldsymbol{A}} K_{\boldsymbol{Q}} \varphi$, etcetera. Indeed, they achieve the "limit notion" of common knowledge, written as $C_{\{\boldsymbol{Q}, \boldsymbol{A}\}} \varphi$. The importance of this notion has been recognized in many areas by now, from philosophy to game theory, computer science, linguistics, and psychology.

---

[116]Both presuppositions fail with *rhetorical questions*: a teacher knows the answer, and need not have any illusions about the students' knowing the answer.

[117]Common knowledge C_G is a higher-order notion, while individual modalities are first-order. The dual modality $\langle C_G \rangle$ is mainly a technical convenience.

The preceding assertions only make precise sense when backed up by a semantics. Here is the formal version of the intuitive idea of "information as range" in the graph models of Chapter 2:

Definition 12.2.2 (Models). *Models* M for the epistemic language are triples $(W, \{\rightarrow_i | \ i \in G\}, V)$, where W is a set of worlds, G is a set of agents, the $\rightarrow_i$ are binary accessibility relations for agents between worlds, and V is a valuation assigning truth values to proposition letters at worlds. We will also use the notation $\sim_i$ for accessibility.

In what follows, our primary semantic objects are *pointed models* M, s where s is the actual world representing the true state of affairs, even though the agents may not know this.

Epistemic models encode collective information states for groups of agents finding themselves in some real situation that they need not know, and may want to learn about. We impose no general structural conditions on the accessibility relation – leaving this choice as a "degree of freedom" for the modeler using the system. But in fact, many of our examples work with *S5*-style equivalence relations (reflexive, symmetric, and transitive; cf. Chapter 8) – and the reader should feel free to keep such special settings in mind throughout.

Example (Setting up realistic models). A real feel for the elegance and utility of epistemic logic only comes from the "art of modeling" real scenarios. Doing so also dispels delusions of grandeur about "worlds". Consider a simple game: three cards "red", "white", "blue" are given to three players: 1, 2, 3, one each. Each player sees her own card, but not that of the others. The real distribution over the players 1, 2, 3 is *red, white, blue* (**rwb**). Here is the resulting information state:

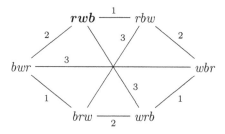

This pictures the 6 relevant states of the world (the "hands", or distributions of the cards), with the appropriate accessibilities (equivalence relations in this case) pictured by the uncertainty lines between hands. E.g., the single 1-line between *rwb* and *rbw* indicates that player 1 cannot distinguish these two situations, whereas 2 and 3 can (they have different cards in them). In particular, the diagram says the following, intuitively: though they are in $\boldsymbol{rwb}$ (as an outside observer can see), no player knows this. Of course, the game itself is a dynamic process yielding further information, which will be our theme in Chapter 15.

Over these structures, which may often be pictured graphically and concretely as a sort of "information diagrams" for a group of agents, we can now interpret the epistemic language:

Definition 12.2.3 (Truth conditions).

$\boldsymbol{M}, s \models p$	iff	V makes p true at s
$\boldsymbol{M}, s \models \neg\varphi$	iff	not $\boldsymbol{M}, s \models \varphi$
$\boldsymbol{M}, s \models \varphi \wedge \psi$	iff	$\boldsymbol{M}, s \models \varphi$ and $\boldsymbol{M}, s \models \psi$
$\boldsymbol{M}, s \models K_i\varphi$	iff	for all t with $s \to_i t$: $\boldsymbol{M}, t \models \varphi$ [118]
$\boldsymbol{M}, s \models C_G\varphi$	iff	for all worlds t that are reachable from s by some finite sequence of arbitrary $\to_i$ steps with $i \in G$ we have $\boldsymbol{M}, t \models \varphi$ [119]

Example (A model for a question/answer scenario). Here is how a question answer episode might start (this is just one of many appropriate concrete initial situations!). In the following diagram, reflexive arrows are presupposed, but not drawn. Intuitively, agent $\boldsymbol{Q}$ does not know whether p, but $\boldsymbol{A}$ is fully informed about it:

$$p \, \bullet \xleftarrow{\quad\quad \boldsymbol{Q} \quad\quad} \circ \, \neg p$$

In the black world, the following formulas are true:

$$p, \quad K_{\boldsymbol{A}}p, \quad \neg K_{\boldsymbol{Q}}p \wedge \neg K_{\boldsymbol{Q}}\neg p, \quad K_{\boldsymbol{Q}}(K_{\boldsymbol{A}}p \vee K_{\boldsymbol{A}}\neg p),$$
$$C_{\{\boldsymbol{Q},\boldsymbol{A}\}}(\neg K_{\boldsymbol{Q}}p \wedge \neg K_{\boldsymbol{Q}}\neg p), \quad C_{\{\boldsymbol{Q},\boldsymbol{A}\}}(K_{\boldsymbol{A}}p \vee K_{\boldsymbol{A}}\neg p)$$

This is an excellent situation for $\boldsymbol{Q}$ to ask $\boldsymbol{A}$ whether p is the case: he even knows that she knows the answer. Once the answer "Yes" has been given, intuitively, this model changes to the following one-point model where maximal information has been achieved:

$$p \, \bullet$$

Now, of course $C_{\{\boldsymbol{Q},\boldsymbol{A}\}}p$ holds at the black world.

The epistemic language sharpens various intuitive distinctions. For instance, saying that "everybody in the group knows something" is not yet common knowledge, but the operator $E_G\varphi$ of *universal knowledge* in a group, being the conjunction of all formulas $K_i\varphi$ for all $i \in G$.

The *social character* of group information suggests further notions.

---

[118]This is of course just the standard universal box modality $\Box$ of Parts I and II.
[119]More precisely, one can define a new accessibility relation $\to_G$ for the whole group G as the *reflexive transitive closure* of the *union* of all separate relations $\to_i$ ($i \in G$). C_G is then the universal modality for this relation.

Example (From implicit to explicit group knowledge)**.** Suppose that both agents have information that the other lacks, say as follows:

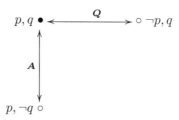

Here, the black dot is the actual world. The most cooperative scenario is for Q to tell A that q is the case (something that Q knows), while A can then tell her that p. This reduces the initial three-point model to the one-point model where $p \wedge q$ is common knowledge.

Another way of describing what happens in the preceding example is that, when Q, A do the best they can in informing each other, they will cut things down to the *intersection* of their individual accessibility relations. This suggests a new natural notion for groups:

Definition 12.2.4 (Distributed knowledge)**.** Intuitively, a formula φ is *implicit* or *distributed knowledge* in a group, written $D_G\varphi$, when agents could come to see it by pooling their information. More technically, this involves intersection of accessibility relations:

$$M, s \models D_G\varphi \quad \text{iff} \quad \text{for all } t \text{ with } s \cap_{i \in G} \rightarrow_i t : M, s \models \varphi \quad 120$$

Intuitively, agents can turn their implicit group knowledge into common knowledge by acts of *communication*: Chapter 14 has more.

12.3 Validity, axiomatic systems, and correspondence

Basic logics Validity of formulas φ in epistemic logic is defined as usual, as truth of φ in all models at all worlds. Consequence from premises to conclusions is then defined as in Chapter 4, through valid conditionals. Our completeness theorem of Chapter 5 then tells us that the minimal modal logic K is at the same time a minimal epistemic logic, at least for individual knowledge operators.[121]

---

[120] Here the relation for D_G runs from world s to all t that are connected to it simultaneously by every agent accessibility relation $\rightarrow_i$. This relates all those worlds that no agent can distinguish from the current one. There have been doubts in the literature whether this is really the best intuitive account of distributed knowledge as "what can be made explicit through communication", partly, because bisimulation invariance fails. We forego such further issues here.

[121] We drop agent subscripts for K-operators when they play no essential role.

Even though this calculus is simple, one of its axioms has sparked continuing debate, viz.

$$K(\varphi \to \psi) \to (K\varphi \to K\psi) \qquad \textit{Epistemic Distribution}$$

This says that agents' knowledge is closed under logical inferences, and this "omniscience" is usually considered unrealistic. At stake here is a distinction between *semantic* and *inferential information*. Semantically, in terms of pure observation, an agent who has the information that $\varphi \to \psi$ and that φ, also has the information that ψ. But in a more fine-grained perspective of inferential information and dynamic processes of *elucidation*, this need not be the case at all.[122]

Systems of deduction like this may be used in two modes. They either describe (a) the agents' own explicit reasoning "inside" our scenarios, or (b) our own "outside" reasoning as theorists about them. In many settings, the difference between the two stances will not matter: the modeler is "one of the boys" – but sometimes, it may.

Stronger logics: correspondence On top of the minimal epistemic logic, we can help ourselves to stronger axioms endowing agents with further informational features. These will impose matching structural conditions on accessibility by *frame correspondence* (cf. Chapter 9). Here are three more axioms with vivid epistemic interpretations:

$K\varphi \to \varphi$	Veridicality
$K\varphi \to KK\varphi$	Positive Introspection
$\neg K\varphi \to K\neg K\varphi$	Negative Introspection

The former is uncontroversial (knowledge is "in synch" with reality), but the latter two have been much discussed. They assume that, in addition to logical omniscience, agents also have unlimited introspection into their own epistemic states. But we are all surrounded by people who do not realize their own ignorance!

Formally, these axioms correspond to the following structural conditions on accessibility, by techniques that you already know:

$K\varphi \to \varphi$	reflexivity	$\forall x : x \to x$
$K\varphi \to KK\varphi$	transitivity	$\forall xyz : (x \to y \land y \to z) \Rightarrow x \to z$
$\neg K\varphi \to K\neg K\varphi$	euclidity	$\forall xyz : (x \to y \land x \to z) \Rightarrow y \to z$

The complete deductive system with all the above axioms is our earlier logic *S5*, or "multi-*S5*" when we have more than one agent.

---

[122]There are many proposals for finely-grained syntactic perspectives on information: cf. the chapter by van Benthem & Martínez in the *Handbook of the Philosophy of Information*. There are also dynamic logics of inference steps and related acts of "awareness raising", that go beyond our present scope.

What may be surprising is that this logic has no "interaction axioms" relating different modalities K_i, K_j. But none are plausible.

Example (Your knowledge and mine do not commute). Here is a counter-example to $K_1 K_2 p \to K_2 K_1 p$. Its antecedent is true in the black world to the left, but its consequent is false:

Such formulas only hold for agents with special informational links.

In the "dynamic epistemic logics" of Chapters 15, 23, some commutation principles do hold, but then between epistemic modalities and action modalities. In between the minimal logic K and $S5$, many other epistemic logics have a following, such as "$KD45$" for belief.

Stronger languages Another earlier theme is extension of *expressive power*, having to do with which modal language we want to use for describing our structures. The basic epistemic language is one candidate, but one may add "universal modalities" ranging over all worlds (accessible or not), or "nominals" picking out single worlds (cf. Chapters 7, 10). The most striking addition in the epistemic setting has been the earlier-mentioned group modality of *common knowledge*.

Theorem 22. The complete epistemic logic with common knowledge is axiomatized by adding the following principles to the minimal logic, with E_G the earlier modality "everyone in the group knows":

$$C_G \varphi \leftrightarrow (\varphi \wedge E_G C_G \varphi) \qquad \text{Fixed-Point Axiom}$$
$$(\varphi \wedge C_G(\varphi \to E_G \varphi)) \to C_G \varphi \qquad \text{Induction Axiom}$$

These axioms are also of independent interest for what they say. The Fixed-Point Axiom expresses an intuition of "reflective equilibrium": common knowledge of φ is a proposition implying φ of which every group member knows that *it* is true. Restated slightly differently, its "fixed point character" says that the agents are in an epistemic state where saying that it is a truth that everyone knows that state adds nothing new. On top of this, the Induction Axiom reflects the usual Induction Axiom of Arithmetic in an obvious manner:

$$(\varphi(0) \wedge \forall n(\varphi(n) \to \varphi(n+1))) \to \forall n \varphi(n)$$

Technically the epistemic Induction Axiom says that $C_G \varphi$ is not just any equilibrium state of its kind, but the largest.[123]

---

[123]Thus, common knowledge is a "greatest fixed-point": cf. Chapter 22 for details.

12.4 Invariance, expressive power, and the balance with complexity

All more advanced topics from our earlier chapters make immediate sense for the epistemic language. We briefly mention a few. First, we can *translate* the whole language effectively into first-order logic, though we would need a "fixed-point extension" of first-order logic called *LFP(FO)* to deal with common knowledge (cf. Chapters 7, 22 for such extensions).

Next, inside this larger arena, we can measure the expressive power of epistemic languages in terms of their invariance for various notions of *bisimulation*. The intuitive interpretation of this invariance relation does acquire a certain local flavour, of course – this time, not as a "process equivalence", but as equivalence of information structure.

Example (Bisimulation-invariant information structures). Our earlier question-answer example has a bisimulation with the following variant:

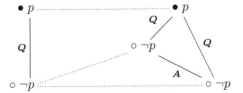

In a natural sense, both models represent the same information state for the agents. Bisimulation also occurs naturally in *information update* changing a current model. Suppose that the initial model is like this, with the actual world indicated by the black dot:

All three worlds satisfy different epistemic formulas, as you can check for yourself. Now, despite her uncertainty, in the actual world, agent 1 does know that p, and can say this – updating to the model

But here the two worlds are intuitively redundant, and there is an obvious bisimulation to just the one-point model

$$p \bullet$$

Defining information states Chapter 3 had model-theoretic results tying bisimulation closely to truth of modal formulas across models. The epistemic perspective suggests one more basic issue. First, note that the intuitive notion of an "information state" has both syntactic and semantic versions. Syntactically, there is the *modal theory* of a world w in a model M: an explicit record of all formulas that are true "internally" at w about the facts, agents' knowledge of these, and their knowledge of what others know. By contrast, modal models M, w locate the same information implicitly in the local valuation of world w plus its global interaction with other worlds via accessibility relations.[124] The following result says essentially that states in an epistemic model and their maximally consistent epistemic theories are equivalent:

Theorem 23. For each finite model M, s, there is an epistemic formula β with common knowledge[125] such that the following are equivalent:

(a) $N, t \models \beta$

(b) N, t has a bisimulation $\equiv$ with M, s such that $s \equiv t$.

The Invariance Lemma of Chapter 3 said that bisimulation has the right fit with the modal language. The new theorem strengthens this to say that each semantic state is captured by one epistemic formula. This result extends to arbitrary models, provided we are willing to use formulas from a language allowing arbitrary infinite conjunctions and disjunctions (cf. Chapter 7, 22). Instead of a proof, we give an illustration of how such complete definitions work.

Example (Defining a model up to bisimulation). Consider the two-world model for our earlier basic question-answer episode. Here is an epistemic formula which defines its φ-state up to bisimulation:

$$p \wedge C_{\{Q,A\}}((K_A p \vee K_A \neg p) \wedge \neg K_Q p \wedge \neg K_Q \neg p)$$

These results allow us to switch, in principle, between semantic and syntactic accounts of information states. Syntactic states have been dominant in areas like belief revision theory, and semantic ones in the dynamic epistemic logics that we will discuss in Chapters 15 and 23.

---

[124]This "external" global feature is sometimes considered a drawback of relational semantics. But really, it is a brilliant move, describing worlds externally through their interactions with other worlds, the same way Category Theory describes mathematical structures through their morphisms with other structures.

[125]Common knowledge is needed to make sure we quantify over all accessible worlds in our models. In fact, even a single reflexive point cannot be defined up to bisimulation in the basic modal language, since any modal formula true in that point can be made true in the root of a finite tree (by unraveling, Chapter 3), which has no bisimulation with it: just consider the irreflexive end points!

Computational complexity While issues of derivability and definability have been the main pillars of logical analysis so far, in recent years, there has been a growing awareness that issues of *task complexity* form a natural complement. Given that all information available to us has to be recognized, or extracted to be of use, it is natural to ask how complex such extraction processes are – cf. our discussion for basic modal logic in Chapter 6. The "complexity profile" of the basic epistemic language is that of the basic modal one. Model-checking takes *PTIME*, satisfiability is *PSPACE*-complete, and model comparison takes *PTIME*. But there are a few nice twists in the epistemic setting. Single-agent satisfiability in *S5* was in *NP*, since *S5* had a normal form without iterated modalities close to propositional logic. But with two agents, involving two equivalence relations as in many of our examples, satisfiability jumps back to *PSPACE*: social life is more complicated than being alone.

These complexity results are affected by the expressive power of the language. For instance, when we add the earlier *common knowledge* modality $C_G\varphi$ to the language, the above profile changes as follows:

Fact. The complexity profile of the epistemic language with C_G is:

Model-Checking	Satisfiability	Model Comparison
PTIME	*EXPTIME*	*PTIME*

Best algorithms for model-checking formulas with common knowledge are quite clever; while the analysis of decidability also changes considerably from what we saw in Chapter 6.

Information and games Finally, we note that computation is not just a routine chore measuring "difficulty" of tasks: it is also a fundamental process in its own right. This comes out particularly well with the earlier *game versions* of basic tasks (Chapters 2, 3), which model the "intensional" procedural activity behind them in a vivid manner. There were games for semantic model-checking, model comparison, and there are even logical games for testing validity or satisfiability via model construction moves. Indeed, games have a more general relevance to epistemic logic. They are typical multi-agent informational processes, whose practice and theory involves epistemic notions in an essential way. We present this link in more detail in Chapter 17.

12.5 Conclusion

We have surveyed epistemic logic as a species of modal logic, emphasizing how our earlier general themes play naturally in this setting. But we have also shown how the peculiarities of an interest in knowledge lead to new modal logical notions. Of course, there are still further issues that might be pursued, and we mention three particular avenues.

A richer *epistemic predicate logic* (cf. Chapter 27) can make further important distinctions about knowledge of properties of individual objects, such as $\exists x K_a \varphi(x)$ ("de re knowledge") versus $K_a \exists x \varphi(x)$ ("de dicto knowledge"). Such richer systems are needed to formalize natural reasoning about knowing objects, such as telephone numbers, or people. As we said in the Introduction to this Part, extending our whole framework to the predicate-logical case is a task that mostly still needs to be done – and who knows, it may be done by *you*!

In addition to declarative knowledge there is *procedural knowledge* and "skills". An account of the intuitive notion of "know-how" versus our present "know-that" would involve knowledge which procedures lead to certain desired (information) states. Some of this will be considered in Chapters 16, 17 using tools from dynamic logic (Chapter 15).

Finally, the philosophical tradition also has the natural notion of justification or *evidence* for knowledge. One option is to add *resources* to our systems with explicit justifications or cost functions for epistemic modalities – say in an indexed format $K[x]\varphi$: "evidence x supports knowledge that φ". Then earlier axioms acquire interesting new formulations, such as modal distribution:

$$K[x]\varphi \rightarrow (K[y](\varphi \rightarrow \psi) \rightarrow K[x+y]\psi),$$

with $+$ some "merge" function for evidence. So, we can know logical consequences of our knowledge, but at a cost indicated by the calculus of evidence. Keeping track of justifications also has independent virtues: it allows for finer-grained analyses of many epistemic notions. Now, "having evidence" is an *existential* quantifier that seems at odds with our universal *quantifier* for $K\varphi$ as "in all current alternatives". But the provability logic of Chapter 21 shows how the two can co-exist happily.

Exercises Chapter 12

Epistemic models always have equivalence relations in what follows, – but in the diagrams, only the minimal set of lines is displayed.

1. Some earlier modal topics in epistemic semantics:
   (a) Find epistemic formulas that uniquely define each world in this model:

   $$p \circ \underset{}{\overset{2}{\rule{3em}{0.4pt}}} \circ p$$
   $$\left. 1 \right| \qquad \left| 1 \right.$$
   $$p \circ \qquad \circ \neg p$$

   (b) The following information model is "over-elaborate". How would you show that technically?

   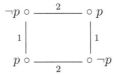

2. Which one of the following two implications is valid in multi-$S5$? Draw a counter-example for the other:

   $$\langle 1 \rangle K_2 \varphi \rightarrow \langle 2 \rangle \langle 1 \rangle \varphi, \qquad \langle 1 \rangle K_2 \varphi \rightarrow \langle 2 \rangle K_1 \varphi$$

3. Here some basics of reasoning with groups:
   (a) Show that $E_G \varphi$ does not imply $C_G \varphi$, while $D_G \varphi$ does not imply $E_G \varphi$.
   (b) Check the validity of the axioms for common knowledge with the semantic explanation in our models.
   (c) Common knowledge is undefinable in terms of ordinary K-operators for single agents in a group, if that group has at least 2 members. Prove this by considering models consisting of finite linear chains of worlds connected by alternating $\sim_1$ and $\sim_2$ links. *Hint*: Use a suitable "Finite Depth Property" for multi-agent epistemic formulas.
   (d) Consider knowledge across different groups. Does $C_{G_1} \varphi \wedge C_{G_2} \varphi$ imply $C_{G_1 \cup G_2} \varphi$, or vice versa? Can you find other valid principles of this sort?

13

Doxastic and conditional logic

13.1 From knowledge to belief as a trigger for actions

While best available information and knowledge are important, our actions are often driven by less demanding attitudes of belief. I am riding my bicycle since I believe that it will get me home, even though my epistemic range includes worlds where the Great Earthquake finally happens. Indeed, decision theory is about choice and action on the basis of beliefs, since waiting for knowledge may last forever. Think of simple scenarios like in Chapter 12. The cards have been dealt. I know that there are 52 of them, and I know their colors. But I have more fleeting beliefs about who holds which card, or how other agents will play.[126]

With this distinction in attitude comes one of dynamics. An event of *hard information* changes irrevocably what I know. If I see the Ace of Spades played on the table, I come to know that no one holds it any more. But there are also events of *soft information*, that affect my current beliefs without affecting my knowledge about the cards. I see you smile. This makes it more likely that you hold a trump card, but it does not rule out that you do not. This soft information motivates the semantics of belief in the sections to follow.

13.2 Basic logic of belief and knowledge: first attempt

A simplest "doxastic logic" works in the same style as epistemic logic, with an accessibility relation that drops Veridicality (reflexivity), because, crucially, beliefs can be *wrong*:

Example (A mistaken belief). Consider the following model with two worlds that are epistemically accessible to each other, but the pointed arrow is the only belief relation. Here, in the actual black world to the

---

[126]I could even be wrong about the cards (a demon replaced the King of Hearts by Clinton's visiting card), but this worry seems morbid in normal scenarios.

left, the atom p is true, but the agent mistakenly believes that $\neg p$:

$$p \bullet \xrightarrow{} \circ \neg p$$

More precisely,

$$B_i\varphi \quad (\text{``}i \text{ believes that } \varphi\text{''})$$

is a universal modality of the sort we know over a new accessibility relation $R_{B,i}$. Here, intuitively, knowledge implies belief: $K_i\varphi \to B_i\varphi$, but not vice versa. One may believe more propositions than those one knows, which gives a *converse* semantic requirement that the relation $R_{B,x}$ should be included in $R_{K,i}$. For belief, I am willing to consider fewer alternatives. I believe that Australia exists (it is there in all worlds I find most plausible), even though I do not strictly *know* this: my only evidence is having seeing the Russell Crowe movie "Heaven's Burning". Again, we see the distinction between hard and soft information.

As for logical systems, one usually takes the minimal modal logic K once more, just as for knowledge, plus the *K4* axiom of positive introspection for belief. The veridicality axiom $B_a\varphi \to \varphi$ is not plausible, but instead, one usually requires

$$B_a\varphi \to \neg B_a\neg\varphi \qquad \text{Belief Consistency}^{127}$$

Further axioms govern the interplay of knowledge and belief. As we said already, it is uncontroversial that knowledge implies belief:

$$K_a\varphi \to B_a\varphi$$

while some authors accept strong introspection laws like

$$B_a\varphi \to K_aB_a\varphi$$

Combinations of knowledge and belief have been used, for instance, in semantic analyses of "assertoric force" of statements in natural language. When an agent a says that φ, then the force of this seems stronger than $B_a\varphi$, but weaker than $K_a\varphi$, and hence the intermediate force $B_aK_a\varphi$ has been proposed. Further epistemic attitudes, such as "be convinced" are studied in Lenzen (1979). These, and even richer notions return in modern computer science, in the so-called *BDI* ("belief-desire-intention") framework for describing interactive agents.

This view of belief, though appealing, still has some problems:

Example. Consider a "public announcement" $!p$ of the true fact p. Applied to our earlier two-world model, the result is the one-world model where p holds, with the inherited empty doxastic accessibility

---

[127]This is still an idealization, of course: our actual beliefs can be inconsistent.

relation. But on the above reading of belief, the agent then believes that p, but also that $\neg p$, as $B\bot$ is true at such an end-point.

In this way, agents who have their beliefs contradicted are shattered and start believing anything. Such a collapse does not sound right.

13.3 Plausibility models

A richer view of belief follows the intuition that an agent believes the things that are true, not in all epistemically accessible worlds, but only in those "most relevant" to her. I believe my bicycle will get me home, even though I do not know that it will not suddenly disappear in an earthquake chasm. But worlds where it stays on the road are more plausible than those where it drops down, and among the former, those where it arrives on time are more plausible than those where it does not. Static models for this setting are easily defined:

Definition 13.3.1 (Epistemic-doxastic models). *Epistemic-doxastic models* are structures $\boldsymbol{M} = (W, \{\sim_i\}_{i \in I}, \{\leq_{s,i}\}_{i \in I}, V)$ where the relations $\sim_i$ stand for epistemic accessibility, and the $\leq_{s,i}$ are ternary comparison relations for agents read as follows, $\leq_{s,i} xy$ if, in world s, agent i considers x at least as plausible as y.

In line with our intuitions, one can impose further conditions on these abstract plausibility relations. For convenience, we will just write the two main arguments, suppressing the world. An often-used minimum is *reflexivity* and *transitivity*, while a lushed version adds

for all worlds x, y, either $x \leq y$ or $y \leq x$ *connectedness*

The latter yields the well-known geometrical systems of "nested spheres" of equiplausible worlds as a concrete picture for our models – that is also known from the possible-worlds semantics for conditional logic, where spheres represent worlds equally "close" to the current one.[128] The latter setting has only three options for worlds x, y:

either strict precedence $x < y$ or $y < x$, or equiplausibility $x \leq y \land y \leq x$.

While this is attractive, there are also scenarios with a fourth option:

$$\neg\, x \leq y \land \neg\, y \leq x \qquad \textit{incomparability}$$

This happens in practice when comparing worlds according to conflicting criteria – and sometimes, the latter partial orders are just the mathematically more elegant and perspicuous approach.

Further natural constraints regulate the interplay of epistemic and doxastic structure. It makes sense to view plausibility as the same re-

---

[128]The natural strict variant of these orderings is $x < y$ iff $x \leq y \land \neg y \leq x$.

lation throughout epistemic equivalence classes, requiring that, when $s \sim_i t$, the worlds s, t agree on their plausibility order. This makes agents know their plausibility order, validating *knowledge introspection* axioms for belief. Instead of pursuing this abstract analysis, we give a concrete illustration of the sort of belief model that we have in mind:

Example (Two-agent knowledge and belief). In the following model, dotted lines mark epistemic accessibility, and within equivalence classes, arrows point at worlds with greater plausibility. In the actual world y with the black dot, looking at his epistemic range y, z, Agent 2 knows that q, does not know that p, and in fact, looking at the world z that he considers most plausible, believes that $\neg p$. For agent 1, these things work analogously, looking at worlds y, x. As for higher-order knowledge, e.g., Agent 2 believes (by looking at world z) that Agent 1 knows that q, whereas actually (in y), 1 does not know that q:

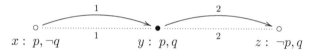

$$x : p, \neg q \qquad y : p, q \qquad z : \neg p, q$$

One can interpret many logical operators in this richer comparative structure. In what follows, we use intuitive "minimality" formulations for belief $B_i \varphi$, though these would have to be modified in models that contain infinitely descending sequences in the world ordering.[129] First of all, there is plain belief, with a modality interpreted as follows (we will often drop agent subscripts for convenience):

Definition 13.3.2 (Belief as truth in the most plausible worlds). In epistemic-doxastic models, knowledge is interpreted as usual, while for *belief*, we now say that $M, s \models B_i \varphi$ iff $M, t \models \varphi$ for all worlds t that are minimal in the ordering $\lambda xy. \leq_{i,s} xy$, restricted to the set $\{t \mid s \sim_i t\}$ of worlds that are epistemically accessible from s.[130]

This semantics with a comparative ordering of worlds gives fine-structure to the earlier bare accessibility relation for doxastic logic. The logic validated by this stipulation depends on the relational properties assumed for the plausibility order – but this is not our concern in this chapter. We rather focus on the models as such, and note that a comparative order like this allows us to interpret further important doxastic notions. Often, absolute belief does not suffice – and the richer plausibility order naturally allows us to interpret *conditional belief*, which

---

[129]We consider such changes for infinite models an orthogonal issue to the main thrust of this chapter, and will only refer to them occasionally.

[130]The lambda term $\lambda xy. \leq_{i,s} xy$ denotes the relation $\{(x, y) \mid \leq_{i,s} xy\}$ for a fixed world s. Also, we use the term "minimal", but "maximal" would be fine, too.

"pre-encodes", so to speak, what beliefs an agent will have after some new information comes in. We write this notion as

$$B^\psi\varphi, \quad \text{with the intuitive reading that, conditional on } \psi,$$
the agent believes that φ.

The semantic account of this notion is close to standard conditional logic, as developed by Lewis and Stalnaker since the 1960s – but explicit doxastic versions seem to have occurred first in computer science, in the work of Boutilier, Halpern, Shoham, and others:

Definition 13.3.3 (Conditional beliefs as plausibility conditionals). In epistemic-doxastic models, $M, s \models B^\psi\varphi$ iff $M, t \models \varphi$ for all worlds t that are minimal for $\lambda xy. \leq_{i,s} xy$ in the set $\{u \sim_i s \mid M, u \models \psi\}$.

Absolute belief $B\varphi$ is a special case of this: $B^\top\varphi$. It can be shown that conditional belief is not definable in terms of absolute belief, so we have a genuine language extension.[131]

13.4 Conditional logic

Conditional logic was developed for *counterfactual assertions* like

"if the match had been struck, an explosion would have occurred".

By now, it has also been applied to a wide range of indicative conditionals. Such a conditional $\varphi \Rightarrow \psi$ is true at the model M, w if

ψ is true in all the minimal or "closest" worlds to w where φ is true, with closeness measured by some comparison order on worlds.[132] This is exactly the above clause. Thus, results from conditional logic apply to conditional belief. For instance, on models with reflexive transitive plausibility orderings, we have the following completeness theorem:

Theorem 24. The logic of $B^\psi\varphi$ is axiomatized by standard propositional logic plus the following laws of conditional logic:

(a) $\varphi \Rightarrow \varphi$

(b) $\varphi \Rightarrow \psi$ implies $\varphi \Rightarrow \psi \vee \chi$

(c) $\varphi \Rightarrow \psi$, $\varphi \Rightarrow \chi$ imply $\varphi \Rightarrow \psi \wedge \chi$

(d) $\varphi \Rightarrow \psi$, $\chi \Rightarrow \psi$ imply $(\varphi \vee \chi) \Rightarrow \psi$

(e) $\varphi \Rightarrow \psi$, $\varphi \Rightarrow \chi$ imply $(\varphi \wedge \chi) \Rightarrow \psi$

On connected orders, we also get the following additional axiom valid:

---

[131] Compare the fact that the binary quantifier *"Most A are B"* is not definable in a first-order logic plus a unary quantifier *"Most objects in the universe are B"*.

[132] Again, we forego some subtle reformulations needed in cases like Lewis' "if I were taller than I am ...", with models allowing for "infinite approach".

(f) $((\varphi \vee \psi) \Rightarrow \varphi) \vee \neg((\varphi \vee \psi) \Rightarrow \chi) \vee (\psi \Rightarrow \chi)$

One can determine its relational content through frame correspondence techniques, but we leave this as a technical exercise.

For much more information on conditional logic and its current ramifications in philosophy, computer science, and game theory, see the chapters on "Modal Logic and Philosophy", and on "Modal Logic, Information and Games" in the *Handbook of Modal Logic*.

13.5 A down-to-earth modal alternative

While we have presented a standard line in the literature, there is a simpler alternative. In this intermezzo, we forget the epistemic structure in our models, and just concentrate on the plausibility order of worlds. Given a binary plausibility relation $\leq$, just introduce a modality making the following "local" assertion at a world w:

$$\boldsymbol{M}, s \models \langle \leq \rangle \varphi \quad \text{iff} \quad \text{there exists a } v \geq s \text{ with } \boldsymbol{M}, v \models \varphi$$

i.e., some world v at least as plausible as s satisfies φ. This simple system can express many natural notions (as observed by Boutilier in the early 1990s). Four dissertations at *ILLC* Amsterdam (Girard (2008), Liu (2008), van Otterloo (2005) and Roy (2008)) provide applications to belief revision, preference, and games.[133] Here we just give one illustration, whose verification we leave to the reader:

Fact. In finite pre-orders, the standard truth definition of a conditional $A \Rightarrow B$ can be written as the following modal combination:

$$U(A \to \langle \leq \rangle (A \wedge [\leq](A \to B)))$$

with U the universal modality of Chapter 7.[134]

13.6 Further topics: system combination, and a first glimpse of information dynamics

Combined epistemic-doxastic logics In actual agency, knowledge and belief occur intertwined, and require combinations of epistemic and doxastic logic. We already noted the elegant semantics making epistemic accessibility an *equivalence relation*, and plausibility a *pre-order over equivalence classes*, the same as viewed from any world inside such a class. This will have the effect of making the following valid:

$$B\varphi \to KB\varphi \qquad \textit{Epistemic-Doxastic Introspection}^{135}$$

---

[133]The dissertation server `http://www.illc.uva.nl` has downloadable versions.
[134]When combining the conditional or doxastic language with an epistemic one, this universal modality can be replaced by a knowledge operator.

Combined epistemic-conditional logics But there are further reasons for combining our modal systems so far. For instance, in epistemology, Nozick proposed that knowledge is true belief with a surplus in terms of "successful tracking" of the facts. The true belief $B\varphi \wedge \varphi$ is held in place by two counterfactual assertions:

(a) if φ persists after a counterfactual change, I still believe it:

$$\varphi \Rightarrow B\varphi$$

(b) if φ were to become false after some counterfactual change, I would come to believe that $\neg\varphi$:

$$\neg\varphi \Rightarrow B\neg\varphi$$

The philosophers are ahead of the logicians here. The complete epistemic logic of this intriguing notion has not yet been found – though it has challenging differences from that in Chapter 12. For instance, Nozick knowledge is not closed under weakening of known propositions φ to propositions $\varphi \vee \psi$ logically entailed by them.

All this shows that rational agency involves a rich repertoire of modal notions: epistemic, doxastic (and beyond to preferences and intentions). But one important step remains to be made toward a complete picture.

A "dynamic turn" Here is a further topic that motivates much of our Chapters 12, 13. Our account of knowledge was really about epistemic models that change when new information comes in. For instance, the point of our card example was not that players' knowledge stays as in the initial diagram. This knowledge gets *updated* every time events happen that produce further information, such as showings of cards, other observations, linguistic statements, or other forms of communication. Thus, we need to move from "statics" to "dynamics". This dynamics plays just as well in our doxastic logics, where being wrong is the engine of progress. As soon as we see that our beliefs are wrong, we engage in dynamic procedures of *belief revision*, or if you wish: *learning*.

To bring this "Dynamic Turn" into the scope of our analysis, we need to design a logic of state-changing actions, and that is the topic of our next Chapter 14 on "dynamic logic" – a major area of contemporary modal logic. Chapter 15 then puts a number of things together, and shows you how combined modal systems can deal with concrete activities of communication or games. Later on, in Chapter 23, we will study some technical issues raised by these developments.

---

[135]There are some complications: e.g., bisimulations now need back-and-forth clauses for the *intersection* of epistemic accessibility and plausibility.

Exercises Chapter 13

1. Verify that Disjunction of Antecedents holds for conditional logic.

2. Show that on models with pre-orders, the conditional logic axiom $((\varphi \vee \psi) \Rightarrow \varphi) \vee \neg((\varphi \vee \psi) \Rightarrow \chi) \vee (\psi \Rightarrow \chi)$ corresponds to connectedness of the order.

3. Show that conditional belief $B^\psi \varphi$ is not equivalent to belief in the corresponding conditional: $B(\psi \to \varphi)$.

4. Prove the adequacy of the stated modal definition $U(A \to \langle \leq \rangle (A \wedge [\leq](A \to B)))$ for conditionals $A \Rightarrow B$ on finite models.

5. Show that Nozick's notion of knowledge does not satisfy monotonicity: you can know A without knowing that $A \vee B$.

14

Dynamic logic of actions and events

This chapter is about logics of programs, action, and process structure. For more details than we can provide here, see the textbook Goldblatt (1987), the comprehensive monograph Harel et al. (2000), or the chapter by Bradfield & Stirling in Blackburn et al. (2006).

14.1 Modal logic over process graphs

A poly-modal language with $[a]$, $\langle b \rangle$ (cf. Chapters 7, 10) describes effects of actions. This was the "process intuition" behind the notion of bisimulation in Chapter 3, but now we pursue it more explicitly. Models $M = (S, \{ R_a \}_{a \in A}, V)$ have *labeled transitions* R_a for successful executions of action a (such models are also called "labeled transition systems", with R_a written as $\rightarrow_a$). Here, S consists of the states of a computer, the world, or any process. The binary relations R_a encode successful program executions, or transitions for any action a at all. The valuation V indicates for each atomic proposition, a "local property" of the process, whether it is true or not, at any state. This is about the simplest logical model of action. It can be pictured as follows:

Example (A process graph). A *process graph* has labeled arrows between nodes, and, when relevant, information about atoms annotating the nodes. In the following picture, the four dots indicate states West, North, East and South – where West is the "starting state":

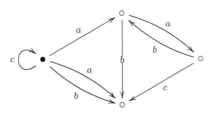

There are three types of action: a, b, c. In West, actions b, c are deterministic: one possible transition. (Here, c "loops", and does not change the state.) Action a is non-deterministic in West: two possible transitions. South is an end state: no action is possible. Actions also have relationships. For instance, above right, b "undoes" the effect of a, as a "converse". But atomic actions also combine to form compound ones. Thus, the sequential action $a; b$ (a followed by b) gives a new transition from West to South, and from North to North. Local state properties might be a proposition letter q ("cold") true in West and North.

In a concrete computational setting, evaluating predicate-logical languages or simple programming languages, the states are usually all *variable assignments* into some fixed domain of objects, transitions are shifts in values for a variable, and the valuation says which atomic predicates hold for every relevant assignment of objects to variables. This analogy will drive our final Chapter 27.

14.2 Program correctness

A basic computational logic is *Hoare calculus of correctness assertions*:

$\{\varphi\}\pi\{\psi\}$ "after every successful execution of program π starting from a state where precondition φ holds, postcondition ψ holds in the final state":

$$\varphi \circ \longrightarrow \bullet\, \psi$$

These statements involve both program expressions π and logical propositions φ, ψ.[136] Non-determinism is allowed: a program may have more than one successful execution starting from the same initial state: ψ is to hold after each of these. Also, in this setting, successful executions are identified "extensionally" with binary transitions ⟨input state, output state⟩ , without "intensional" information on how this was achieved. Finally, $\{\varphi\}\pi\{\psi\}$ expresses *partial correctness*: it does not require that any execution of π *terminates*.[137]

Hoare "correctness rules" can analyze imperative "While Programs" constructed from atomic instructions $x := t$ using the operations of

Sequential composition $\pi_1; \pi_2$
Guarded choice   *IF φ THEN π_1 ELSE π_2*
Iteration   *WHILE φ DO π*

Starting from assignments $x := t$ involving terms t constructed with variables, 0, and the successor $+1$, these programs have universal com-

---

[136]Likewise, an *IF φ THEN π_1 ELSE π_2* involves both assertions and programs.
[137]Dijkstra's "total correctness assertions" do include strong termination.

puting power on the natural numbers $\mathbb{N}$: any computable (recursive) function whatsoever can be defined by a program of this kind.

Definition 14.2.1 (Rules of the Hoare Calculus).

$$\frac{\{P\}S\{A\} \qquad \{A\}T\{R\}}{\{P\}S;T\{R\}} \qquad \text{composition}$$

$$\frac{\{P \wedge E\}S\{Q\} \qquad \{P \wedge \neg E\}T\{Q\}}{\{P\}IF\ E\ THEN\ S\ ELSE\ T\{Q\}} \qquad \text{guarded choice}$$

$$\frac{\{I\}S\{I\}}{\{I\}\,WHILE\ E\ DO\ S\{I \wedge \neg E\}} \qquad \text{iteration}[138]$$

$$\frac{\{P\}S\{Q\}}{\{P \wedge A\}S\{Q \vee B\}} \qquad \text{monotonicity}$$

Here are some simple examples of true correctness statements:

$\{x = 4 \wedge y = 3\}(IF\ x < y\ THEN\ (z := x; y := y + 1)$
$\qquad ELSE\ z := y); z := z + 1\{x = 4 \wedge y = 3 \wedge z = 4\}$

$\{x = 3 \wedge y = 4\}(IF\ x < y\ THEN\ (z := x; y := y + 1)$
$\qquad ELSE\ z := y); z := z + 1\{x = 3 \wedge y = 5 \wedge z = 4\}$

These assertions can be derived systematically using the above rules, starting from the following initial axiom

$$\{[t/x]A\}x := t\{A\}$$

For a methodology of developing well-structured imperative programs in tandem with correctness proofs, cf. Kaldeway (1990).

A key observation motivating our next step is this: program correctness statements are modal implications $\varphi \to [\pi]\psi$!

14.3   Propositional dynamic logic, semantics and proof

Language and semantics   The following system (*PDL*, for short) generalizes all earlier ideas about describing effects of programs.

Definition 14.3.1 (Language of dynamic logic). The *PDL* language has two components, one of programs and one of propositions:

$F := atomic\ propositions \mid \neg F \mid (F \wedge F) \mid \langle P \rangle F$
$P := atomic\ actions \mid (P; P) \mid (P \cup P) \mid P^* \mid (F)?$

---

[138]Here, I is called the "loop invariant": and finding one is usually an art.

Note the mutual recursion: the modality $\langle P\rangle F$ uses programs to construct assertions, while the test (F)? uses assertions to construct programs. The existential modality $\langle\pi\rangle\varphi$ is a "weakest precondition", true at those states where program π can be performed to achieve the truth of φ. The program operators are now the *regular operations* of

relation composition, Boolean choice, Kleene iteration, and tests for formulas.

This system defines the earlier standard operators on programs:

Conditional Choice   IF ε THEN π_1 ELSE π_2 $((\varepsilon)?;\pi_1)\cup((\neg\varepsilon)?;\pi_2)$

Guarded Iteration   WHILE ε DO π $((\varepsilon)?;\pi)^*;(\neg\varepsilon)?$

This system extends both modal logic and relational algebra.

Definition 14.3.2 (Semantics of dynamic logic). The semantics matches the mutual recursion in the syntax. $M, s \models \varphi$ says that *formula φ is true at state s*, while $M, s_1, s_2 \models \pi$ says that *the transition from state s_1 to state s_2 corresponds to a successful execution of the program π*:

$M, s \models p$	iff	$s \in V(p)$
$M, s \models \neg\psi$	iff	*not* $M, s \models \psi$
$M, s \models \varphi_1 \wedge \psi_2$	iff	$M, s \models \varphi_1$ *and* $M, s \models \psi_2$
$M, s \models \langle\pi\rangle\varphi$	iff	*there is an s' with* $M, s, s' \models \pi$ *and* $M, s' \models \varphi$
$M, s_1, s_2 \models a$	iff	$(s_1, s_2) \in R_a$
$M, s_1, s_2 \models \pi_1;\pi_2$	iff	*there is an s_3 with* $M, s_1, s_3 \models \pi_1$ *and* $M, s_3, s_2 \models \pi_2$
$M, s_1, s_2 \models \pi_1 \cup \pi_2$	iff	$M, s_1, s_2 \models \pi_1$ *or* $M, s_1, s_2 \models \pi_2$
$M, s_1, s_2 \models \pi^*$	iff	*some finite sequence of π-transitions in M connects the state s_1 with the state s_2*
$M, s_1, s_2 \models (\varphi)?$	iff	$s_1 = s_2$ *and* $M, s_1 \models \varphi$

Again, the semantics does not represent details of program execution as such, only its input-output relations.

Axiomatic proof system Propositional dynamic logic has a natural minimal logic generalizing our system of Chapter 5:

Definition 14.3.3 (Axiom system for PDL). The logic *PDL* has rules of Modus Ponens and Necessitation plus the following axioms:

· All principles of the minimal modal logic for all modalities $[\pi]$
· Computation rules for decomposing program structure:

$$\langle\pi_1;\pi_2\rangle\varphi \leftrightarrow \langle\pi_1\rangle\langle\pi_2\rangle\varphi$$
$$\langle\pi_1 \cup \pi_2\rangle\varphi \leftrightarrow (\langle\pi_1\rangle\varphi \vee \langle\pi_2\rangle\varphi)$$
$$\langle\varphi?\rangle\psi \leftrightarrow (\varphi \wedge \psi)$$
$$\langle\pi^*\rangle\varphi \leftrightarrow (\varphi \vee \langle\pi\rangle\langle\pi^*\rangle\varphi)$$

- The Induction Axiom: $(\varphi \wedge [\pi^*](\varphi \to [\pi]\varphi)) \to [\pi^*]\varphi$.

Fact (Soundness). All theorems of *PDL* are universally valid.

This requires a simple check of validity for the given axioms.

This elegant axiomatic calculus generalizes the algebra of regular expressions in formal language theory, propositional modal logic, the earlier Hoare Calculus for correctness assertions $\{\varphi\}\pi\{\psi\}$, and even the epistemic logic of Chapter 12.[139] Here is an illustration:

Fact. Under the transcription $\varphi \to [\pi]\psi$, plus the above definitions for *IF THEN ELSE* and *WHILE DO*, the logic *PDL* derives all Hoare rules for sequencing, conditional choice and guarded iteration.

A proof is postponed to the Exercises for this chapter. For instance, the Hoare *WHILE* rule is really this fact about transitive closure:

$$\{I\}S\{I\} \quad \text{implies} \quad \{I\}S^*\{I\}.$$

This proof-theoretic strength reflects a general fact:

Theorem 25. The logic *PDL* axiomatizes universal validity in propositional dynamic logic.

The completeness proof is as in Chapter 5, but over a finite set of formulas (the "Fisher-Ladner closure" of the initial formula).

Decidability The preceding proof method also yields the following

Corollary. Validity in *PDL* is decidable.

But, compared with Chapter 6, computational complexity for this more expressive language goes up from the *PSPACE*-completeness of the basic modal logic to *EXPTIME*-complete.

What makes *PDL* special compared with our earlier logics is the "in-finitary" operation of iteration, repeating an action an arbitrary finite number of times. This is crucial to recursive computation and long-term action, including strategies in games (Chapter 17). One surprising thing about *PDL* is that, while adding transitive closure to *first-order* logic drives up the complexity to high levels (one can define the natural numbers up to isomorphism, and validity gets high second-order complexity), *PDL* expresses the "bare bones" of computability while staying decidable, thanks to its weak modal base (cf. Chapter 7). This theme will return in the fixed-point logics of Chapter 22.

---

[139]The accessibility relation for common knowledge is defined by the program $(\bigcup \sim_i)^*$. The laws for common knowledge are then special cases of the $*$ laws. Chapter 23 even uses a more baroque system of "epistemic *PDL*".

14.4 Background: relational algebra

The program component of *PDL* is related to an important part of first-order logic: viz. the algebraic study of logical operations on binary relations. This so-called *Relational Algebra* has the following operations, indicated with their set-theoretic interpretation:

Boolean operations $\quad -, \cap, \cup \quad$ *complement*, *intersection* and *union*
Ordering operations $\quad \circ, \check{} \quad\quad$ *composition* and *converse*
Identity element $\quad\quad \Delta \quad\quad\quad$ *the identity relation*

Here, $\cup$ models choice, $\circ$ sequential composition and $\check{}$ converse for binary relations. Interpretation of algebraic terms proceeds inductively:

$$
\begin{aligned}
-R &= \{(x,y) \mid \neg Rxy\} \\
R \cap S &= \{(x,y) \mid Rxy \wedge Sxy\} \\
R \cup S &= \{(x,y) \mid Rxy \vee Sxy\} \\
R \circ S &= \{(x,y) \mid \exists z : Rxz \wedge Szy\} \\
R\check{} &= \{(x,y) \mid Ryx\} \\
\Delta &= \{(x,y) \mid x = y\}
\end{aligned}
$$

Definition 14.4.1 (Basic relational algebra). The calculus for relational algebra contains all valid equations of Boolean Algebra, plus the following equations for composition, converse, and diagonal:

$$
\begin{aligned}
R \circ \Delta = R = \Delta \circ R &\quad\quad R\check{}\check{} = R \\
(-R)\check{} = -R\check{} &\quad\quad (R \cup S)\check{} = R\check{} \cup S\check{} \\
(R \circ S)\check{} = S\check{} \circ R\check{} &\quad\quad (R \circ S) \circ T = R \circ (S \circ T) \\
R \circ (S \cup T) = (R \circ S) \cup (R \circ T) &\quad\quad (R \cup S) \circ T = (R \circ T) \cup (S \circ T) \\
(R\check{} \circ -(R \circ S)) \cup -S = -S
\end{aligned}
$$

Relational Algebra started in the 19th century as a general algebraic theory of binary relations, just as Boolean Algebra treated elementary operations on sets (unary relations). This shows as follows:

Definition 14.4.2 (First-order translation). The following *translation* sends relation-algebraic terms R to first-order formulas $\underline{R}(x, y)$:

$$
\begin{aligned}
\underline{-R}(x,y) &= \neg \underline{R}(x,y) &\quad \underline{R \cap S}(x,y) &= \underline{R}(x,y) \wedge \underline{S}(x,y) \\
\underline{R \cup S}(x,y) &= \underline{R}(x,y) \vee \underline{S}(x,y) &\quad \underline{R \circ S}(x,y) &= \exists z : \underline{R}(x,z) \wedge \underline{S}(z,y) \\
\underline{R\check{}}(x,y) &= \underline{R}(y,x) &\quad \underline{\Delta}(x,y) &= (x = y)
\end{aligned}
$$

With proper care, "recycling variables" in the composition step, this translation can make do with a *three-variable fragment* (compare the two variables needed for basic modal logic in Chapter 7):

Fact. Each first-order relational operation definable using only three variables can be defined using the basic operations of Relation Algebra.

This first-order translation has uses like those for modal logic. Known properties of first-order predicate logic transfer – but this time, Relational Algebra also inherits some of the bad. In particular, the equational theory of full set relation algebras is *undecidable*.

But there are also natural *infinitary* operations on binary relations. These encode unlimited actions, such as repetition ("Kleene star"), or in other words, *reflexive transitive closure*:

$$R^* = \{\, (x, y) \mid some\ finite\ sequence\ of\ successive\ R\ transitions\ links\ x\ to\ y \,\}$$

The Kleene star satisfies principles of "regular algebra", such as[140]

$$R \cup R^* = R^* \qquad R^{**} = R^* \qquad (R \cup S)^* = (R^* \circ S^*)^*$$

Now one of the virtues of propositional dynamic logic is that it encodes many of these principles in a perspicuous decidable calculus – at least for those operations of Relational Algebra that have a reflection inside *PDL*. In particular, all relation-algebraic validities involving $\cup, ; ,^*$ can be derived in *PDL*, using the following transcription:

Fact. An equation $R = S$ is valid in Relational Algebra iff the *PDL*-formula $\langle R \rangle p \leftrightarrow \langle S \rangle p$ is valid – where p is some new proposition letter.

It is an illuminating exercise to give *PDL*-proofs for laws like

$$\langle R \circ (S \cup T) \rangle p \leftrightarrow \langle (R \circ S) \cup (R \circ T) \rangle p$$
$$\langle (R \cup S)^* \rangle p \leftrightarrow \langle (R^* \circ S^*)^* \rangle p$$

Again the "Balance" of Chapter 7 returns: you have now seen a modal language provides perspicuous decidable fragments of complex classical systems, this time, for computational processes.

14.5 A tiny bit of process theory: invariance, safety, and process equivalences

Invariance The expressive power of *PDL* may be measured via modal bisimulations. One can prove invariance for all formulas – but there is a new aspect. Intertwined with the old inductive argument, one has to show that the back-and-forth clauses are inherited by the regular program constructions: indeed, each binary transition relation $[\pi]$ shows this behaviour, upward from the atomic ones:

Proposition 14.5.1. Let $\equiv$ be a modal bisimulation between two models M, M', with $s \equiv s'$.

(a) s, s' verify the same formulas of propositional dynamic logic,

---

[140] Algebraic versions of *PDL* were proposed in the early 1980s by Dexter Kozen.

(b) if $sR_\pi^M t$, then there exists t' with $s'R_\pi^{M'} t'$ and $s' \equiv t'$, and similarly in the opposite direction.

Proof. By a simultaneous induction on formulas and programs. Here is a typical step. If $sR_{\pi_1;\pi_2}^M t$ then, by the *PDL*-truth definition, there is a state x with $sR_{\pi_1}^M x$ and and $xR_{\pi_2}^M t$. By the inductive hypothesis for π_1 with respect to $s \equiv s'$, there is then an x' with $x \equiv x'$ and $s'R_{\pi_1}^{M'} x'$. Next, by the inductive hypothesis for π_2 with respect to $x \equiv x'$, there exists a state t' with $t \equiv t'$ and $x'R_{\pi_2}^{M'} t'$. Then, by the truth definition we have $s'R_{\pi_1;\pi_2}^{M'} t'$ – and we are done. Similar arguments work for the other regular program constructions. In particular, the inductive step for tests recurses toward the opposite formula side. □

Safety This motivates a new notion for program operations:

Definition 14.5.1 (Safety for bisimulation). An n-ary operation $O(R_1, \ldots, R_n)$ on programs is *safe for bisimulation* if, whenever the relation $\equiv$ is a bisimulation between two models for their respective transition relations $R_1, \ldots, R_n$, then the same $\equiv$ is also a bisimulation for the relation $O(R_1, \ldots, R_n)$.

The core of the program induction in the invariance proof is that the three regular operations ; $\cup$* of *PDL* are safe for bisimulations. Non-regular program operations outside of standard *PDL* that typically lack safety are Boolean negation or *conjunction*:

Example (An unsafe program operation). The dotted lines in the following picture shows a bisimulation for the relations a, b that does not bisimulate for the intersection $a \cap b$:[141]

Safe again is the following operation called *test negation*

$$\neg(R) = \{ (x, x) \mid \text{for no } z: Rxz \}$$

PDL has a program companion to the Modal Invariance Theorem of Chapter 7. The "Modal Safety Theorem" says this (cf. Chapter 25):

Theorem 26. First-order definable programs (in the language for relational algebra) are safe for bisimulations of their atomic relations iff

---

[141]With essentially the same example, it can also be shown that the notion of *distributed knowledge* in Chapter 12, which involved intersection of epistemic accessibility relations, is not bisimulation invariant.

they can be defined from the latter using only the safe operations ; , ∪ and test negation ¬: dynamic counterparts of Boolean ∧, ∨ and ¬.

Process equivalences Any fundamental theory of processes must specify two things together:

(i) a representation format – say, process graphs – plus (ii) a notion of invariance saying when two representations stand for the same process.

Now bisimulation is definitely not the only reasonable invariance. If observable behaviour is your only concern, a *coarser* view suffices: just compare all finite sequences of actions that can occur from the initial state. This so-called *finite-trace equivalence* is used in formal language theory: two automata are equivalent if they recognize the same language, viewed as a set of strings.[142] Most computer scientists, however, see local internal choices as relevant process structure – and the back-and-forth clauses of bisimulation capture that.

Example (Process differences). The following models lead to the same finite traces (viz. *ab*, *ac*), but they are not bisimilar:

Finer process invariances than bisimulation include *isomorphism* of process graphs, which fits better with a first-order language of process properties (cf. Chapter 7). There is a broad spectrum of process theories, a variety comparable to the "geometries" of Chapter 19.

14.6 Infinitary translation and correspondence

The first-order translation of Chapter 7 for modal logic extends to *PDL*. Naturally, there are now two parts to the procedure. One component $^\$$ takes propositions to unary formulas $\varphi(x)$, while its companion $^\#$ takes programs to binary ones $\pi(x, y)$, in a mutual recursion:

Definition 14.6.1 (Standard translation for dynamic logic).

$$(p)^\$ = Px \qquad (\neg\varphi)^\$ = \neg(\varphi)^\$$$
$$(\varphi \wedge \psi)^\$ = (\varphi)^\$ \wedge (\psi)^\$ \qquad (\langle\pi\rangle\varphi)^\$ = \exists y((\pi)^\# \wedge [y/x](\varphi)^\$)$$

---

[142]It is also used by newspapers when comparing senators' voting records, regardless of internal differences (one's decision process may be fast, another's involves sleepless nights full of dilemmas). But for other purposes, like deciding whether to live with someone, you may want to know all about that internal structure.

$$(a)^\# = R_a xy \qquad (\pi_1 \cup \pi_2)^\# = (\pi_1)^\# \vee (\pi_2)^\#$$
$$(\varphi?)^\# = x = y \wedge (\varphi)^\$ \qquad (\pi_1 \circ \pi_2)^\# = \exists z([z/y](\pi_1)^\# \wedge [z/x](\pi_2)^\#)$$
$$(\pi^*)^\# = \bigvee_{n \in N}(\pi \circ \cdots (\text{ } n \text{ } times \text{ }) \cdots \circ \pi)$$

The latter clause, of course, makes the formalism infinitary.

Proposition 14.6.1. The translation is correct from dynamic logic into a countably infinitary first-order logic over state transition models.

This translation has various uses. First, without iteration, it shows that dynamic logic is first-order. With it, we end up in a small "constructively defined" countable fragment of the *infinitary* first-order logic $L_{\omega_1 \omega}$, or also: first-order logic with fixed-points *LFP(FO)*.

Our earlier *frame correspondences* of Chapter 9 also have a use here. There are no obvious action logics stronger than minimal *PDL*. But we can encode basic relationships between specific actions. For instance, consider this abstract version of the Composition Axiom:

$$\langle c \rangle p \leftrightarrow \langle a \rangle \langle b \rangle p.$$

This is a "Sahlqvist form", and its first-order frame correspondent can be computed with the substitution method of Chapter 9:

$$\forall x \forall y : (R_c xy \leftrightarrow \exists z(R_a xz \wedge R_b zy)).$$

This says that the binary transition relation c is just the relational composition $a; b$! Thus, the Composition Axiom of *PDL* defines the latter operation *precisely*. A similar analysis may be given for all *PDL*-axioms: they fix the intended meanings of their operations.

14.7 Richer languages, more complex logics

Like our modal languages in Parts I, II, *PDL* is an open-ended enterprise. For instance, adding *converse* of programs, running them backwards, gives a temporal variant of the system. Also, the missing Boolean program operations $\cap$ and $-$ may be brought in after all. The former addition is known to preserve decidability, but the latter does not, as we can then encode the undecidable full algebra of set relations.[143] Another useful extension of propositional dynamic logic has a *loop operator* (π) for programs π, true at those states s where $sR_\pi s$. Other extensions are the modal μ-calculus of Chapter 22, and temporal languages in computer science (see Chapter 18).

14.8 The charms of propositional dynamic logic

Our final point is this. *PDL* started as a logic for program analysis in computer science, proposed by Vaughan Pratt around 1976 (with some

---

[143]Harmless-looking extensions of *PDL* can have skyrocketing complexity.

prehistory in Poland), and it enjoyed some success for that purpose. Even so, people observed around 1980 that *PDL* cannot easily deal with distributed computation and concurrent processes, and hence it quickly lost favour. But scientific theories often have an unpredictable subsequent history not foreseen by their founders. Gradually, it has become clear that *PDL* is a nice general-purpose theory of action, since program structures occur everywhere. You can see this already in Harel's lovely book *Algorithmics, the Spirit of Computing* (Harel, 1987) where key examples of sequential composition, guarded choice, and iteration come from cooking recipes ("if not up to taste, keep adding salt", etc.). More generally, *PDL* is very much alive today in philosophy and other areas. We will see examples in Chapters 15, 17.[144] This chapter ends with an excursion showing *PDL*-style ideas at work in linguistics.

14.9 ENCORE: *PDL* takes a look at first-order logic

The following is an extra, but you may find it well worth-while!

Natural language meets logical form The following system has become quite influential in the semantics of natural language. *Dynamic predicate logic* (*DPL*) "dynamifies" the first-order predicate logic that we were all were raised with. Here is why and how. Given a not quite perfect match with natural language, you are usually drilled in "translation folklore" to make first-order formulas fit actual linguistic forms. Here are some typical examples:

1	A man came in. He whistled.	Underlined phrases can co-refer.
2	*No man came in. He whistled.	Co-reference impossible.
3	*He whistled. A man came in.	Co-reference impossible.
4	If a man came in, he whistled.	Underlined phrases can co-refer.
5	* If no man came in, he whistled.	Co-reference impossible.
6	A man came in. So, he came in.	Underlined phrases can co-refer.

Let us first summarize what you have probably been taught:

The naive direct translation for 1: $\exists x C x \wedge W x$, does not give the intended scope, and hence one uses a bracket-trick (notice that natural language has no such device): $\exists x (C x \wedge W x)$.

The direct translation for 2: $\neg \exists x C x \wedge W x$, does give the intended scope, no binding occurs from the quantifier to the "free pronoun" in $W x$, and hence no tricks are needed.

---

[144]van Benthem (2007a) explains how program structure, both sequential and parallel, is essential to general conversation and argumentation.

The direct translation for 3: $Wx \wedge \neg \exists x Cx$, does give the intended scope, no binding occurs from the quantifier to the free pronoun in Wx, and again no tricks are needed.

The direct translation for 4: $\exists x Cx \to Wx$, does not give the intended scope, and you are taught a bracket trick plus a quantifier change (by contrast, the natural language sentence has $\to$ as its main operator): $\forall x (Cx \to Wx)$.

The direct translation for 5: $\neg \exists x Cx \to Wx$, gives the right scope, as no binding goes from the quantifier to the free pronoun in Wx.

The direct translation for 6: $\exists x Cx.Cx$ (note that this inference is a text with two sentences, separated by a punctuation mark), does not give the intended cross-sentential scope, and it is hard to model inference with anaphora from premise to conclusion coherently at all.

"Dynamifying" standard first-order semantics Now, the idea of *DPL* is this: stop being ad-hoc, and change the "static" interpretation of predicate logic, so that the dynamic meaning of the "naive translations" for natural language works without tricks. To achieve this, first-order formulas φ are now re-interpreted as semantic *evaluation procedures*, denoting transition relations between variable assignments.

This is like operational semantics for simple imperative programming languages, whose successive instructions change states, viewed as assignments of data-objects to variables. Think of registers filled with transient objects: say, the instruction $x := 2$ replaces the current content of register x with the value 2. This is also like *PDL* actions:

Atoms are tests:
$M, s_1, s_2 \models Px$ iff $s_1 = s_2$ and $I^M(P)(s_1(x))$

Conjunction is composition:
$M, s_1, s_2 \models \varphi \wedge \psi$ iff   there is s_3 with $M, s_1, s_3 \models \varphi$ and $M, s_3, s_2 \models \psi$

Negation is a failure test:
$M, s_1, s_2 \models \neg \varphi$ iff $s_1 = s_2$ and there is no s_3 with $M, s_1, s_3 \models \psi$

Existential quantification is random assignment:
$M, s_1, s_2 \models \exists x$ iff $s_2 = s_1[x := d]$ for any object d in the domain

Note that only existential quantifiers can drive the state forward. And in doing so, existential formulas $\exists x \varphi$ are read like *compositions* $\exists x \wedge \varphi$: first reset x, then successfully execute φ. Finally, the *DPL* negation is the "safe" relational algebra version of Section 14.5.

Example (Dynamic evaluation and binding). (1) Dynamic evaluation of $\exists x Cx \wedge Wx$ composes one random assignment with two successive test actions. This moves from any state s to some state $s[x := d]$ where both $C(d), W(d)$ hold. This explains the binding in the first example. (2) Evaluation of $Wx \wedge \exists x C x$ composes a test, a random assignment, and one more test. This moves from any state s where $W(s(x))$ holds to some state $s[x := d]$ where $C(d)$ holds: no co-reference achieved. (3) The non-binding in the third example is explained by the nature of the negation test, which leaves no new value for x to co-refer. (4, 5) To get the given implication examples right, we first define $\varphi \to \psi$ dynamically as $\neg(\varphi \wedge \neg\psi)$. This works out to (check!) a new test operation:

every successful execution of φ can be followed by one of ψ.

Check for yourself that this does what it should for both implications. (6) The final "text" example follows directly by reading an intra-sentential dot as a composition operator.

Logic as evaluation algebra DPL makes predicate logic into a dynamic logic for "variable reassignment" plus "atomic test". Even non-well-formed expressions like $Px.\exists x$ can be interpreted now (think of overhearing part of a conversation that breaks off). And we can also add new operators: say, *substitutions* $[t/x]$ as specific assignments, or parallel conjunction of actions. The effect is a mix of general relation algebra, plus specific features of first-order actions.

Example (Some background explanation). The algebraic reason for the scope behaviour in (1) is just the *associativity* of composition. Also, we can define a *universal quantifier* $\forall x\varphi$ as $\neg\exists x\neg\varphi$, and observe that, dynamically, the two translations for (4): $\exists x C x \to W x$ and $\forall x(Cx \to Wx)$ are equivalent in relational algebra. As for atomic actions, $\exists x$ is the same procedure as $\exists x; \exists x$ (why?). Also, $Px; Qy$ is the same procedure as $Qy; Px$. The latter are specific facts, not general algebraic ones.

One can study all this in PDL.[145] The reader may try with this relation-algebraic law for embedded disjunctions:

$$\neg(\varphi \cup \psi) \quad \text{is the same relation as} \quad \neg\varphi; \neg\psi$$

In this setting, Hoare-style correctness statements acquire a delightful ambiguity. Between the braces, first-order formulas stand for their usual static meanings – while, in the middle, they denote programs for evaluation procedures. Here are two correctness axioms:

$$\{\varphi\}\exists x\{\exists x\varphi\}, \qquad \{\varphi\}Px\{\varphi \wedge Px\}.$$

There is a translation lurking here from DPL into standard logic.

Inference Finally, what is valid inference for DPL? The standard "if the premises are true, the conclusion is true" no longer makes sense.

---

[145]Note the related acronyms "PDL", "DPL": LPD still seems free for the taking.

Procedures are not "true" or "false". We define

Dynamic inference: Once you have successfully processed all successive premises, you can successfully execute the conclusion.

This dynamic style of inference is non-classical. For instance, it is *non-monotonic*. If $A \models B$, then $A, C \models B$ need not hold, take:

$$A = \exists x P x, \qquad B = P x, \qquad C = \exists x \neg P x.$$

We do retain "left-monotonicity": you can add an extra premise C on the left: what you said prior to the premises cannot invalidate a conclusion, what you say after them may.[146]

DPL views natural language as a cognitive programming language. This may seem strange: logic is usually considered "declarative" rather than "imperative". But again, it exemplifies the Dynamic Turn in Chapter 13, that includes "dynamic semantics", "belief revision theory", and other systems placing cognitive actions at centre stage.

---

[146]These properties of dynamic inference, too, can be studied in *PDL*, using the modal pattern $[A]\langle B \rangle true$ that expresses the essence of dynamic inference.

Exercises Chapter 14

1. Which of these two formulas is valid in *PDL*, which is not?

   $[(a \cup b)^*]p \to ([a^*]p \wedge [b^*]p)$ $([a^*]p \wedge [b^*]p) \to [(a \cup b)^*]p$

   Give a counter-example for the invalid one, and motivate the other.

2. Explain the following validities of *PDL*, and give a formal proof:

   $[a^*]p \leftrightarrow [a^*][a^*]p, \qquad [(a \cup b)^*]p \leftrightarrow [(a^*; b^*)^*]p$

3. Show that the Hoare rule for *WHILE DO* is valid in the *PDL* semantics. Analyze it also syntactically via the *PDL* iteration axioms, showing how the rule mentioned in the text from $\{I\}S\{I\}$ to $\{I\}S^*\{I\}$ is crucial.

4. Consider a simple "action version" of propositional logic:

   (a) Correctness assertions $\{A\}S\{B\}$ are like "action conditionals" $A \to_S B$: "if A, then you need not have B, but you get it by performing action S". Find the valid and the invalid cases among the following, where A, B, C are arbitrary formulas, while S is any program. Explain your answers.
   - $\{A\}S\{A\}$
   - $\{A\}S\{B\} \Rightarrow \{A \wedge C\}S\{B\}$
   - $\{A\}S\{B\} \Rightarrow \{A\}S\{B \vee C\}$
   - $\{A\}S\{B\} \Rightarrow \{\neg B\}S\{\neg A\}$
   - $\{A\}S\{B\}, \{A\}S\{C\} \Rightarrow \{A\}S\{B \wedge C\}$

   (b) The principle $\{A\}S\{B\}, \{B\}S\{C\} \Rightarrow \{A\}S\{C\}$ is not valid. How could you make it valid by using a *PDL*-style program construction? The same question for $\{A\}S\{B\} \Rightarrow \{\neg B\}\#(S)\{\neg A\}$ for some suitable operation $\#$.

5. Write a^* as a new action b. Find the frame correspondence for

   $\langle b \rangle p \leftrightarrow p \vee \langle a \rangle \langle b \rangle p :$

   what should be the relationship between R_a and R_b?
   Can you also find the property matching the Induction Axiom:

   $(p \wedge [b](p \wedge [a]p)) \to [b]p \ ?$

6. Explain how bisimulation safety for programs arises in an inductive proof of the Invariance Lemma for *PDL*.

7. Explain the properties of common knowledge by defining it in *PDL*, viewing epistemic logic as a special dynamic logic.

8. Let ¬ be the strong negation of dynamic predicate logic. That is:

$$\neg(R)st \quad \text{iff} \quad s = t \text{ and there is no } u \text{ such that } Rsu.$$

(a) Give a valid axiom of the form $\langle\neg(R)\rangle\varphi \leftrightarrow \cdots$
(b) Prove the following algebraic law by translation into *PDL*:

$$\neg(R; S) = \neg(R; \neg\neg S).$$

15

Logic and information dynamics

In Chapters 12 and 13, we described one major paradigm for modal logic: the knowledge and beliefs that agents have on the basis of information. Then in Chapter 15, we described another major source of modal intuitions, the dynamic logic of actions. In recent years, the two perspectives have come together in various ways, and in this chapter, we give a few illustrations. The reason for doing this is quite simple: agents change their knowledge and beliefs continually on the basis of incoming information, and such processes of information flow seem so "logical" that a logical theory should be able to deal with them explicitly.

15.1 Information flow in card games

For a start, consider a follow-up to an example in Chapter 12. Cards "red", "white", "blue" were dealt to players: 1, 2, 3. Each player sees his own card only. The real deal was 1:*red*, 2:*white*, 3:*blue* (**rwb**). The following epistemic model was the group information state:

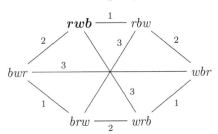

Now the following two conversational moves take place:

> 2 *asks* 1   *"Do you have the blue card?"*,
> 1 *answers truthfully*   *"No"*.

Who knows what then? Here is the effect in words:

Assuming that the question is sincere, 2 indicates that she does not know the answer, and so she cannot have the blue card. This tells 1 at once what the deal was. But 3 does not learn, since he already knew that 2 does not have blue. When 1 says she does not have blue, this now tells 2 the deal. 3 still does not know even then.

We now give the updates in the diagram, making them geometrically transparent. Here is an "update video":

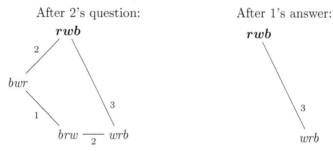

We see in the final diagram that 1, 2 know the initial deal now, as they have no uncertainty lines left. But 3 still does not know, but she does know that 1, 2 know – and in fact, the latter is common knowledge. Similar analyses exist for other conversation scenarios, and indeed, for a wide variety of puzzles, and parlour games such as "Clue".

15.2 Modeling update by hard information

Here is a common sense view: new information eliminates possibilities from the current range. In particular, *public announcements* of true propositions P give "hard information" that changes the current model irrevocably, discarding worlds which fail to satisfy P:

Definition 15.2.1 (Updating via definable sub-models). For any epistemic model M, world s, and formula P true at s, the *updated model* $M|P, s$ ("M relativized to P at s") is the sub-model of M whose domain is the set $\{t \in M \mid M, t \models P\}$.

Drawn in a simple picture, such an update step goes

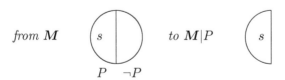

You can think of this as a typical step of communication, but it is also an act of public *observation*, regardless of language. These diagrams of a jump from one model to another visualize arguments about logical principles in this setting. Crucially, truth values of formulas may change in an update step as depicted here: most notably, since agents who did not know that P now do after the announcement.

This update mechanism explains many puzzles – one of them an evergreen packing many relevant topics into one story:

Example ("Muddy Children"). After playing outside, two of three children have got mud on their foreheads. They can only see the others, so they do not know their own status. (This is an inverse of our card games.) Now their Father says: "At least one of you is dirty". He then asks: "Does anyone know if he is dirty?" Children answer truthfully. As questions and answers repeat, what happens?

> Nobody knows in the first round. But in the next round, each muddy child can reason like this: "If I were clean, the one dirty child I see would have seen only clean children, and so she would have known that she was dirty at once. But she did not. So I must be dirty, too!"

In the initial model, eight possible worlds assign D or C to each child. A child knows about the others' faces, not her own, as reflected in the accessibility lines in the diagrams below. Now, the successive assertions made in the scenario update this information:

Example, continued (Updates for muddy children). Updates start with the Father's public announcement that at least one child is dirty. This communicative act eliminates those worlds from the initial model where the stated proposition is false. i.e., CCC disappears:

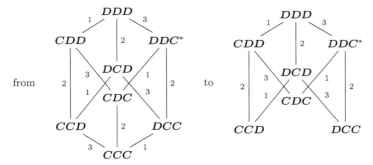

When no one knows his status, the bottom worlds disappear:

The final update is to

DDC*

In this sequence of models, domain size decreases size stepwise: 8, 7, 4, 1. With k muddy children, k rounds of the simultaneous assertion "I do not know my status" yield common knowledge which children are dirty. A few final assertions by those who now know achieve common knowledge of the distribution of the **D** and **C** for the group.

15.3 Dynamic logic of public announcement: language, semantics, axioms

Now we bring the update steps into a suitable combination of epistemic and dynamic logic:

Definition 15.3.1 (Language and semantics of public announcement). The language of *public announcement logic PAL* is the epistemic language with added action expressions, as well as dynamic modalities for these, defined by the syntax rules:

Formulas $\quad P: p \mid \neg\varphi \mid (\varphi \vee \psi) \mid K_i\varphi \mid C_G\varphi \mid [A]\varphi$
Action expressions $\quad A: !P$

The epistemic language is interpreted as before in Chapter 12, while the semantic clause for the new dynamic action modality is "forward-looking" among models as follows:

$$M, s \models [!P]\varphi \quad \text{iff} \quad \textit{if } M, s \models P, \text{ then } M|P, s \models \varphi$$

This language can make characteristic assertions about knowledge change such as $[!P]K_i\varphi$, which states what φ agent i will know after having received the hard information that P.

Now, reasoning about information flow through public update revolves around the following dynamic "recursion equation" that relates new knowledge to old knowledge the agent had before:

Fact. The following equivalence is valid for *PAL*:

$$[!P]K_i\varphi \leftrightarrow (P \rightarrow K_i(P \rightarrow [!P]\varphi)).$$

Proof. Compare the models M, s and $M|P, s$ before and after update:

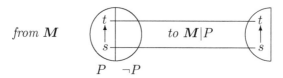

from **M** $\qquad\qquad\qquad\qquad$ *to* **M**|**P**

$\qquad\qquad\qquad\qquad P \quad \neg P$

The formula $[!P]K_i\varphi$ says that, in $M|P$, all worlds $t \sim_i$-accessible from s satisfy φ. The corresponding worlds t in M are those $\sim_i$-accessible from s *that satisfy* P. As truth values of formulas may change in an update step, the right description of these worlds in M is not that they satisfy φ (which they do in $M|P$), but rather $[!P]\varphi$: they *become* φ after the update. Finally, $!P$ is a partial function: P must be true for its announcement to be executable. Thus, we make our assertion on the right conditional on $!P$ being executable, i.e., P being true. Putting this together, $[!P]K_i\varphi$ says the same as $(P \to K_i(P \to [!P]\varphi))$.[147] □

Here is how this functions in a calculus of public announcement:

Theorem 27. *PAL* without common knowledge is axiomatized completely by the laws of epistemic logic over our static model class[148] plus the following recursion axioms:

$$[!P]q \qquad \leftrightarrow \quad P \to q \qquad \qquad \textit{for atomic facts } q$$
$$[!P]\neg\varphi \qquad \leftrightarrow \quad P \to \neg[!P]\varphi$$
$$[!P](\varphi \wedge \psi) \leftrightarrow \quad [!P]\varphi \wedge [!P]\psi$$
$$[!P]K_i\varphi \qquad \leftrightarrow \quad P \to K_i(P \to [!P]\varphi)$$

Proof. First, consider soundness. The first axiom says that update actions do not change ground facts in worlds. The negation axiom interchanging $[\,]\neg$ and $\neg[\,]$ is not a modal base law, and it says that update is a *partial function*. The conjunction axiom is valid in the minimal modal logic. And we have seen the crucial knowledge axiom already.

Next, we turn to completeness. Suppose that formula φ of *PAL* is valid. Start with some *innermost* occurrence of a dynamic modality in a sub-formula $[!P]\psi$ in ψ. Now the axioms allow us to push this modality $[!P]$ through Boolean and epistemic operators in ψ until it attaches only to atoms, where it disappears thanks to the base axiom. Thus, we get a provably equivalent formula with $[!P]\psi$ replaced by a purely epistemic formula. Repeating this process until all dynamic modalities have disappeared yields a purely epistemic formula φ' provably equivalent to φ. Since φ', too, is valid, it is provable in the base logic, which is complete by assumption, and hence, so is our φ itself. □

Example (Announcing an atomic fact makes it known). Here is a typical calculation using the recursion axioms:

$$[!q]Kq \leftrightarrow (q \to K(q \to [!q]q)) \leftrightarrow (q \to K(q \to (q \to q))) \leftrightarrow (q \to K\top) \leftrightarrow \top.$$

---

[147]The consequent even simplifies to the equivalent formula $P \to K_i[!P]\varphi$.
[148]Think of poly-modal K, or multi-agent $S5$, with equivalence relations $\sim_i$.

15.4 Exploring the framework: learning, agency, communication

Modal logic of information dynamics raises many new issues.

Learning Public announcement of atomic facts p makes them common knowledge. But not all events $!\varphi$ result in common knowledge of φ. A counter-example are so-called "Moore-type" sentences. In a question-answer scenario, let the answerer A say truly

$$p \wedge \neg K_Q p \qquad \text{"p, but you don't know it"}$$

This removes Q's ignorance about p, and thus makes itself false: true sentences like this lead to knowledge of their negation! This also occurred with the Muddy Children, where the last assertion of ignorance led to knowledge. Similar phenomena occur in philosophy:

Example (Verificationism and the "Fitch paradox"). The general verificationist thesis says that *what is true can be known* – or formally:

$$\varphi \rightarrow \Diamond K \varphi \qquad ^{149} \qquad \textbf{VT}$$

A neat argument by Fitch trivializes this principle, taking the instance

$$P \wedge \neg KP \rightarrow \Diamond K(P \wedge \neg KP)$$

Then we have a chain of three conditionals (say, in modal T):

(a) $\Diamond K(P \wedge \neg KP) \rightarrow \Diamond(KP \wedge K \neg KP)$
(b) $\Diamond(KP \wedge K \neg KP) \rightarrow \Diamond(KP \wedge \neg KP)$
(c) $\Diamond(KP \wedge \neg KP) \rightarrow \bot$

Thus, a contradiction follows from $P \wedge \neg KP$, and we have shown overall that P implies KP, making truth and knowledge equivalent. Now, it seems plausible to read the modality $\Diamond$ as referring to an event of hard information, and then the point is again that the Moore sentence $P \wedge \neg KP$ cannot be truly announced without making itself false.

This is just a beginning. Dynamic logics of information can classify types of assertions: "self-refuting", "self-fulfilling", etcetera, depending on the shape of announced formulas, leading to more sophisticated versions of "Verificationism" and actions of learning.

Agency Basic epistemic logics, say $S4$, highlight some assumptions about agents' powers that have become a focus of debate:

> The axiom $K(\varphi \rightarrow \psi) \rightarrow (K\varphi \rightarrow K\psi)$ describes agents' powers of deduction,[150] and the .4 axiom $K\varphi \rightarrow KK\varphi$ powers of introspection.

---

[149] The $\Diamond$ is an existential modality whose precise nature is irrelevant here.
[150] This is often called "epistemic closure" of knowledge under known consequences.

Here, PAL adds what one might call a

"*Knowledge Gain Axiom*" $[!P]K\varphi \leftrightarrow (P \to K[!P]\varphi)$

This principle interchanges knowledge after an event with knowledge before that event. What this means is easier to see when we adopt a more abstract stance. Consider

$$K[a]\varphi \leftrightarrow [a]K\varphi$$

This says that I know now that action a will produce effect φ if and only if, after a has occurred, I know that φ. For many actions and assertions, this is fine. But there are counter-examples. I know now, that after drinking, I get boring. But after drinking, I do not know that I am boring. Vice versa, after the exam I know that I have failed, but I need not know right now that after the exam I have failed.

This involves two new features of agents, which have received far less attention in the epistemological literature: their powers of *memory*, and their powers of *observation* of relevant events. Drinking is an action that impairs both of these epistemic powers, whereas the public announcements of PAL leave an agent in full possession of both.

Common knowledge We did not give a PAL recursion axiom for formulas $[!P]C_G\varphi$. Such a principle can only be found by suitably extending the modal language: one of our standard themes.

Definition 15.4.1 (Conditional common knowledge). The operator $C_G^P\varphi$ says that φ is true in all worlds in model M reachable from the current world s via some finite path of accessibilities running entirely through worlds satisfying P. Plain $C_G\varphi$ is the special case $C_G^\top\varphi$.

It is not hard to see that the following equivalence is valid:

$$[!P]C_G\varphi \leftrightarrow (P \land C_G^P[!P]\varphi)$$

The next result shows that the hierarchy stops here:

Theorem 28. PAL with conditional common knowledge is axiomatized completely by adding the valid recursion law

$$[!P]C_G^\varphi\psi \leftrightarrow (P \to C_G^{P\land [!P]\varphi}[!P]\psi)$$

Example (Atomic announcements produce common knowledge).

$$[!q]C_Gq \leftrightarrow (q \to C_G^q[!q]q) \leftrightarrow (q \to C_G^q\top) \leftrightarrow (q \to \top) \leftrightarrow \top$$

Conversation PAL may also be used as a logic of longer-term conversations, or complex observation procedures, by iterating single update steps. Here is a relevant observation:

Fact. The formula $[!P][!Q]\varphi \leftrightarrow [!(P \land [!P]Q)]\varphi$ is valid.

The proof should be easy given your familiarity with *PAL* by now. You will find it rewarding to see why we cannot just use $!(P \land Q)$.

Further conversational structures would arise by enriching *PAL* with *program constructs* from *PDL*, expressing conditional assertions ("if φ, then say P, else Q") or guarded iterations like "as long as not all children know the solution, keep asking the Father's question". While this can be dealt with in the style of Chapter 15, it has been discovered in 2004 that such logics of long-term conversation can be extremely complex – for reasons explained in Chapters 23, 24.

Optimal communication What can agents in a group achieve by maximal communication? Consider two agents in some collective information state M with actual world s. They can tell each other things they know, thereby cutting down the model to smaller sizes. Suppose they wish to be maximally cooperative.

Example (The best agents can do by internal communication). What is the best that the agents can achieve in the following model?

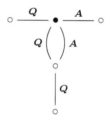

Geometrical intuition suggests that this must be:

Indeed, a two-step conversation getting there is the following:

Q sighs: "I don't know", then A sighs: "I don't know either"

This particular scenario also works in the opposite order.

Successive updates in any finite model must eventually end in a submodel that can no longer be reduced, where everything agents know is common knowledge. This "communication core" often consists of the actual world plus all worlds linked to it by the intersection of all uncertainty relations[151], as with distributed knowledge in Chapter 13.

---

[151]Technical subtleties with the "communication core" go beyond this course.

Thus, communication can turn implicit knowledge of a group into common knowledge. This is a new theme in dynamic logic of information – but not in neighbouring fields like computer science[152] and economics: see the classics Aumann (1976) and Geanakoplos and Polemarchakis (1982).[153] More extensive links to economic game theory will return in Chapter 17 on modal logic and games.

15.5 Technical themes: bisimulation, correspondence, complexity

Bisimulation Recall the bisimulation of Chapter 3. *PAL* still fits:

Fact. All formulas of *PAL* are invariant for bisimulation.

Proof. This follows from the earlier reduction to purely epistemic formulas. But a more informative proof goes via the following observation about update, viewed as an operation O on models. We say that such an operation *respects bisimulation* if, whenever two models M, s and N, t are bisimilar, then so are their values $O(M, s)$ and $O(N, t)$. □

Fact. Public announcement update respects bisimulation.

Proof. Let ≡ be a bisimulation between M, s and N, t. Consider their sub-models $M|\varphi, s$, $N|\varphi, t$ after public update with φ. Now the point is that the restriction of ≡ to these is still a bisimulation. Here is the proof of the relevant zigzag clause. Suppose that some world w has an $\sim_i$-successor v in $M|\varphi, s$. This same v is still available in the other model: it remained in M since it satisfied φ, but then v also satisfied φ in N, t, because of the Invariance Lemma for the bisimulation ≡ – and so it stayed in the updated model $N|\varphi, t$, too. □

Frame correspondence *PAL* is a concrete way of taking new hard information, subject to the general laws in its completeness theorem. One can also reverse the perspective, state abstract postulates governing information update, and then see *which concrete operations on models* validate these, using the frame correspondences of Chapter 9. We give a brief sketch:

Consider abstract model-changing operations ♠p taking epistemic models (M, s) with a distinguished set of worlds named by a proposition letter p, to new models $(M♠p, s)$ – where the domain of worlds

---

[152]An excellent and influential book linking epistemic logic with computer science, from distributed protocols on the internet to communication and rational agency, is R. Fagin, J. Halpern, M. Vardi & Y. Moses Fagin et al. (1995).

[153]Geanakoplos (1992) also has Muddy Children update scenarios.

remains the same. By *link elimination*, we mean the process that cuts all epistemic links between p-worlds and $\neg p$-worlds.

Theorem 29. Link elimination is the only model-changing operation that satisfies the following equivalence for all sets q:

$$[\spadesuit p]Kq \leftrightarrow (p \rightarrow K(p \rightarrow [\spadesuit p]q))$$

Proof. From left to right, let q be the set of worlds that are $\sim$-accessible from the current world s after the operation $\spadesuit p$ has been applied to the model. This makes the left-hand side true. Assume also that s is in p. Then the right-hand side says that all worlds in the set p that are $\sim$-accessible from s are still accessible after the operation $\spadesuit p$. Thus, the relation change leaves all already existing links from p-worlds to p-worlds. In the converse direction, we let q be the set of $\sim$-accessible worlds in $M \spadesuit p$ that were $\sim$-accessible p-worlds from s in M. The left-hand side then tells us that all new accessibilities came from old ones. Together, we see that the p area after the update has just its old links, and none sticking out into its complement. This is one half of the link-cutting version of epistemic update; the other half follows by applying the same analysis to the complement set of p.[154]   □

This is just one version in a sequence. We state one next step. Now assume that the domain of worlds may change from M to $M \spadesuit p$. To zoom in on *PAL*-style eliminative update, we also need the *existential* modality $E\varphi$ of Chapter 7. We state the following result without proof, though it is well within reach of the techniques of Chapter 9:

Theorem 30. Eliminative update is the only model-changing operation that satisfies the following three principles:

(a) $\langle !p\rangle\top \leftrightarrow p$
(b) $\langle \spadesuit p\rangle Eq \leftrightarrow (p \wedge E\langle \spadesuit p\rangle q)$, and
(c) $[\spadesuit p]Kq \leftrightarrow (p \rightarrow K(p \rightarrow [\spadesuit p]q))$.

Complexity Chapter 6 emphasized computational complexity of logical tasks. Here is the score for information dynamics:

Theorem 31. Validity in *PAL* is decidable.

Proof. The reduction that proved completeness is an effective algorithm from *PAL*-formulas into equivalent epistemic ones. After that, use the decision procedure for the epistemic base logic.   □

This does not settle the *complexity* – as the translation may increase formula length exponentially. But here is the true profile of the logic:

---

[154]The veteran reader will recognize a substitution argument from Chapter 9.

Theorem 32.

- The complexity of satisfiability in *PAL* is *PSPACE*-complete.
- Model-checking for *PAL* formulas takes *PTIME*.
- Model comparison for *PAL* formulas takes *PTIME*.

Thus, though it shows us much more, *PAL* has the same balance of expressive power and complexity as its static epistemic base logic.

15.6 Belief change under hard information

The same ideas work for changes in belief, as introduced in Chapter 13.[155] A capacity for learning from new facts contradicting our earlier beliefs seems typical of rational agency, and here is how it goes:

Fact. The formula $[!P]B\varphi \leftrightarrow (P \rightarrow B^P([!P]\varphi))$ is valid for beliefs after events of hard information.

Of course, this is not enough to keep our full language in harmony. We need to know, not just which beliefs are formed after new information, but rather which *conditional beliefs* arise:[156]

Theorem 33. The logic of conditional belief under public announcements is axiomatized completely by

- Any complete static logic for the model class chosen,
- the *PAL* recursion axioms for atomic facts and Boolean operations,
- the following new recursion axiom for conditional beliefs:

$$[!P]B^\psi\varphi \leftrightarrow (P \rightarrow B^{P\wedge[!P]\psi}[!P]\varphi)$$

Proof. First we check the soundness of the new axiom. On the left hand side, it says that in the new model $M|P, s$, φ is true in the best ψ-worlds. With the usual precondition for the announcement, on the right-hand side, it says that in M, s, the best worlds that are P now and will become ψ after announcing that P, will also become φ after announcing P. This is indeed equivalent. The remainder of the proof is our earlier stepwise reduction analysis, noting that the above axiom is recursive, pushing announcement modalities inside.[157] □

The present simple setting hides some tricky scenarios:

---

[155] We will often drop agent subscripts of modalities, for greater readability.

[156] Again, for simplicity, we suppress the interplay with epistemic structure.

[157] This logic relates two notions that are close: *conditional belief* $B^\psi\varphi$, and *belief after information has been received*: $[!\psi]B\varphi$. The two are equivalent in case φ, ψ are modality-free "factual" formulas. But they may diverge with epistemic-doxastic formulas, since conditional belief evaluates φ in the original model M, while $[!\psi]B\varphi$ evaluates φ in the updated model $M|\psi$, where truth values may have changed.

Example (Misleading with the truth). Consider a model where an agent believes that p, which is indeed true in the actual world depicted to the far left, but for "the wrong reason": she thinks that the most plausible world is the one to the far right. For convenience, assume that each world also verifies a unique proposition letter:

$$\bullet \xrightarrow{\hspace{2cm}} \circ \xrightarrow{\hspace{2cm}} \circ$$
$$p, q_1 \qquad\quad \neg p, q_2 \qquad\quad p, q_3$$

Now giving the true public information that we are not in the final world (say, in the form of "$!\neg q_3$") updates this model to

$$\bullet \xrightarrow{\hspace{2cm}} \circ$$
$$p, q_1 \qquad\quad \neg p, q_2$$

in which the agent believes mistakenly that $\neg p$.

Observations like this have been made in philosophy, computer science, and game theory. Thus, further epistemic-doxastic attitudes make sense, as hinted at in Chapter 13. Here is a new notion, intermediate between knowledge and belief, stable under new true information:

Definition 15.6.1 (Safe belief). The modality of *safe belief* $B^+\varphi$ is defined as follows: $M, s \models B^+\varphi$ if, for all worlds t in the epistemic range of s with $t \geq s$, $M, t \models \varphi$. Thus, φ is true in all epistemically accessible worlds that are at least as plausible as the current one.[158]

This modality is stable under hard information, at least for factual assertions φ that do not change their truth value as the model changes. And indeed, the new notion is the base modality $[\leq]\varphi$ for the plausibility ordering that we already considered in Chapter 13:

Example (Three degrees of doxastic strength). Consider this picture, now with the actual world in the middle:

$$\circ \xrightarrow{\hspace{2cm}} \bullet \xrightarrow{\hspace{2cm}} \circ$$

$K\varphi$ is what we know: φ must hold in all three worlds in the epistemic range, less or more plausible than the actual one. $B^+\varphi$ describes our safe beliefs in further investigation: φ is true in the two worlds from the middle toward the right. $B\varphi$ describes the most fragile thing: our beliefs as true in all worlds in current topmost position on the right.

Fact. The following *PAL*-style axiom holds for safe belief:

$$[!P]B^+\varphi \leftrightarrow (P \to B^+(P \to [!P]\varphi))$$

---

[158]Safe belief uses an *intersection* of epistemic accessibility and plausibility order.

15.7 Belief change under soft information

In more general revision scenarios, an agent can also take incoming signals in a softer manner, without throwing away options forever. But then, we need a general mechanism that makes new information P more plausible, without burning our ships behind us.

Example (Default rules). A default rule $A \Rightarrow B$ does not say that all A-worlds are B-worlds. It rather says that the counter-examples: i.e., the $A \wedge \neg B$-worlds, *become less plausible* until further notice. This "soft information" does not eliminate worlds, it changes their ordering.

An event making us believe that P need only *rearrange worlds* making the most plausible ones P by "promotion" rather than elimination. Thus, on the earlier models $\boldsymbol{M} = (W, \sim_i, \leq_i, V)$, we change the relations $\leq_i$, rather than the set of worlds W or the epistemic $\sim_i$. One very strong policy is a radical social revolution where the underclass P becomes the upper class. In a picture, we get a reversal:

from $\boldsymbol{M}, s$ $\left(\begin{array}{c} s \\ \hline P \quad \neg P \end{array} \right)$ *to* $\boldsymbol{M} \Uparrow P, s$ $\left(\begin{array}{c} s \\ \hline \end{array} \right) \begin{array}{c} P \\ \neg P \end{array}$

Definition 15.7.1 (Radical, or lexicographic upgrade). A *lexicographic upgrade* $\Uparrow P$ changes the current ordering $\leq$ between worlds in $\boldsymbol{M}, s$ to a new model $\boldsymbol{M} \Uparrow P, s$ as follows: all P-worlds in the current model become better than all $\neg P$-worlds, while, within those two zones, the old plausibility ordering remains.

We take a matching "upgrade modality" in our dynamic language:

$$\boldsymbol{M}, s \models [\Uparrow P]\varphi \quad \text{iff} \quad \boldsymbol{M} \Uparrow P, s \models \varphi$$

Theorem 34. The dynamic doxastic logic of lexicographic upgrade is axiomatized completely by

(a) any complete axiom system for conditional belief on static models,

(b) the following recursion axioms:

$$
\begin{array}{lll}
[\Uparrow P]q & \leftrightarrow & q \qquad \textit{for all atomic propositions } q \\
[\Uparrow P]\neg\varphi & \leftrightarrow & \neg[\Uparrow P]\varphi \\
[\Uparrow P](\varphi \wedge \psi) & \leftrightarrow & [\Uparrow P]\varphi \wedge [\Uparrow P]\psi \\
[\Uparrow P]K\varphi & \leftrightarrow & K[\Uparrow P]\varphi \\
[\Uparrow P]B^\psi\varphi & \leftrightarrow & (\Diamond(P \wedge [\Uparrow P]\psi) \wedge B^{P \wedge [\Uparrow P]\psi}[\Uparrow P]\varphi) \vee \\
& & (\neg\Diamond(P \wedge [\Uparrow P]\psi) \wedge B^{[\Uparrow P]\psi}[\Uparrow P]\varphi) \quad \text{159}
\end{array}
$$

Proof. Most axioms are simpler than for *PAL*, since unlike !*P*, ⇑*P* has no precondition. The first axiom says that upgrade does not change truth values of atomic facts. The second says upgrade is a function on models, the third is a general law of modality, and the fourth says that there is no change in epistemic accessibility. The fifth axiom is the locus for the specific change in the plausibility ordering. The left-hand side says that, after the *P*-upgrade, all best ψ-worlds satisfy φ. On the right-hand side, there is a case distinction. Case (1): there are epistemically accessible *P*-worlds in the model M that become ψ after the upgrade. Then lexicographic reordering ⇑*P* makes the best of these worlds in M the best ones over-all in the ψ-zone of M⇑*P*. Now, in the original model M – more precisely, its epistemic range from the current world s – the latter worlds are just those satisfying the formula $P \wedge [⇑P]\psi$. Thus, the formula $B^{P \wedge [⇑P]\psi}[⇑P]\varphi$ says that the best among these in M will satisfy φ after the upgrade. But these best worlds are just those described earlier, since lexicographic reordering does not change plausibility ordering inside the *P*-area. Case (2): no *P*-worlds in the original M become ψ after upgrade. Then lexicographic reordering ⇑*P* makes the best worlds satisfying ψ after the upgrade just the same as the best worlds before that satisfied $[⇑P]\psi$. The formula $B^{[⇑P]\psi}[⇑P]\varphi$ in the recursion axiom says these best worlds become φ after upgrade. The rest of the completeness proof is a reduction argument as before. □

More conservative belief revision policies can be axiomatized as well. A general method uses the dynamic logic of Chapter 14. First note that:

Fact (Radical upgrade). ⇑*P* is definable as a program, where "*T*" stands for the universal relation between all worlds:

$$⇑P(R) := (?P; T; ?\neg P) \cup (?P; R; ?P) \cup (?\neg P; R; ?\neg P).$$

A definition for a relation R on models is *in PDL-format* if it can be stated using the old relation, *union, composition*, and *tests*.[160]

Theorem 35. Each relation change in *PDL*-format has a complete set of recursion axioms that can be derived via an effective procedure.

Proof. Computing modalities for the new relation after a model change uses the program axioms of *PDL*. We use the existential epistemic modality ◇ when dealing with the universal relation. For instance:

---

[159] Here, "◇" is the dual *existential epistemic modality* $\neg K \neg$ of Chapter 12.

[160] A further example is the "suggestion" operator #*P* of Chapter 16 that takes out all pairs from the old relation with "$\neg P$ over *P*": $\#P(R) = (?P; R) \cup (R; ?\neg P)$.

$$\langle \Uparrow P(R) \rangle \varphi \; \leftrightarrow \; \langle (?P;T;?\neg P) \cup (?P;R;?P) \cup (?\neg P;R;?\neg P) \rangle \varphi$$
$$\leftrightarrow \; \langle ?P;T;?\neg P \rangle \varphi \vee \langle ?P;R;?P \rangle \varphi \vee \langle ?\neg P;R;?\neg P \rangle \varphi$$
$$\leftrightarrow \; \langle ?P \rangle \langle T \rangle \langle ?\neg P \rangle \varphi \vee \langle ?P \rangle \langle R \rangle \langle ?P \rangle \varphi \vee \langle ?\neg P \rangle \langle R \rangle \langle ?\neg P \rangle \varphi$$
$$\leftrightarrow \; (P \wedge \Diamond(\neg P \wedge \varphi)) \vee (P \wedge \langle R \rangle (P \wedge \varphi)) \vee (\neg P \wedge \langle R \rangle (\neg P \wedge \varphi)).$$

This transforms into an axiom for safe belief after radical upgrade $\Uparrow P$.

□

15.8   Conclusion

Methods from dynamic logic of programs turn epistemic and doxastic logics into rich descriptions of information flow and attitude change. The same methodology applies to preference change (Chapter 16), and other features of rational agency – and you now have the tools in hand for "dynamification" of many other logical systems.

Exercises Chapter 15

1. Suppose that in our card example, Child 2's question is not treated as informative. What happens then? Draw the updates.

2. Let us change the Muddy Children a little bit:
   (a) Let the Muddy Children in our scenario with 3 kids speak in turn. What happens? Draw the successive diagrams.
   (b) Suppose the father says "At least one of you is clean", while the same procedure is followed as before. Compute the update sequence, and explain what happens.

3. Three men are standing on a ladder, each wearing a hat. Each can see the colours of the hats of people below him, but not his own or those higher up. It is common knowledge that only red and white occur, and that there are more white hats than red ones. The actual order is *white, red, white* from top to bottom.
   (a) Draw the information model.
   (b) The top person says: "I know the color of my hat". Is that true? Draw the update.
   (c) Who else knows his color now? If that person announces that he knows his colour, what does the bottom person learn?

4. Consider the system *PAL* of Public Announcement Logic:
   (a) Give equivalent versions for the *PAL* axioms with existential modalities $\langle !P \rangle$.
   (b) Why does not *PAL* need an additional axiom for the operator combination $[!P][!Q]\varphi$?

5. What does the interchange axiom $K[a]\varphi \rightarrow [a]K\varphi$ express in terms of frame correspondence?

6. Three cards r, w, b are distributed over three people 1, 2, 3, with an actual world $\langle r, w, b \rangle$ as before. But this time, nobody reads their card, or that of the others. Using some suitable extended form of update, describe the following scenarios:
   (a) 1 reads his card publicly, and says: "2 does not have red".
   (b) 1 reads his card, and then shows it to 2 – while 3 observes just the showing.
   (c) 1 shows his card to the others without reading it himself.

7. Let 3 agents have only ordinary telephone lines, without a facility for conference calls. One of them knows that p.

(a) Can they achieve common knowledge of p by phone calls if a non-involved person cannot see if a phone call is being made, or even if he can: but cannot check its content?

(b) What should you assume about the "protocol" to make sure that common knowledge results from the phone calls?

8. Reasoning with belief:

(a) Give a concrete example showing that conditional belief is not always the same as belief following the information that the antecedent holds.

(b) Check the soundness of the axioms for hard and soft belief change in our text.

(c) Check that these axioms still hold if we interpret beliefs within epistemic equivalence classes as in Chapter 13.

(d) Using the earlier modal definition of conditional belief in terms of safe belief, derive the recursion axiom for conditional belief after hard update $!P$ from the stated recursion axiom for safe belief after hard update.

(e) Give a valid recursion axiom for safe belief after radical soft update $\Uparrow P$.

16

Preference and deontic logic

So far, we have looked at agents processing information. But human activity is goal-driven, and hence we also need to describe agents' evaluation of states of the world, or outcomes of their actions. All these things come together in even such a simple scenario as a *game*, where we need to look at what players want, what they can observe and guess, and which moves and long-term strategies are available to them in order to achieve their goals. That will be the topic of Chapter 17 – but for now, we concentrate on preference logic per se. We will merely show how modal patterns arise, with some new themes special to this area.

16.1   Modal logic of betterness

We start with a simple setting. Modal models $M = (W, \leq, V)$ consist of worlds W (or any sort of objects subject to evaluation and comparison), a *"betterness" relation* $\leq$ between worlds ("at least as good as"),[161] and a valuation V for proposition letters at worlds (properties of objects). The comparison may vary among different agents, but as usual, we suppress agent subscripts $\leq_i$ for greater readability. We use the artificial term "betterness" to stress that this is an abstract comparison. Still, this semantics is natural in decision theory, where worlds (standing for outcomes of actions) are compared by utility, or game theory, where end nodes of a game tree (standing for different final histories of the game) are related by preferences for the different players.[162]

Over these models, we can interpret a modal language, and see which patterns of reasoning it can be define. In particular, a formula $\langle \leq \rangle \varphi$ makes a "local" assertion at a world w:

$$M, w \models \langle \leq \rangle \varphi \quad \text{iff} \quad \text{there exists a } v \geq w \text{ with } M, v \models \varphi$$

---

[161] *Warning.* In this chapter $\leq$ stands for betterness, not plausibility order!

[162] A helpful analogy: compare the plausibility orders for belief in Chapter 13.

This logic can express many notions about preference-driven action.

Which properties should betterness have? *Total orders* with reflexivity, transitivity, and connectedness are common, as these properties are enforced by numerical utilities. But the logical literature on preference often has reflexive and transitive *pre-orders*, with *four* intuitively irreducible basic relations between worlds:

$$
\begin{aligned}
&w \leq v, \neg v \leq w \ (w < v) &&w \text{ strictly precedes } v \\
&v \leq w, \neg w \leq v \ (v < w) &&v \text{ strictly precedes } w \\
&w \leq v, v \leq w \ (w \sim v) &&w, v \text{ are indifferent} \\
&\neg w \leq v, \neg v \leq w \ (w\#v) &&w, v \text{ are incomparable.}
\end{aligned}
$$

One may also take an independent weak order $w \leq v$ ("at least as good"), and a strict $w < v$ ("better") satisfying $w \leq v \wedge \neg v \leq w$.

16.2 Defining global propositional preference

Concrete modal systems bring their own special topics. In particular, many authors consider preference a relation between *propositions*. Technically, this calls for comparison of sets of worlds. For a given relation $\leq$ among worlds, this may be achieved by *lifting*. One ubiquitous proposal in relation lifting is the $\forall\exists$ stipulation that

a set Y is preferred to a set X if $\forall x \in X \ \exists y \in Y : x \leq y$.

But there are alternatives. Von Wright, the father of preference logic, favoured the $\forall\forall$ stipulation that

a set Y is preferred to a set X if $\forall x \in X \ \forall y \in Y : x \leq y$.

Such options are a feature, not a bug. In a *game*, when comparing sets of outcomes that can be reached by moves, players have options. They might prefer a set whose minimum utility value exceeds the maximum of another (this is like the $\forall\forall$ reading) – or settle for the maximum of one set exceeding that of the other, like the $\forall\exists$ reading.

Many liftings are definable in our modal base logic when extended (as in Chapter 7) with a universal modality $U\varphi$: "φ is true in all worlds". For instance, the $\forall\exists$ reading runs as follows:

$$
U(\varphi \rightarrow \langle \leq \rangle \psi)
$$

We will use the notation $P\varphi\psi$ for lifted propositional preferences.

Priorities One can also *derive* betterness on worlds from a primitive relation of "priority" between propositions, or properties of objects. This perspective occurs, e.g., in Social Choice Theory, and linguistic Optimality Theory, where one orders sentence parses and meanings in terms of linguistically desirable properties. One might start with a finite linear sequence $\boldsymbol{P}$ of properties, and then order objects as follows:

$x \leq y$ if, when y lacks some property P in $\boldsymbol{P}$ that x has, there is a P' with higher priority than P in $\boldsymbol{P}$ that y has and x lacks.

This is just one option: "lowering" has a its diversity, like "lifting".[163]

16.3 Ceteris paribus clauses

Many preferences are defeasible: they hold only *ceteris paribus*. This can mean two things. The normality sense says we only make comparisons "under normal circumstances". Thus, I prefer beer over wine, but not when dining at the Paris Ritz. This refers to the most plausible worlds of a model, linking preference to the doxastic logic of Chapter 13 – combining modal logics of betterness and belief.

But there is also von Wright's equality sense of ceteris paribus: involving comparison under the proviso that certain propositions do not change their truth values. A ceteris paribus preference for φ over ψ with respect to proposition A says that

both (i) among the A-worlds I prefer φ over ψ, and
also, (ii) among the $\neg A$-worlds I prefer φ over ψ.

This, too, fits a modal logic, with the following operators:

$\boldsymbol{M}, w \models [\Gamma]\varphi$ iff $\boldsymbol{M}, v \models \varphi$ for all t with $s \equiv_\Gamma t$,

$\boldsymbol{M}, w \models [\Gamma]^{\leq}\varphi$ iff $\boldsymbol{M}, v \models \varphi$ for all t with $s \equiv_\Gamma t$ and $s \leq t$,

$\boldsymbol{M}, w \models [\Gamma]^{<}\varphi$ iff $\boldsymbol{M}, v \models \varphi$ for all t with $s \equiv_\Gamma t$ and $s < t$,

Here $s \equiv_\Gamma t$ holds iff the worlds s, t agree on the truth values of all formulas in the set Γ.[164] Then Γ-equality-based ceteris paribus preference $P\varphi\psi$ can be defined like this:

$$U(\varphi \to \langle\Gamma\rangle^{\leq}\psi)$$

The logic of this system is completely axiomatizable. We merely list one valid axiom that allows us to shift a ceteris paribus set:

$$(\alpha \wedge \langle\Gamma\rangle^{\leq}(\alpha \wedge \varphi)) \to \langle\Gamma \cup \{\alpha\}\rangle^{\leq}\varphi$$

16.4 Entanglement: preference, knowledge, and belief

Natural notions of preference mix modal logic of pure betterness with other considerations. This "entanglement" can take many forms:

Combining separate operators Consider a system with knowledge and preference, whose models have both epistemic accessibility relations

---

[163]The dissertations *Changing for the Better* (Liu, 2008) and *Modal Logic for Belief and Preference Change* (Girard, 2008) have many more details.

[164]In Chapter 3, the symbol $\equiv$ stood for bisimulation: a wholly unrelated use.

and a preference order. The language has betterness modalities $\langle\leq\rangle$, the universal modality, and epistemic K as in Chapter 12. It can interpret nested operator combinations such as

$KP\varphi\psi$ knowing that some global betterness relationship holds,
$PK\varphi K\psi$ preferring to know certain things over others.

The semantics allows betterness comparison with epistemically inaccessible worlds, which can express a sense of "regret".[165] The language improves on the earlier global preferences $P\varphi\psi$, reading the earlier $U(\varphi \to \langle\leq\rangle\psi)$ with a universal modality in epistemic terms:

$$K(\varphi \to \langle\leq\rangle\psi)$$

Intersection modalities The preceding formula refers to ψ-worlds that are better than epistemically accessible φ-worlds, but the ψ-worlds themselves need not be accessible. But the normality sense of ceteris paribus made comparisons inside the normal worlds. This requires a new modality for the *intersection* of epistemic $\sim$ and betterness $\leq$:

$$M, w \models \langle\leq \cap \sim\rangle\varphi \quad \text{iff} \quad \text{there is a } t \text{ with } s \sim t \text{ and } s \leq t \text{ s.t. } M, t \models \varphi$$

Now we can define versions of "internally epistemized" preference as $K(\varphi \to \langle\leq \cap \sim\rangle\psi)$. This richer logic is no longer bisimulation-invariant (cf. Chapters 12, 14). Similar points hold for belief instead of knowledge, using intersection modalities for betterness and plausibility relations.

16.5   Dynamics of preference change

Like information, agents' preference can change when new events happen. There are many triggers for this. First, pure *information changes* can modify preference, if the latter was entangled with what agents know or believe. In particular, one can combine the logic *PAL* of hard information of Chapter 15 with modal betterness logic, leading to valid principles for betterness after public announcement:

$$[!\varphi]\langle\leq\rangle\psi \leftrightarrow (\varphi \to \langle\leq\rangle(\varphi \wedge [!\varphi]\psi))$$

Similar laws hold for merely belief-changing events of soft information.

But there are also *intrinsic events* that change betterness order, such as following a command, or a suggestion. Consider the following action $\#\varphi$ of "suggestion", removing just blatant infractions:

For each model M, w, the model $M\#\varphi, w$ is M, w with the new relation $\leq' = \leq -\{(x, y) \mid M, x \models \varphi \text{ and } M, y \models \neg\varphi\}$.

Now, we enrich the static language by adding action modalities:

---

[165] Realists will not use this facility, and the logic does not force them to.

$$\boldsymbol{M}, w \models [\#\varphi]\psi \quad \text{iff} \quad \boldsymbol{M}\#\varphi, w \models \psi$$

These operations state what agents will prefer after their betterness relation has changed. Say, if you suggest that it is better to drink beer than wine, and I accept this, then I now come to prefer beer over wine, even if I did not do so before.

As in the dynamic logics of Chapter 15, the crux is the "recursion equation" stating when a preference obtains after an action. Here is the relevant principle for suggestions, whose two cases follow the definition of the above model change:

$$\langle\#\varphi\rangle\langle\leq\rangle\psi \;\leftrightarrow\; (\neg\varphi \wedge \langle\leq\rangle\langle\#\varphi\rangle\psi) \vee (\varphi \wedge \langle\leq\rangle(\varphi \wedge \langle\#\varphi\rangle\psi))$$

Just this once, we give a complete axiom system, so you can see concretely what a dynamic logic of preference change looks like:

Theorem 36. The dynamic logic of preference change under suggestions is axiomatized completely by

1. the static modal logic of the underlying model class, plus
2. the following equivalences for the dynamic modality:

$$\begin{aligned}
[\#\varphi]p &\;\leftrightarrow\; p \\
[\#\varphi]\neg\psi &\;\leftrightarrow\; \neg[\#\varphi]\psi \\
[\#\varphi](\psi \wedge \chi) &\;\leftrightarrow\; [\#\varphi]\psi \wedge [\#\varphi]\chi \\
[\#\varphi]U\psi &\;\leftrightarrow\; U[\#\varphi]\psi \\
[\#\varphi]\langle\leq\rangle\psi &\;\leftrightarrow\; (\neg\varphi \wedge \langle\leq\rangle[\#\varphi]\psi) \vee (\varphi \wedge \langle\leq\rangle(\varphi \wedge [\#\varphi]\psi)).
\end{aligned}$$

This logic automatically derives a dynamic logic of lifted propositional preferences. For instance, we can compute as follows how the earlier $\forall\exists$-type preferences $P\varphi\psi$ arise:

$$[\#\varphi]P\psi\chi \;\leftrightarrow\; P([\#\varphi]\psi \wedge \neg\varphi)[\#\varphi]\chi \wedge P([\#\varphi]\psi \wedge \varphi)(\varphi \wedge [\#\varphi]\chi)$$

It is easy to combine this with the logic *PAL* of knowledge update under hard information (Chapter 15), and the same style of analysis also applies to entangled intersection modalities:

$$\langle\#\varphi\rangle\langle\leq \cap \sim\rangle\psi \;\leftrightarrow\; (\neg\varphi \wedge \langle\leq \cap \sim\rangle\langle\#\varphi\rangle\psi) \vee (\varphi \wedge \langle\leq \cap \sim\rangle(\varphi \wedge \langle\#\varphi\rangle\psi))$$

16.6 Excursion: deontic logic

Deontic logic is the study of *obligation* and *permission*, traditionally with modalities $O\varphi$: "φ ought to be the case" and $P\varphi$: "it is permitted that φ". These notions are usually studied with abstract deontic accessibility relations. But in our setting, they relate directly to betterness orderings: what is obligatory is what holds *in all best worlds*: presumably, the ones we should strive for. The relevant ordering here need not be our own, but it may be given by some moral or legal authority.

This ties in with all our topics so far. For instance, note the strong analogy between obligation and *belief*, as truth in all most plausible worlds (Chapter 13). Indeed, deontic logic has undergone a very similar formal development, including the notion of *conditional obligation*, comparable to conditional belief. Also, the counterpart to acts of belief revision are dynamic events that change the deontic betterness order, say, the promulgation of a new law. Viewed in this way, deontic logic is really about multi-agent preferences (me, the law-giver, other people), and how these interact. And dynamics describes how our obligations change under changes in the law, or just in our information.

16.7 Multi-agent interaction and group preference

While preference logic has been mainly studied for individual agents, most scenarios of interest involve social interaction. *Games* are driven by players' moves, their preferences over outcomes, and beliefs about what other players will do (Chapter 17). Another basic social setting are *groups* that deliberate and take decisions – as in Social Choice Theory. There has been some logical analysis of this sort of group behaviour, in particular, merging individual betterness relations into collective ones.[166] These analyses assume that the group G has enough structure to resolve conflicts in the process of aggregating individual preference relations. Here is one concrete way of doing this, generalizing the earlier derivation of object preference from priority sequences:

Definition 16.7.1 (Object order induced by priority graphs). Consider a *priority graph* $\mathbf{G} = (G, <)$ of indices (which may have multiple occurrences), standing for agents, issues, or any other relevant items. The over-all *induced object order* is this:

$$x \leq_{\mathbf{G}} y \quad \text{iff} \quad \text{for all indices } i \in \mathbf{G}, \text{ either } x \leq_i y,$$
$$\text{or there is some } j > i \text{ in } \mathbf{G} \text{ with } x <_i y$$

Powerful aggregation mechanisms like this invite the logics of our chapters so far. Even so, the systematic job of developing epistemic, doxastic, and preferential logics for groups, considered as serious entities in their own right, has not been done yet.

We leave matters here – but this open end is important. The dynamics of preference change under information and other triggers is crucial for understanding deliberation, fair procedure, and social organization.

---

[166] An analogous natural task is *belief merge* for a group of agents.

Exercises Chapter 16

1. We can introduce a modality $\langle < \rangle \varphi$ for a strict order saying that φ is true in some strictly better world (with 'strictly better' as defined in the text). This will validate several axioms for the combination of $\langle \leq \rangle$, $\langle < \rangle$, such as $\langle < \rangle \varphi \to \langle \leq \rangle \varphi$ (but not the converse). Can you find other valid axioms?

2. Show the validity of the ceteris paribus axiom

$$(\alpha \wedge \langle \Gamma \rangle^{\leq}(\alpha \wedge \varphi)) \to \langle \Gamma \cup \{\alpha\} \rangle^{\leq}\varphi$$

3. Show the validity of the stated reduction axiom for betterness change under suggestion.

4. Consider subsets of a connected pre-order $\leq$. A set Y is preferred to a set X if $\forall x \in X \, \forall y \in Y : x \leq y$. Which basic properties hold for this set order? Must it be linear?

5. Let us derive betterness order from given properties:
   (a) Consider a finite "priority sequence" P of properties, and order objects as follows:
   $x < y$ iff x, y differ in at least one property in P, and the first $P \in P$ where this happens is one with $Py, \neg Px$.
   Show that this induced object order $<$ is reflexive, transitive, and connected. Show that every finite connected order can be obtained from some P in this way.

   (b) Consider a priority graph $G = (G, <)$ as introduced in Section 16.7. Show how its induced object ordering generalizes the object ordering of the previous item. Which ordering do we get when we take the disjoint union of two such graphs? And what about sequential composition of priority graphs?

17

Modal logic and games

A concrete area where information and action meet is that of games, where players' strategies involve interaction over time with other players' moves. We will just show you a number of ways in which modal logic is involved here, without any pretense at systematic theory. In particular, we assume that the reader is familiar with basic game-theoretic notions, or can pick up the needed from the present text.[167]

17.1 Extensive games as process models

An *extensive game* is a tree with labeled relations going from node to node (the available moves), in which intermediate nodes indicate players' turns, and end nodes carry information about players' utilities when the game stops. Histories in such a tree can also be infinite, but most examples in this chapter are about games of finite depth. Such a tree is a modal model process with nodes as worlds, labeled actions, and markings for local properties of stages.

Example (An extensive game tree). Consider a game for two players A, E with four actions c, d, a, b, and a special property p holding at two of the four possible end states, yielding this process graph:

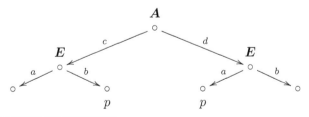

---

[167]An excellent text is M. Osborne & A. Rubinstein, *A Course in Game Theory* (Osborne and Rubinstein, 1994). Interfaces with logic are in my lectures *Logic in Games*, ILLC, Amsterdam, 2001, van der Hoek & Pauly, 2006, in the *Handbook of Modal Logic*, and the 2008 ESSLLI lectures by E. Pacuit & O. Roy.

Here is a typical modal formula that is true at the root of this model:

$$[c \cup d]\langle a \cup b\rangle p$$

each of the actions c and d leads to a state where either a or b can be executed to get to a final state where p holds. This says in the given graph that player E has a strategy ensuring that the outcome of the game satisfies p. Here, p might be the property that E wins, in which case the modal formula expresses that "E has a winning strategy".

More complex strategies than a single response give rise to longer modal $\Box, \Diamond$ sequences. Here is a more technical example of the power of modal languages (read "zero-sum" here as "win/lose only"):

Theorem 37 (Zermelo's Theorem). Each finite 2-player zero-sum game is *determined*: one of the two players has a winning strategy.

Proof. Here is a procedure for computing the player with the winning strategy at any node in a finite 2-player game with end nodes marked win_i or $\neg win_i$ for players i. One starts in end nodes, and works upwards as follows. First, colour end nodes *black* that are wins for player I, and the other ones *white*. Then extend this stepwise as follows:

> If all children of a node x have been coloured, do one of the following: (a) player I is to move, and at least one child is black: colour x *black*; if all children are white, colour x *white*, (b) likewise for player II, with *white* and *black* interchanged.

Working upward to the root, this eventually gives black to all nodes where player I has a winning strategy, and white to those where II has a winning strategy. Here is the colouring for a simple game tree:

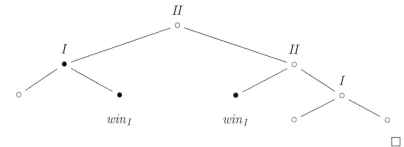

$\Box$

Zermelo was concerned with Chess, which also allows draws. His result implies that one of the two players has a *non-losing strategy*.[168] The difference between theory and practice: right now, a century later, it is still unknown *which player* has the non-losing strategy!

---

[168]The result was rediscovered by the Dutch world Chess champion Euwe.

Here is what drives the algorithm:

Fact. Player I has a winning strategy in a node iff either

(i) it is an end node which is winning for I, or

(ii) it is I's turn, and at least one move is available to a node where I has a winning strategy, or

(iii) it is II's turn, but all II's available moves lead to nodes where I has a winning strategy.

But now we see a modal logic pattern! Let *move* be the union of all available actions. Then the rule for i's winning positions win_i may be defined by the following modal recursive definition:

$$win_i \leftrightarrow (end \wedge win_i) \vee (turn_i \wedge \langle move \rangle win_i) \vee (\neg turn_i \wedge [move] win_i)$$

The technical background is the modal fixed-point logic of Chapter 22.

Zermelo's reasoning yields a mechanical *algorithm* that traverses finite game trees, and determines node-by-node which player has the winning strategy. This algorithm is the basis for all sophisticated methods that solve games using computers, a form of "meta top sport". Recently, for the board game Checkers, 15 years of computer labour yielded the Zermelo answer: the starting player has a non-losing strategy.

17.2 Dynamic logic of strategies

This modal description does not yet define the *strategies* that players follow in a game, i.e., the rules that guide their behaviour. But the dynamic logic of Chapter 14 can do just that. For a start, the total *move* relation was a program union of atomic transition relations $move_i$, and the statement about a winning strategy in our first example of an extensive game involved these:

$$[a \cup b]\langle c \cup d \rangle p$$

More generally, strategies are *partial transition functions* defined on players' turns by rules "if she plays this, then I play that". Functions are also binary relations, and indeed, arbitrary binary transition relations make sense in games. These allow more choices at nodes, a bit like general *plans* of action. Now *PDL* was our modal language for defining transition relations, and it makes sense here as well: on top of the "hard-wired" moves in a game, we get *PDL*-style relations that define strategies. And once we have these, we can use a modal language to state what players can achieve by following these (interactive) plans:

Fact. For any *PDL* strategy term σ, *PDL* can define the following "forcing modality" $\{\sigma, i\}\varphi$: σ *is a strategy for player i forcing the game, against any play of others, to pass only through states satisfying* φ.

Here is a related result. Giving strategies for both players, we get to a unique end-point of a game, and here is how:

Fact. PDL can define the outcome of running joint strategies σ, τ.

Proof. The formula is $[((turn_E; \sigma) \cup (turn_A; \tau))^*](end \rightarrow p)$ [169] □

We conclude with another use of PDL. As a binary relation, a strategy σ for player i in a finite game M is just a finite set of ordered pairs (s, t). Thus, it can be defined by a PDL program union, if we can define the singleton relations $\{(s, t)\}$. Now call a model M *expressive* if all its states s are uniquely definable by modal formulas def_s. Then define $\{(s, t)\}$ by the program expression

$?def_s; U; ?def_t$ where U stands for the universal relation.

This simple observation proves:

Fact. In expressive finite extensive games, PDL defines all strategies.

17.3 Games with imperfect information

Many games have *imperfect information*: players need not know exactly where they are in the tree – for instance when playing at cards.

Example (An extensive game with imperfect information). Consider this variant of the game of Section 17.1, now with an uncertainty for player E about the first move played by A. (Perhaps, A put his move in an envelope.) This models a combined *modal-epistemic* language:

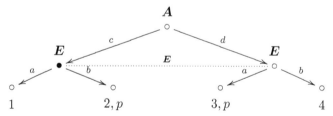

The modal formula $[c \cup d]\langle a \cup b\rangle p$ is still true at the root. But we can make more subtle assertions now, using the dotted lines as an accessibility relation for knowledge, just like in Chapter 12. At stage s, a player knows those propositions that are true throughout the "information set" to which s belongs. Thus, after A has played move c from the root, in the black state, by the standard semantics of epistemic logic, E *knows* that playing either a or b will give her p – because the disjunction $\langle a\rangle p \vee \langle b\rangle p$ is true at both middle states:

$$K_E(\langle a\rangle p \vee \langle b\rangle p)$$

---

[169] Dropping the *end* $\rightarrow$ describes effects of strategies at intermediate nodes.

On the other hand, there is no specific move of which E knows that it guarantees an outcome satisfying p – which shows in the black node, witness the truth of the epistemic-dynamic formula

$$\neg K_E \langle a \rangle p \wedge \neg K_E \langle b \rangle p$$

We recognize the *de re/de dicto* distinction from Chapter 11.

17.4   Preferences, rationality, and solving games

Real game theory arises only when players get payoffs, and have preferences between outcomes. Then, the Zermelo colouring algorithm must be extended to a numerical procedure called *Backward Induction* (*BI*). We do not give details of the method, but just an illustration.

Example (A Backward Induction computation). Here is a simple case of this ubiquitous method for computing optimal interactions – with outcome values indicated for A and E in that order:

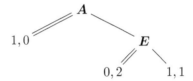

If player E gets to play, she will choose left, since she prefers 2 over 1. This is a standard assumption of "rationality": I choose what is best for me, given my options.[170] Anticipating that, A chooses left, since that gives him 1, while going right would give him only 0. Thus, optimal strategies for the players are those marked by the double lines.

Analyzing this reasoning suggests modal logics of action and preference. Finite game trees are not only models for a dynamic logic of moves, but also for players' preferences. Here is just one definability result out of many recent ones, in a modal correspondence version:[171]

Fact. The *backward induction solution* of a finite game is the unique function *bi* satisfying this modal law for all formulas φ:

$$\langle bi \rangle [bi^*](end \to \varphi) \to [move]\langle bi^* \rangle(end \wedge \langle \leq \rangle \varphi)$$

The formula says that there is no alternative to a *BI*-move all of whose outcomes would be better than following that *BI*-move. You will see the analogy with the Geach convergence axioms of Chapter 9.

---

[170]More sophisticated versions have a doxastic aspect: agents choose what they think is best for them, given *what they believe* about their options.
[171]This simplified version assumes that end nodes are uniquely definable.

Backward Induction finds a so-called *Nash equilibrium*: a set of strategies where no player can achieve a better outcome for herself by unilaterally changing her strategy, while the others stick to theirs. Stated differently, each player's strategy is a "best response" to those of the others. Notions of equilibrium, locking interactive behaviour into place, are typical for game theory, and economics in general. They, too, have a ring of preference logic – and logics for defining equilibria and studying their properties are a lively research area.

More generally, the entanglement of modal notions, noted in Chapter 16, is very noticeable in this setting. Reasoning about games, and by players inside games, involves a mix of actions, knowledge, belief, and preference. Moreover, it is important to understand that reasoning, since game solution methods may have surprising outcomes.

Example (The darker sides of Backward Induction). Consider the following simple numerical variant of our earlier game:

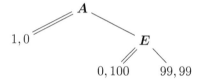

As before, Backward Induction computes an equilibrium with outcome (1, 0) by bottom-up reasoning about players' "rationality" – making both hugely worse off than the right-most outcome (99, 99).

So, why does this happen? It pays to analyze the reasoning more closely. It derives expectations from betterness among end nodes, and chooses moves accordingly. This is a dynamic doxastic process like in Chapter 15. Each complete history of the game is a world, and the backward induction algorithm creates a plausibility order among these, the same for both players. In our example this ordering eventually has world (1, 0) on top, then (0, 100) and then (99, 99). Thus in games, the plausibility relations stipulated in earlier models for belief are now created by a dynamic analysis connecting belief with preference.[172]

Clearly, this is just the start of a study of games where all logics of Part III so far can be put to use, static and dynamic. And this study is not confined to justifying standard game-theoretic rationality. It can equally well undermine received notions, by analyzing quite different assumptions about players' behaviour.

---

[172]This involves crucial betterness comparisons with worlds that we believe will *not* happen: it is precisely those that keep the actual prediction "in place".

17.5 Dynamic logics of game change

Finally, the dynamic logics of Chapter 15 also make sense. For instance, one can break a bad Backward Induction solution by *changing a game.*

Example (Promises and game change). In our earlier game, the Nash equilibrium $(1, 0)$ can be avoided by $\boldsymbol{E}$'s *promise* that she will not go left. This is a public announcement that some histories will not occur (we make this binding by a huge fine on infractions) – and the new equilibrium $(99, 99)$ results. Interestingly, this makes both players better off by restricting the freedom of one of them!

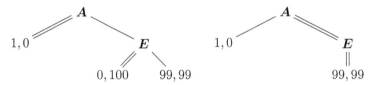

Our earlier methods apply here at once:

Theorem 38. The dynamic logic of changing games by announcement is axiomatized by a modal logic of moves and strategies,[173] the *PAL* axioms for atoms and Boolean operations, plus one law for moves:

$$\langle !P \rangle \langle a \rangle \varphi \leftrightarrow (P \wedge \langle a \rangle (P \wedge \langle !P \rangle \varphi))$$

We can also talk about explicit strategies. Using *PDL* as before, this leads to a logic *PDL + PAL*. It is easy to show that *PDL* can *relativize* strategies π to $\pi|P$ in the submodel defined by P, and we need this for the following result about the earlier forcing modalities:

Theorem 39. *PDL + PAL* is axiomatized by the logic of Theorem 38 plus the following reduction axiom for strategy modalities:

$$[!P]\{\sigma\}\varphi \leftrightarrow (P \rightarrow \{\sigma|P\}[!P]\varphi)$$

PAL-style model-changing logics also suggest new analyses for game solution methods. Many such methods involve pruning game trees in successive rounds. This can be modeled as "internal deliberation" between players, driven by *repeated announcements* of "Rationality":

Theorem 40. The Backward Induction solution is obtained through iterated announcement, as long as possible, of the assertion "No player chooses a move all of whose further histories end worse than all histories after some other available move".[174]

---

[173]This static modal game logic could be *PDL* again, as earlier on this chapter.

[174]In game theory, the nodes eliminated in this way are called the "strictly dominated" ones. Our iterated announcement procedure leaves one with only topmost *BI*-moves. For lower nodes, one has to keep track of intermediate stages.

Proof. This is a simple induction on finite trees. We show the procedure for a "Centipede game", with three turns, branches indicated by name, and pay-offs for A, E in the given order:

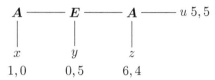

Stage 0 of the announcement procedure rules out branch u, which is the only one to violate the stated form of Rationality. Next, Stage 1 rules out z, which now violates Rationality after branch u has disappeared – while Stage 2 rules out y. What remains is the BI solution x, which on its own satisfies Rationality. Elimination stops. □

This iterated announcement procedure necessarily ends in largest sub-games that cannot be further compressed: i.e., the Rationality assertion holds throughout. When this sub-game is non-empty, through deliberation, players have achieved *common knowledge of rationality*.

17.6 Conclusion

We have shown by examples how modal logics apply to games in a natural manner. We worked with games in extensive form, but similar methods apply to the usual matrix games in *strategic form*.

Finally, the reader may want to think about our first use of games, in the evaluation and model comparison tasks for basic modal logic (Chapters 2 and 3). Thus you see that, while *logic can be used to analyze games*, conversely also, *games can be used to analyze logic*. This intriguing duality is far from being completely understood.

Exercises Chapter 17

1. Using formulas of dynamic logic, express the following assertion: "No matter what player II does in the course of the game, the result of player I's playing strategy σ is always an end state satisfying p".

2. Consider a finite game where no two worlds satisfy the same formulas. Show that every strategy for a player is PDL-definable.

3. Consider the following epistemic-dynamic axiom for imperfect information games: $(turn_i \wedge K_i[a]\varphi) \to [a]K_i\varphi$. Which game-theoretic form of "Perfect Recall" is expressed by this?

4. Show that the stated modal-preference axiom for Backward Induction is valid. Give a more formal equivalence proof using a frame correspondence argument.

5. Show the soundness of all dynamic axioms for game change stated in our text.

6. Finite games satisfy a version of "Löb's Axiom" (Chapter 21): state which one.

7. Re-analyze our "hard" public announcement analysis of Backward Induction, now using a dynamic scenario of suitable "soft information" events (Chapter 15) that change plausibility ordering in a game tree without eliminating nodes.

8. Turn the Card update example of Chapter 15 into a "knowledge game" by adding a purpose and pay-offs, and analyze players' best conversational strategies. For such games with Muddy Children-like features: see

    http://spotlightongames.com/summary/abbey.html.

9. In a two-step game, either the first player has a move such that all further countermoves lead to a win for her, or, for every move of the first player, there is a countermove making the second player win. Which classical logical law justifies this? Turn this into a general proof of Zermelo's Theorem. Why does not this "pure logic method" work for infinite games?

Introducing chapters 18 through 21: Mathematical structures

While the preceding chapters dealt with many aspects of agency, modal logic also has quite different applications. The following group of chapters follows another line, running through mathematics and computation. First we deal with modal structures in Time and Space, then we move to mathematical reasoning itself, viewing proof from two foundational perspectives: intuitionism, and classical provability logic.

While this looks like a more traditional line, it is not at all disjoint from our earlier concerns. For instance, temporal logic is also important in the study of language, computation and agency, and intuitionistic logic may be viewed as a knowledge-related paradigm providing an alternative to our earlier epistemic logic. But the topics to come also stand on their own.

Again, many of our general modal themes will return, and you may be surprised to see what they have to say about these classical areas, that have also been well-studied from other logical perspectives.

18

The structure and flow of time

18.1   Origins and habitats of temporal logic

Time is a long-standing concern in many disciplines, from philosophy to physics, psychology, and computer science – and logic joins in this endeavour, too. Temporal discourse and reasoning show logical structures, and many of these are modal. Temporal logics were initially proposed for analyzing famous arguments from the philosophical tradition involving time, but it soon became clear that such reasoning involves presuppositions about the ontology of temporal entities and their order, which can be brought out by logical means. Afterwards, techniques developed in this way were applied to linguistic semantics, and the repertoire of temporal expressions in natural languages.

In recent decades, temporal logic has been used extensively in computer science and artificial intelligence as a vehicle for describing processes, and general cognitive agency (Chapter 15). Temporal logic today is a vast area of research, and we will only skim the surface. All earlier modal themes of Parts I, II return, but often with a very special flavour.

18.2   Tense logic: languages, semantics, and invariance

Basic language We start with a propositional system with operators

$F\varphi$ at least once in the future, φ will be the case
$P\varphi$ at least once in the past, φ has been the case

Derived from these, we have two dual universal modalities:

$G\varphi$ always in the future from now φ
$H\varphi$ always in the past up until now φ

This simple formalism already generates interesting patterns:

Example (Temporal expressions).

$GF\varphi$ φ is always going to be true at some later stage

$PH\varphi$ once upon a time, φ had always been the case

$G(\varphi \to F\varphi)$ φ will always "enable" φ to become true afterwards.

Semantics The usual modal models M for this language can now be interpreted as "flows of time" $(T, <, V)$, where $<$ is an *earlier than* relation between points in time. The only special feature is that we use both the relation itself and its converse in the truth definition:

$$M, t \models F\varphi \quad \text{iff} \quad \text{for some } t' > t : M, t' \models \varphi$$
$$M, t \models P\varphi \quad \text{iff} \quad \text{for some } t' < t : M, t' \models \varphi$$

Of course, we may want special principles to hold for the relation of temporal precedence, and these can often be found systematically using the modal frame correspondences of Chapter 9. For instance, the axiom $G\varphi \to GG\varphi$, or alternatively $H\varphi \to HH\varphi$, enforces transitivity of the temporal order. Here are some further examples:

Fact. Rightward Linearity of temporal order: $\forall y \forall z((x < y \land x < z) \to (y < z \lor z < y \lor z = y))$, is defined by the tense-logical axiom $(Fp \land Fq) \to (F(p \land q) \lor F(p \land Fq) \lor F(q \land Fp))$.[175] Density $\forall x \forall y(x < y \to \exists z(x < z \land z < y))$ is defined by $F\varphi \to FF\varphi$, the converse *4*-axiom. *(Forward) discreteness* $\exists y(x < y \land \forall z(z < y \to (z = x \lor z < x)))$ is defined by "Hamblin's Axiom" $\varphi \to FH(\varphi \lor F\varphi)$.

All these facts follow from the substitution method of Chapter 9. But some natural principles for temporal precedence are second-order:

Example (Two higher-order principles). *Continuity* says that temporal flow is "as full as can be": every subset with an upper bound has a supremum (a lowest upper bound).[176] Next, *homogeneity* says that all points in time are "essentially the same": every point can be mapped onto any other one by some order-isomorphism of the temporal frame.

No consensus has emerged, and temporal logic studies many different patterns of time: linear or branching, dense or discrete, and so on.

Basic model theory The notion of modal bisimulation applies here without further ado, provided we add clauses for backward steps in the converse relations. But is bisimulation the right measure of identity for temporal structure? This depends on the level of detail. For instance, with successive events, temporal *betweenness* seems essential, a relation not preserved by bisimulation. In that case, we need stronger semantic invariances, and stronger temporal languages.

---

[175] Leftward Linearity of the order may be defined likewise using P.

[176] We will see a tense-logical axiom expressing Dedekind Continuity a bit later on.

Many further issues make sense. For instance, we are often interested in special temporal properties defined only by special formulas. A typical example is *forward persistence* of propositions φ over time, making $\varphi \to G\varphi$ valid. Here is a sufficient syntactic condition:

Fact. On *transitive* models, all formulas constructed from atoms $\bot, \top$ and arbitrary formulas $P\varphi, G\varphi$ using $P, G, \wedge, \vee$ are forward persistent.

Extended languages The tense system of natural language goes beyond future and past. Consider a progressive tense ("Baby is cry-ing"):

$$M, t \models \Pi\varphi \quad \text{iff} \quad \exists t_1 < t \exists t_2 > t \forall u(t_1 < u < t_2 \to M, u \models \varphi)$$

Fact. The progressive is not definable in the temporal base language.

Proof. $\Pi\varphi$ is not invariant for temporal bisimulation, witness the following two models, where numbers mark points to be identified:

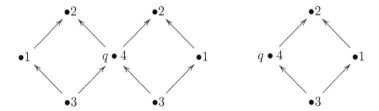

Set $V(q) = \{4\}$ in both cases. Then, Πq is true on the left in the point 4 (consider some upper point 2 and its diagonally opposite 3) – but, it fails in its counterpart 4 on the right. □

The progressive tense is still first-order definable under an obvious translation. The same is true for many temporal operators.

Example (Next time). The following useful operator O ("next time", "tomorrow") only makes sense on discrete models:

$$M, t \models O\varphi \quad \text{iff} \quad M, t + 1 \models \varphi$$

And here are two stronger temporal notions from Chapter 7 that translate into the 3-variable fragment of first-order logic:

Example (Since and Until).

(a) $M, t \models S\varphi\psi$ iff *for some point* $t' < t$, $M, t' \models \varphi$ *and for all* x *with* $t' < x < t$, $M, x \models \psi$.

(b) $M, t \models U\varphi\psi$ iff *for some point* $t' > t$, $M, t' \models \varphi$ *and for all* x *with* $t < x < t'$, $M, x \models \psi$.

A famous result is "Kamp's Theorem" on *functional completeness*:

Theorem 41. On *continuous* linear orders, every first-order statement with one free variable is definable in the $\{S, U\}$ formalism.

The underlying fact is that on linear orders $<$ with a first-order language expressing unary properties, the 3-variable fragment already suffices for defining all first-order assertions.[177]

Multiple indices Another type of extension in temporal logic are *multiple indices*, keeping track of more than one point together. This makes sense, for instance, in formal systems describing the ubiquitous tenses of natural language. A famous proposal is the "three-point scheme" of Reichenbach, casting sentences as describing events E that happened at some time, while there is also a point of speech S where the sentence is uttered, plus an auxiliary "point of reference" R. Tenses then differ in the way in which they set up a narrative:

Present	"I am sinning"	E, R, S	$(E = R = S)$
Perfect	"I have sinned"	$E\ \ R, S$	$(E < R = S)$
Imperfect	"I sinned"	$E, R\ \ S$	$(E = R < S)$
Past Perfect	"I had sinned"	$E\ \ \ R\ \ \ S$	$(E < R < S)$

Similar schemes explain sentences involving also future tenses. "Double-indexing" in a format $M, t, t_0 \models \varphi$ [178] has also been proposed to model the properties of the fundamental temporal indexical expression NOW, which refers back, no matter how deeply embedded in a formula, to the original point t_0 of evaluation:

$$M, t, t_0 \models NOW\varphi \quad \text{iff} \quad M, t_0, t_0 \models \varphi$$

In the limit of this approach, there is a whole family of extended temporal languages describing properties of pairs or longer tuples of worlds, up to the expressive power of a full first-order language.

18.3 Tense logic: deduction and complete logics

Minimal logic and beyond The minimal tense logic is exactly like the minimal modal logic K, but with the following additional axioms expressing that future and past are converses:

$$\varphi \to GP\varphi \qquad \varphi \to HF\varphi$$

Interesting features include "anisotropy" (no preferred direction):

> *Mirror Image Property* for Future versus Past:
> if $\models \varphi(F, P, G, H)$, then $\models [P/F, F/P, H/G, G/H]\varphi$

The pair $\varphi \to GP\varphi$, $\varphi \to HF\varphi$ exemplifies this substitution.

---

[177]There exist many sophisticated generalizations of Kamp's Theorem.
[178]This technique keeps getting rediscovered, since it makes sense more widely.

On top of this logic, specific temporal structures add further axioms.

Theorem 42. The complete tense logic of the rational number line $\mathbf{Q}$ is given by the minimal tense logic plus the above axioms for (a) linear order, (b) density, and (c) two principles ensuring existence of successors toward past and future: PT and FT.

Theorem 43. The complete tense logic of the reals $\mathbf{R}$ extends that of $\mathbf{Q}$ with the following axiom of "Dedekind Continuity": $(FHp \wedge F \neg p \wedge G(\neg p \rightarrow G\neg p)) \rightarrow F((p \wedge G\neg p) \vee (\neg p \wedge Hp))$.

Although completeness theory has enjoyed an immense success in temporal logic, the area has also seen the first set-backs: natural logics for which no complete set of temporal frames exists.

Example (An Incomplete Tense Logic). Consider the past-looking Löb's Axiom $H(Hp \rightarrow p) \rightarrow Hp$, that expresses (a) transitivity, plus (b) well-foundedness of the temporal order (cf. Chapters 9, 21). Add the McKinsey Axiom $GFp \rightarrow FGp$, which now expresses "future stabilization". On transitive frames, the latter enforced the existence of (reflexive) *end-points*: $\forall x \exists y (x < y \wedge \forall z (y < z \rightarrow z = y))$. Together, these two principles form a consistent tense logic, but they hold on no temporal frame. More details can be found in Chapter 26.

Looking in the opposite direction, there is also no guarantee that natural temporal structures have well-behaved axiomatizable logics. In practice, however, many such logics have been found: from the standard number lines to complex relativistic structures (cf. Chapter 10). One explanation may be found in Chapters 7, 24; many temporal structures are tree-like, and hence fall in the scope of Rabin's Theorem guaranteeing even decidability. Another, much easier observation is that the complete tense logics of classes of structures defined by a *first-order sentence* must always be recursively enumerable.

Complexity We forego decidability and computational complexity here, though temporal logic is one of the best-researched areas of modal logic in this respect.[179] Complexity of satisfiability for tense logics ranges from *NP*-complete (for instance, on linear orders) through *PSPACE*-complete (like K and $S4$) to *EXPTIME*-complete (when models include binary trees), while undecidable tense logics have also been constructed – some of extremely high second-order complexity.

In addition, since temporal languages are widely used to specify properties of processes, the complexity of model-checking, too, has been extensively researched. As the reader will recall from Chapter 6, model-

---

[179]See the chapter by Hodkinson & Reynolds in the *Handbook of Modal Logic*.

checking for modal languages on finite models can be very efficient, and many computational resources exist for temporal logics.

18.4 An alternative: interval ontology

Structures and axioms Durationless points have been a prevalent image, but alternative intuitions take Time as having extended periods or *intervals* as its primary stuff. Motivations have come from philosophy, linguistics, and artificial intelligence, as being closer to common sense conceptions and simple algorithms for temporal information.

Definition 18.4.1 (Interval models). Temporal *interval models* consist of a set of temporal intervals, with suitable relations such as

$$i < j \qquad i \text{ wholly precedes } j$$
$$i \subseteq j \qquad i \text{ is included in } j$$
$$iOj \qquad i \text{ overlaps with } j$$

Here are some familiar pictures that use linear stretches:

precedence i ———   ——— j

inclusion   ————————————— j
                          i ———

overlap i —————————
                          ————————— j

There is no uniform choice of relations or operations in the field. Sometimes, one includes all possible relative positions between bounded linear intervals. Of these, there are exactly thirteen, as may be shown by listing the possible positions for i and j in the above picture.

Example (Concrete intervals). Typical interval models arise as *convex sets* X in the ordering on point models, that is:

$$\forall t_1 \in X \forall t_2 \in X \forall t \in T : ((t_1 < t \wedge t < t_2) \to t \in X)$$

Think of linear intervals, convex sets in a plane, etcetera.

On the other hand, interval models can be taken as primary temporal pictures without any point-based underpinning, satisfying some suitable constraints. We merely formulate a few candidates, showing how various primitive relations between intervals might interact:

$$<, O \quad \forall x \ \neg x < x$$
$$\forall x \ xOx$$
$$\forall x \forall y \ (xOy \to yOx)$$
$$\forall x \forall y \ (xOy \to \neg x < y)$$
$$\forall x \forall y \forall z \forall u \ (x < yOz < u \to x < u)$$

$adding \subseteq$ $\forall x \; x \subseteq x$

$\forall x \forall y \forall z \; (x \subseteq y \subseteq z \rightarrow x \subseteq z)$

$\forall x \forall y \; (x \subseteq y \subseteq x \rightarrow x = y)$

$\forall x \forall y \forall z \forall u \; (x \subseteq y < z \supseteq u \rightarrow x < u)$

$\forall x \forall y \; (x \supseteq yOz \subseteq u \rightarrow xOu)$

All these formulas are *universal Horn clauses* of the form

$\forall x_1 \cdots \forall x_k$: *conjunction of atoms involving* $x_1, \ldots x_k$
implies atom involving $x_1, \ldots x_k$

that do not require existence of points, but merely drive a "composition table" for temporal relations. In addition, there are more negotiable requirements on interval models, such as

Convexity	$\forall x \forall y \forall z \forall u (u \supseteq x < y < z \subseteq u \rightarrow y \subseteq u)$
Linearity	$\forall x \forall y (x < y \vee y < x \vee xOy)$

Languages and modal axioms Basic tense logic extends to interval models with valuations for proposition letters, while adding operators taking advantage of the new structure. Thus, with two primitive relations $<$ and $\subseteq$, one gets two new modalities:

$\Box_{down}\varphi$	φ *holds in all subintervals*
$\Box^{up}\varphi$	φ *holds in all superintervals*

This logic can be studied by our techniques from Part II.

Fact. The following pairs are frame correspondences for inclusion:

reflexivity	$\Box_{down}p \rightarrow p$
transitivity	$\Box_{down}p \rightarrow \Box_{down}\Box_{down}p$
atomicity	$\Box_{down}\Diamond_{down}p \rightarrow \Diamond_{down}\Box_{down}p$

As for the interaction with temporal precedence, we have, for instance:

right monotonicity	$Fp \rightarrow \Box_{down}Fp$
left monotonicity	$Pp \rightarrow \Box_{down}Pp$

This richer structure can be studied using bisimulation and other known techniques, but it also raises many new issues. For instance, verbs in natural language have different aspectual behaviour in terms of persistence under changes in intervals. Important properties are preserved under going to sub-intervals, like "being in love" or "going to get married". Such forms of "temporal inertia" are also important in data bases or reasoning about causation and action:

Fact. Truth of temporal formulas constructed from arbitrary formulas $P\varphi$, $F\varphi$, $\Box_{down}\varphi$ and $\Diamond^{up}Pp$ using $\wedge$ and $\vee$, is always preserved downward along inclusion of intervals.

Our earlier Progressive *"be V-ing"* turns an event description V into a "state description", which is downward persistent. Likewise, a Perfective *"have V-ed"* turns V into a downward persistent state description, as reflected in the monotonicity of the above past operator P.

The translation methods from Chapter 7 still apply. Our modal languages translates into either a first-order logic over primitive intervals, or a second-order logic over point models where interval quantifiers range over suitable subsets, say convex ones. In this setting of richer classical languages, many extended modal formalisms can be devised.

Example (Extended modal interval logics). Here are some modal operators in a richer calculus of aspectual structure and reasoning:

$BEGIN$ φ is true at $[t_1, t_2]$ iff *there exists* $t_3 < t_2$ *with* φ *true at* $[t_1, t_3]$

$START$ φ is true at $[t_1, t_2]$ iff *there exists* $t_3 > t_2$ *with* φ *true at* $[t_1, t_3]$

$BEFORE$ φ is true at $[t_1, t_2]$ iff *there exists* $t_3 \leq t_1$ *with* φ *true at* $[t_3, t_1]$.

Also, the binary modalities of Chapter 10 express sums of intervals.

Different views and representations The different paradigms are related. We have already seen how point models induce intervals as special subsets. A converse strand in the literature, going back to Russell and Wiener, retrieves points as maximally overlapping families of intervals. This is one way how the interval structure of our common sense experience gives rise to mathematical "public time".

18.5 Branching temporal logic

The most widely used temporal formalisms in philosophy and computer science today involve a richer structure than our point- or interval-based models so far. We also want to have a *tree of possible histories* around, modeling some unfolding process, or the total "playground" of a game (cf. Chapter 17). There are many logics for this purpose. Some are extensions of the *dynamic logic PDL* of Chapter 14, now used over unraveled tree models. For instance, one popular formalism *CTL* extends *PDL* to an expressive and yet computationally still quite manageable fragment of the modal μ-*calculus* of Chapter 22.

Just for illustration, we define a richer structure making histories ("paths", "branches") into independent objects. This gives the language a combined temporal and modal flavour, where temporal operators stay inside one history, while modal operators cross the lines. Think of this setting as a *tree of finite sequences of events*, with a selection made among all possible branches in the tree, leaving just the "legal runs" obeying some relevant *protocol*:

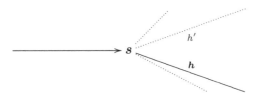

Language and models The basic language has proposition letters standing for local process properties of nodes, Boolean operations, as well as temporal and modal operators.

Definition 18.5.1 (Branching temporal semantics). Formulas are interpreted at nodes s on histories h, in the following format:

(a) $\boldsymbol{M}, h, s \models F_a \varphi$ iff $s^\frown \langle a \rangle$ lies on h and $\boldsymbol{M}, h, s^\frown \langle a \rangle \models \varphi$

The standard operator F ("at some point in the future") is the transitive closure of this modality, taken over all possible events a.

(b) $\boldsymbol{M}, h, s \models P_a \varphi$ iff $s = s'^\frown \langle a \rangle$ and $\boldsymbol{M}, h, s' \models \varphi$

Again, P ("at some point in the past") is the transitive closure.

(c) $\boldsymbol{M}, h, s \models \Diamond \varphi$ iff $\boldsymbol{M}, h', s \models \varphi$ for some history h' which coincides with h up to stage s.[180]

Ontological and epistemic interpretations One can read the modality $\Diamond$ as absolute historical possibility in some ontological sense, but also, as an epistemic possibility for agents, referring to future continuations which they think possible.[181] In the latter vein, branching temporal models become a good extended setting for information flow, knowledge update, and belief revision performed by rational agents, as studied in Chapter 15. In particular, if players i also have *beliefs* about the future course of the process, we add binary relations $\leq_i$ of *relative plausibility*, and a matching doxastic modality

(d) $\boldsymbol{M}, h, s \models B_i \varphi$ iff $\boldsymbol{M}, h', s \models \varphi$ for all histories h' that coincide with h up to stage s and are most plausible for i according to the given relation $\leq_i$.

These languages can faithfully translate the dynamic epistemic, doxastic, and preferential logics of Chapters 12, 13, and 15. Special modal-temporal axioms express special features of branching structures, such

---

[180]Enriching this language describes event trees more fully. E.g., a "sideways" modality for *simultaneity* might refer to truth at sequences of the same length.
[181]This interpretation needs *agent-relative* accessibility relations on histories.

as behaviour over time of agents with *perfect memory* that may be studied via frame correspondences. There is a growing literature on these logics and their connections with process theories in computer science and accounts of strategic equilibrium in game theory.

18.6 Further linguistic and mathematical perspectives

Temporal logic is a vast area, and we have just opened a few windows. Natural language has a much richer repertoire of temporal expressions, where verb tenses, aspects, and adverbials structure a narrative.

Likewise, much more can be said about time in the sciences. We conclude with a tiny sample, reflecting our theme of invariance. Consider any frame $(T, <)$. Temporal propositions denote subsets of T, and so temporal operators are *unary operations* f on the power set of T. Not all a priori functions are plausible, however: certain constraints must be obeyed. It may be demanded that genuine temporal operators f be insensitive to inessential shifts in temporal order:

Temporal automorphism invariance
$\pi[f(A)] = f(\pi[A])$ for all $A \subseteq T$ and all $<$-*automorphisms* π.

This induces a uniformity on the transformation f. For instance, on the real number line $\mathbb{R}$, f-images of singleton propositions $\{t\}$ must now arise through one uniform choice of the f-value in the form of a union of the three relevant regions $\{t\}$, $\{t' \mid t' < t\}$, $\{t' \mid t < t'\}$. Further constraints include a requirement of local computability:

Continuity of temporal operators
f commutes with arbitrary unions of all its arguments.

For such temporal operators, computation of $f(A)$ amounts to taking the union of all values at singletons $f(\{t\})$ with $t \in A$. Together, the two constraints characterize basic tense logic:

Fact. On the reals, the automorphism-invariant continuous temporal operators are the basic tenses F, P plus all disjunctions of these.

Similar notions apply to extended tenses, such as the Progressive, leading to a temporal hierarchy in terms of invariance behaviour. This invariance analysis also extends to the interval setting, provided we now look at combined precedence/inclusion-automorphisms.

18.7 Conclusion

As we said at the start, time is a phenomenon with many aspects, and a province of many disciplines. We have shown that logic is one of these.

Exercises Chapter 18

1. Give some concrete examples for the Mirror Image property, and then prove it.

2. Prove the stated frame correspondence for Hamblin's Axiom and forward discreteness.

3. Define the "serial sets" of reals as finite unions of convex intervals. Show that the serial sets are closed under the Boolean operations, plus the set operations matching the operators F and P.

4. Find a characteristic axiom for interval models with convexity.

5. Consider any interval model. A *filter* F is a non-empty set of intervals closed under super-intervals. Set $F < G$ if $\exists f \in F, g \in G, f < g$. The "point interval" $p(i)$ for the interval i is the set of filters to which it belongs. Investigate some properties of the map p: is it an isomorphism, a homomorphism?

6. Let us do some temporal logic:
   (a) Which of the following principles is valid in branching temporal logic, and which ones have counter-examples?:
   $$\Diamond F\varphi \to F\Diamond\varphi \qquad F\Diamond\varphi \to \Diamond F\varphi$$
   $$\Box F\varphi \to F\Box\varphi \qquad F\Box\varphi \to \Box F\varphi$$
   (b) Define a branching time analogue of the earlier axiom for Perfect Recall in dynamic epistemic logic (Chapter 15), and show what condition it imposes.

7. Give a more detailed argument that the incomplete tense logic over $K4$ with the backward Löb and forward McKinsey axioms holds on no frames.

8. Show that all first-order definable classes of frames have recursively enumerable sets of tense-logical validities.

19

Modal patterns in space

19.1 Spatial structures

When thinking about the physical world, logicians have taken Time as their main interest, maybe also because of its natural fit with computation and action in general. Despite the evident significance of Space and geometry, spatial logics have been more marginal – even though historically, the axiomatic method was largely geometrical. An exception to this neglect was Tarski's famous decidable first-order axiomatization of elementary geometry, going one step further than Hilbert's famous *Grundlagen der Geometrie*. Today Space has a growing importance in many disciplines, and you can get a good impression of spatial reasoning in the *Handbook of Spatial Logics* (Aiello et al., 2007).

Space can be studied at many levels, that come with their own mathematical transformations. You must first choose some level of structure (topological, affine, metric), and determine its invariances (homeomorphism in topology, Euclidean transformations in geometry, etc.). At each of these levels, a logician will then design languages that bring out interesting laws, preferably in a calculus of some reasonable complexity. In this chapter, we look at a few such patterns from a modal perspective starting from a "coarse" theory of space: topology.[182]

---

[182]We assume that the reader already knows some topology, the mathematics of Space up to transformations that, intuitively, shift and compress it, but without breaking or tearing up essential "inside outside" structure. Here is a crash course in one footnote, with the absolute basics. A *topological space* is a pair (X, O) of a set X and a family O of subsets of X (the "open sets", or "opens") containing the the empty set and X itself, while being closed under taking finite intersections and arbitrary unions. An open set containing a point is called a "neighbourhood" of that point. Any set X contains a largest open set, its "interior" – and the opens and the interior operation encode the same thing. Dually, everything might be formulated in terms of *closed sets*, the complements of open sets. The opens are often given by a *sub-base*: some family of sets which is then closed under the given two operations to get all opens. Typical examples are *metric spaces*, where the "unit

19.2 Modal logic and topology

Let M be a *topological model* $(X, \mathcal{O}, V)$ with points X, a family of open sets $\mathcal{O}$ satisfying the usual conditions for a topology, and in addition, a valuation V as in modal models. A modal language fits very well:

Definition 19.2.1 (Topological semantics). $\Box\varphi$ is *true at point* s in M (written $M, s \models \Box\varphi$) if s is in the topological interior of $[\![\varphi]\!]^M$: that is, the set of points satisfying φ in M. Formally, one can write $\exists O \in \mathcal{O} : s \in O \wedge \forall t \in O : M, t \models \varphi$.[183]

Dually, the existential modality $\Diamond$ denotes a topological closure operator. Typical examples of topologies are metric spaces like the real line, or real Euclidean planes or *3D* spaces, but later on, we will also look at different more abstract topologies, derived from trees. Please think of our semantics as concretely as you can, in visual pictures. That is precisely the charm of this interpretation of the modal language:

Example (Defining parts of spoons). Let the proposition letter p denote the following "spoon" in $\mathbb{R}^2$. We explain the topological regions defined by some other modal formulas (these need not be open!):

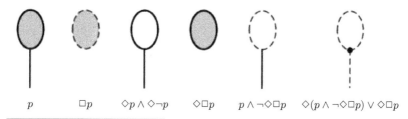

| p | $\Box p$ | $\Diamond p \wedge \Diamond\neg p$ | $\Diamond\Box p$ | $p \wedge \neg\Diamond\Box p$ | $\Diamond(p \wedge \neg\Diamond\Box p) \vee \Diamond\Box p$ |

spheres", consisting of all points around some point up to a given distance, generate the familiar open sets in n-dimensional spaces like the real line, or the plane. This is one major source of topological spaces. The other source are *tree models* with reflexive transitive orders, where a sub-base is given by the "cones" consisting of points with all their successors in the ordering. Typically, in the latter topologies, points have a smallest neighbourhood, whereas in the familiar metric spaces, this is not true at all: e.g., 0 has no smallest open interval around it in the reals. Both extremes will play a role in what follows. Next, as for invariances, a *homeomorphism* is a bijection between two topological spaces that preserves open sets both ways. Homeomorphic spaces are "the same", even though they might be very different in terms of geometric properties like what lies between what on lines, or metric distance structure. Perhaps of even greater interest are rougher *continuous functions* from one space M onto another N that preserve open sets only from image to source: if the set X is open in N, then the inverse image $f^{-1}[X]$ is open in M. These preserve many topologically relevant properties already. Finally, while topology started as a theory of space, it also has informational interpretations, with the open sets standing for "information pieces" of some sort, and "points" as limits of inquiry. This makes topology connected to the intuitionistic logic of our next chapter, but we will not pursue this analogy in any detail here.

[183]This is reminiscent of the neighbourhood models of Chapter 10: see below.

You see how modal formulas of various operator depths define the interior, the boundary, the handle, and even the single special point connecting the handle to the main oval part.

This interpretation is attractive because of the following

Fact. The modal axioms of *S4* express basic topological properties:

$\Box \varphi \to \varphi$	inclusion
$\Box \Box \varphi \leftrightarrow \Box \varphi$	idempotence
$\Box(\varphi \wedge \psi) \leftrightarrow (\Box \varphi \wedge \Box \psi)$	intersection closure of opens

There is no analogue of closure under arbitrary unions in our finite formulas, but we do have the following theorem in the logic *S4*:

$$(\Box \varphi \vee \Box \psi) \leftrightarrow \Box(\Box \varphi \vee \Box \psi)$$

More generally, one can prove this general completeness result:

Theorem 44. A modal formula is topologically valid iff it is provable in the logic *S4*.

The proof is by "sleeping with the enemy". Soundness is seen by direct inspection, as we just did. For completeness, one just finds an *S4*-style reflexive-transitive possible worlds model for a consistent formula (as in Chapter 5). Now, any such model generates a topology:

Fact. Each pre-order induces a topology, where topological modal evaluation amounts to standard modal evaluation on relational models.

Proof sketch. The opens are all subsets of the model that are closed under taking $\leq$-successors. In particular, an open basis is given by all "upward cones" $s^{\leq} = \{\, t \in W \mid s \leq t \,\}$. With this transformation, truth throughout some open neighbourhood of a world is equivalent to truth in all its relational successors. $\Box$

Structures of this special kind are called "Alexandroff topologies", in which arbitrary intersections of open sets are open, not just finite ones. Our earlier relational modal models are such topologies and vice versa, and this link can be made quite precise. For instance, over relational models, in an infinitary modal language, we have an unrestricted distribution law matching the Alexandroff property:

$$\Box \bigwedge_{i \in I} \varphi_i \leftrightarrow \bigwedge_{i \in I} \Box \varphi_i$$

But the most central topologies came from metric spaces, so one main interest is how modal logic behaves in that less familiar territory.

Example (Unlimited distribution fails on metric spaces). Interpret the proposition letters p_i as the open real interval $(-1/i, +1/i)$, for $i \in \mathbb{N}$.

Then the modal formulas $\Box p_i$ denote the same intervals, and hence their conjunction denotes the intersection of them all, i.e., $\{0\}$. But the formula $\Box \bigwedge_{i \in I} p_i$ denotes the topological interior of the singleton set $\{0\}$, which is the empty set $\emptyset$.

The following intriguing point is often overlooked. Historically, the first semantic interpretation for modal languages was in topological terms, by Tarski in the 1930s, and the "standard relational semantics" of the 1950s then switched to tree-like topologies. Only nowadays, broader topological models are picking up interest again.

19.3 Special topics: invariance, expressive and deductive power

All the earlier topics from general modal logic return with new twists.

Comparison games One can analyze expressive power of the modal language with games comparing points in topological models, probing their degree of analogy:

Definition 19.3.1 (Topo-games). A *topo-game* has a Spoiler claiming that two models M, s and N, t are different, while Duplicator claims that they are analogous. Rounds proceed as follows, starting from some current match $s - t$. Spoiler takes one of these points, and chooses one of its open neighbourhoods U in its model. Duplicator responds with an open neighbourhood V of the other current point. Still in the same round, Spoiler chooses a point $v \in V$, and then Duplicator chooses a point $u \in U$, making $u - v$ the new match. Duplicator loses if the two points differ qua atomic properties.

This looks abstract, but it is concrete. Here are some illustrations:

Example (Comparing cutlery). In the above spoon models, compare the following sets of intuitively different points:

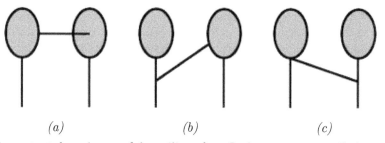

(a)   (b)   (c)

For a start, here is a useful auxiliary fact. It does not matter if players choose small or large open neighbourhoods in the game. You can see this by trying a few moves, but there is also a general result, like the earlier fact that on relational models, evaluation of formulas only needs to look at R-closed "generated submodels" around the current point:

Fact (Locality Lemma). For any model M, s and modal formula φ, and any open neighbourhood O of s, the following are equivalent:

(a) $M, s \models \varphi$,

(b) $M|O, s \models \varphi$, with $M|O$ the model M restricted to the subset O.

This Fact is an easy induction on modal formulas. Now we consider games for the above three situations, where black lines indicate the initial match between points.[184] For vividness, things will be stated largely from the perspective of Spoiler, since we have chosen cases with a topologically significant difference. If you want to see a winning strategy for Duplicator, just let a game start with two points in the interior of the spoon: whatever Spoiler does, Duplicator serenely tags along.

Case (a). If Spoiler chooses a neighbourhood to the left, Duplicator chooses a small interior disk to the right, and whatever Spoiler chooses, there will be an inside point that Duplicator can match in the open to the left. So, this is a bad idea. But if Spoiler starts with a small disk on the right, Duplicator must respond with a disk on the edge to the left, which then allows Spoiler to choose an object outside of the spoon, and every response by Duplicator is losing, since it falls inside the spoon. So, Spoiler has a winning strategy in one round. This is reflected in the earlier modal difference formula of operator depth 1 distinguishing the two positions – say $\Box p$.

Case (b). Spoiler's winning strategy starts with an open on the handle to the left, and Duplicator must choose an open on the rim of the oval. Now Spoiler picks an object there inside the spoon, and Duplicator can only respond by choosing outside of the spoon (an immediate loss), or on the handle. But the latter reduces the game to case (a), which Spoiler could already win in one round. The difference formula this time has modal depth 2.

Case (c) is the most complicated, since the point connecting rim and handle is most like an ordinary rim point, but Spoiler has a winning strategy in 3 rounds, matching a modal difference formula of modal depth 3, for instance, $\Diamond(p \wedge \neg\Diamond\Box p) \wedge \Diamond\Box p$.

As in Chapter 3, one can prove an Adequacy result by induction:

Fact. Duplicator has a winning strategy in the comparison game over k rounds starting from two models M, s and N, t iff these two pointed models satisfy the same modal formulas up to modal operator depth k.

---

[184]We are comparing points, not figures as a whole. To do the latter, we could let Spoiler first mark two points that he wants to play from.

The proof is like that for relational models: you might give it a try.

Topo-bisimulation Here is a matching relation for topological models:

Definition 19.3.2 (Topo-bisimulation). A *topo-bisimulation* is a relation E between points in two models M, M' connecting only points verifying the same proposition letters, and satisfying the zigzag clauses

(a) Whenever sEt and $s \in U \in \mathcal{O}$, there is an open V with (a1) $t \in V \in \mathcal{O}'$ and (a2) $\forall v \in V \exists u \in U : uEv$. (b) The same vice versa.[185]

Topo-bisimulation is a coarse variant of homeomorphism. By a simple induction, it leaves the modal language invariant, and even its infinitary extension with arbitrary set conjunctions and disjunctions.

Still, the other basic topological transformation of a *continuous map* is coarser than this, as it only preserves open sets in one direction, backward from image to source. Even so, such maps preserve much topological structure, and part of the reason is logical preservation. Consider a continuous map f from M onto N, and let V be a propositional valuation on N. Then taking inverse images $f^{-1}[V(p)]$ induces a corresponding valuation on M:

Fact. Continuous maps with their induced valuations preserve, going *from N to M*, all modal formulas created by the following syntax: $p \mid \neg p \mid \wedge \mid \vee \mid \Box$.[186]

To find concrete applications, we move to key topological notions:

Extended modal languages Many topological notions require slight extensions of the modal base language. For instance, call a topological space *connected* if it cannot be written as a disjoint union of two nonempty open sets. A topo-bisimulation argument shows that this is not definable in our basic modal language. But an extended language with the *universal modality* U of Chapter 3 provides a correspondence:

Example (Connectedness). A topological space (considered as a "frame" without a valuation) is connected iff the following modal formula holds for all valuations: $(U(\Box p \vee \Box q) \wedge Ep \wedge Eq) \rightarrow E(p \wedge q)$.

Now, note two things. First, given that continous maps are surjective functions, the preceding preservation result easily extends to allow for two more syntactic operators in the preserved formulas: the universal

---

[185]This is similar to the bisimulations for neighbourhood models in Chapter 10.

[186]These shapes look like "universal formulas" in the basic modal language, preserved when going to relational sub-models. But here, these formulas are preserved under, amongst others, *extensions* of topologies on the same base domain. There is more to this connection, but we will stick to a minimum in our discussion.

modality U and the existential E. Next, the negation of the connect-edness axiom can be written in this modal syntax. That is why it is preserved from a continuous image to the source, and hence: if the original space is connected, so is its image.[187]

Special completeness theorems Deductive power and completeness of modal logics also make sense for topological structures. Here is a famous result by McKinsey & Tarski in the 1940s: $S4$ is not just adequate for tree topologies, but also for the other major branch of topologies:

Theorem 45. The complete modal logic of any metric space without isolated points equals $S4$.

The proof is difficult, and simplifications and variants are still appearing. This theorem shows how little the modal language can say about topological structures: not even a rich metric space like the reals can elicit more music from it than $S4$. But in another sense, by its very weakness, the completeness gives attractive concrete connections between the modal language and spatial patterns. For instance, it follows that any consistent modal formula in reflexive transitive $S4$-models can be made true by choosing a suitable valuation on the reals. This is highly non-trivial:

Example (Satisfying consistent formulas on the reals). Consider this tree, with numbers for unique proposition letters true at the nodes:

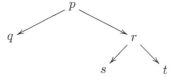

In this reflexive transitive $S4$-model (we omitted some arrows for convenience), formulas true at end points are necessarily true there. We first make p true at some real number r. The fact that the root sees a q-world

---

[187]We can also test this analysis against another major feature of continuous maps: they preserve *compactness*. (What follows corrects an argument in van Benthem and Bezhanishvili (2007).) First, the obvious logical form of Compactness is in an infinitary modal language:

$$U \bigvee_{i \in I} \Box \varphi_i \ \rightarrow \ \bigvee_{J \text{ finite} \subseteq I} U \bigvee_{j \in J} \Box \varphi_j$$

But its negation is not of the right form, since the negated consequent would contain existential modalities. However, we can redefine compactness in a way that does fit: start with an antecedent saying that all formulas φ_i imply $\Box\varphi_i$, and then state the finite cover property in terms of the φ_i rather than the $\Box\varphi_i$. There are many technical model-theoretic questions here that have not been explored yet.

means that r is in the closure of the set of q-worlds, and hence in the reals, there must be a convergent sequence of q-points toward it. In fact, given that the q-world is an endpoint satisfying $\Box q$, we see a convergent sequence of *open q-intervals* toward the initial point. Looking at the node with r, we have to put another convergent sequence, of r-points which themselves have converging sequences of open s- and t-intervals around them. The resulting nested pattern on the reals quickly gets complicated, and the procedure for satisfying consistent statements on $S4$-trees on the reals, involves *fractal*-style nested figures.

Stronger logics than $S4$ arise with special structures. For instance, suppose we only want *serial sets* of real numbers: finite unions of convex sets (proposed as a model for temporal "events"). The modal logic of the serial sets is much stronger, since fewer sets are available as denotations for modal formulas.

Fact. Serial sets validate the principle $(\neg\varphi \wedge \Diamond\varphi) \to \Diamond\Box\varphi$.

You will find it rewarding to check the concrete spatial reason.[188]

Generalization: neighbourhood models Topological models are special cases of the neighbourhood models of Chapter 10, where the latter dropped even the $S4$-properties, validating a minimal logic below K. The two semantics have essentially the same complexity. While relational models read one modality as one quantifier, topological semantics reads a modal box as a classical quantifier combination $\exists\forall$: "every point in some neighbourhood". This explains all the additional effort in defining games, topo-bisimulation, and the like.[189]

19.4   Geometrical modal logics

Next, we increase descriptive power (cf. Chapter 10), and change the similarity type of our models to include geometrical notions.

Affine geometry Models $M = (W, B, V)$ get a primitive ternary relation B of betweenness, which supports a new "convexity modality":

$$M, s \models C\varphi \quad \text{iff} \quad s \text{ lies in between two points satisfying } \varphi, \text{ i.e.,}$$
$$\exists t, u : Bs, tu \text{ with } M, t \models \varphi \text{ and } M, u \models \varphi.$$

Again this language has appealing concrete spatial models:

---

[188] Actually, the modal logic of the serial sets is exactly that of the "2-fork": a 3-world tree model with a root and just two daughters.

[189] To do away with this, one would have to use a *bimodal translation* to two-sorted models with "points" and "sets", where points can belong to sets and open sets can be neighbourhoods of points. This involves a neighbourhood relation N plus membership $\in$, yielding a transcription $\langle N \rangle [\in]$ for $\Box$.

Example (Convexity formulas on a tetrahedron). Consider the proposition letter p interpreted as the vertices of the following tetrahedron:

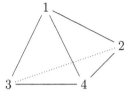

The formula Cp holds on just the edges, CCp in the whole solid.[190]

Now dimensionality of metric spaces $\mathbb{R}^n$ shows up in the logic:

Fact. The reals validate the equivalence $CC\varphi \to C\varphi$.

Equivalences with higher indices hold in higher dimensions. Valid combined principles with the earlier modal topological language include

$$C\Box p \to \Box Cp$$

Complete logics are unknown – and this whole area is replete with open problems (see the *Handbook of Spatial Logics*).

But we can also have a more powerful polyadic betweenness modality (cf. Chapter 10), satisfying full distributivity. It says that the current point lies on an interval whose endpoints have properties φ and ψ:

$\boldsymbol{M}, s \models \langle B \rangle \varphi \psi$ iff $\exists t, u : Bs, tu$ with $\boldsymbol{M}, t \models \varphi$ and $\boldsymbol{M}, u \models \psi$.

In a picture:

Chapter 10 gave a concrete illustration, that we copy here:

Example (Triangle models). In the following "annotated triangle", the worlds are the vertices, while the lines just help to indicate betweenness and proposition letters are true at marked points.

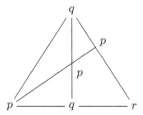

---

[190]You will find the proof a very useful exercise in *3D* visualization.

The right-most vertex is uniquely defined by the formula r, the one in the middle by $p \wedge \Diamond qq$, the right-most p-point by $p \wedge \Diamond qr$ – and continuing, each vertex has a unique modal definition.[191]

There are also links with standard geometry via frame correspondences. Consider the natural modal axiom of *Associativity*:

$$\langle B \rangle \, p \, \langle B \rangle qr \;\rightarrow\; \langle B \rangle \langle B \rangle pq \, r$$

This syntactic Sahlqvist form yields to the techniques of Chapter 9 – but it acquires a classical meaning from affine geometry:

Fact. On betweenness frames, Associativity defines *Pasch's Axiom*.

Proof. Pasch's Axiom says that "Every line drawn through a vertex of a triangle into its interior can be continued to intersect the opposite side". This is easily expressed in first-order terms, using the following picture. The correspondence is then a straightforward exercise.

$$\forall xyvzu((Bv,yz \wedge Bu,xv) \rightarrow \exists s(Bs,yx \wedge Bu,sz))$$

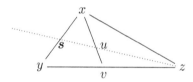

□

Metric geometry The same analysis extends to metric structure. This requires adding a quaternary predicate of "equidistance", or ternary "relative nearness":

$$Nx,yz \qquad y \text{ is closer to } x \text{ than } z \text{ is to } x$$

This relation satisfies nice laws, including "Triangle Inequalities" like

$$(Nx,yz \wedge Nz,xy) \rightarrow Ny,xz$$

This is like similarity "sphere models" for conditional logic (Chapter 13), but complete logics for this geometrical version are unknown.

19.5 Mathematical morphology

Theories of space are still emerging. We end with one that recently turned out to involve modal logic. "Mathematical morphology" is a new

---

[191]Chapter 10 had more details for modal definabilities in this triangle example.

theory of shapes in computational image processing. Spatial or visual regions are taken as sets of *vectors*, that can typically be "added". In addition to the ordinary Booleans, this yields two key operations for manipulation of images or pictures. One involves vector addition in the usual parallelograms, as in the following diagram with vectors coming from two sets A and B:

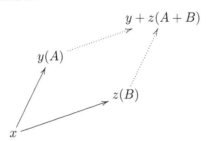

The other operation smoothes a rough figure A by "subtracting" some suitable B, say a small circle rolling around A's inside edges:

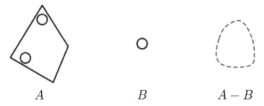

The resulting notions on sets of vectors A, B (also $X, Y, \ldots$) are:

Definition 19.5.1 ("Minkowski operations"). *Addition of regions* is the sum $A + B = \{\, x \mid \exists y {\in} A, z {\in} B : x = y + z \,\}$. *Subtraction* uses vector differences: $A - B = \{\, x \mid \forall y {\in} B : x + y \in B \,\}$.

Here are some valid principles in this algebra of images:

Fact. The following laws hold for all regions in Euclidean space:

$$(X \cup Y) + S = (X + S) \cup (Y + S), \quad (A \cup B) - C = (A - C) \cup (B - C)$$

There are also useful defined operations with special laws, such as

$$\text{morphological opening } X \circ S =_{def} (S - X) + S$$

Fact. Morphological opening satisfies idempotence $(X \circ S) \circ S = X \circ S$.

Typically non-valid is the idempotence law $A + A = A$. The reason in words: adding an image to itself may create quite a different image.

Excursion: linear logic There is a surprising link here with *linear logic* in proof theory and computation, which views propositions as multi-sets of "resources", making, say, a multi-set $\{P, P\}$ with two occurrences different from the singleton $\{P\}$. This changes the usual laws of conjunction and implication:

Theorem 46. Morphological addition and subtraction satisfy the laws of *multiplicative linear logic*, with $+$ for the product conjunction, and $A - B$ for the implication $B \to A$.

The two directions of the above "opening" law $(X \circ S) \circ S = X \circ S$ are literally the following two derivable sequents in linear logic:

$$(S \to X) + S \Rightarrow (S \to ((S \to X) + S)) + S$$
$$(S \to ((S \to X) + S)) + S \Rightarrow (S \to X) + S$$

Completeness for this geometrical version of linear logic is open.

Arrow logic of vector spaces For a modal perspective on the same structures, we go back to the *Arrow Logic* of Chapter 10, with a binary modality for a ternary relation Cx, yz that we now read as: "vector x is the sum $y + z$". The Boolean connectives of Arrow Logic match those of mathematical morphology. Finally, it had a unary modality for a binary relation of converse Ix, y, that is now the linear minus operation: $x = -y$. This generalizes the linear logic analysis, though a fortiori, the complete arrow logic of mathematical morphology is unknown.

A further resemblance between mathematical morphology and modal logic is the use of language extensions when convenient. For instance, special letters are often used to formulate valid laws involving single vectors. Here is an identity that holds in this way, but not with arbitrary sets of vectors:

Fact. The identity $S \to (X + \{t\}) = (S \to X) + \{t\}$ is valid.

From right to left, this is derivable as a generally valid implication

$$(S \to X) \cdot A \Rightarrow S \to (X \cdot A)$$

in both linear logic and arrow logic. The converse has counter-examples, but it does become derivable when we treat the singleton as a *nominal* (cf. Chapter 7): a proposition letter only true in one world. One can now appeal to a special nominal principle for the modal derivation:

$$S \Rightarrow (S + \{t\}) - \{t\}.$$

19.6 Conclusion

Logic of space is a rich and relatively unexplored research area with an old tradition. This chapter has shown how modal structures come up naturally in topology, geometry, and linear algebra. All notions and techniques of Parts I, II made sense – on their own, or in combination with other logical perspectives.

Exercises Chapter 19

1. Consider some basic facts about topological models:
   (a) Prove the topological Locality Lemma in the text.
   (b) Prove that a topo-bisimulation leaves modal formulas invariant. Show how the Locality Lemma follows from this fact.
   (c) Prove that two finite modally equivalent topological models have a topo-bisimulation between them.
   (d) Prove the extended preservation lemma with universal modalities for continuous maps.

2. Recall the special logic of "serial sets":
   (a) Show why the "two-fork" satisfies the axiom in the text.
   (b) Show why the "two-fork" frame captures precisely the modal logic of the serial sets.

3. Look at the picture of a tetrahedron in our text:
   (a) Explain in detail why the tetrahedron is defined by the modal formula CCp.
   (b) Show why the reals satisfy the principle $C\varphi \rightarrow CC\varphi$.

4. Now move to metric geometry:
   (a) Find as many valid first-order triangle inequalities for relative nearness as you can.
   (b) Using nearness in the real plane as a similarity relation for conditionals, do we get new laws of conditional logic valid beyond those in Chapter 13?

5. Check the soundness of some of the principles stated in the text for mathematical morphology.

20

Intuitionistic logic

Our final topics in Part III come from the foundations of mathematics, but they also have a broader thrust for computation and epistemology.

20.1 Implicit versus explicit knowledge

The epistemic logic of Chapter 12 has explicit operators for knowledge. But there are older traditions where the semantics of logical languages itself gets "epistemized". Then the standard logical operations (Booleans, quantifiers) acquire epistemic meanings, without any special K-operators. The paradigm of this "implicit epistemics" is *intuitionistic logic*, originating in a view of mathematics as intuitive construction of objects and proofs for their properties.

20.2 The logic of constructive proof

Intuitionistic logic describes constructive proof, with high standards. Here is a famous unprincipled (though rather clever) non-constructive classical proof:

Fact. There exist two irrational numbers x, y such that x^y is rational.

Proof. Consider $\sqrt{2}^{\sqrt{2}^{\sqrt{2}}}$. This is equal to $\sqrt{2}^{(\sqrt{2} \cdot \sqrt{2})} = (\sqrt{2})^2 = 2$, which is rational.

Case 1: $\sqrt{2}^{\sqrt{2}}$ is rational – and we are done: let $x = y = \sqrt{2}$.
Case 2: $\sqrt{2}^{\sqrt{2}}$ is irrational: and we take $x = \sqrt{2}^{\sqrt{2}}$, $y = \sqrt{2}$.

$\square$

This proof gives no conclusive information about the actual objects the theorem is about! There is also a constructive proof showing that Case 2 in fact obtains (a deep result). The distinction between mere proof and explicit construction dates back to Antiquity: geometrical "constructions" occur intertwined with proofs in Euclid's *Elements*.

Intuitionism rejects all laws of classical logic that support non-constructive reasoning, retaining only those with a proof-theoretic underpinning. In particular, Excluded Middle $\varphi \vee \neg\varphi$ is rejected, as we have no general way of knowing which disjunct is the case. Here is the systematic thinking behind this critical position. Consider a mathematician who constructs objects, and proves their properties. Typically, proofs for complex assertions can be constructed from proofs for component assertions. For the Boolean key notions, this works as follows:

A proof for a conjunction $A \wedge B$ is a pair of proofs, for A, and for B. A proof for a disjunction $A \vee B$ is a proof for A or one for B. And a proof for a negation $\neg A$ is a refutation of A, that is: an effective method transforming each proof of A into one for a manifest contradiction.

Read in this way, Excluded Middle says that each statement A is provable or refutable. But Gödel's Theorems tell us that "incompleteness" is frequent in mathematics: some statements are neither provable nor refutable in arithmetic, analysis, or set theory (assuming that these theories are consistent).[192] [193]

The proof interpretation of the logical notions validates a system of laws of its own. For instance, the Law of *Non-Contradiction* still holds. Assuming that we have both a proof and a refutation for A is untenable, and this observation itself is a proof for $\neg(A \wedge \neg A)$. And many other useful classical principles remain correct. What does happen is that classical reasoning often "splits" into variants, some intuitionistically correct, others not. A beautiful example is the famous method of proof by contradiction. In classical logic, one can establish an assertion $\neg A$ by first assuming A, and then deriving a contradiction. This pattern is unproblematic to an intuitionist. But classical logic also has a more magical variant: prove an assertion A by deriving a contradiction from its negation $\neg A$. This second method is intuitionistically unacceptable: "refuting refutability" is not the same as positive proof. The former does establish something, but only the double negation $\neg\neg A$. Thus, intuitionists reject the classical equivalence between $\neg\neg A$ and A. They find the first weaker than the second.[194]

---

[192]Even so, intuitionists agree that mathematical structures admit of reasoning with Excluded Middle if they are "simple enough" – say: *finite*. But automatic extrapolation of classical logic to infinite structures is problematic.

[193]You might object that the objection does not affect classical Excluded Middle. For, a meaning shift has taken place from *truth* to *provability*. So, Brouwer, the founder of intuitionism, did not fight classical logic on its own territory: as so often with revolutionaries, he changed the agenda.

[194]Proposing marriage by refuting non-proposing works rarely. A witty Dutch logician once proposed a funerary inscription "L.E.J. Brouwer: not not dead".

Proof theory is a stronghold of intuitionistic logic. The standard natural deduction rules for implication (Modus Ponens, Conditionalization) give intuitionistic, not classical logic! Intuitionistic proof calculi and type theories have proofs with an algorithmic surplus constructing objects whose existence is derived. This is appropriate in computer science. If you can prove intuitionistically that every sequence of numbers has a sorted version, then that proof will contain a sorting algorithm, that you can try to extract. Or, you can design algorithms and correctness proofs at the same time in natural intuitionistic calculi.[195]

20.3 Information models for intuitionistic logic

It is also possible to interpret intuitionistic logic in a semantics of *information stages*, from poorer to richer, where formulas describe stages of the process.[196] A mathematician, or a rational agent in general, gradually acquires more information, moving upward in this order. At final stages of the process, where all information is in, classical logic holds. But in intermediate stages, classical laws may fail. Let us call a negation *not-A* true at a stage of the model when A has been refuted right now already: no further richer stage makes A true. Under this interpretation, it is easy to see that Excluded Middle can fail:

Example (Refuting Excluded Middle). Take an extremely simple information model with only two stages, an initial one where we do not have A yet, followed by a final stage where we do have it:

$$1 \circ \xrightarrow{\quad A \quad} \bullet 2$$

At the first stage 1, A fails by assumption, but neither does *not-A* hold, since we do get A at stage 2 after all. Thus, the disjunctive statement $A \vee \neg A$ does not hold at stage 1.

This semantics has a delicate difference between saying "A does not hold" at a stage, and saying that "$\neg A$ holds". Indeed, an intuitionist cannot use her own strong negation *not* to deny the law of Excluded Middle: $\neg(A \vee \neg A)$ is a contradiction also intuitionistically. The following principle is intuitionistically valid:

$$\neg\neg(A \vee \neg A)$$

This is not Excluded Middle, as $\neg\neg A \leftrightarrow A$ was intuitionistically invalid. The distinction is easily seen in our models: $\neg\neg A$ unpacks to the

---

[195]For more information, see the two volumes *Constructivism in Mathematics* by Troelstra and van Dalen (Troelstra and van Dalen, 1988).

[196]Such models were first devised by Brouwer's colleague Beth in Amsterdam, himself not an intuitionist. Later versions of the semantics are due to Kripke.

assertion that each stage has a later stage where A is made true (A is "inevitable"), but this is not to say that A is true right here and now. In stage 1 of the above picture, $\neg\neg A$ is true, but A is not.

More generally, intuitionistic logic is the logic of a process of acquiring knowledge by an agent moving toward ever richer epistemic states.[197] This is just our basic modal semantics with a new epistemic interpretation. Think of each model $\boldsymbol{M} = (W, \leq, V)$ as a research program with a set of information states W, a growth relation $\leq$, and a valuation V that records which atomic facts are known at each stage. In line with this interpretation, we demand persistence of atomic facts:

Heredity   If $\boldsymbol{M}, s \models p$ and $s \leq t$, then also $\boldsymbol{M}, t \models p$.

By induction, Heredity holds for all propositional formulas given the intuitionistic truth conditions. We saw the clause for negation already, while conjunction and disjunction are interpreted as usual. As an illustration, we saw a failure of Excluded Middle, but here is a failure of an even weaker variant:

Example (Refuting Weak Excluded Middle). Weak Excluded Middle $\neg p \vee \neg\neg p$ fails in the root of the following model:

Finally, an implication $\varphi \rightarrow \psi$ holds at a stage if *in all further stages* where φ holds, the ψ holds as well. Thus, a negation $\neg\varphi$ is equivalent to $\varphi \rightarrow \bot$, with $\bot$ an "absurd" statement that never holds.

At end points, intuitionistic and classical evaluation coincide. Thus, intuitionistic logic generalizes classical logic to intermediate stages of investigation – and being weaker in this richer setting, it can make sophisticated new distinctions. For instance, intuitionistically, connectives are not inter-definable as in classical logic. One can even define *new* ones without classical counterparts.[198]

20.4   Model theory of intuitionistic logic

All earlier modal topics make sense for intuitionistic logic – including bisimulation, axiomatic proof, first-order translation, correspondence,

---

[197]Ordinary mortals like us eventually start moving backwards through this landscape. These models suggest a systematic comparison with the epistemic information models of Chapters 12, 13 and 15, but we will not undertake this task here.

[198]Similar points apply to *quantifiers*, a topic not treated in this chapter.

and complexity. The underlying reason is that the system is much like the basic modal language over *pre-orders*, under the so-called

Gödel translation sending proposition letters p to $\Box p$, $\wedge$ to $\wedge$, $\vee$ to $\vee$, $\varphi \to \psi$ to $\Box(\varphi \to \psi)$, and $\neg\varphi$ to $\Box\neg\varphi$.[199]

Viewed in this way, the intuitionistic language is a "hereditary fragment" of the full modal language, being those formulas φ for which $\varphi \to \Box\varphi$ is valid. The *completeness theorem* for intuitionistic propositional logic (its proof is like for modal K in Chapter 5) identifies the universal validities as the theorems of "Heyting's calculus" *HPC*. We can then prove facts like those for K, such as the "Disjunction Property" of *HPC*: if $\varphi \vee \psi$ is a theorem, then so is either φ or ψ. This clearly fails for classical logic!

The complexity of satisfiability for intuitionistic propositional logic is that of K and $S4$: *PSPACE*-complete. This is worth noting, as many people think that intuitionistic logic is simpler than classical logic. This is false: the price of constructivism in propositional reasoning is a jump up from the *NP*-completeness of classical propositional logic.[200]

On top of *HPC*, further axioms give intermediate logics between intuitionism and classical proof – whose meaning can be made explicit by frame correspondences. Excluded Middle makes every point an end-point, and takes us up to classical logic. Weak Excluded Middle $\neg p \vee \neg\neg p$ imposes *confluence*: akin to the relational confluence conditions in Chapters 7, 9, and 24.

Two kinds of information The modal setting suggests merging "implicit" and "explicit" epistemic logic, since we can introduce an explicit modality $\Box$ for the stage inclusion order. But this modality is not the epistemic K of Chapter 12. Quantifying over future stages in an intuitionistic model mixes two intuitively different notions:

(a) *factual information* about the world and what other people know about it,

(b) *procedural information* about how we can find out such things.

Even the dynamic epistemic logic of Chapter 15 has no counterpart for the latter notion, unless we extend it with temporal operators over admissible histories of investigation (Chapter 18).[201] Other neighbours

---

[199]This translation is to be applied recursively, working inside out.

[200]This is just one instance of the unfortunate scarcity of insights from computer science in philosophical circles.

[201]Recent versions of dynamic epistemic logic add *protocols* regulating admissible sequences of events in the informational process. As to basic events occurring in such protocols, if you look more closely at intuitionistic models, their upward steps

are the dynamic doxastic logics in Chapter 15. *Backtracking* along the stage inclusion order leads to appealing notions of belief revision.[202]

20.5   Aside: intuitionistic mathematics

On this logical foundation, intuitionistic *mathematics* has new kinds of behaviour. In particular, its weaker base allows for theorems that *contradict* those of classical mathematics, such as Brouwer's famous result that every function from real numbers to real numbers is continuous. Also, the algorithmic aspect of intuitionistic proofs has a thriving literature by itself. Indeed, our emphasis on information models is somewhat suspect to staunch intuitionists, as our informal reasoning about these models was *classical!*[203] Should not the meta-theory of intuitionistic logic be intuitionistic *itself*? See again the book by Troelstra & van Dalen (Troelstra and van Dalen, 1988).

20.6   The story goes on: intuitionism and games

Intuitionism is associated with foundations of mathematics, and proofs of extraterrestrial precision. But it also relates to a different tradition going back to Antiquity, of logical patterns in *dialogue* and debate. After all, even a formal proof is not just a "conversation stopper", but an ultimate attempt at clarity and inter-subjective communication. In the mid 1950s, this was seen by Lorenzen, when looking for an underpinning of logic in daily practices of argumentation. His idea was that the logical core operations "or", "and" and "not" function as a sort of switches, not just in a computer, but also in discussion. The resulting *dialogue games* have rules like this:

> When I defend $A \vee B$, you can press me as to which of the two I will defend. Thus, a disjunction is a choice for its defender. Likewise, a conjunction $A \wedge B$ is a choice for the attacker: as the defender of a conjunction is committed to both its parts.

In this manner, an argumentation game unrolls between the defender of an assertion and its attacker, and this explains in a dynamic manner why conjunction and disjunction are so analogous. They are the same

---

are of *two* interesting kinds. One is public announcements of facts as in Chapter 15, ruling out further histories. But there are also non-eliminative steps of "explicitly realizing" facts that were already implicitly known. The latter acts relate to the epistemological problem of "omniscience" mentioned in Chapter 12: some implicit information still needs to be made explicit.

[202] One retreats to the nearest earlier stage where the new proposition P was still consistent, and then moves up to a closest information stage enforcing P.

[203] An intuitionist colleague of mine compares uses of Excluded Middle to taking drugs. The first time, you feel a moral barrier – but the next time, you feel less compunction, until you are hooked on classical stuff.

act, namely choice, but performed by different players. Moreover, in a dialogue, interesting interactions arise through the operation of logical negation, which triggers a *role switch*:

defending $\neg A$ is attacking A, and vice versa.

Being able to put yourself in another person's place seems an essential cognitive achievement. Dialogues become *games* by stipulating that players lose when they must say something (i.e., engage in a legitimate attack or defense), but are prevented from doing so by the game rules. Then all notions from Chapter 17 apply. In particular, Lorenzen called an inference *valid* if the defender of the conclusion has a *winning strategy*: a rule that will always lead her to win the game against any defender granting the premises.

Example (Winning with the Sudoku Rule). When you defend a conclusion B against someone defending premises $A \vee B$ and $\neg A$, then first attack that disjunction, forcing him to choose.[204] If his answer is B, then you win at once – and if his choice is A, then you can now safely attack A, since he has just placed himself in the shameful conversational position of "self-contradiction": $A, \neg A$.

General winning strategies in argumentation may of course be much more complex that this simple gambit.

Now Lorenzen observed that Excluded Middle is not plausible in this game setting. The defender of $A \vee \neg A$ need not have a strategy telling her infallibly which disjunct to choose, and win. In fact, the logical validities backed up by winning strategies in these dialogue games are precisely those of intuitionistic logic! By now, dialogue games have been found that do match classical logic, and the difference is instructive. Their debating rules, quite humanely, allow the defender of a disjunction to *revise* her initial choice later on.

We already saw a connection between Excluded Middle and games in Chapter 17. Here is a paraphrased proof of Zermelo's Theorem:

Suppose the game lasts for only 1 move, and Player I starts. Then either I has a move that makes her win (and her winning strategy "I choose such a winning move"), or all initial moves lead to loss for I, and in that case, it is Player II who has a winning strategy ("just wait, and win"). When a game lasts for two rounds, we just repeat the given reasoning. Either the starting player has a move taking her to a position where she has a winning strategy, and then she has a winning strategy in the whole game – or all moves of the starting player lead

---

[204]This is the principle of *Sudoku* puzzles: there must be one of k digits, we can rule out one of these, leaving one of $k - 1$ digits – and so on.

to a position with a winning strategy for the other player, and then the latter player has a winning strategy. And so on for longer games.

The pivotal role of Excluded Middle will be clear. Of course, intuitionists would not object: our games here were finite. In infinite games, matters are more delicate, as studied in descriptive set theory.

New logical operations We end with a surprising twist. Argumentation is all about interaction unfolding over time. But in such a setting, our interpretation of the disjunction $A \vee B$ as a choice for one of the sub-games A, B seems too drastic. Why make this choice right at the start, when we know nothing yet about what happened in those sub-games? For this reason, it has been proposed to add a second logical form of choice. Now the sub-games A, B are played in *parallel*, and the player who has to choose may decide locally, at each of her turns, in which of the two games the next move is to be played. A much-cited example again comes from Chess. Here is a method that makes you beat even the world champion, the "Copy Cat" strategy:

Play two games at once, one as White and one as Black. Let Champion open as White, then copy his move to the other game as White, and stay there, forcing him to respond as Black to your (i.e., his own) opening move. Next copy this answer in the other game (you have the power to switch), etcetera. Both games get exactly the same sequence of moves, and you must win one of them (or draw in both).

So now we have a new logical operation of "parallel disjunction" $A + B$ (where the + refers to parallel play as in our switching scenario). As we saw, in Lorenzen dialogues, Excluded Middle does not always hold for the choice disjunction $\vee$. But the Copy Cat argument shows that quite generally, "interactive choice" $A + B$ satisfies Excluded Middle:

the logical principle $A + \neg A$ is valid without any restrictions!

Thus, we see a new world of logical operations with their own laws, and Boolean algebra is now just one corner of a beautiful general theory of complex interactive behaviour.[205]

---

[205] An elegant exposition of these ideas in computer science and beyond is found in the chapter "Information, Processes and Games" (Abramsky, 2008) in the *Handbook of the Philosophy of Information*.

Exercises Chapter 20

1. Look at the two classically valid De Morgan laws:

   $$\neg(\varphi \lor \psi) \leftrightarrow (\neg\varphi \land \neg\psi), \qquad \neg(\varphi \land \psi) \leftrightarrow \neg\varphi \lor \neg\psi$$

   Of the four implications, three are valid intuitionistically, one is not. Motivate the valid ones in terms of the proof interpretation, and give a counter-example for the invalid one.

2. Show that intuitionistic logic has the Disjunction Property.

3. Find a notion of bisimulation that is appropriate for the intuitionistic language.

4. Analyze intuitionistic information models with a dynamic epistemic logic of public announcement, where "protocol" restrictions may occur on the true assertions that can be announced at a stage. Also explain the steps that do not fit this format, since no branching occurs: can you define an act of "realization" as in Footnote 201?

5. Analyze the temporal belief revision sketched in Footnote 202.

6. Reasoning with games:
   (a) Show there is a winning strategy in a dialogue game for Proponent in defending the formula $p \land \neg(p \land q) \to \neg q$. Also for $((p \to q) \land r) \to (p \to (q \land r))$.
   (b) Show that there is a winning strategy for Opponent when Proponent puts forward the formula $\neg(p \land q) \to (\neg p \lor \neg q)$.
   (c) What standard logical objects correspond to winning strategies for Proponent and Opponent in dialogue games?

7. Intuitionistic predicate logic, too, has the Heredity property. How would you interpret quantifiers to make sure that this holds?

21

Provability logic

Our final topic concerns any sort of proof, intuitionistic or classical.

21.1 Modal logic of provability and proofs

We noted in Part I that a modal box $\Box\varphi$ can also be read as provability: the existence of a proof or evidence for φ. This is an existential quantifier view of knowledge, rather than our usual semantic universal one. Here is an illustration: the modal distribution axiom

$$\Box(\varphi \to \psi) \to (\Box\varphi \to \Box\psi)$$

now says that, if $\varphi \to \psi$ is provable and also φ, then ψ is provable:

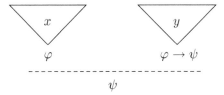

In particular, if x is a proof of φ, and y a proof of $\varphi \to \psi$, then merging x, y by a final application of Modus Ponens is a proof for ψ: the axiom is a constructive form of Modus Ponens.

Remark on co-existence The provability interpretation sees necessity as having compelling reasons for an assertion. There is no contradiction with the semantic account. For instance, the completeness theorem for first-order logic matches these two faces. Validity quantifies universally over models, and the equivalent notion of provability quantifies existentially, but over the *different domain* of syntactic proofs.

21.2 Gödel-Löb logic

With provability for specific mathematical theories, modal formulas can express facts in the foundations of mathematics. The earlier highway to Un (Chapter 8) contains an important case:

Definition 21.2.1 (Gödel-Löb provability logic). The *Gödel-Löb logic* GL extends the minimal modal logic K with the axiom

$$\Box(\Box\varphi \to \varphi) \to \Box\varphi$$

Specifically, the modal box $\Box\varphi$ is meant to say that φ is provable in a theory crucial to the foundations of mathematics, viz. Peano Arithmetic. The axiom looks strange for an Id-route traveler, as it says that the formerly harmless T-axiom of Veridicality can only hold for provable formulas. But it really reflects a deep result about Peano Arithmetic called "Löb's Theorem", as explained later.

Valid principles on this account of $\Box$ include, as already observed by Gödel: (a) the laws of K (we saw this for modal distribution by "proof combination"), and (b) the transitivity law $\Box\varphi \to \Box\Box\varphi$ of $K4$, which now says that one can prove that provable formulas are provable, for instance, by running a "proof-checker". In this setting, even simple modal derivations can be non-trivial:[206]

Example (Löb's axiom implies $K4$). The following elegant proof was found by Dick de Jongh in the 1970s. Substitute the formula $\Box\varphi \wedge \varphi$ for φ in Löb's Axiom $\Box(\Box\varphi \to \varphi) \to \Box\varphi$. This yields the theorem:

$$\Box(\Box(\Box\varphi \wedge \varphi) \to (\Box\varphi \wedge \varphi)) \to \Box(\Box\varphi \wedge \varphi)$$

Now note that the following principle is derivable in K alone:

$$\Box\varphi \to \Box(\Box(\Box\varphi \wedge \varphi) \to (\Box\varphi \wedge \varphi))$$

Therefore, again in the minimal modal logic K, we can prove

$$\Box\varphi \to \Box(\Box\varphi \wedge \varphi)$$

and from this, still in the minimal modal logic K, we get

$$\Box\varphi \to \Box\Box\varphi \qquad \text{[207]}$$

We elaborate a bit, to show modal logic at work in this new setting. Gödel's famous arithmetical Liar Sentence φ now has this modal form:

$$\varphi \leftrightarrow \neg\Box\varphi \quad \text{says "I am not provable"}$$

The top-level pieces of Gödel's proof can then be clarified as follows:

Theorem 47. If $\vdash \varphi \leftrightarrow \neg\Box\varphi$, then $\vdash \neg\Box\bot \to \neg\Box\varphi$.

---

[206] A publishable formal first-order proof was the derivation of the *Russell Paradox*.
[207] The student may find it worthwhile to write out a complete formal derivation.

This simple modal notation expresses a deep foundational fact: the liar sentence cannot be proved if no contradiction is provable. In other words, we have the gist[208] of the First Incompleteness Theorem: *if arithmetic is consistent, it cannot prove Gödel's liar sentence.*

Proof. This is a basic modal deduction using only principles from $K4$:

1) $\varphi \leftrightarrow \neg\Box\varphi$ (assumption)
2) $\Box\varphi \to \neg\varphi$ (from 1, by propositional logic)
3) $\Box\varphi \to \Box\neg\varphi$ (from 2, by Necessitation, Distribution, and $K4$)
4) $\Box\varphi \to \Box\varphi \wedge \neg\varphi$ (from 3, in the minimal K)
5) $\Box\varphi \to \Box\bot$
6) $\neg\Box\bot \to \neg\Box\varphi$

$\square$

The origins of Löb's Axiom lie in the Paradox of the Truth Teller:

"what I am saying right now is true".

No truth value seems applicable for this cousin of the Liar. The arithmetical version is a formula φ stating its own provability. Is φ right or wrong? Here is the answer for Peano Arithmetic:

Theorem 48 (Löb's Theorem). If $\vdash \Box\varphi \to \varphi$, then $\vdash \varphi$.

Proof. Using Gödel's "diagonalization technique",[209] create an arithmetical sentence σ with the following intriguing self-referential property ("my own provability implies φ"):

$$\vdash \sigma \leftrightarrow (\Box\sigma \to \varphi)$$

Now comes a "magical" piece of modal reasoning that has delighted generations. Put in reasons for each step by yourself!

1) $\sigma \to (\Box\sigma \to \varphi)$
2) $\Box\sigma \to \Box(\Box\sigma \to \varphi)$
3) $\Box\sigma \to (\Box\Box\sigma \to \Box\varphi)$
4) $\Box\sigma \to \Box\Box\sigma$
5) $\Box\sigma \to \Box\varphi$
6) $\Box\sigma \to \varphi$ using that $\vdash \Box\varphi \to \varphi$!
7) $(\Box\sigma \to \varphi) \to \sigma$
8) σ
9) $\Box\sigma$
10) φ

$\square$

---

[208] Caveat: there is much more depth to Gödel's complete argument!

[209] An accessible modern exposition of these ideas is P. Smith, 2007, *An Introduction to Gödel's Theorems*, Cambridge University Press, Cambridge.

Löb's Axiom is just the formalized form of Löb's Theorem.

21.3 Semantic analysis and completeness

Recall a statement from Chapter 9 about the models for GL:

Theorem 49. $F \models \Box(\Box p \to p) \to \Box p$ iff (1) R is transitive, and (2) R is *reversely well-founded*, i.e., there are no chains $x_1 R x_2 R x_3 R \cdots$.

Proof. First, we show that Löb's Axiom implies transitivity. Let Rsx and Rxy, but not Rsy. Setting $V(p) = W - \{x, y\}$ makes Löb's Axiom false at s. Next, let (1) hold. If (2) fails, then there is an ascending sequence $s = s_0 R s_1 R s_2 \cdots$ – and setting $V(p) = W - \{s_0, s_1, s_2, ...\}$ refutes Löb's Axiom at s. Conversely, if Löb's Axiom fails at s, there must be an infinite upward sequence of $\neg p$-worlds. This arises by taking any successor of s where p fails, and repeatedly applying the truth of $\Box(\Box p \to p)$ – using the transitivity of the frame. □

The transitivity clause (1) is surprising, as the $K4$-axiom had originally been postulated separately in provability logic – but we saw a modal derivation just above. Also, one can see that Löb's Axiom in its second-order translation is close to well-foundedness. This correspondence analysis suggests a completeness result:

Theorem 50. The theorems of Löb's Logic are precisely the modal formulas that are valid in all transitive reverse well-founded orderings.

And by a Henkin-style argument over finite sets of formulas:

Theorem 51. Löb's Logic has precisely the modal formulas valid in all *finite trees*, with accessibility the dominance relation.

The same method shows validity in provability logic to be *decidable*.

This semantics is formal. The intended use is the arithmetical interpretation, where proposition letters range over formulas in the first-order arithmetic of the natural numbers with zero 0, successor S, addition $+$, and multiplication $\times$. The modal operator then refers to the arithmetized *provability predicate* in Peano Arithmetic:

$$\Box\varphi = \exists y Proof_{PA}(y, \#(\varphi)), \text{ with } \#(\varphi) \text{ the Gödel code of } \varphi.$$

In 1975, Solovay proved that Löb's Logic is *arithmetically complete*. The above axioms derive every valid modal principle of provability in Peano Arithmetic. Please contrast this with Gödel's Incompleteness Theorem: we cannot axiomatize all of arithmetic, but we can axiomatize significant parts of its meta-theory.

21.4 Further theory: the fixed-point theorem

The attraction of this system is again a balance: a poor but perspicuous modal language captures key phenomena in arithmetic. A celebrated result (due to de Jongh and Sambin) is a modal version of the arithmetical Fixed-Point Lemma underlying the proof of Gödel's Theorem:

Theorem 52. Consider any modal formula $\varphi(p, q)$ in which the proposition letter p only occurs in the scope of a modality, with q a sequence of other proposition letters.[210] There exists a formula $\psi(q)$ such that $\psi(q) \leftrightarrow \varphi(\psi(q), q)$ is provable in Löb's Logic, and also, any two solutions to this fixed-point equation w.r.t. φ are provably equivalent.

There is also a simple algorithm for computing the fixed-point $\psi(q)$.

Example (Solving fixed-point equations in provability logic.). Here are a few typical cases, which explain some of our earlier illustrations:

$$\begin{array}{ll}
\text{Equation:} \quad p \leftrightarrow \Box p & \qquad \text{Solution:} \quad p = \top \\
\qquad\qquad\quad p \leftrightarrow \neg \Box p & \qquad\qquad\qquad p = \neg \Box \bot \\
\qquad\qquad\quad p \leftrightarrow \Box p \to q & \qquad\qquad\qquad p = \Box q \to q
\end{array}$$

More complex recursions work when the body $\varphi(p, q)$ has multiple occurrences of p. There are also algorithms that solve simultaneous recursions with tuples of proposition letters p.

Excursion: analysis and extensions Two noteworthy aspects of the preceding result are (a) existence and uniqueness of the new predicate p, and (b) its explicit definability in the modal base language. The first is a general property of all recursive definitions over well-founded orderings. But we also get the concrete information that this recursive predicate can be defined inside the original modal language. A general reason for this beautiful fact seems to be unknown. We do know that it also happens elsewhere:

Theorem 53. Explicit definability for fixed-point equations with all occurrences of p under some operator holds for all propositional languages with "generalized quantifiers" Qp over sets of worlds satisfying

(a) $Q(P)$ is true at x iff $Q(P \cap R_x)$ is true at x [211]   Locality
(b) $Qp \to \Box Qp$ Heredity

This covers quantifiers Q like modal "in some successor", but also first-order "in at most five successors", or even second-order quantifiers like "in most successors of each successor".

---

[210] For instance, what is allowed is $q \vee \Box p$ or $q \vee \Box \neg p$, but not, say, p, $\neg p$, or $q \vee p$.
[211] Here R_x is the set $\{y \mid Rxy\}$ of all worlds in M that are accessible from x.

We will compare provability logic with other fixed-point languages in Chapter 22 on the modal "μ-calculus". To end here, we link up with fixed-point extensions of classical logic.

21.5 Coda: correspondence moves to fixed-point logic

This digression can be skipped if you had enough provability logic.

Löb's Axiom is beyond the Sahlqvist Theorem of Chapter 9, as its antecedent has a modal box over an implication. But the Löb frame-equivalent of transitivity plus well-foundedness is definable in a natural extension of first-order logic – viz. *LFP(FO): first-order logic with fixed-point operators*. Here is a brief explanation.

The antecedent $\Box(\Box p \to p)$ of Löb's Axiom still allows for the minimal valuation step in the substitution algorithm. For, if this modal formula holds anywhere in a model M, x, then there must be a smallest predicate P for p making it true at M, x – because of the following set-theoretic property guaranteeing a minimal verifying predicate:

Fact. If $\Box(\Box p_i \to p_i)$ holds at world x for all $i \in I$, then, with $[\![p_i]\!]$ the set of worlds with p_i in M, $\Box(\Box P \to P)$ holds at x for $P = \bigcap_{i \in I} [\![p_i]\!]$.

Here is the more general notion behind this observation:

Definition 21.5.1 (Intersection Property). A formula $\varphi(P, \boldsymbol{Q})$ has the *intersection property* if $\varphi(P, \boldsymbol{Q})$ holds in a model M for all predicates P in $\{P_i \mid i \in I\}$, we also have $M, \cap P_i \models \varphi(P, \boldsymbol{Q})$.[212]

The Löb antecedent displays a syntactical format that ensures this:

Definition 21.5.2 (*PIA* format). A first-order formula is called a *PIA condition* ("positive antecedent implies atom") if it has the form $\forall x(\varphi(P, \boldsymbol{Q}, x) \to Px)$, with P occurring only positively in $\varphi(P, \boldsymbol{Q}, x)$.

The Löb antecedent has the first-order *PIA* form

$$\forall y((Rxy \land \forall z(Ryz \to Pz)) \to Py).$$

It is easy to see that this format implies the Intersection Property. Moreover, we have this syntactic observation:

Fact. Minimal predicates for *PIA*-conditions are definable in *LFP(FO)*.

Example (Computing a minimal valuation for Löb's Axiom). Analyzing $\Box(\Box p \to p)$ closely, the minimal predicate satisfying it at a world x describes exactly the following set of worlds: $\{y \mid \forall z(Ryz \to Rxz)$ and no infinite sequence of R-successors starts from $y\}$. Substi-

---

[212]The formula $\varphi(P, \boldsymbol{Q})$ holds for a predicate P in $\{P_i \mid i \in I\}$ if $M \models \varphi(P, \boldsymbol{Q})$ when we interpret the predicate letter P as the predicate P.

tuting this description in the Löb consequent $\Box p$ yields precisely the earlier-mentioned frame condition.

Thus we can generalize the correspondence results in Chapter 9:

Theorem 54. Modal axioms with *PIA* antecedents and syntactically positive consequents define frame conditions in *LFP(FO)*.

Not all modal axioms yield: it can be shown that the McKinsey Axiom $\Box\Diamond\varphi \rightarrow \Diamond\Box\varphi$ still has no frame-equivalent in *LFP(FO)*. There is more theory behind these observations, but the main point here is again that provability logic naturally connects with fixed-points.[213]

21.6 Conclusion

Provability logic is a beautiful theory where modal logic blends with arithmetical facts. There are elegant publications by Boolos and others unfolding much more of this rich theory, and in particular, one exciting new development are "logics of proofs" or justifications where modal boxes now come with explicit proof terms.[214]

---

[213]It has been proved recently that modal provability logic and the modal μ-calculus of Chapter 22 are very close under mutual translations, a surprising unification of the area of modal logic with added recursive definitions.

[214]For details on this system, classical provability logic, as well as many other subjects, cf. Artemov's Chapter on *"Modal Logic and Mathematics"* in the *Handbook of Modal Logic* (Artemov, 2008).

Exercises Chapter 21

1. Correspondence for provability principles:
   (a) Analyse the following Löb variant semantically:

   $$\Box(\Box\varphi \leftrightarrow \varphi) \rightarrow \Box\varphi.$$

   What corresponding frame property do you find?
   (b) Also find a correspondent for this generalized variant:

   $$[a]([b]p \leftrightarrow p) \rightarrow [c]p.$$

2. Try a Henkin-style argument like in Chapter 5 to establish completeness of the Gödel-Löb logic. How can you keep things finite to get decidability?

3. (Cf. Chapter 22 for relevant notions.) Show how the Gödel-Löb logic can be faithfully translated into the modal μ-calculus.

Part IV

Recent Theoretical Themes

Theory and applications often go together, though perhaps with a phase difference. Modal logics were developed in the 1950s and 1960s for the analysis of philosophical, linguistic and mathematical notions, and the 1970s saw a first wave of mathematical theory about the resulting systems. We have seen some major themes from this phase in Parts I and II. Then in Part III, we looked at a broad spectrum of recent developments, including applications to information, computation, and agency, as well as new studies of perennial mathematical structures like time, space, and proof. Both ways, modal logic now also extends into computer science, artificial intelligence, and even economics. But this phase, too, raises its theoretical issues, that play across fields, and provide new unity to the expanding universe of the field. In this final part, we will look at some theoretical issues that have been prominent since the 1990s, giving the student a glimpse of threads that run across the current diverse area. While some people see the unity of modal logic in maintaining some vast Platonic Museum of formal systems, I see major issues and styles of answers as truly keeping a field together.

This part is even less of a textbook than Part III – but the interested reader may at least get a sense of what lies behind the material presented in the mainstream of this course.

22

Fixed-points, computation, and equilibrium

Computation has been a major theme throughout these lectures – but the best logical take on it is still a matter of study. Some people think that Recursion Theory, starting from the 1930s provides all the answers, but that approach mixes two things: computational *process structure*, and the coding power of one particular *data structure*, viz. the natural numbers. Thus, major results in Recursion Theory are an entangled mixture of both influences. But then, in the 1970s, people started separating the former from the latter in *fixed-point logics* of computation, working over arbitrary data structures. These provide abstract accounts of program or process structure, including the crucial notions of iteration and recursion. Now, adding operators for fixed-points to first-order logic yields an intriguing but highly complex system *LFP(FO)*, where one can define the natural numbers up to isomorphism after all. One surprising discovery around 1975 was the propositional *dynamic logic PDL* of Chapter 14 that showed how modal theories of computation can be both illuminating and decidable. Later on, even stronger modal fixed-point logics were discovered, in particular, the *modal μ-calculus* that will also be discussed briefly in this chapter. These fields picked up much interest around 1980, but were then gradually abandoned in favour of systems hat could deal with *parallel computation*, still the reality of modern computing. Still, today, they are being revived for their intriguing mathematical structure, and the insights that this holds for at least the foundations of sequential computation.[215]

---

[215]More could be said about modal logic and concurrency, including links with Process Algebra, but we must set a limit somewhere.

22.1 Recursion and fixed-points

Many natural notions have "circular definitions", such as the transitive closure of a relation:

$$\underline{tc}(R)(x, y) \;\leftrightarrow\; (Rxy \vee \exists z(Rxz \wedge \underline{tc}(R)(z, y))).$$

Which predicate is defined here? One concrete intuitive reading is this: if R stands for the "parent" relation, then $\underline{tc}(R)$ stands for the family relation of "ancestor". More abstractly, starting from the empty relation ("false") as an initial approximation, the given schema can be used to produce, step by step, the following *approximation sequence*:

$$R, \qquad R \cup (R; R), \qquad R \cup (R; R) \cup (R; R; R) \cup \cdots$$

and in the countable limit, the usual definition of the transitive closure of R, as reachability via a finite sequence of R-steps, as used for instance in the dynamic logic of Chapter 14.

This recursive format will not always work. Unacceptable circular definitions exist, too – but they tend to involve negations, such as the following post-modern family relation:

$$Parent^{\#}\ xy \;\leftrightarrow\; Parent\ xy \vee \neg Parent^{\#}\ xy$$

Its approximation sequence, starting from *False*, oscillates between the two predicates $Parent^{\#}\ xy$ and *True*.[216]

Still, recursive definitions occur widely in mathematics, computer science, and linguistics – but also in our agency-related Chapters 12 through 17. Transitive closure was essential to propositional dynamic logic, which described iterated structures in actions, but also in information structure, where common knowledge was an "equilibrium notion" defined by the recursion

$$C_G \varphi \;\leftrightarrow\; \varphi \wedge E_G C_G \varphi$$

More general equilibrium conditions on strategies for players underlie the solution concepts of game theory. Indeed, the provability logic of Chapter 21 involved "cracking" definitions of this sort. All these notions call for logical systems that can capture the essentials in a perspicuous manner, and allow us to reason about, and with recursive definitions.

The underlying mathematical theory studies "fixed-points" for functions on sets of objects P, as the current value for some predicate p,[217] and computing, for some given description φ, the *next approximation* as

---

[216] The Liar Sentence "The statement I am now making is not true" is a more famous example where negation inside a circular definition wreaks havoc.

[217] Think of how, generally, modal proposition letters denote sets of worlds.

the set of states satisfying $\varphi(P)$. This works under general conditions, described by the Tarski-Knaster Theorem, a result about *monotone operators* F on partial orders $\leq$ satisfying

$$x \leq y \rightarrow F(x) \leq F(y).$$

Theorem 55. On complete partial orders $\leq$ (where all suprema and infima exist), monotone operators always have *fixed-points* x where $F(x) = x$. There is even always a *smallest* and a *greatest* fixed-point in the order $\leq$, that need not coincide.[218]

Here is a modal logic extending our basic system with a systematic format for recursive definitions via fixed-point operators:

22.2 Modal μ-calculus

The language includes the basic modal syntax, but it adds one operator

$$\mu p \cdot \varphi(p) \quad \text{provided that } p \text{ occurs only positively in } \varphi.$$

Here *positive occurrence* is defined in the style of Chapter 9, say as being inside an even number of negations, since negation is the only "polarity-switcher" among $\wedge, \vee, \Box, \Diamond, \mu p \cdot$. Here the μ-operator stands for a *smallest fixed-point* in the following semantic sense:

Definition 22.2.1 (Fixed-point semantics). In any model M, the formula $\varphi(p)$ defines an inclusion-monotone set transformation

$$F_\varphi(X) = \{\, s \in W \mid (M, p := X), s \models \varphi \,\}$$

By the Tarski-Knaster Theorem, the operation F_φ must have a smallest fixed-point on the power set of the domain W. Now $M, w \models \mu p \cdot \varphi(p)$ iff world w belongs to the latter set.

Here is a simple auxiliary semantic result behind the syntax restriction. If a formula $\varphi(p)$ in our language has only positive occurrences of the proposition letter p, then it is semantically monotone in p:

If $M, s \models \varphi(p)$, and $V(p) \subseteq Q$, then $(M, p := Q), s \models \varphi(p)$, with $(M, p := Q)$ the model M with the value of p reset to Q.

This smallest fixed-point can be reached bottom-up by an ordinal sequence of approximation stages

$$\varphi^0, \dots \varphi^\alpha, \varphi^{\alpha+1}, \dots, \varphi^\lambda, \dots$$

with $\varphi^0 = \emptyset$, $\varphi^{\alpha+1} = F_\varphi(\varphi^\alpha)$, and $\varphi^\lambda = \bigcup_{\alpha < \lambda} \varphi^\alpha$.

The smallest fixed-point formula $\mu p \cdot \varphi(p)$ denotes the first stage where $\varphi^\alpha = \varphi^{\alpha+1}$. Likewise, we can define a formula $\nu p \cdot \varphi(p)$ for the

---

[218]The smallest fixed-point is in fact the *infimum* of the set $\{x \mid F(x) \leq x\}$.

greatest fixed point of the operator F_φ, starting from the whole domain of M as its first approximation, and going downward to smaller sets. Both fixed-points exist by the Tarski-Knaster theorem. Indeed, one can see that the following definability holds between them:

Fact. $\nu p \cdot \varphi(p) = \neg \mu p \cdot \neg \varphi(\neg p)$.

Try to prove this for yourself.[219] We can use this fact as a definition of $\nu p \cdot \varphi(p)$. In general, smallest and greatest fixed-points need not coincide in a model, and others may be in between.

This system generalizes propositional dynamic logic (cf. Chapter 14).

Example (Transitive closure and dynamic logic). "Some φ-world is reachable in finitely many R_a-steps" is $\langle a^* \rangle \varphi = \mu p \cdot (\varphi \vee \langle a \rangle p)$.

But other fixed-point formulas define notions beyond *PDL*:

Example (Well-foundedness). $\mu p \cdot \Box p$ defines "the well-founded part" of the accessibility relation for $\Box$ in any modal model: that is, the set of points from where no infinite ascending R-sequence starts.[220]

Greatest fixed-point operators define still further notions:

Example (Infinity). In any model, $\nu p \cdot \Diamond p$ defines the set of points where some infinite sequence starts.

This is sometimes described negatively as "non-termination", but it is also the set of states from where our process never breaks down. Computer science is long past the traditional bias from recursion theory toward finitely terminating programs, since some crucial programs on your computer, like its operating system, are meant not to terminate. The μ-calculus can describe termination via μ-operators, but it can also describe infinite process behaviour such as "safety" or "fairness" by ν-operators. This feature is in line with the branching temporal logics of Chapter 18, that typically allow for infinite histories for general processes and games.

Formulas with stacked fixed-point operators, allowed by our syntax, express much more complex process behaviour.

Major properties of this system keep it "modal" and attractive:

Theorem 56. μ-calculus formulas are invariant for bisimulation.

Theorem 57. The μ-calculus is decidable.

---

[219]You may be surprised to see that three negations occur instead of two. But note at least that this feature gets the positive occurrence right in the μ-formula.

[220]It is illuminating to trace the approximation sequence for $\mu p \cdot \Box p$ in the ordinal model $\omega + \omega$ (two copies of $\mathbb{N}$ in a row) with the relation "greater than" downward.

Theorem 58. The μ-calculus validities are effectively axiomatized by two simple proof rules on top of the minimal logic K:

(i) $\mu p \cdot \varphi(p) \leftrightarrow \varphi(\mu p \cdot \varphi(p))$ *Fixed-Point Axiom*

(ii)   if $\vdash \varphi(\alpha) \rightarrow \alpha$, then $\vdash \mu p \cdot \varphi(p) \rightarrow \alpha$ *Closure Rule*

The Closure Rule tells us that we really have a smallest fixed-point.

22.3   A few further topics

Generalizing earlier themes All of our earlier basic theory in Parts I and II still makes sense in this extended framework. For instance, concerning its model theory, there is a celebrated result by Janin & Walukiewicz extending the modal Invariance Theorem of Chapter 7:

Theorem 59. The language of the μ-calculus consists precisely of the bisimulation-invariant formulas of the system *MSOL*: *monadic second-order logic* over binary orderings.

The proof of this result involves methods from Automata Theory, and indeed, the modern theory of the μ-calculus involves *automata* and *games*, far beyond classical modal logic. These methods are so powerful that they sometimes yield improved versions of classical results. For instance, a famous result by Lyndon says that, in first-order logic,

A formula $\varphi(P)$ is semantically monotone with respect to a predicate P (in the above-defined sense) iff $\varphi(P)$ is logically equivalent to a formula all of whose occurrences of P are positive.

But the latter definition cannot always be found effectively: and it is even undecidable whether a first-order formula is monotone with respect to a given P. By contrast, in the μ-calculus, we have a stronger uniform Lyndon theorem: the positive equivalent can be found effectively using a transformation on associated automata.

In this setting, bisimulation invariance implies that, like the basic modal logic (Chapter 2), the μ-calculus is insensitive to the difference between general models and unraveled *tree models*. This tree-oriented character explains many of its features, including the decidability.

Next, with frame correspondences, we can extend our theory of Chapter 9 to systematically determine properties corresponding to modal axioms stated using fixed-point operators.

Example (A Löb variant). $\square^*(\square p \rightarrow p) \rightarrow \square^* p$ defines upward well-foundedness of R, without transitivity.[221]

---

[221] Here, if $\square$ is the modality $[R]$, $\square^*$ is the corresponding one for $[R^*]$.

Example (Term rewriting). The formula $\Diamond\Box^*p \to \Box\Diamond^*p$ expresses Weak Confluence: points diverging from a common root still have a common successor in the transitive closure of the relation.[222]

Connections to provability logic The new system subsumes the provability logic of Chapter 21:

Theorem 60. Löb's Logic is axiomatized by the two principles

$$\text{(a) } \Box p \to \Box\Box p, \qquad \text{(b) } \mu p \cdot \Box p$$

Proof. We do this as a practical combinatorial exercise in working with these systems. From Löb's Logic to (a) was a purely modal deduction. Next, (b) is derived as follows. By the fixed-point axiom of the μ-calculus, we have $\Box\mu p \cdot \Box p \to \mu p \cdot \Box p$. So it suffices to get $\Box\mu p \cdot \Box p$. Now Löb's Axiom implies:

$$\Box(\Box\mu p \cdot \Box p \to \mu p \cdot \Box p) \to \Box\mu p \cdot \Box p$$

and the antecedent of this is derivable by modal Necessitation from the converse direction of the μ-calculus fixed-point axiom.

Next, assume (a) and (b). We show that, in the modal logic $K4$,

$$\mu p \cdot \Box p \to (\Box(\Box p \to p) \to \Box p).$$

The proof rule for smallest fixed-points gives $\mu p \cdot \Box p \to \alpha$ for any formula α if $\Box\alpha \to \alpha$ can be proved. Now us this law of $K4$ (try!):

$$\Box(\Box(\Box q \to q) \to \Box q) \to (\Box(\Box q \to q) \to \Box q)$$

$\Box$

One can recast this link between provability and fixed-point logics:

Theorem 61. Löb's Logic faithfully embeds into the μ-calculus.

The converse is more tricky. Albert Visser has shown recently that there is an effective translation from the μ-calculus into provability logic, though not a faithful one. This leaves open an option of merging the two major approaches to fixed points in the modal literature.

22.4 Further languages

Beyond computation Patterns like the above also occur in logics of information, such as epistemic logic. In Chapter 12, we saw that common knowledge in groups of agents G had a typical equilibrium character, and indeed, it can be defined by a greatest fixed-point:

$$C_G\varphi \leftrightarrow \nu p \cdot (\varphi \wedge E_G p)$$

---

[222]Basic laws of term rewriting are implications between modal properties.

where E_G ("everybody knows") is the conjunction of all single-agent knowledge operators. In Chapter 23, we will see more of these connections with dynamic logics of information.

Fragments While the μ-calculus is modal, it makes sense to look at better fragments. *Propositional dynamic logic* was one. Here is another:

Definition 22.4.1 (Continuous fragment). The $\omega - \mu$-calculus only allows fixed-point operators in the following existential format:

$$\mu p \cdot \varphi(p) \quad \text{with } \varphi \text{ constructed according to the syntax rule}$$
$$p \mid \text{all } p\text{-free formulas} \mid \wedge \mid \vee \mid \Diamond \mid \mu {}^{223}$$

This syntax guarantees that smallest fixed-points are always reached, in any model, in at most ω approximation steps. A typical example is the transitive closure of a binary relation. This "uniformity" fits well with examples from practice. Its mathematical core is called *Scott Continuity*: the approximation map F_φ for formulas φ from this fragment has the following property:

For all worlds w and sets X,
$w \in F_\varphi(X)$ iff $w \in F_\varphi(X_0)$ for some *finite* $X_0 \subseteq X$.[224]

PDL is a still weaker fragment inside the $\omega - \mu$-calculus where the recursion formula may not even use conjunctions $\wedge$.

Second-order extensions But there are also extensions. In particular, the μ-calculus is related to the much stronger system *SOML* of modal logic with second-order *quantifiers over proposition letters*. μ-calculus formulas are definable in *SOML* plus a *PDL*-style iteration modality $\Box^*$ for transitive closure.

LFP(FO) But the most obvious comparison is the earlier-mentioned logic *LFP(FO)* that extends first-order logic with smallest and greatest fixed-point operators over formulas $\varphi(P)$ with positive occurrences of the relevant predicates P, now of any arity. Its syntax is an obvious generalization of that for the μ-calculus. This natural extension of first-order logic loses Compactness and Completeness. As we said, one can easily define the standard natural numbers up to isomorphism, so the valid formulas of *LFP(FO)* include True Arithmetic, and even form a highly complex Π_1-complete set (cf. Chapters 10, 24).[225] Semantically, this system is not very well-understood, though we know that its formulas are invariant for potential isomorphism (cf. Chapter

---

[223]We omit a technicality in the precise syntax of the continuous fragment.
[224]A semantic characterization theorem was proved recently by Gaëlle Fontaine.
[225]Such logics have the complexity of *second-order arithmetic* with quantifiers over sets of natural numbers, an incredibly strong system encoding much of Analysis.

7 and the Appendix on first-order logic), and *LFP(FO)* also satisfies a downward Löwenheim-Skolem Theorem. We used this system already as a frame-correspondence language for Löb's Axiom in Chapter 21.

The interesting point here in a modal perspective is how adding fixed-points explodes the complexity of expressive power and validity on top of first-order logic, but not on top of the weaker language of modal logic. And this phenomenon extends to other modal-like fragments of first-order logic. For instance, the system *LFP(GF)* of the Guarded Fragment (Chapter 7) with fixed-point operators is still decidable. Thus, going the "modal way": weakening classical logic often gives a more solid ground for then adding features that would be harmful in general. This seems a nice mystery to conclude this chapter with.

Exercises Chapter 22

1. Explain the meaning of the μ-calculus formula $\mu p \cdot \Box p$ in some detail. Show how the approximation sequence for this smallest fixed-point can take up to any ordinal length, in arbitrary models.

2. Show the soundness of the proof system for the μ-operator.

3. Define the operator $[\pi]\varphi$ of *PDL* as a greatest fixed point.

4. Prove that all formulas of the μ-calculus are invariant for bisimulation. One way you can do this is by translation into infinitary modal logic: a separate exercise in itself.

5. Derive the *induction axiom* of propositional dynamic logic:

$$\Box\varphi \wedge [^*](\varphi \rightarrow \Box\varphi) \rightarrow [^*]\varphi$$

from Löb's Axiom and appropriate Fixed-Point Axiom here: $[^*]\varphi \leftrightarrow (\Box\varphi \wedge \Box[^*]\varphi)$

6. Discuss the following non-analogy between *PDL* and the μ-calculus: the former has explicit programs telling us how to reach certain points. What would be a way of adding programs to the μ-calculus after all – where would that make sense?

7. The *inflationary μ-calculus* allows for arbitrary approximation maps without any monotonicity or positive occurrence conditions on $\mu p \cdot \varphi(p)$. We just define the approximation map using an *union*: $F_\varphi(X) = \{ s \in W \mid (M, p := X), s \models \varphi \} \cup X$. Prove that smallest fixed-points always exist for any such operator.

8. Prove that the μ-calculus is closed under taking simultaneous fixed-points (how do you define these; why do they exist?).

9. Prove that De Jongh-Sambin fixed-points (Chapter 21) can be defined in the μ-calculus by the following simultaneous inflationary inductive definition: $r \leftrightarrow \Box r$, $p \leftrightarrow \Box r \wedge \varphi(p, q)$.

23

Issues in information dynamics

The public announcements $!P$ in Chapter 15 were simple events, but real information flow is much more complex. In real life, agents need not get the same information out of events that they witness. When I take a new card from the stack in a game, I see the one I get, but you do not. When I overhear what you tell your friend, you may not notice that I do. At the website of your bank, you have an encrypted private conversation that as few people as possible should learn about. The most enjoyable games are all about different information for different players. In all these cases, modeling the dynamics poses a challenge, and simple elimination of worlds is definitely not the right mechanism.

This chapter gives an introduction to a significant extension of PAL that deals with partially private information, and its broader temporal setting in the branching perspective of Chapter 18.

23.1 Multi-agent information flow

We start with a simple scenario of information flow of a private nature:

Example (Two envelopes).

> We have each drawn a closed envelope. It is common knowledge that one holds an invitation to a lecture on logic, the other to a wild night out. We are both ignorant of the fate in store for us. Now I open my envelope, and read the contents, without showing them to you. Yours remains closed. Which information has passed because of my action? I know now which fate is in store for me. But you have also learnt something, viz. that I know – though not what I know. Likewise, I did not just learn what is in my envelope. I also learnt something about you, viz. that you know that I know. The latter fact has even become common knowledge between us. And this may not even be all.

What general principle lies behind this scenario? Intuitively, we need to eliminate links now instead of worlds. The initial information state has collective ignorance, the update removes my uncertainty link – but both worlds are still needed to model your ignorance:

In the resulting model, all observations from our story come out right.

This kind of update occurs in many games, and the system to be presented in this chapter has been used to completely analyze the parlour game of Clue. Here is another phenomenon all around us:

Example (*CC* and *BCC* in email). Sending an email with a *CC* is like a public announcement. But what if you send one with *BCC*? Now some people receive the message, while others do not realize that. Scenarios like this go beyond link cutting, as they may *add new worlds*. Here is a simplest case. Initially, we are both ignorant whether *P* is true. An initial model again looks as follows:

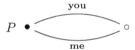

Now you hear a public announcement that *P*, but you are not sure if I heard it. Then we need two things: a copy of the model where you think nothing happened, and an "update copy" for the information that I received. This requires at least 3 worlds, and we need a new update mechanism that can increase the number of worlds.

These phenomena pose real challenges. It is not easy to write the right epistemic models by hand, and the usual "art of modeling" has to become more of a science. And this is not just "information engineering", since maintaining different information for different agents is the reality of social organization, and perhaps even civilization.

23.2   Event models and product update

Here is the red thread through the above examples: agents learn from events to which they may have different access. This idea was turned into logic by a group of young researchers over the last 10 years, cf. the recent textbook by van Ditmarsch, van der Hoek & Kooi (van Ditmarsch et al., 2007)[226] For a start, the epistemic models of Chapter

---

[226] An up-to-date survey is the chapter "Epistemic Logic and Information Update" by Baltag, van Ditmarsch & Moss (Baltag et al., 2008) in the *Handbook of the Philosophy of Information* (Adriaans and van Benthem (2008)).

12 have a natural companion, when we look at the events involved in scenarios of communication or interaction:

Definition 23.2.1 (Event models). An *epistemic event model* $E = (E, \{\sim_i\}_{i \in G}, \{Pre_f\}_{f \in E}, e)$ has a set of events E, epistemic uncertainty relations $\sim_i$ for each agent,[227] a map assigning *preconditions* Pre_f to events f, stating when these are executable, and an *actual event e*.

Here agents' uncertainty relations encode which events they cannot distinguish in the relevant scenario, because of their observational limitations. When I open my envelope, you know it must be either Lecture or Night-Out, but you cannot distinguish the two events "my reading L", "my reading N". Hence both are in the event model, though not other events that we can all distinguish from these two, such as Mount Etna erupting. Next, an event model has no valuation, but events come with *preconditions* for their occurrence. A public announcement $!P$ has truth of P for its precondition, reading Night-Out has the precondition that this card is in fact in my envelope, my asking a genuine question meant I did not know the answer. Most events carry information about when and where they occur. That is precisely why they are informative!

The following mechanism describes how new worlds after update with an event model (i.e., one step of observation in an epistemic scenario) are pairs of old worlds with an event that has taken place:

Definition 23.2.2 (Product update). For any epistemic model (M, s) and event model (E, e), the *product model* $(M \times E, (s, e))$ is an epistemic model with the following main components. Its domain is the set $\{(s, e) \mid s$ a world in M, e an event in E, $M, s \models Pre_e\}$ and its accessibility relations satisfy the rule

$$(s, e) \sim_i (t, f) \quad \text{iff} \quad \text{both } s \sim_i t \text{ and } e \sim_i f.$$

The valuation for atoms p at (s, e) is the same as that at s in M.[228]

$M \times E$ is a product of the epistemic model M and the event model E, and this explains its possible growth in size. But some pairs are eliminated by the preconditions, and this makes information flow. Next, the *product rule* for epistemic accessibility has the following motivation: we cannot distinguish two new worlds if we could not distinguish them before, and the new events do not distinguish them either.

Even so, the definition is incomplete: *what language did the preconditions come from?* For simplicity, we assume here they are from our

---

[227]The $\sim_i$ are often equivalence relations – but using directed accessibility one can even model more complex "mistaken beliefs".

[228]There are also versions with real world change: van Benthem et al. (2006). Beyond preconditions, these also stipulate post-conditions on effects of events.

epistemic base language, by atomic propositions ("I have the red card") or epistemic ones ("I think you may know whether P"). The intuitive understanding in our update mechanism is that the preconditions are common knowledge in the group.

This mechanism can model a wide range of phenomena:

Example (Public announcement). The event model for a public announcement $!P$ has just one event with precondition P, and reflexive accessibility arrows for all agents. The product model $\boldsymbol{M} \times \boldsymbol{E}$ then just retains the pairs $(w, !P)$ with $\boldsymbol{M}, w \models P$, thus producing an isomorphic copy of our earlier PAL-style model $\boldsymbol{M}|P$.

Example (The two envelopes). Our initial epistemic model was like this ("L" is my having the lecture, "N" the NightOut):

You could not distinguish between the two events of my reading "Lecture" and my reading "NightOut" – and this shows in the following event model, where the black event is actual:

We also assume all reflexive arrows for both agents. The resulting product model $\boldsymbol{M} \times \boldsymbol{E}$ looks like this. Of the 4 possible pairs, 2 drop out by the preconditions, but this time, we do not just copy the original model, but perform link-cutting, yielding the intended outcome:

Example (The doubtful signal). Here is how model size can increase. Consider our ubiquitous earlier model

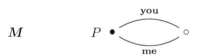

Now take an event model for the earlier scenario where I hear $!P$, while perhaps you merely experienced an identity event Id:

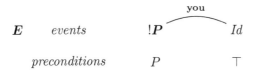

$$E \qquad events \qquad !P \qquad Id$$

$$preconditions \qquad P \qquad \top$$

This time, the product model $M \times E$ has 3 worlds, arranged as follows:

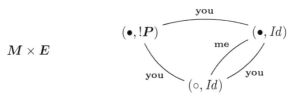

This clearly satisfies our intuitive expectations described earlier.

Product models for realistic scenarios can increase size considerably. Successive uses of BCC in emails (a device that can be modeled here) may explode the initial model, as we all know when trying to keep track of who is supposed to know what. Parlour games like "Clue" start with simple models, evolve to complex models in mid-play where players know very different things, and only get simpler again in the end game. In this practical setting, computer programs have been developed that perform product update and related symbolic calculations.

23.3   Exploring the mechanism further

There is more to this system than meets the eye, and here is some:

Under-informed versus misinformed When you buy a board game, its rules on the cover may make things complicated, but they will not mislead you. Likewise, using BCC in an email system need not mislead recipients, provided they are aware that it is an available move. Indeed, product update helps classify various kinds of "public ignorance". For instance, public resolution of a known question does not increase domain size, but cuts links. But a *secret* observation of a card will mislead you: cheating crosses a complexity threshold.

Product update describes the latter scenario, too, provided we increase generality. Instead of epistemic equivalence relations, we can just as well use pointed accessibility arrows in models that indicate what the current world, or event, might be like according to you. In particular, that world itself is not among these when you are mistaken.[229]

---

[229]In this way, dynamic epistemic logic is also a dynamic doxastic logic of *belief* – though the latter topic has further complexities that we do not purse in this chapter.

Example (A secret peep). We both do not know if P is the case, but I secretly look and find out. The initial model is

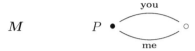

$$M \qquad P \bullet \qquad \circ$$

Here is the event model, with the pointed arrows read as just indicated:

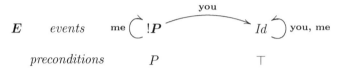

$$\boldsymbol{E} \quad events \qquad \text{me} \quad !\boldsymbol{P} \qquad Id \quad \text{you, me}$$

$$preconditions \qquad P \qquad \top$$

We get a model $\boldsymbol{M} \times \boldsymbol{E}$ with 3 worlds, ordered as in the next picture (for convenience, leaving out a reflexive arrow for me in the actual world, and reflexive arrows for us both in the other two):

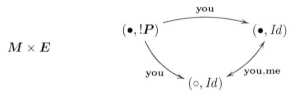

$$\boldsymbol{M} \times \boldsymbol{E}$$

This fits intuitive expectations. In the actual world, I know exactly what has happened – while you still think, mistakenly, that we are in one of the other two worlds, where everything is just like before.

23.4 Language and logic of DEL

The logic for *DEL* is similar to that of *PAL* in Chapter 15. The only new feature in what follows is the use of event models inside modalities, which takes some guts, but there is nothing to it really:

Definition 23.4.1 (*DEL* language and semantics). The dynamic epistemic language is defined by the following inductive syntax rule:

$$p \mid \neg\varphi \mid \varphi \vee \psi \mid K_i\varphi \mid C_G\varphi \mid [\boldsymbol{E}, e]\varphi$$

where $\boldsymbol{E}, e$ is any event model with distinguished event e.[230] The semantic interpretation of this language is standard for all these clauses, except for the dynamic modality, where we set:

$$M, s \models [\boldsymbol{E}, e]\varphi \quad \text{iff} \quad \text{if } M, s \models Pre_e \text{ then } \boldsymbol{M} \times \boldsymbol{E}, (s, e) \models \varphi$$

This formalism is a sort of watershed. If you are "born to be wild",

---

[230]This recursion is tricky when event preconditions come from the same language.

DEL is for you.[231] Axiomatizing this language goes by the PAL methodology of recursion axioms:

Theorem 62. DEL is effectively axiomatizable, and decidable.

Proof. The recursion axioms are like for PAL, with two adjustments:

$$[\boldsymbol{E}, e]q \quad \leftrightarrow (Pre_e \to q)$$
$$[\boldsymbol{E}, e]K_i\varphi \leftrightarrow (Pre_e \to \bigwedge_{e \sim_i f \in \boldsymbol{E}} K_i[\boldsymbol{E}, f]\varphi)$$

The latter equivalence holds since worlds (t, f) that are accessible from (s, e) in $\boldsymbol{M} \times \boldsymbol{E}$ are those whose world component t is accessible from s in $\boldsymbol{M}$, and whose event-component f is accessible from e in $\boldsymbol{E}$.[232]

The final completeness argument reducing all formulas to equivalent ones in the epistemic base language runs as in Chapter 15. □

The system also supports basic notions of Parts I and II:

Fact. All formulas of DEL are invariant for epistemic bisimulation.

Proof. One proof is by reduction to basic EL formulas. More informative is a direct induction, where the dynamic modality uses this

Fact. For bisimilar epistemic models $\boldsymbol{M}, s$ and $\boldsymbol{N}, t$, the product model $(\boldsymbol{M}, s) \times (\boldsymbol{E}, e)$ is bisimilar with the model $(\boldsymbol{N}, t) \times (\boldsymbol{E}, e)$.[233]

□

23.5 Excursion on extensions: common knowledge

Is the dynamic epistemic language right for our intended uses of information models? New modalities make sense, too, such as common knowledge (Chapter 12). This connects up with the fixed-point logics of Chapters 14, 22, and we sketch an illustration (van Benthem et al. (2006) has details), only for the intrepid reader. We will work with arbitrary models, not necessarily with equivalence relations. Here is the simplest illustration of what we want to analyze:

Example (Secret observation, or private subgroup announcement). Consider the following two-event model involving two agents 1, 2 – where 1 learns that the precondition of e holds, say p, while 1 thinks that nothing has happened ($\top$). What group knowledge arises?

---

[231] In practice, one often uses finite event models, though this is not required.
[232] If the event model is infinite, this axiom contains an *infinitary conjunction*!
[233] One could call two event models "the same" if, for all $(\boldsymbol{M}, s)$, $(\boldsymbol{M}, s) \times (\boldsymbol{E}_1, e_1)$ and $(\boldsymbol{M}, s) \times (\boldsymbol{E}_2, e_2)$ are bisimilar. A structural characterization of this notion of *action emulation* has been found, but it is quite complex.

First, agent 2 learns nothing significant here. This is because the second event (that 2 takes to be the real one) with its accessibilities acts as a public announcement of its precondition $\top$. Now here is a general law:

Fact. $\langle !\top\rangle\varphi \leftrightarrow \varphi$ is valid in *PAL*.

The reason is, semantically, that announcing $\top$ does not change a model – or alternatively, just use the *PAL* recursion axioms. Of course, 1 does learn that p is the case, which can be seen through the *DEL* reduction axiom (note that only e is accessible to e for 1):

$$[\boldsymbol{E}, e]K_1 p \leftrightarrow (p \to K_1[\boldsymbol{E}, e]p) \leftrightarrow (p \to K_1(p \to p)) \leftrightarrow (p \to \top) \leftrightarrow \top$$

But now for groups. Try to write a recursion axiom for common knowledge $[\boldsymbol{E}, e]C_{\{1,2\}}\varphi$ in this setting: it is not at all obvious! Here is a solution, written for convenience with existential modalities, that may be computed by the techniques that prove our next theorem:

$$\langle \boldsymbol{E}, e\rangle\langle C_G\rangle\varphi \leftrightarrow \langle(1 \cup 2)^*\rangle\varphi$$

$$\langle \boldsymbol{E}, e\rangle\langle C_G\rangle\varphi \leftrightarrow (p \wedge \langle(?p; 1)^*\rangle(p \wedge \varphi)) \vee (p \wedge \langle(?p; 1)^*\rangle(p \wedge \langle(1 \cup 2)^*\rangle\varphi))$$

To see the issue, draw a picture of $C_G\varphi$ in a product model $\boldsymbol{M} \times \boldsymbol{E}$, with a finite accessibility sequence $(s_1, e_1), \ldots, (s_k, e_k)$, and try to write that information in $\boldsymbol{M}$, with only s-sequences.

The only known solution drastically extends our epistemic language:

Definition 23.5.1 (The system EDL). The *epistemic dynamic-language EDL* is defined by the following inductive syntax rules:

formulas	$p \mid \neg\varphi \mid (\varphi \wedge \psi) \mid [\pi]\varphi$
programs	$i \mid \pi \cup \pi \mid \pi; \pi \mid \pi^* \mid ?\varphi$

The semantics is over the standard epistemic models of Chapter 12, in a mutual recursion. Formulas are interpreted as in Chapter 14, with $\boldsymbol{M}, s \models [\pi]\varphi$ saying that φ is true at all successors of s in $\boldsymbol{M}$ according to the relation denoted by the program π. Programs denote binary accessibility relations between worlds: atomic i are agents' epistemic uncertainty relation, $\cup$ stands for *union* ("choice"), ; for *sequential composition*, and * for *reflexive transitive closure* ("Kleene star"). Moreover, $?\varphi$ is the *test* program $\{(s, s) \mid \boldsymbol{M}, s \models \varphi\}$.

Warning EDL is unlike *DEL*, which changes models. *EDL* stays in one model, where programs denote accessibility relations for complex agents. E.g., common knowledge $C_G\varphi$ is $[(\cup_{i \in G} i)^*]\varphi$, i.e., knowledge for the "complex agent" $(\cup_{i \in G} i)^*$. Conditional common knowledge $C_G^\psi \varphi$ as in Chapter 15 even involves "agents" with tests: $(?\psi; \cup_{i \in G} i; ?\psi)^*$. Of course, not every program defines a natural epistemic "agent".

The important point is that EDL does provide recursion axioms for common knowledge, and in fact much more. Consider DEL as earlier in this chapter, but now with EDL as its static language. The crucial recursion axiom will analyze $\langle \boldsymbol{E}, e \rangle \langle \pi \rangle \varphi$, for any program expression π of EDL, using existential modalities for convenience.

Definition 23.5.2 (Product closure). A language L is *product closed* if for every $\varphi \in L$, the formula $\langle \boldsymbol{E}, e \rangle \varphi$ interpreted using product update, is equivalent to a formula already inside L. *Effective* product closure requires an algorithm producing the equivalents.

Our completeness result showed that epistemic logic EL is product-closed for *finite event models*: the recursion axioms drive an effective algorithm. We use only finite event models henceforth:

Theorem 63. The logic E-PDL is effectively product-closed.

Proof. The argument involves two simultaneous inductions. First, fix some finite pointed event model $\boldsymbol{E}, e$, and, without loss of generality, enumerate its event domain as a finite set of numbers $\{1, \ldots, n\}$.

Fact. For φ in EDL, $\langle \boldsymbol{E}, e \rangle \varphi$ is in EDL.

The steps for atomic formulas and Booleans are as for DEL. The essential case $\langle \boldsymbol{E}, e \rangle \langle \pi \rangle \varphi$ with a program π is analyzed as follows:

Definition 23.5.3. Given any EDL program π, and any two events e, f in the given event model $\boldsymbol{E}$, we define the EDL program $T(e, f, \pi)$ by the following induction on programs:

$$T(e, f, i) \quad = \begin{cases} ?Pre_e\,;\, i\,;\, ?Pre_f & \text{if } e \sim f \text{ in } \boldsymbol{E} \\ ?\bot & \text{otherwise} \end{cases}$$

$$T(e, f, \pi_1 \cup \pi_2) = T(e, f, \pi_1) \cup T(e, f, \pi_2)$$

$$T(e, f, \pi_1; \pi_2) \quad = \textstyle\bigcup_{g \in \boldsymbol{E}} (T(e, g, \pi_1)\,;\, T(g, f, \pi_2))$$

$$T(e, f, ?\varphi) \quad = \begin{cases} ?Pre_e\,;\, ?\langle \boldsymbol{E}, a \rangle \varphi\,;\, ?Pre_f & \text{if } e = f \\ ?\bot & \text{otherwise} \end{cases}$$

$$T(e, f, \pi^*) \quad = P(e, f, n, \pi) \qquad n \text{ largest in } \boldsymbol{E}$$

The auxiliary program $P(e, f, i, \pi)$ is defined by induction on i:

$$P(e, f, 0, \pi) = \begin{cases} T(e, f, \pi) \cup ?\top & \text{if } e = f \\ T(e, f, \pi) & \text{if } e \neq f \end{cases}$$

$$P(e, f, i+1, \pi) = P(e, f, i, \pi) \cup$$
$$\begin{cases} P(e, i, i, \pi) \,;\, P(i, i, i, \pi)^* \,;\, P(i, f, i, \pi) & \text{if } i \neq e, \, i \neq f \\ P(e, i, i, \pi) \,;\, P(i, i, i, \pi)^* & \text{if } i \neq e, \, i = f \\ P(i, i, i, \pi)^* \,;\, P(i, f, i, \pi) & \text{if } i = e \end{cases}$$

All these programs are in EDL. Their meanings are in the next claim, proved simultaneously with all other claims in the main proof:

Claim.

(a) $(w, v) \in [\![T(e, f, \pi)]\!]^M$ iff $((w, e), (v, f)) \in [\![\pi]\!]^{M \times E}$

(b) $(w, v) \in [\![P(e, f, i, \pi)]\!]^M$ iff there exists a finite sequence of transitions in $M \times E$ of the form $(w, e)[\![\pi]\!]x_1 \cdots x_k [\![\pi]\!](v, e)$ such that no stage $x_j = (w_j, e_j)$ has an event e_j with index $j \geq i$.

The inductive proof is obvious from the definition. In particular, the complex clause for $P(e, f, i+1, \pi)$ says that a finite path from e to f pass at worst through the event i some finite number of times – and marking these, it decomposes into an initial part from e to i of lower index i for intermediate stages, an iteration of trips from i to i with lower index, and a final part from i to f with lower index.

With this explanation, here is our desired equivalence:

Lemma.
$$\langle E, e \rangle \langle \pi \rangle \varphi \;\leftrightarrow\; \bigvee_{i \in E} \langle T(e, i, \pi) \rangle \langle E, i \rangle \varphi$$

The proof follows easily from the explanation for the relations $T(e, i, \pi)$.

This proof is also an effective *algorithm* for writing correct recursion axioms for common knowledge and other *EDL*-defined notions.[234] □

23.6 Games, update evolution, and long-term temporal perspective

Like public announcement, product update can be *repeated* to model successive assertions, observations, or other informational events. We saw this with the puzzle of the Muddy Children in Chapter 15, where the Father creates a model with two announcement events (with standard preconditions) that can be distinguished by all participants:

---

[234]The result generalizes to epistemic μ-calculus: van Benthem and Ikegami (2008).

"Child i says that it knows (or: does not know) whether it is dirty" This gets repeated until the epistemic model no longer changes. Scenarios like this generate trees or "forests" whose nodes are finite sequences of events (cf. Chapter 18), starting from worlds in an initial epistemic model. As an illustration, consider games of imperfect information (Chapter 17). Moves in a game have preconditions that restrict what is playable at nodes of the game tree. Now collect all moves into one event model E, while also recording the right information about which players can observe which move. Then successive rounds of the game correspond to forming successive update with this model E:

Definition 23.6.1 (Update evolution models). Consider an initial epistemic model M, with event model E. Then $Tree(M, E)$ is the possibly infinite epistemic tree model whose successive layers are disjoint copies of all successive product update models $M \times E, (M \times E) \times E, \ldots$

Example (Updates in play: propagating ignorance along a game tree).

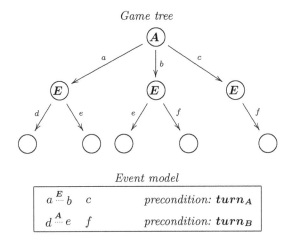

Game tree

Event model

Here are the successive updates creating the right uncertainty links:

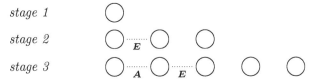

stage 1

stage 2

stage 3

There is more to updates evolution. For instance, successive levels may stabilize in that they become bisimilar to each other – as happens in some games. But here we move on to our final perspective:

23.7   Dynamic epistemic logic in temporal logic

While dynamic logics describe stepwise events and induced changes in agents' knowledge and belief, a global perspective also makes sense (as in Chapter 18, though we will deviate in a moment), with tree pictures:

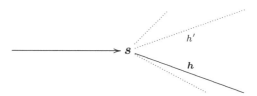

Branching temporal models provide a "Grand Stage" view of agency, with histories standing for runs of some information-driven process, that can be described by languages with both epistemic and temporal operators.[235] As we already saw in an example, such trees may arise as unfoldings of some initial epistemic model M via successive DEL product updates $M \times E$ with event models E by "update evolution". We will see in a moment just how this works.

Basic epistemic-temporal logic Take a set $\mathcal{A}$ of agents and $\mathcal{E}$ of events. This time, we change the perspective a bit from Chapter 18, and take a *history* to be a finite sequence of events, that can be an initial part of some longer history. $\mathcal{E}^*$ is the total set of histories. For a history h, write he for h followed by the event e. Write $h \leq h'$ if h is a prefix of h', and $h \leq_e h'$ if $h' = he$ for the event e.

Definition 23.7.1 (ETL Frames). A *protocol* is a set of histories $\mathcal{H} \subseteq \mathcal{E}^*$ closed under prefixes. An *ETL frame* is a tuple $(\mathcal{E}, \mathcal{H}, \{\sim_i\}_{i \in \mathcal{A}})$ with $\mathcal{H}$ a protocol, and the $\sim_i$ epistemic accessibility relations.

An *ETL* frame describes knowledge evolving over time in some process. The protocol captures the admissible histories, with he the point in time after e has happened in h. The relations $\sim_i$ represent uncertainty of agents about how the current history has evolved, due to their limited powers of observation. $h \sim_i h'$ means that from agent i's perspective, history h' looks the same as history h.

A temporal language L_{ETL} for these structures is generated by the following grammar (AT is a set of atomic propositions):

$$p \mid \neg\varphi \mid \varphi \vee \psi \mid [i]\varphi \mid \langle e \rangle \varphi \qquad \text{where } i \in \mathcal{A}, e \in \mathcal{E}, \text{ and } p \in AT.$$

Formulas are interpreted at finite histories in the following structure:

---

[235]Some well-known Grand Stage views are Interpreted Systems (Fagin et al., 1995), Epistemic-Temporal Logic (Parikh and Ramanujam, 2003), STIT (Belnap et al. 2001), Process Algebra/Game Semantics (Abramsky, 2008).

Definition 23.7.2 (*ETL* Model). An *ETL model* M is a tuple $(\mathcal{E}, \mathcal{H}, \{\sim_i\}_{i \in A}, V)$ with $(\mathcal{E}, \mathcal{H}, \{\sim_i\}_{i \in A})$ an *ETL* frame, and V a valuation map sending proposition letters to sets of histories in $\mathcal{H}$.

Definition 23.7.3 (Truth of L_{ETL} formulas). Let $M = (\mathcal{E}, \mathcal{H}, \{\sim_i\}_{i \in A}, V)$ be an *ETL* model. *Truth* of a formula φ at a history $h \in \mathcal{H}$, denoted $M, h \models \varphi$, is defined inductively as follows:

(a) $M, h \models p$ iff $h \in V(p)$
(b) Booleans are interpreted as usual
(c) $M, h \models [i]\varphi$ iff   *for each* $h' \in \mathcal{H}$, *if* $h \sim_i h'$, *then* $M, h' \models \varphi$
(d) $M, h \models \langle e \rangle \varphi$ iff   *there exists* $h' = he \in \mathcal{H}$ *with* $M, h' \models \varphi$

Modal correspondence for special agents Further constraints on these models reflect special features of agents, or of the informational process. Such constraints come either as conditions on epistemic and action accessibility, or as epistemic-temporal axioms, with the two related by modal frame correspondences (Chapter 9):

Fact. The axiom $K[e]\varphi \to [e]K\varphi$ corresponds to *Perfect Recall*:

if $he \sim k$, then there is a history h' with $k = h'e$ and $h \sim h'$.[236]

This says that agents' current uncertainties can only come from previous uncertainties: expressing a strong form of perfect memory. In particular, this implies the following property:

Synchronicity: $h \sim k$ only occurs between h, k at the same tree level.

In a similar fashion, we have a dual modal correspondence fact:

Fact. The axiom $[e]K\varphi \to K[e]\varphi$ corresponds to *No Miracles*:

for all ke with $h \sim k$, we also have $he \sim ke$.

This says that, although learning can take place by observing events, there are no miracles: current uncertainties can only be resolved by differential observation of different events.

Representation theorems Now we can say how *DEL* and *ETL* relate:

Definition 23.7.4 (Induced *ETL* forests). An epistemic model M and sequence of event models $\mathcal{E}$ have an *induced ETL-model Forest*$(M, \mathcal{E})$ whose histories are all sequences $(w, e_1, \ldots, e_k)$ produced by successive product update, with epistemic accessibility and valuation as in *DEL*.

Induced models of this sort have three striking properties:

Fact. *ETL*-models $\mathbf{H}$ of the form *Forest*$(M, \mathcal{E})$ satisfy these three principles, where $h, h', k, \ldots$ range only over histories present in M:

---

[236]The elementary proof is Sahlqvist substitution argument. Details simplify by letting transition relations for events e in our trees be *partial functions*.

(a) *Perfect Memory*: if $he \sim k$, then for some f, $k = h'f$ and $h \sim h'$.

(b) *Uniform No Miracles*: if $h \sim k$, and $h'e \sim k'f$, then $he \sim kf$.

(c) *Definable Executability*: The domain of any event e is definable in the epistemic base language.

Clause (c) stipulates definability of preconditions for events e, i.e., the domains of the partial functions he in the tree model $\mathbf{H}$. Chapter 3 has an alternative of *bisimulation Invariance*: closure of event domains under *epistemic bisimulations* in the *ETL*-model $\mathbf{H}$. Combining these results yields a representation for "*DEL* inside *ETL*":

Theorem 64. For *ETL* models $\mathbf{H}$, the following are equivalent:

1. $\mathbf{H}$ is isomorphic to some model $Forest(\mathbf{M}, \mathcal{E})$,
2. $\mathbf{H}$ satisfies Perfect Memory, Uniform No Miracles, and Bisimulation Invariance.

Using this, we can translate *DEL* into epistemic-temporal logic.

This tells us how special *DEL* is as an account of informational processes over time. It takes idealized observing agents with perfect memory, and its protocols have only local conditions on executability. Current generalizations include more complex temporal preconditions, other types of epistemic agent (say, with limited memory), and also: *revising beliefs* instead of knowledge (cf. Chapters 13, 15).

Protocols To conclude, we show how, with links like this, frameworks can share ideas. Recall the above *protocols*: constraints on runs of a computational process. Human interaction, too, has conventions ruling out some histories: think of conversation rules like "do not repeat yourself", "let others speak in turn", "be honest". Other protocols occur in puzzles (the Muddy Children could only make limited assertions) or physical experiments. All this immediately changes our logics. With procedural information present, what is the logic of arbitrary protocols?[237] *PAL* itself no longer qualifies: two of its axioms fail.

Example (Failures of *PAL* validities). *PAL* had a valid axiom $\langle !P \rangle q \leftrightarrow (P \wedge q)$. As a special case, this implied the earlier $\langle !P \rangle \top \leftrightarrow P$. From left to right, this holds with arbitrary protocols: $!P$ can only be executed if P holds. But the direction from right to left is no longer valid: P may be true at the current world, but there is no reason why the protocol would allow a public announcement of this fact at this stage. Next, consider the crucial knowledge recursion law, in its existential version

$$\langle !P \rangle \langle i \rangle \varphi \leftrightarrow (P \wedge \langle i \rangle \langle !P \rangle \varphi)$$

---

[237]Think of epistemic models plus all models reachable via some protocol.

This, too, will fail in general, again from right to left. Even when P is true right now, and the agent thinks it possible that P can be announced to make φ true, she need not *know the protocol* – and indeed, the protocol need not allow the action $!P$ in the actual world.

The point is this: assertions $\langle !P \rangle \top$ now express genuine *procedural information* about the informative process agents are in, and hence, they no longer "reduce" to basic epistemic statements. PAL expressed factual and epistemic information only. We now remedy this.

Definition 23.7.5 (The logic TPAL). The logic $TPAL$ of arbitrary protocols has the same language as PAL, and its axioms are (a) the epistemic base logic, (b) the minimal modal logic for each announcement modality, and (c) modified recursion axioms

$$\langle !P \rangle q \quad\quad \leftrightarrow \langle !P \rangle \top \wedge q \quad\quad\quad\quad \textit{for atomic facts } q$$
$$\langle !P \rangle (\varphi \vee \psi) \leftrightarrow \langle !P \rangle \varphi \wedge \langle !P \rangle \psi$$
$$\langle !P \rangle \neg \varphi \quad\quad \leftrightarrow \langle !P \rangle \top \wedge \neg \langle !P \rangle \varphi$$
$$\langle !P \rangle K_i \varphi \quad \leftrightarrow \langle !P \rangle \top \rightarrow K_i(\langle !P \rangle \top \rightarrow \langle !P \rangle \varphi)$$

Theorem 65. $TPAL$ is complete for PAL protocol models.

Clearly, this is just a starting point for further dynamic logics of agency, with knowledge, belief, but also preferences and other features.

Exercises Chapter 23

1. Consider the Three Card game in Chapters 12, 15. This time, player 2 shows his card in public, but *only to player 1*. Draw the update. Explain how this would work with event models.

2. Consider an epistemic model M with two worlds satisfying $p, \neg p$, between which agent 1 is uncertain, though 2 is not. The actual world has p. Now a true announcement of p takes place, and agent 1 hears this. But agent 2 thinks it might just be a statement "True" that could occur anywhere. Draw the initial model M and the event model E. Next, compute the successive models $M \times E, (M \times E) \times E$, etc. At some stage, one "level" becomes bisimilar to the next: where?

3. Prove that, if M and E are both transitive, then so is the product model $M \times E$. Refute this implication for the property of linearity of accessibility relations. What is the difference? Can you state a general "preservation principle"?

4. In the proof of completeness for DEL with common knowledge, do all the easy inductive steps involving program composition.

5. Show that Perfect Recall implies Synchronicity in our tree models.

6. Find principles in the epistemic-temporal language ETL that correspond to the two implications in the crucial DEL recursion axiom for knowledge.

7. Check the soundness of the logic $TPAL$ on protocol models.

8. If we want to formalize the whole Muddy Children scenario, which epistemic temporal notions do we need? Where would we require the extensions in this chapter?

System combination and undecidability

24.1 System combination and complexity

Modal logics usually isolate one particular modal notion, say of knowledge or of time, and then study its properties in expressively weak languages, often decidable. But what happens when we put these separate modalities together – as we must do when painting all the strokes needed for a full picture of agency, space-time, or other structures in reality? When both component logics are simple, a "divide and conquer" view would suggest that the behaviour of the whole system will be simple, too. But things are more delicate. One telling discovery in the 1990s has been that modal system combination can lead to high complexity, depending crucially on the way the separate modalities "interact". Here is a typical result, that illustrates a genre:

Theorem 66. The minimal modal logic of two modalities [1], [2] satisfying the axiom $[1][2]\varphi \rightarrow [2][1]\varphi$ in a language with the *universal modality* U over all worlds is undecidable.

Several features here deserve attention. The first is the semantic structure of the models for this logic, reflecting an important "parameter" that determines complexity: the *mode of combination* of the separate logics. What the axiom really says is easily seen through frame correspondence (Chapter 9). It makes frames for the logic look like a *grid structure* satisfying this first-order convergence property:

$$\forall xyz : (xR_1y \wedge yR_2z) \rightarrow \exists u : (xR_2u \wedge uR_1z).$$

The most typical example of such a structure is $\mathbb{N} \times \mathbb{N}$, where we take two relations: *NORTH* moving one step from (i,j) to $(i, j + 1)$ and

$EAST$ moving from (i,j) to $(i+1,j)$:

$$\vdots$$

$$(0,1) \dashrightarrow (1,1)$$
$$\uparrow \qquad \wedge$$
$$(0,0) \longrightarrow (1,0) \qquad \cdots$$

While this structure looks geometrically simple and regular, it hides a lot of complexity. The other major feature involved in the high complexity over these geometrical structures is expressive power of the modal language (cf. Chapter 7) – but we will get to that below.

24.2 Tiling problems

Here is a well-known undecidable computational benchmark problem, the *Tiling Problem*. Let a finite set of "tiles" be given, with colours on each side, that form patterns like this:

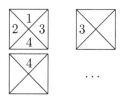

Matching tiles must have the same colours on adjacent sides. Now the geometrical *Tiling Problem* asks

Can we cover the whole plane with matching tiles from our set?

Do a few concrete examples, and you will see this is non-trivial.

Theorem 67. The Tiling Problem is *undecidable*.

Actually, the geometrical Tiling Problem has the same complexity as the computational "Non-Halting Problem": that is, determining if a given Turing machine will keep computing forever on a given input. Indeed, the two problems are equivalent, as one can show by mimicking Turing computations over time with successive horizontal rows in a grid as tape contents, and the vertical sequence as the "computation". It is essential in making this work that positions on successive rows can be compared in the right way, and this is what the grid structure does. Tilings are easier to visualize than Turing machines, and they have gained popularity as a way of showing high complexity of logics.

Aside on complexity Upon reflection, you might find the Tiling Problem complex and second-order, since a tiling is really an infinite function defined on $\mathbb{N} \times \mathbb{N}$ sending positions to suitable tiles. But this is only apparent: such a global tiling of the whole grid exists if and only if *each finite left quadrant can be tiled*.[238] Given an initial finite set of tiles, the latter property is decidable for each finite quadrant, and hence the complexity of the Tiling Problem is of the so-called "Π_1^0-form": "all natural numbers have some decidable property". This syntactic shape is just like that for the Non-Halting Problem.

The problem changes dramatically with an added constraint that some given tile must occur infinitely often on the bottom-most row. The complexity of this *Recurrent Tiling Problem* goes up to non-arithmetically definable. It is "Σ_1^1-*complete*": as difficult as checking the arithmetical properties that hold for some choice of sets of natural numbers. This is often considered to be as bad as a logic can get.[239]

24.3 A key to undecidability in first-order logic

One application of tiling problems is a celebrated result by Church:

Theorem 68. Satisfiability for first-order logic is undecidable.

Proof. We sketch the essence of the method. Consider a set T of square tiles $\{t_1, ..., t_m\}$. The Tiling Problem asks us to put one tile on each point in the grid $\mathbb{N} \times \mathbb{N}$ so that all adjacent edges have the same colour. Now we reduce this problem effectively to a *satisfiability problem* in first-order logic. To achieve this, we take a language with enough vocabulary to express the basic grid structure. That is, we have two binary relations *North xy* ("*y* lies to the north of *x*") and *East xy* (likewise) to define the grid, as well as unary predicates T_i for each tile *i*. You might think we also need predicates for colours, but we do not. Now we write a number of first-order formulas in this language:

Grid says that *North* and *East* are discrete linear orders with a beginning but no end, lying intertwined by the above confluence property.

To make the structure look more like $\mathbb{N} \times \mathbb{N}$, you can add features like disjointness of the two relations, etcetera. The first-order formula *Grid* can be written so that all its models look as follows: they start with a

---

[238]The latter implies the former by *Koenig's Lemma*, and it takes a little insight.

[239]Perhaps surprisingly, complexity goes down again when we ask for existence of a *constructive* recurrent tiling: a *computable* map from grid positions to tiles satisfying the recurrence condition.

copy of $\mathbb{N} \times \mathbb{N}$, and may have further points at "infinity" beyond this.[240] Next, write a first-order formula

Tile: each point has exactly one tile, and colours must match.

The latter feature is simple. Given a concrete list of tiles, we know what it means for them to match horizontally and vertically, and we can just write a finite number of conjuncts like

$$\forall x \forall y ((\mathit{East}\ xy \wedge \neg \exists z (\mathit{East}\ xz \wedge \mathit{East}\ zy) \wedge T_i) \rightarrow$$
$$\bigcup_j \text{ matches horizontally with } {}_i T_j).$$

Now the formula φ_T is the conjunction of *Grid* and *Tile*. Note that it can be constructed effectively from the given tiling.

Lemma. φ_T is satisfiable iff the given set T can tile the $\mathbb{N} \times \mathbb{N}$-plane.

From right to left this is obvious, since a tiled plane is itself a model for our formula. Conversely, if φ_T has a model $\boldsymbol{M}$, we just look at the initial part of that model that formed a copy of $\mathbb{N} \times \mathbb{N}$, and use the interpretation of the predicates T_i to read off the tiling. □

So, first-order satisfiability is undecidable, since it can effectively encode the Tiling Problem. The same is then true for first-order validity. On the other hand, the *completeness theorem* for first-order logic says validity is effectively axiomatizable, and that fixes the complexity as undecidable but "recursively enumerable".[241]

24.4 But why are things sometimes decidable?

Syntax restriction and guards Against this background, we can understand what happened in Chapters 3 and 10. One way of lowering complexity is by restricting syntax, noting which patterns are crucial in setting up the above formulas *Grid* and *Tile*. As it happens, many of these formulas are already in the decidable *Guarded Fragment* of Chapter 7, but the crucial exception is the quantifier pattern in the confluence property defining the grid. The latter is typically not guarded, since the branching prefix in its quantification

---

[240]Compare how one describes the natural numbers as a discrete linear order. Models of its complete first-order theory may also contain infinite numbers living in copies of the integers.

[241]A worry: can the same method encode *Recurrent Tiling*? See the Exercises.

does not relate all of x, y, z at the same time. It is not even *"loosely guarded"* in our weaker sense that also guaranteed decidability, since there is no atom guarding the pair y, z.

Thus, while the Guarded Fragment arose by working "from below" keeping distinct features of basic modal syntax intact, we can also approach it now "from above", seeing where first-order logic has become overly expressive – and what needs to be dropped.

Trees versus grids But our analysis seems to raise a problem. How can it be that, despite all this bad news about grids and undecidability, so many complex-looking first-order and modal logics are *decidable*? The reason is that, sometimes, the special structures one works with help, making the complete logic simple and well-behaved. In particular, many natural logics do not involve a grid-like pattern. Their models rather behave like trees, perhaps with many successor relations – the "normal form" for modal logics modulo bisimulation. And in that case, the counterpart of our tiling troubles is a classical positive result, that applies not just to first-order logic but even to its extension $MSOL$ with second-order quantifiers over subsets of the domain:

Theorem 69 (Rabin's Theorem). The complete monadic second-order logic over a countable tree with finitely many unary successor functions plus the binary relation of *precedence* between nodes is decidable.

This key result explains the decidability of many modal logics.[242]

Here is the crucial contrast between the two types of structure. Trees are "loose", with no interaction between successors of a point ("separation is forever"), whereas grids do: whence their complexity. What you might just take away from this as a rule of thumb is:

Modal logics of *trees* are harmless, modal logics of *grids* are dangerous!

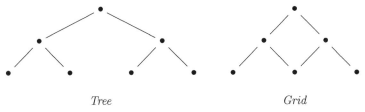

Tree   *Grid*

Thus, finding the complexity of satisfiability or validity for a combined modal logic may require non-trivial "good sense" concerning its

---

[242]Still further sources of decidability arise in logics of geometrical structures like the reals, that admit of so-called *quantifier elimination*. In this case, it is strength, rather than weakness of the theory that explains the decidability.

semantic modeling.[243] There are some powerful methods of analysis and design, but nothing like a complete classification.

The contrast is often quite drastic: logics tend to be either decidable or highly complex. Logics like first-order logic are, if not decidable, at least recursively axiomatizable, but once this property gets lost through extension, they often tend to be Π_1^1-complete. The same is true as a rule of thumb for many modal logics, as we will see below.

24.5   Combined modal logics

Having understood all this, we now see how modal logics can get complex. Consider the bimodal logic of Section 24.1 with two modalities $[1], [2]$ satisfying the axiom $[1][2]\varphi \rightarrow [2][1]\varphi$ plus a *universal modality* U. One can mimic the argument for first-order logic roughly as follows. The Tiling Problem is now reduced effectively to a satisfiability problem in the characteristic grid models for this modal logic, by constructing a formula φ_T with the following property:

Lemma. φ_T is satisfiable in a characteristic Grid model for our modal logic iff the given set T can tile the $\mathbb{N} \times \mathbb{N}$-plane.

If we can prove this, then we are done: the satisfiability problem for the modal logic will be at least as hard as that of the Tiling Problem. This is a lower bound, of course, and we may have to also supply an upper bound. We will make some comments on this aspect later.

Proof. Here is a sketch of the argument for this undecidability result. The formula φ_T is constructed as follows. We choose proposition letters p_t for each tile t, and write up what a tiling amounts to, using our modalities. The "adjacent colours" condition is just a relation from tiles to a finite set of "fitting tiles", in each direction. Each point must then satisfy three properties:

(a) the finite disjunction T of all tiling propositions p_t, while also forbidding overlap (a Boolean formula),

(b) $p_t \rightarrow [North]$ "disjunction of all $p_{t'}$ with t' fitting to the north", $p_t \rightarrow [East]$ "disjunction of all $p_{t'}$ with t' fitting to the east", altogether a finite conjunction,

(c) $\langle North \rangle \top \wedge \langle East \rangle \top$

Prefix a universal modality to make this hold in every point.

It will be clear how to satisfy this formula from a tiling. Conversely, if this formula holds at some point s in a grid-like model, the denotations

---

[243]To show the subtlety, adding a relation "same-level" or "simultaneity" to the Rabin Tree yields a sort of "grid", and its logic jumps to Π_1^1-complete.

of the proposition letters p_t help tile the plane $\mathbb{N} \times \mathbb{N}$. We first use s to read off the tiling for $(0,0)$, and then proceed inductively tiling in triangles, using the grid property of the model to place the next edge in a way that avoids conflicts in the placement pattern:

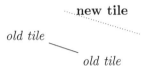

$\Box$

This type of argument only gives a *lower bound* on complexity. Satisfiability in the logic might still be worse than that for the encoded tiling problem. *Upper bounds* may come from known complexities of classical logics. Many modal logics are complete for some simply definable class of frames, and then complexity is at most that of monadic second-order logic over that frame class.[244]

Finally, bimodal logics like the above are not artificial. Consider a modal language combining *action and knowledge*, as in Chapters 15 and 23. One axiom that is used a lot here is the interchange of knowledge and action, with the following intuitive interpretation:

$$K[a]\varphi \to [a]K\varphi$$

This says that, if I know that after doing a result φ will hold, then after doing a, I know that φ holds. This seemed a harmless assumption of "perfect observation" and "perfect recall". But modal logics of "well-behaved agents" tend to be quite complex: undecidable, or worse. The reason is the tiling pattern lurking behind them, and its geometrical richness. Indeed, agents with perfect memory are complex objects of study, and their complete logic is as rich as some standard mathematical theories. Similar points hold for logics of spatial patterns, complementing our analysis in Chapter 19: complex *two-dimensional* spaces quickly get very complex modal theories.

24.6   A case of balance: epistemic-temporal logics

To conclude, we briefly discuss how the preceding issues play in the concrete study of rational agency of Part II and Chapter 23. This technical section mainly gives pointers to what lies beyond.

---

[244]With more expressive power in the language, our method encodes Recurrent Tiling, making complexity of satisfiability explode. To achieve this, we must make sure that the distinguished tile repeats infinitely often on a horizontal line of successors from the origin – which can be enforced, for instance, by using an iteration modality $[East^*]$ from dynamic logic (Chapter 15).

One important insight from the computational literature is that increases in expressive power may lead to big upward jumps in complexity of logics of knowledge and time. The first systematic investigation of these phenomena was made in Halpern and Vardi (1989). Here is a Table with a few relevant observations from their work showing where dangerous thresholds lie for the complexity of validity in this area:

	K, P, F	K, C_G, F_e	K, C_G, F_e, P_e	K, C_G, F
All ETL models	*decidable*	*decidable*	*decidable*	RE
Perfect Recall	RE	RE	RE	Π_1^1-complete
No Miracles	RE	RE	RE	Π_1^1-complete

Here complexities run from decidable through axiomatizable (RE) to Π_1^1-complete.[245] As we see, general epistemic-temporal logic over arbitrary ETL-models is simple even with rich vocabularies, but things change with special assumptions on agents such as Perfect Recall. The mathematical explanation is, of course, the grid encoding. Modulo some technicalities, Perfect Recall[246] forces epistemic accessibility and future moves in time to behave like $\mathbb{N} \times \mathbb{N}$, and given enough resources in the logic, it can even express "Recurrent Tiling". This requires a balance between grid structure and expressive power. In order to really perform a tiling argument, the language also needs sufficient expressive power, say, a universal quantifier ranging over all points in the grid. This is precisely what is supplied by the combination of an unbounded future modality ranging over the forward direction of the tree, plus a common knowledge modality accessing every reachable point at the same "horizontal" tree level. If one of these resources is not available, say we have common knowledge but no unbounded future, complexity may drop, as shown in the table.

We suppress many issues here. van Benthem and Pacuit (2006) explains in detail how Perfect Recall enforces tiling even though it merely requires the basic cell structure "downward" in a tree. Also, there is a subtle difference between the *forest* models of Chapter 23, where the bottom-most level may have many points (say, the worlds in initial epistemic models M for update evolution), and *trees* with just one root.

---

[245]There is a huge a priori gap between the complexities RE and Π_1^1-complete for logical systems, but no epistemic-temporal logics that we know of fall "in between". This gap that we saw earlier also occurs with extensions of first-order logic. Being able *to define a copy of the natural numbers* $\mathbb{N}$ acts as a "watershed". If you cannot, like first-order logic, then complexity stays low – whereas, if you can, like in first-order fixed-point logics or second-order logic, then complexity jumps.

[246]Similar observations hold for the converse principle of No Miracles.

The results of Halpern and Vardi (1989) work immediately in forests. To encode grid structure in tree models with single roots, and perhaps finite horizontal levels, we need to create basic cells in another way, looking "obliquely" at (part of) the tree as a grid:

DEL as an ETL-logic Against this background, we can now "place" *DEL* and understand its earlier behaviour. Its language is the K, C_G, F_e slot in the earlier Table, over models satisfying both Perfect Recall and No Miracles. Thus, there is grid structure, but the expressive resources of the language stay away from exploiting it to the full, since we only have one-step future operators $\langle !P \rangle$ or $\langle E, e \rangle$. If we add unbounded future operators, however, the same complexity arises as for *ETL*. Indeed, Chapter 15 mentioned a result in Miller and Moss (2005) that the logic of public announcement with common knowledge and Kleene iteration of assertions $!P$ becomes Π_1^1-complete.

Still, these observations leave loopholes for lower complexity – e.g., on finite models and their sub-models reached by announcements. Or, consider temporal extensions beyond the above Table. Adding one-step *past* does not endanger decidability.[248] But *DEL* might even stay decidable over *ETL*-models with an unbounded past modality, going back finitely many steps to the root. This can define preconditions in the earlier conversational protocols.

24.7 Conclusion

Altogether, we have seen that combining modal logics is a delicate business, and since we *must* combine components when analyzing real phenomena, the ways in which we do that are crucial. Even so, it also has to be said that the high-complexity results mentioned here are often

---

[247]Here we reach the bottom corner of a cell by a "horizontal" epistemic move plus a "vertical" event move, as shown to the right in the picture. To make use of the latter, the language needs to iterate mixed epistemic and temporal moves in patterns $(\sim_i; e)^*$. The most straightforward formalism for this is a *propositional dynamic logic* PDL_{et} with both epistemic accessibility and temporal event moves as basic transition relations. The validity problem for PDL_{et} is Π_1^1-complete.

[248]A one-step past modality Y ("Yesterday") also makes a lot of sense in the basic dynamic logic PAL of Chapter 15: a public announcement $!P$ achieves common knowledge that P *was true* just before the event: $[!\varphi]C_G Y \varphi$.

just thunder in the distance. Modal logics that are theoretically complex contain many nice principles that lend themselves to simple study. Why this is so, is another matter. Maybe we need a more delicate style of system combination[249] – or maybe, a better understanding of which parts of the total syntax of a system one is really using in practice.

---

[249]Cf. Dov Gabbay's work on "fibering logics", and the resulting research program.

Exercises Chapter 24

1. Use Koenig's Lemma to prove that the Tiling Problem is equivalent to the existence of tilings for all finite quadrants of the plane.

2. Provide some details for the crucial steps in the undecidability proof for first-order logic via a tiling argument.

3. A subtlety about complexity:
   (a) A worry in the preceding proof might be here that our coding method could simply encode the infinite repetition required by *Recurrent Tiling*, by a simple quantifier combination ∀∃. Why does this not happen?
   (b) But if this danger does not materialize in first-order logic, why *can* we encode recurrent tiling problems in some modal logics? Are not they expressively weaker?

4. Prove that the temporal logic of the natural numbers with the relations of immediate successor and general precedence ≤ is decidable using Rabin's Theorem.

5. Consider memory-impaired epistemic agents who only remember the last-observed event. Define their knowledge modality purely in terms of temporal operators for past events. What does this mean for the complexity of their epistemic-temporal logics?

6.
   (a) Explain how Rabin's Theorem fails when trees also have a *simultaneity* relation. Connect the key trick to the complexity proof mentioned in the final section for epistemic temporal logics on trees with complex *DEL*-style agents.
   (b) Given the stated "danger thresholds", what epistemic temporal logic on tree models might still have low complexity?

25

Abstract model theory

A logical system yields its secrets through mathematical analysis, and there is more to what makes modal logic tick than what we have seen so far. In particular, there is a good deal of model theory about modal languages, and we saw glimpses in Part II. More can be found in the *Modal Logic* textbook by Blackburn, de Rijke & Venema Blackburn et al. (2001), and the chapters by van Benthem & Blackburn, and especially, Goranko & Otto in Blackburn et al. (2006). In this chapter, we give a few basic results in the area, as well as a recent new perspective.

25.1 Bisimulation invariance and modal definability

We recall a basic fact from Chapter 3.

Proposition 25.1.1 (Bisimulation implies modal equivalence)**.** Let $\equiv$ be a bisimulation between two models M, N with $s \equiv t$. Then, for all modal formulas φ, $M, s \models \varphi$ iff $N, t \models \varphi$.

There is no general converse, though, as we have seen, modal equivalence does imply the existence of a bisimulation for *finite* models. Now we will work toward a different type of converse result, analyzing what *does* follow from modal equivalence. For a start, here are two relevant model-theoretic notions.

Definition 25.1.1 (Elementary extension)**.** Model N is an *elementary extension* of M if (a) M is a submodel of N, and (b) for each first-order formula φ and tuple of M-objects s, $M, s \models \varphi$ iff $N, s \models \varphi$.

Definition 25.1.2 (ω-saturated model)**.** A model is ω-*saturated* if, for each set Σ of first-order formulas (with finitely many names for objects in M) with a finite set x of free variables occurring in them, the following holds: if each finite subset of Σ has a satisfying tuple of objects for x in M, then so does the whole set Σ.

This notion says that the model M is "full" with witnesses to the-

293

ories of objects that are consistent inside M . The natural numbers $\mathbb{N}$ are typically not saturated: consider the infinite set of formulas $\Sigma(x)$ saying that x lies at any finite distance from the origin. To satisfy this, a linear order needs infinite "supernatural" numbers. By standard model-theoretic arguments, one has that

Fact. Each model has an ω-saturated elementary extension.

Proof. Consider a model M together with all sets of formulas $\Sigma(x_\Sigma)$ that are finitely satisfiable inside M. (Here we subscript the variables to make them unique to each of these sets.) Now take the first-order theory of the expanded model (M, M) where we have added names for each object in M to the language, and add this to Σ. Each finite subset of this new set has a model, since it only involves a finite number of sets Σ, and we can just "add" the given witnesses for their different variables x_Σ – where the subscripting avoids clashes. Hence, by the Compactness Theorem for first-order logic, the whole set has a model N. It is easy to see that (a) N is an elementary extension of M, and (b) N witnesses every set of formulas that is finitely satisfiable in M. Now we repeat this process through countably many stages. The result is a countable *elementary chain* of models under inclusion (we trust the reader understands what this intuitive notion means) whose union M^+ is an elementary extension of all its members. Moreover, this union itself is an ω-saturated model. The reason is the usual one that, if a set is satisfiable *using only finitely many objects* from the union, it will in fact use only finitely many objects from some large enough stage, and then a witness had been added already at the next stage.[250] □

Now we can prove a converse direction for the case of modal logic. Recall that, under the Standard Translation, modal formulas were first-order formulas with one free variable.

Proposition 25.1.2 (From modal equivalence to bisimulation). Let $M, s \models \varphi$ iff $N, t \models \varphi$, for all modal formulas φ. Then there exist Σ-saturated elementary extensions M^+, N^+ of M, N, respectively, and a bisimulation $\equiv$ between M^+, N^+ such that $s \equiv t$.

Proof. By the preceding fact, take two ω-saturated elementary extensions M^+, s and N^+, t of M, s and N, t, respectively.Note that the worlds s, t still satisfy the same modal formulas in these extended models. Now we prove that, in such saturated models, this relation of modal equivalence *is* a bisimulation. First, modal equivalence implies the atomic clause of bisimulation, since proposition letters are

---

[250]This argument is not fully precise yet, but we leave the last details to the reader.

included. Next, the key observation lies in the back-and-forth clauses. If some world u in M^+ is modally equivalent with v in N^+, and $R^M uw$ holds, then the following set of formulas is finitely satisfiable in N^+:

$\{Rvx\}$ plus the full modal theory of w in M^+ for the variable x.

But then, by ω-saturation, some world must exist satisfying all of these formulas in N^+: and that is precisely is the required match for bisimulation. The converse is symmetric. □

In particular, *finite* models M, N are ω-saturated, and this explains our earlier observation, since elementary extensions of finite models must be those models themselves.

Now comes our main result, stating that modal logic and bisimulations are a perfect match in a first-order perspective (cf. Chapter 7):

Theorem 70 (Modal invariance theorem). For formulas $\varphi = \varphi(x)$ in the first-order language of modal models, the following two assertions are equivalent: (a) φ is logically equivalent to a modal formula, (b) φ is invariant for bisimulation.

Proof. From (a) to (b): that all modal formulas are invariant was shown before. Conversely, suppose that $\varphi = \varphi(x)$ is an invariant first-order formula. Let $mod(\varphi)$ be the set of all modal first-order consequences of φ. We prove the following implication:

Claim. $mod(\varphi) \models \varphi$

From this, by an easy application of the Compactness Theorem, φ will follow from some finite conjunction of its modal consequences – and hence it will be equivalent to the latter.

It remains to prove the Claim. Let M, s be any model for $mod(\varphi)$. Take the complete set of all modal formulas true at s in M and add $\{\varphi\}$. This set is easily seen to be finitely satisfiable, using the fact that $mod(\varphi)$ holds at M, s. By Compactness, it then has a model N, t modally equivalent to M, s. But then, the preceding observations give us elementary extensions M^+, N^+ of M, s and N, t, respectively, and a bisimulation $\equiv$ between M^+, N^+ with $s \equiv t$:

M, s	modal equivalence	N, t
elem. ext.		elem. ext.
M^+, s	bisimulation	N^+, t

Now we can clinch the proof by "diagram chasing". For a start, by our construction we had that $N, t \models \varphi$, and hence $N^+, t \models \varphi$ (by elementary extension), whence $M^+, s \models \varphi$ (by bisimulation invariance), and so $M, s \models \varphi$ (passing to an elementary submodel). □

This argument extends to many modal-like languages, modulating the link between zigzag clauses and restricted quantifier patterns.

25.2 Two excursions

Complexity of fragments The above result captures modal logic inside first-order logic by means of simple invariance. But it does so "up to logical definability". While it is easy to see if a first-order formula has explicit modal syntax, it is much harder to see whether it is *equivalent to* such a formula. Indeed, in the latter sense, natural fragments of first-order logic may be *undecidable*. The modal formulas are a case in point, because of the following effective reduction of the undecidable validity problem of first-order logic. Let $\alpha = \alpha(x)$ be any first-order formula, and P (unary), R (binary) new predicate letters outside of α.

Fact. The following two assertions are equivalent:

(a) α is universally valid,

(b) $\exists y P y \wedge (\neg\alpha)^\rho$ is bisimulation invariant, where $(\neg\alpha)^\rho$ is the formula $\neg\alpha$ syntactically relativized to the subdomain $\lambda z \cdot (Rxz \vee x = z)$.

Proof. If α is universally valid, then $\exists y P y \wedge (\neg\alpha)^\rho$ is equivalent to a contradiction, and the latter is trivially bisimulation invariant. Conversely, if α is not universally valid, then $\neg\alpha(x)$ is true in some model M at some world s. Now let R be the universal relation in M – and then, add one unrelated point t where P holds to obtain a model N:

In the new model N, the point s satisfies $\exists y P y \wedge (\neg\alpha)^\rho$. But this formula fails in the R-closed sub-model of N generated by s, thus clearly violating invariance for bisimulation. □

From invariance of formulas to safety of programs A few points from Chapter 14 put the preceding in perspective. The Modal Invariance Theorem also extends to other modal constructions. Consider the programs of dynamic logic (Chapter 14) that denoted binary transition relations between states in a model. These involved a special property:

Definition 25.2.1 (Safety for bisimulation). An n-ary operation $O(R_1, \ldots, R_n)$ on programs is *safe for bisimulation* if every bisimulation $\equiv$ between two models for their basic transition relations $R_1, \ldots, R_n$ is also a bisimulation for the relation $O(R_1, \ldots, R_n)$.

Thus, safe operations on programs or actions "stay inside" the invariance level of basic modal logic. The three regular program operations ; $\cup^*$ of *PDL* were safe for bisimulation, and so was the following operation, related to the test operation of dynamic logic:

$$\sim (R) = \{ (x, y) \mid x = y \text{ and for no } z\colon xRz \} \quad \text{strong test negation}$$

A non-regular program operation outside of standard *PDL* that lacked safety was Boolean *intersection* of relations. These observations suggest a more general characterization. Recall that program operations could be defined in Relational Algebra, and hence, at least the first-order ones among these were definable in standard first-order logic:

Theorem 71 (Modal safety theorem). A first-order relational operation $O(R_1, \ldots, R_n)$ is safe for bisimulation iff it can be defined using (a) atomic relations $R_a xy$ and atomic tests (q)? for propositional atoms q, plus (b) the three relational operations ; , $\sim$ and $\cup$.

The proof of this result involves somewhat laborious "tree surgery", but what it says is clear. The safe first-order operations are precisely three dynamic counterparts of the classical Booleans $\wedge$, $\neg$ and $\vee$.

25.3 A modal Lindström theorem

Here is another, still more abstract way of analyzing a logic. It was initiated in the 1960s by the "Lindström Theorem" that captured first-order logic (*FOL*) as the strongest extension of *FOL* satisfying abstract versions of the Compactness and Löwenheim-Skolem properties. Another important version combines a model-existence property (Compactness) with one of semantic invariance (often called the "Karp Property"):

Theorem 72. An abstract logic L extending *FOL* equals *FOL* iff

(a) all formulas of L are invariant for potential isomorphism,[251]

(b) L has the Compactness property.

Note that the invariance (a) is not part of the general definition of abstract logics: these just satisfy invariance for isomorphism.[252] The same style of thinking applies to extended abstract logics.

---

[251] For the notion of "potential isomorphism", see Chapter 7 and the Appendix.

[252] The version with Compactness and Löwenheim-Skolem follows from the one with isomorphism invariance, using the fact that potential isomorphisms between countable models are true isomorphisms.

We will not go into the proof of this result, except to note that it crucially involves the expressive power of a first-order language. The latter can typically encode how successive finite partial isomorphisms behave that satisfy the basic *back-and-forth properties* in the definition of a potential isomorphism.[253] And perhaps not surprisingly, the first-order ∀∃ quantifier pattern that is needed here turns out to be just the confluence diagram behind the *grid properties* of Chapter 24.

But now, when we want to do a similar analysis for modal logic, we have a problem. Encoding the notion of bisimulation would also involve such a grid pattern.[254] As we have seen repeatedly, this is about the anti-thesis of modal expressive power, and so we must follow another road, much closer to basics of the modal language.

To be wholly precise, we should first define an *abstract modal logic* L like in abstract model theory, with truth referring to pointed models M, w. But we trust that the reader will understand what follows without being exposed to these somewhat boring details. Of all such core conditions on what we call a "logic", we do high-light one:

Definition 25.3.1 (Relativization). A logic L has *relativization* if, for any L-formula φ and new unary proposition letter p, there is an L-formula $Rel(\varphi, p)$ true at a model M, w iff φ is true at $M|p, w$: the submodel of M with just the points in M satisfying p for its domain.

Most good logics satisfy Relativization (compare *PAL* and *DEL* in Chapters 15, 23), and it is also crucial to the above proof of the Lindström Theorem for first-order logic. Now we state our result, a so-called "maximality characterization" of the basic modal language:

Theorem 73. An abstract modal logic L extending the basic modal language equals the latter iff L satisfies (a) Invariance for Bisimulation, and (b) Compactness.

Proof. The direction from left to right is well-known to you. Next, assume that L has the stated two properties, and consider any formula φ in it. We start by proving a striking semantic property for L that the basic modal logic had, as we have seen in Parts I and II:

> *Finite Depth Property* For any formula φ, there is a natural number k such that, for all models, $M, s \models \varphi$ iff $M|k, s \models \varphi$, where $M|k$ is the submodel of M with its domain restricted to points reachable from s in k or fewer successive R-steps.

---

[253]See van Benthem et al. (2007) for a modern exposition.
[254]This is a bit weird: a strong bi-modal logic of bisimulation is undecidable!

Lemma. In a compact abstract modal logic L that is invariant for bisimulation, any formula has the Finite Depth Property.

Proof. Let φ be any formula in L. Suppose, for the sake of reductio ad absurdum, that it lacks the Finite Depth Property. Then for any natural number k, there exists a model M_k, s and a cut-off version $M_k|k, s$ that disagree on the truth value of φ. Without loss of generality, assume that the following happens for arbitrarily large k:

$$M_k|k, s \models \varphi \text{ while } M_k, s \models \neg\varphi.^{255}$$

Now, take a new proposition letter p, and consider the following infinite set Σ of L-formulas:

$$\neg\varphi, \; Rel(\varphi, p), \; \{ \, \Box^n p \mid n \text{ is a natural number} \, \}.$$

Given our assumptions, this set is clearly finitely satisfiable: we choose k sufficiently large, and make p true in the k-reachable part of one of the above sequence of models. But then, by Compactness for our abstract modal logic L, there must be a model N, v for the whole set Σ at once. But this leads to a contradiction. We focus on the *generated sub-model* N_v, v consisting of v and all points finitely reachable from it. Clearly, the identity relation is a bisimulation between any pointed model and its unique generated sub-model. Hence by the invariance for bisimulation of our logic, formulas of L have the same truth value in any pointed model and its generated sub-model. Now, given the first formula in Σ, $\neg\varphi$ holds in N, v and hence also in N_v, v (i). On the other hand, since $N, v \models Rel(\varphi, p)$, also $N|p, v \models \varphi$. But by the truth of the infinite third set of formulas, p holds in the whole generated sub-model N_v, v. Therefore, it is easy to see that the generated submodel of $N|p, v$ is also just N_v, v, and so we have that φ holds in N_v, v (ii). This is a contradiction. $\Box$

Now we move on to a crucial next property:

Lemma. If L-formula φ has the Finite Depth Property for distance k, then φ is preserved under modal equivalence up to operator depth k.

Proof. Let two models M, w, N, v agree on all modal formulas up to depth k, while $M, w \models \varphi$. By a standard technique from Chapter 3, these models are bisimilar to their *tree unraveling*: $Tree(M, w)$, $Tree(N, v)$. Now, since the latter tree models have the same modal theory up to depth k in their roots, we can define an obvious *"cut-off" bisimulation* between them up to the first k tree levels starting from

---

[255]Here we use the fact that abstract modal logics are closed under negations.

the root. More precisely, the relevant relation is, for nodes lying at the same distance i from the respective roots w, v:

satisfying the same modal formulas up to depth $k - i$.

It is easy to see that this relation between nodes in the two trees satisfies the back-and-forth clauses of bisimulation up to at most k times. And what is more, it is a *full* bisimulation between the "cut-off models" $Tree(M, w)|k$ and $Tree(N, v)|k$. By the Finite Depth Property plus invariance for bisimulation, φ then holds, successively, in

$$(M, w), \ Tree(M, w), \ (\ Tree(M, w)|k, w), \ (\ Tree(N, v)|k, v) \text{ and } (N, v).$$

$\square$

The proof of the theorem is clinched by a well-known observation:

Lemma. If an L-formula φ is preserved under modal equivalence up to some finite operator depth k, it is definable by a modal formula of operator depth k.

Proof. Here we first observe the fact that formulas of the logic L depend on only finitely many proposition letters.[256] Next, we use that the basic modal language is *logically finite*: on finitely many proposition letters, it has only finitely many non-equivalent formulas.[257] Finally, it is easy to see from our closure assumption that

Any class K of pointed models that is closed under modal k-equivalence is defined by the disjunction of all finite complete modal depth-k theories satisfied in K.

This disjunction is a modal formula defining our L-formula φ.

$\square$

25.4 Further perspectives and omitted topics

The modal Lindström theorem is the beginning of a broader set of questions. Traditional abstract model theory has looked at extensions of first-order logic. In line with the "small is beautiful" slogan of modal logic, however, it is of equal interest to analyze weaker first-order languages in this way. This area includes the study of many extended modal logics from Part II, and it has revealed lots of surprises: see the dissertation *Model Theory of Extended Modal Languages* of Balder ten Cate (ten Cate, 2005) or the cited paper on "weak abstract model theory" by van Benthem, ten Cate & Väänänen (van Benthem et al.,

---

[256]We can either stipulate that any L-formula φ depends on only finitely many proposition letters, or use Compactness to derive it from "renaming properties".

[257]We used this fact when proving adequacy of bisimulation games in Chapter 3.

2007). One major challenge right now is generalizing this style of Lindström analysis to the modal fixed-point logics of Chapter 22. It seems we still lack the right basic properties here.[258]

Frame theory While all this is about theory of models, there is also a flourishing literature on modal logics as describing *frames* in the second-order sense of Chapter 9, where a modal formula is true if it holds under all valuations for its proposition letters. Modal correspondence theory has many results not mentioned in these lectures. Just as a teaser, we recall one fundamental result stated in Chapter 9, due to Goldblatt & Thomason, which explains modal definability in terms of a few elegant model-theoretic closure properties:

Theorem 74. A first-order definable class of frames is defined by a set of modal formulas iff it is closed under the formation of (a) *generated subframes*, (b) *disjoint unions*, (c) *p-morphic images*, and (d) its complement is closed under *ultrafilter extensions*.

If you want to know what these frame-theoretic notions mean, and how a characterization result like this might be proved, please refer to the Modal Logic book by Blackburn, de Rijke & Venema cited throughout these lectures (Blackburn et al., 2001), or the chapters by Goranko & Otto and by Venema in the *Handbook of Modal Logic*: Blackburn et al. (2006). There are algebraic proofs linking modal frames with structures in Universal Algebra, but also model-theoretic ones more in the spirit of this chapter, employing saturated models.

Modal algebra Perhaps the most glaring omission in these lectures are the important *algebraic methods* in contemporary modal logic. While I would typically teach these in an advanced course, including the representation theory of modal algebras and their duality with so-called "general frames", I have not included them in this book, since most of my topics do not require them.[259]

---

[258]One can step up the abstraction level even further, and make the choice of the invariance relations like bisimulation itself a "parameter": for results along those lines, cf. van Benthem and Bonnay (2008).

[259]But to my many friends working with algebraic methods, I say: the omission weighs heavily on my conscience, and I may change my mind in a next edition.

Exercises Chapter 25

1. State a Modal Invariance Theorem for the modal language with an added universal modality. What needs to change in the proof that we have given for the basic language?

2. Invariance and interpolation:
   (a) Prove the following fact: If φ, ψ are first-order formulas, and α is a modal formula such that $\varphi \models \alpha \models \psi$ (such a formula a is called a "modal interpolant"), then "φ *entails ψ along bisimulation*", that is, whenever $M, s \models \varphi$, and there is a bisimulation between M, s and N, t, then $N, t \models \psi$.
   (b) Formulate a converse of this result, as a "Modal Interpolation Theorem". Show that this result implies the Modal Invariance Theorem.

3. There is no modal Lindström theorem when we replace invariance for bisimulation by the Löwenheim-Skolem property. Why not?

4. Derive the Modal Invariance Theorem from the Modal Lindström Theorem by an argument about abstract logics.

5. Try to extend the proof of the Modal Lindström Theorem to the modal language with an added universal modality. Which step typically breaks down?

26

Deductive incompleteness

26.1 Modal deduction and proof theory

I admitted at the start of these lectures that I have no great affinity with drill in formal modal deduction. Interesting formal proofs are scarce in logic (if you except the Russell Paradox), and also in modal logic – even though we have seen a few good examples in provability logic (Chapter 21). So why drill students in things that we hardly touch ourselves? Also, it has often been observed that there is no well-developed subject of modal proof theory, though the *Handbook of Modal Logic* does have a chapter where you can see much of what exists. Indeed, many results in this area seem routine colonization from standard proof theory: things would get livelier if there were something proof-theoretically intrinsic to the restricted notations of the modal language.[260] [261] But having said this, modal logic has turned out to be an interesting area of tension between what seem natural semantics and "matching" proof systems that do not quite match up in the final analysis. We discuss a few of these incompleteness phenomena in this final chapter.

26.2 Another balance: semantics and deductive power

First-order logic may be undecidable, but it does have a completeness theorem telling us that it can capture all its valid reasoning in a perspicuous proof system. This feature is not automatic. Second-order logic, too, seems semantically natural, but it has no complete proof system, and its complexity is beyond the wildest imagination. But these well-known observations are just the start of a thought process. For

---

[260] One intriguing sui generis perspective is in the dissertation *Coming to Terms with Modal Logic* (Borghuis, 1994) where modal boxes and diamonds are a sort of "file management system" for deductions in type theory.

[261] Interesting proof theory occurs also in hybrid logics, with Cut Elimination theorems linked to the choice of expressively well-balanced fragments.

instance, with second-order logic, the mismatch between validity and deduction has raised the issue whether the usual "standard models" (a popular question-begging phrase) of second-order logic are the really natural ones. Famously, Leon Henkin introduced his *"general models"* where second-order quantifiers range over restricted families of predicates, extending the class of models far beyond the original one, restoring axiomatizability. While Henkin's models are generally seen as a mere technical tool or even trick – quite unjustly – they do point at a ubiquitous and serious phenomenon: rethinking existing semantics for proof-theoretic reasons. Let us look at modal logic in the same vein.

26.3 Incompleteness in propositional modal logic

Originally, it seemed as if completeness was the norm in modal logic when relational models arrived in force around 1960. This even worked in two ways. Existing syntactic proof calculi for modal logics like *K*, *S4* or *S5* turned out to have complete semantics, often via frame classes with properties that corresponded to these axioms in the technical sense of Chapter 9. And also conversely, when modal logicians looked at natural classes of models, sometimes even single ones, they found complete axiomatic logics.[262] Against this background, the following result by Steve Thomason in 1973 came as a complete surprise:

Theorem 75. The tense logic axiomatized by the two axioms (a) $H(H\varphi \rightarrow \varphi) \rightarrow H\varphi$ (Lö's Axiom for the past) and (b) $GF\varphi \rightarrow FG\varphi$ (McKinsey Axiom for the future) is not complete with respect to any class of relational frames.[263]

Proof. Suppose there is a class of frames K whose modal theory is this logic. This means that both axioms (a) and (b) hold in each frame in K. And we know what they say, from Chapters 9, 21. The Löb Axiom says that the relation is well-founded: there are no downward infinite chains – while it is also transitive.[264] But on transitive frames, the McKinsey Axiom said that there exist end-points: $\forall x \exists y (Rxy \wedge \forall z (Ryz \rightarrow z = y))$. In particular, these end-points have successors, too, and so they must be reflexive. But now note that the combination of these two properties is inconsistent: any reflexive point is an infinite sequence $sRsRsR\cdots$ of the sort forbidden by well-foundedness. Thus, the class K is empty.

---

[262] The latter success is limited by a cardinality count: there are $2^{\aleph_0}$ possible modal logics, but many more model classes. Still, we have seen that the modal logic of any *first-order definable* class of frames is axiomatizable.

[263] We stated this result briefly in Chapter 18, but we provide more details now.

[264] To be precise, if the converse of a relation is transitive, so is that relation itself.

But the modal theory of the empty class of frames is the inconsistent set of *all formulas*, and this cannot be. For the logic that we just defined is consistent! We can see this as follows. Consider the frame F of the natural numbers $(\mathbb{N}, <)$ but give it only the special family of the *finite* and *cofinite* subsets (these have a finite complement). It is easy to see that, in this structure, all principles of the form (a) and (b) are true, no matter how we evaluate proposition letters in finite or cofinite sets.[265] The Löb Axiom holds because the frame is in fact transitive and well-founded. Of course, $(\mathbb{N}, <)$ has no reflexive end-points, but the crux is that, with formulas denoting finite and cofinite sets only, the McKinsey Axiom must hold: its antecedent says that the formula φ denotes a cofinite set, and this definitely has a future stage where it will contain all greater natural numbers. $\qquad \square$

So what does this mean? Thomason went on to show that *modal frame consequence* $\varphi \models \psi$ defined as "truth of φ in any frame F implies truth of ψ in F" has the same complexity as valid consequence in all of second-order logic. The second-order nature of frame truth reared its head. There is no way that simple modal deduction can capture this, and the success of modal logic so far rested perhaps on thin ice. Now there is much more to be said here. For instance, the Sahlqvist Theorem of Chapter 9 also has a proof-theoretic version saying that modal logics with axioms of the special shape that we described are frame-complete. The ice is quite thick in some places.

What we are really seeing is a mismatch between two styles of deduction. After all, the argument we just gave for the semantic frame inconsistency of the Thomason logic *is* clearly a formal proof. But the issue is *where it lives*. If you spell out details, the proof uses obvious steps in first-order logic, but also, in its assertion about the McKinsey Axiom and atomicity on transitive frames, an appeal to a second-order Axiom of Choice. So, is the mismatch just that some second-order deductions cannot be mimicked in modal deduction? (van Benthem, 1979) showed that things are much worse. It presents a modal logic (no tense logic needed) that has a modal frame consequence obtainable by a trivial first-order proof, and yet there is no modal deduction available yielding this modal consequence.

This result still leaves many roads open. One is to employ stronger proof systems for the basic modal language, adding some first-order, and perhaps even second-order features. Another road increases the

---

[265] It is also easy to show that, based on such special valuations, *all* modal formulas, atomic or complex, come to denote finite or cofinite sets.

expressive power of the modal language, thereby endowing its existing proof principles with greater strength, and trying again. This has removed some incompleteness phenomena – though by Thomason's result, we know that there is no cure that restores complete harmony between frame semantics and effective modal deduction.

A final and different road might lead toward rethinking the very semantics of modal logic. In particular, we can replace frames by *general frames* in Henkin's sense, that can impose restrictions on the available sets that can be denotations of modal formulas. The above structure $(\mathbb{N}, <)$ with just the finite and cofinite sets was in fact an appealing example. This move leads us to algebraic semantics for modal logic, a topic beyond these lectures – but see the chapters by Yde Venema and by Marcus Kracht in the *Handbook of Modal Logic*. And it will make the minimal modal proof calculus complete again.

While the incompleteness phenomena of propositional modal logic seem to have largely lost their sting, the way former dreaded epidemics turn into household diseases like a common cold, such phenomena continue to disturb the area of modal predicate logic (Chapter 11).

26.4 Incompleteness in modal predicate logic

In the 1960s, both Lindstroem and Scott observed that, on natural semantic structures, the success of completeness theorems in propositional tense logic may fail to extend to their predicate-logical companions. For instance, the propositional tense logic of the natural numbers (cf. Chapter 18) had been axiomatized by Segerberg, but the complete tense logic over even constant domains of objects on the natural numbers is not axiomatizable at all.

Unreliable companions Even so, starting with Kripke in 1959, completeness theorems had been found for many predicate-logical versions of existing modal logics such as K, $S4$ and $S5$. These seemed so straightforward that the theory of modal predicate logic might just be an uneventful lift from the propositional case. Indeed, the following conjecture appeared in a 1984 textbook (Hughes and Cresswell, 1984)):

> Whenever a modal propositional logic is complete with respect to some class of frames, its modal predicate-logical version is complete with respect to this same frame class allowing arbitrary cumulative domains.

Here the "companion" is a logic with the former propositional schemata now allowing all substitution instances in the modal predicate-logical language, plus all the usual principles of first-order logic.[266]

---

[266]This innocuous-looking merge is not harmless: using old schemata with substi-

This statement was refuted independently by Ono and Shehtman & Skvortsov in the 1980s, showing how natural complete propositional modal logics may fail to have frame-complete predicate-logical companions. An example is the modal predicate logical companion for the propositional logic *S4.1* of transitive atomic orders. In the 1990s, Ghilardi[267] analyzed the general situation, and proved results like this:

Theorem 76. Among the propositional extensions of *S4*, the modal logics L whose predicate companion LQ is frame-complete have either $L \supseteq S5$ or $L \subseteq S4.3$.

Here *S4.z* is the complete modal logic of linear orders. As we just said, a natural modal logic like *S4.1*, the complete logic of atomic reflexive transitive orders in which each point sees an end-point, neither contains *S5* nor is contained in *S4.3*, and hence its predicate companion *S4.1Q* is deeply incomplete. Thus, the "obvious" standard semantics for modal predicate logic seems to have mathematical problems – an echo of Quine's original problems with the framework.

"Unrealizable" frame correspondences Incompleteness abounds with modal predicate-logical axioms beyond the minimal companion. As we noted in Chapter 11, such axioms impose semantic constraints on models that can be determined by correspondence arguments, as in propositional modal logic.

Example (Frame correspondence in modal predicate logic). Correspondences now constrain world ordering and object occurrence together. The following list gives examples:

$$\exists x \Box Px \rightarrow \Box \exists x Px \quad \forall w : \forall v (Rwv \rightarrow \forall x (Exv \rightarrow Exv)) \quad \textit{Domain Cumulation}$$
$$\Diamond \exists x Px \rightarrow \exists x \Diamond Px \quad \forall w : \forall v (Rwv \rightarrow \forall x (Exv \rightarrow Exw)) \quad \textit{Anti-Cumulation}$$

We also observed that behind these observations, there is a generalized Sahlqvist theorem. But here was a principle beyond the method of minimal substitution analysis of Chapter 9:

Theorem 77. $\Box \exists x Px \rightarrow \exists x \Box Px$ has no first-order correspondent.

We did note a positive correspondence fact on special frames:

Fact. On frames satisfying Domain Cumulation, the modal predicate-logical axiom $\Box \exists x Px \rightarrow \exists x \Box Px$ is first-order definable.

Proof. The equivalent is the conjunction of two first-order properties:

(a) domain anti-cumulation, (b) "partial function": each world whose domain has more than one object has at most one world successor.

---

tutions in the much richer combined language can be very strong.

[267] A co-author on modal predicate logic in the *Handbook of Modal Logic*.

First, if these two first-order properties hold, then so does $\Box\exists x Px \rightarrow \exists x \Box Px$. If a world has just one object d, with domain cumulation and anti-cumulation, all successors have just that d, and the antecedent implies that this object has property P throughout. And if a world has at most one accessible successor, then truth of $\Box\exists x Px$ implies that of $\exists x \Box Px$, either trivially, or because some object d in the unique successor world satisfies P, and that same d will satisfy $\Box Px$ in w.

Next, we show that frame truth of $\Box\exists x Px \rightarrow \exists x \Box Px$ implies the two stated first-order conditions. First consider domain anti-cumulation (a). Suppose that wRv where v has an object d not occurring in w. We can use any such situation to refute our modal axiom:

> In world v, make the predicate P true for d only, and in all other successor worlds of w, make P true for all the objects.

By domain inclusion, the stipulation about world v alone refutes the consequent $\exists x \Box Px$ at w, while the two stipulations together make $\Box\exists x Px$ true at w. Next, take condition (b). Let world w have at least two objects 1, 2 and more than one successor, say v_1, v_2 and perhaps others. Now define a valuation for the predicate P as follows:

> P holds of 1 and of no other object in v_1, P holds of 2 and no other object in v_2, and P holds of all objects in all other successor worlds.

This makes $\Box\exists x Px$ true at w while no object at w has P in all successor worlds. Contradiction: w has at most one successor. $\quad\Box$

The preceding proof, though elementary, cannot work in the substitution style of Chapter 9. To see this, consider the following model where $\Box\exists x Px \rightarrow \exists x \Box Px$ fails at w:

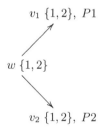

$$v_1 \ \{1,2\}, \ P1$$

$$w \ \{1,2\}$$

$$v_2 \ \{1,2\}, \ P2$$

Given the symmetry between v_1, v_2, there is no uniform definition for the predicate P purely within the language L_{corr} that witnesses this failure. Moreover, since a version of the semantic property (b) can be expressed in modal predicate logic (we forego details), we can turn this into a case of non-derivability in the modal base language.

Natural examples of incompleteness occur in intuitionistic predicate logic (cf. Chapter 20) when analyzing the frame content of intuitionistically invalid classical principles such as "Plato's Law":

$$\exists x(\exists y Py \to Px) \quad [268]$$

26.5   An alternative: semantic re-analysis

Again, one can respond to this situation in many ways, proof-theoretic or more semantic. One interesting proposed remedy has been to go back to the drawing board, and rethink the semantics of modal predicate logic. In particular, we can now change to *functional models*

$$M = (W, F, V)$$

with W a set of individual object domains, and F a family of maps between such domains, including all identity maps and closed under compositions,[269] while V is a valuation as before. There is no explicit accessibility relation, but the maps in F encode one in a sense. The truth definition now inductively describes the notion

$$M, w, a \models \varphi$$

of a formula φ being true at a world w in a model M under assignment a of objects to variables. Here is the key new clause:

$M, w, a \models \Box\varphi$ iff for all maps $f \in F$ with domain D_w and range D_v, $M, v, f \circ a \models \varphi$ – with $f \circ a$ the composition of map f with map a.

To see the power of this semantics compared with standard possible-worlds models, consider just a simple one-world reflexive frame:

Example (Divergences from modal propositional logic.). In standard semantics, this validates propositional $p \to \Box p$, and no matter which domain of objects we attach, we also get

$$\varphi(x) \to \Box\varphi(x)$$

But in the new semantics, one-world frames can refute the latter principle![270] Take a model M with one world w carrying an object domain $\{1, 2\}$, and a function set $F = \{f_1, f_2\}$ with f_1 the identity map, and f_2 the constant map sending both objects to 2. We have $P(1)$ true at w in M, but not $P(f_1(1))$.

---

[268] On intuitionistic frames, Plato's Law defines the conjunction of a surprising bunch of properties: (a) There is a constant domain D for each world, (b) Accessibility is a linear order if that domain D has at least two objects, (c) If D is infinite, then the accessibility relation is also well-founded.

[269] These two conditions ensure that the logic validates a least modal $S4$.

[270] This shows again how old schemata in new languages can be extremely strong.

Interestingly, this technical semantics is closer to Lewis' "counterpart semantics" for modal predication across worlds from the 1960s, which at the time had a purely philosophical motivation. Further remodeling approaches to modal predicate logic are the algebraic semantics of Ono (1999), and the general frames of Goldblatt and Mares (2006).

26.6 Modern perspectives

We repeat a point from Chapter 11. The technical reason for the complications with modal predicate logic is that this system is not straightforward at all – though it seems just a simple merge of two notations. We are merging two different logics, each with its own semantics: the modal propositional realm of worlds and accessibility, and first-order predicate logic over domains of individual objects. Now, as we will see soon in Chapter 27, first-order logic itself is a modal logic over spaces of variable assignments, with accessibility relations R_x corresponding to moving from one assignment to another by changing the value for the variable x. Modal predicate logic is then a product of two modal logics, and we have seen in Chapter 24 that product logics can be very unlike their components.[271]

Finally we mention that natural language semantics involves much more complex modal logics, adding the operators $\Box$, $\Diamond$ to *second-order* logic or even *type theory*. This raises many further issues about the nature of objects and properties – but for further details, we refer to the chapter by Reinhard Muskens in the *Handbook of Modal Logic*.

---

[271] In particular, modal predicate logic requires a merge between two model-theoretic invariances: *bisimulation* for worlds, and *potential isomorphism*, or some Ehrenfeucht-game version thereof, for the objects.

Part V

Coda

This final chapter is mainly an after-thought, to show you that nothing is quite what it seems in logic. In these lectures, we have mostly presented modal logic as a sort of fine-structure laboratory for classical systems, in particular, first-order logic. And the main tool here was the "standard translation" of Chapter 7, making modal logic a weak "fragment" of first-order logic. But things are more delicate. The analogies between modal and classical logic in terms of basic invariances and meta-theory are so striking that they continue to invite new research.[272] The chapter "Modal Logic, A Semantic Perspective" in the *Handbook of Modal Logic* (Blackburn et al., 2006) surveys some kinds of explanation, while recent studies have found new connections between bisimulation and the classical invariance relation of potential isomorphism (first introduced in Chapter 7) at the level of abstract model theory. The upshot of all this is that first-order logic and modal logic are close in many respects. We are now going to demonstrate this very concretely, by turning the tables, and showing how *first-order logic itself* can be viewed as a special case of modal logic. In taking that unusual perspective, we also learn something new about first-order logic, viz. the fact that its undecidability is largely the effect of imposing a particular sort of models on top of a decidable core mechanism of interpretation. This shows that modal techniques can be used to "deconstruct" classical systems into what one might call "core" versus "wrappings". We will develop some further consequences of this as we go.

This chapter may shake up cherished convictions, so take a breath!

---

[272]Of course, modal logic also improves on first-order logic: its complexity is decidable, it has stronger interpolation theorems, etcetera.

27

Modal foundations for classical logic

27.1 The modal core of predicate logic

The standard semantics for predicate logic has this key clause

$$M, \alpha \models \exists x \varphi \text{ iff for some } d \in |M|\colon M, \alpha_d^x \models \varphi$$

The key is the use of variable assignments α that decompose quantified statements $\exists x \varphi$ with possibly free variables in their matrix φ. But looking more closely at this definition, a compositional semantics for first-order quantification really only needs this abstract core pattern:

$$M, \alpha \models \exists x \varphi \text{ iff for some } \beta : R_x \alpha \beta \text{ and } M, \beta \models \varphi$$

Here, assignments α, β become abstract states, and the concrete relation $\alpha =_x \beta$ between α and α_d^x becomes just any binary relation R_x. This involves poly-modal models $M = (S, \{R_x\}_{x \in VAR}, I)$ with S a set of states, R_x a binary update relation for each variable x, and I an interpretation function giving a truth value to atomic formulas $Px, Rxy, \ldots$ in each state α. Then, existential quantifiers $\exists x$ become unary existential modalities $\langle x \rangle$. This modal semantics has an independent appeal: first-order evaluation is an informational process that changes computational states. The first-order language then becomes a *dynamic logic*, with a special choice of atoms and without explicit compound programs – as in the "dynamic semantics" of Chapter 14.

Looking in the opposite direction, from this modal point of view, standard semantics arises by insisting on three additional mathematical choices, not enforced by the core semantics:

(a) States are identified with variable assignments,

(b) update between states must use the specific relation $=_x$, and

(c) all assignments in the space D^{VAR} are available to evaluation.

The former are issues of implementation, the latter a strong existence assumption.[273] Henceforth, we regard these choices as negotiable. This view lends further support to the abstract modal approach. E.g., it is often felt that the usual set-theoretic tricks making predicates sets of tuples should be orthogonal to the nature of logical validity.

Our modal semantics validates the *minimal poly-modal logic*, whose principles consist of (reading a universal quantifier $\forall x$ on the analogy of a modal box $[x]$):

- all classical Boolean propositional laws
- Modal Distribution: $\forall x(\varphi \rightarrow \psi) \rightarrow (\forall x\varphi \rightarrow \forall x\psi)$
- Modal Necessitation: if $\vdash \varphi$, then $\vdash \forall x\varphi$
- a definition of $\exists x\varphi$ as $\neg\forall x\neg\varphi$

This logic is complete, and it has the usual properties of first-order logic, such as Craig Interpolation or Los-Tarski Preservation. One can now usefully pursue standard first-order model theory in tandem with its modal counterpart. For instance, consider modal *bisimulations* for these models, relating states making the same atoms true, with back-and-forth conditions for the relations R_x. Specializing these to standard models leads to the standard notion of *potential isomorphism*. And in all this, this minimal modal logic of evaluation is *decidable*.

The modal perspective suggests a whole landscape below standard predicate logic, with a minimal modal logic at the base, ascending to standard semantics via frame constraints. This landscape contains *decidable sub-logics* of predicate logic, sharing its desirable meta-properties. Thus, the "undecidability of predicate logic" largely reflects accidents of its Tarskian modeling, encoding set-theoretic facts about mathematical function spaces D^{VAR} – rather than the core logic of quantification and variable assignment.

We shall explore the resulting view of first-order semantics, including richer languages. In particular, abstract core models support interesting distinctions between various forms of quantification ("monadic" and "polyadic") that get collapsed in standard predicate logic.

27.2   Dependency models

There are natural inhabitants of the landscape between standard logic and its modal core. One may retain the general mechanism of Tarski semantics (the above (a), (b)), while giving up its existence assumption (c). The result are *general assignment models* (M, V) with V some

---

[273]Actually, standard predicate logic can get by with the set of partial assignments on all *finite* sets of variables – but even that is a strong existence requirement.

family of assignments in the usual sense – not necessarily the full space D^{VAR} – and the R_x the standard relations $=_x$.

Example (General assignment models). With two variables x, y, an object domain $\{1, 2\}$ supports 2^4 assignment sets. One is the standard model with all four maps from variables to objects. Another has just assignments α, β with $\alpha(x) = 1$, $\alpha(y) = 2$ and $\beta(x) = 2, \beta(y) = 1$.

		present	x	y	*absent*	x	y
1	2		1	2		1	1
			2	1		2	2

"Assignment gaps" model the intuitive phenomenon of *dependencies* between variables: when changes in value for one variable x may induce, or be correlated with, changes in value for another variable y. This phenomenon, well-known from probability theory and the semantics of natural language, cannot be modeled in standard first-order semantics, where we can change values for variables completely independently. Starting from any state α, one can move to any α_d^x. But in a model with assignment gaps, the only way to change values for x, starting from some assignment, may be by incurring a change in y. In the above two-assignment model, any shift in value for x produces one for y.

In general assignment models (M, V), a "modal" existential quantifier $\exists x \varphi$ says that some x-variant of the current state exists *inside* V satisfying φ. Standard first-order models are the degenerate cases where all dependencies between variables have been suppressed. This shows clearly in the standard quantifier exchange principle

$$\exists x \exists y \varphi \leftrightarrow \exists y \exists x \varphi$$

that is typically invalid on our general models. Dependence is a popular topic these days in various areas of logic.[274]

27.3 What do first-order axioms say?

The above picture has fine-structure through constraints on modal frames or assignment models, reflecting aspects of dependence. But one can also analyze candidate axioms via *frame correspondences*. In this light, what is expressed by the laws of predicate logic? Usually,

---

[274] Cf. van Benthem (1996), for sources of this chapter, plus an extended analysis of dependency using *sets of assignments*, inspired by work in linguistic semantics of plural expressions. New sophisticated dependence logics with more computational and mathematical motivations are in Väänänen (2007).

these are all in one big bag. But now, they express different facts about states and accessibility, with a computational slant.

For a concrete illustration, we use modal correspondence to deconstruct the axioms for first-order logic in the textbook (Enderton, 1971). We stated these already in our account of the minimal modal logic in Chapter 5. The system has all universal closures of the Boolean propositional laws plus the three quantifier axioms

(1) $\forall x(\varphi \to \psi) \to (\forall x\varphi \to \forall x\psi)$

(2) $\varphi \to \forall x\varphi$ *provided that x does not occur free in φ*

(3) $\forall x\varphi \to [t/x]\varphi$ *provided that t is free for x in φ*

There is one inference rule, Modus Ponens. From a modal perspective, the propositional part is valid. The first quantifier axiom is Modal Distribution. Universal closure of axioms is a technique which amounts to having a rule of Necessitation for universal quantifiers. Indeed, the first part of the Enderton axiomatization by itself is a complete calculus for the minimal modal logic![275] This sub-system of first-order logic is of interest by itself, since it captures many forms of syllogistic *monotonicity-based* inference, of which linguists and philosophers have claimed that they make up the bulk of first-order reasoning in practice.

Now to the other axioms. We start with the least conspicuous one:

$\varphi \to \forall x\varphi$.

We analyze this principle inductively, in a syntax with literals, $\wedge, \vee, \exists, \forall$. Our argument is heuristic, looking at various instances independently. The first instance is the atomic pair:

(2.1) *Atomic* $Py \to \forall xPy$, $\neg Py \to \forall x\neg Py$. This makes truth values for x-free atoms invariant for R_x-transitions: R_x implies $=_x$. Thus, we have a *Heredity Principle* for abstract interpretation functions I:

if $I(\alpha, Py)$, then $I(\beta, Py)$ for all states β with $R_x\alpha\beta$.[276]

(2.2) *Boolean cases* $\varphi_1 \wedge \varphi_2$, $\varphi_1 \vee \varphi_2$. Let $\vdash \varphi_1 \to \forall x\varphi_1$ and $\vdash \varphi_2 \to \forall x\varphi_2$. The base logic automatically yields $\vdash (\varphi_1 \wedge \varphi_2) \to \forall x(\varphi_1 \wedge \varphi_2)$. The case for disjunction is analogous.

(2.3) *Quantifiers* $\exists x\varphi$, $\forall x\varphi$. *Subcase (2.3.1)*. The quantified variable y *is* x *itself*. Then we have that

$$\exists x\varphi \to \forall x\exists x\varphi, \qquad \forall x\varphi \to \forall x\forall x\varphi$$

These are *S5*-axioms: $\langle x \rangle\varphi \to [x]\langle x \rangle\varphi$, and $[x] \to [x][x]\varphi$. Their frame content makes the relation R_x is *transitive* and *euclidean*.

---

[275]It is tempting to see the Hand of Providence at work here.

[276]Compare the Heredity constraint on intuitionistic models in Chapter 20.

If we add the simplest instance of Enderton's axiom (3), viz. $\forall x \varphi \to \varphi$ (expressing *reflexivity* of the R_x), we get full $S5$, where all R_x, like the $=_x$, are *equivalence relations*. Henceforth, we assume the $S5$-principles, that hold anyway in all general assignment models.

Subcase (2.3.2). The variables x, y are distinct. Heuristically, we assume that $\vdash \varphi \to \forall x \varphi$, and then we need the implications

$$\exists y \varphi \to \forall x \exists y \varphi, \qquad \forall y \varphi \to \forall x \forall y \varphi$$

Modulo $S4$, these express well-known first-order quantifier shifts. The rule "$\vdash \varphi \to \forall x \varphi$ implies $\vdash \exists y \varphi \to \forall x \exists y \varphi$" is equivalent with the axiom $\exists y \forall x \varphi \to \forall x \exists y \varphi$. The rule "$\vdash \varphi \to \forall x \varphi$ implies $\vdash \forall y \varphi \to \forall x \forall y \varphi$" is equivalent with the axiom $\forall y \forall x \varphi \to \forall x \forall y \varphi$. Both resulting axioms are Sahlqvist forms (cf. Chapter 9):

Fact.

(a) $\forall y \forall x \varphi \to \forall x \forall y \varphi$ expresses Path Reversal:

$$\forall \alpha \beta \gamma ((R_x \alpha \beta \wedge R_y \beta \gamma) \to \exists \delta (R_y \alpha \delta \wedge R_x \delta \gamma))$$

(b) $\exists y \forall x \varphi \to \forall x \exists y \varphi$ expresses Confluence:

$$\forall \alpha \beta \gamma ((R_y \alpha \beta \wedge R_x \alpha \gamma) \to \exists \delta (R_x \beta \delta \wedge R_y \gamma \delta))$$

We recognize earlier "diamond pictures" from Chapters 7 and 24:

Next comes Enderton's last axiom: "$\forall x \varphi \to [t/x]\varphi$ provided t is free for x in φ". Here, we extend our modal language:

27.4 Quantifiers and substitutions

One can view a substitution $[t/x]$ as a modal operator in its own right,[277] referring to the controlled value assignment $x := t$ that is the natural semantic companion to the random assignment for the existential quantifier $\exists x$. So we enrich our modal models with abstract relations $A_{x,y}$, whose concrete standard interpretation is as follows:

$A_{x,y} \alpha \beta$ iff $\beta(x) = \alpha(y)$ and $\alpha(z) = \beta(z)$ for all z distinct from x.[278]

Here is the obvious truth definition:

$$M, \alpha \models [y/x]\varphi \quad \text{iff} \quad \text{for all } \beta \text{ with } A_{x,y}\alpha\beta : M, \beta \models \varphi$$

---

[277] Maybe the standard box notation for substitution was pre-ordained.
[278] We only consider substitutions of variables for variables.

Again there is a minimal logic, and further axioms put constraints. The usual syntactic definition of substitution now gets semantic import:

(a) *Atomic Cases* $[y/x]Px \leftrightarrow Py$, $[y/x]Pz \leftrightarrow Pz$ (z distinct from x)

These express heredity constraints on admissible propositional valuations. On concrete assignment frames, they express that the relations $A_{x,y}$ are to behave as in the usual concrete clauses.

(b) *Boolean Cases* $[y/x](\varphi \wedge \psi) \leftrightarrow ([y/x]\varphi \wedge [y/x]\psi)$,
$[y/x]\neg\varphi \leftrightarrow \neg[y/x]\varphi$

The first is valid in the minimal modal logic. The second axiom makes the relation $A_{x,y}$ into a *function* (cf. the *PAL* negation axiom in Chapter 15). For convenience, we make this assumption henceforth.

(c) *Quantified Cases* $[y/x]\exists x\varphi \leftrightarrow \exists x\varphi$, $[y/x]\forall x\varphi \leftrightarrow \forall x\varphi$,
$[y/x]\exists z\varphi \leftrightarrow \exists z[y/x]\varphi$ (z distinct from x, y),
$[y/x]\forall z\varphi \leftrightarrow \forall z[y/x]\varphi$ (z distinct from x, y)

These are simple interactions between $A_{x,y}$ and R_x, that we do not spell out. We leave the remaining $[z/x]\exists z\varphi$, $[z/x]\forall z\varphi$ to the reader.

Finally, "$\forall x\varphi \rightarrow [y/x]\varphi$, with y free for x in φ" says

$$A_{x,y} \text{ is contained in } R_x.$$

27.5   Landscape of deductive strength

The upshot of the preceding re-analysis of "standard first-order semantics" is this. First-order predicate logic is really a dynamic logic for variable-to-value assignment, whose atomic processes shift values in registers $x, y, z, \ldots$. This view opens up a hierarchy of fine-structure, and first-order logic becomes the special (undecidable) theory of a particular mathematical class of "rich assignment models". We get a broad semantic landscape with a minimal modal logic at the bottom, where intermediate systems arise by imposing some, though not all of the usual requirements on assignments and their R_x (and $A_{x,y}$) structure:

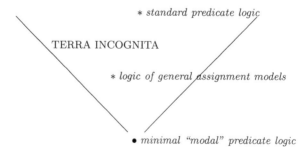

One important intermediate system is the logic of all general assignment models. It is axiomatized by the axioms of poly-modal *S5* plus the earlier Heredity principles for atoms. The system is decidable, and it has been investigated extensively in algebraic logic.[279]

The reason for the potential *undecidability* of systems higher-up will be clear to the reader. Many non-minimal principles of first-order logic have existential effects, requiring the existence of "enough" states in our computation space of assignments. In particular, the preceding "diamond principles" impose grid structure on these computation spaces that was the root of the high complexity results in Chapter 24.

27.6 Extending the language: polyadic quantifiers

The present language suggests extensions. A standard tuple notation $\exists xy.\varphi$ is just shorthand for either $\exists x \exists y \varphi$ or $\exists y \exists x \varphi$. But in general assignment models, $\exists xy.\varphi$ says there is an assignment agreeing with the current one *up to* $\{x, y\}$ *values* where φ holds. Such transitions encode a form of *concurrency* for the single relations R_x and R_y. This does not reduce to either iterated version, as these require existence of intermediate states.

Abstract state models admit general *polyadic quantifiers* $\exists x_1 \cdots x_k$ $.\varphi$ stating that some $R_{\langle x_1,\ldots,x_k\rangle}$-accessible state exists where φ holds. In standard first-order logic, this is equivalent to any linearized version $\exists x_1 \cdots \exists x_k \varphi$. But with possible gaps in our models, it is not. Polyadic quantification has linguistic interest: in natural reasoning, one may treat sequences of variables as dependent or independent. Technically, adding polyadic quantifiers leaves general assignment logic *decidable* – even when we add simultaneous substitutions.

27.7 Conclusion: two perspectives in tandem

There is much more to this modal analysis of first-order logic. First, generalized models are not a trick: they highlight the fundamental notion of *dependence*. The analysis of this phenomenon is by no means over, and we mentioned sophisticated extensions of our modal semantics using sets of assignments as indices of evaluation. Thus, despite the sacred nature of first-order logic as the holiest of holies, there may be room for rethinking. For instance, our state-based models for shifting assignments provide concrete geometrical content to the system that may eventually be more appealing than set-theoretic models.

---

[279] It is also the logic of general assignment models satisfying all *universal properties* of standard first-order models, preserved to smaller assignment sets.

To conclude, we state what we see as a broader thrust of our "deconstructionist" study. One is simply this: it is *fun* to use the techniques you have learnt for the special area of modal logic, and then see how, surprisingly, they apply also in the very heartland of logic.

The next point is the *duality of two perspectives*. These lectures have presented modal languages as fragments of first-order logic, interpreted over standard models, allowing us to study fine-structure. On the other hand, we can now also see first-order logic *itself* as a modal language, but then interpreted over generalized models. The two viewpoints are not in conflict. For instance, it is possible to embed the logic of general assignment models faithfully into the Guarded Fragment (cf. Chapter 7), using guards to constrain the tuples of values the variables can take simultaneously. And vice versa, it is possible to embed the Guarded Fragment into a first-order logic over general assignment models.[280] And this is not an isolated observation: the same duality extends to non-first-order systems. For instance, we can view the modal μ-calculus of Chapter 22 as a modal fragment of the full fixed-point extension of first-order logic $LFP(FO)$ over standard models, but we can also see it, under the same Gestalt Switch as here, as the full language of $LFP(FO)$ itself, but now interpreted over general assignment models. Both perspectives are natural and useful.

A final point emerging from this chapter is as follows: *What, really, is first-order logic?* It is amazing how this familiar system continues to generate new fundamental questions. In particular, if modal models are a natural semantics for first-order logic, received dogmas must be challenged. In textbooks, or treatises on the philosophy of logic, "predicate-logical validity" is a unique notion, locked in place by Gödel's Completeness Theorem. Moreover, it is inherently complex, being undecidable by Church's Theorem: Leibniz's ideal Calculus Ratiocinator just will not work. On the present view, however, standard predicate logic arose historically from decisions that could have gone differently. The genuine logical core of first-order reasoning may well be decidable after all. And the real interest then lies not in one unique completeness theorem, but in the joint model-theoretic and proof-theoretic analysis of a rich family of options for reasoning with quantifiers.

---

[280]Detailed proofs are in the survey of the Guarded Fragment in van Benthem (2005).

A

First-order predicate logic

Here is a quick tour of basic notions in first-order logic, as background to these lectures. Of the many excellent introductions to this area, we mention Enderton (1971) and Hodges (1983). Please note that this Appendix is not a first course, but a reminder!

A.1 Syntax and semantics

Alphabet First-order languages refer to objects having properties and standing in relations, from abstract mathematical spaces to real-life situations. They do so with an alphabet of *individual variables* $x, y, \ldots$, *individual constants* $c, d, \ldots$, *predicate symbols* $P, Q, \ldots$ (with arities indicated), an *identity predicate* $=$, *Boolean connectives* $\neg, \wedge, \vee, \rightarrow, \leftrightarrow$, *quantifiers* $\forall, \exists$, and *brackets* $), ($. Using these, one writes terms and formulas in the usual way.

Example (First-order languages over modal graph models). First-order languages whose vocabulary fits the modal models of these lectures can express various properties of computation or process graphs by means of quantification over states:

Action a is deterministic $\quad \forall xyz((R_a xy \wedge R_a xz) \rightarrow y = z)$
Action a is confluent $\quad \forall xyz((R_a xy \wedge R_a xz) \rightarrow \exists u(R_a yu \wedge R_a zu))$
Action a enables b $\quad \forall xy(R_a xy \rightarrow \exists z R_b yz)$

One can also take a second domain of *actions*, with matching quantifiers and variables, and a ternary predicate $\xrightarrow{a}$ (action a takes state x to state y). Modal models are also models for this "two-sorted" first-order language, and one can express new computational properties:

Endpoints exist	$\exists x \neg \exists y \; x \xrightarrow{a} y$
Every action has a converse	$\forall a \exists b \forall xy(x \xrightarrow{a} y \leftrightarrow y \xrightarrow{b} x)$
Actions are extensional	$\forall ab(\forall xy(x \xrightarrow{a} y \leftrightarrow x \xrightarrow{b} y) \rightarrow a = b)$

323

Syntax *Terms* are individual variables and constants. (We disregard function symbols here.) *Atomic formulas* are of the form $Pt_1 \cdots t_k$ with P of arity k with terms $t_1, \ldots, t_k$. *Formulas* are defined inductively as usual, either by inductive clauses, or the much sparser computer science syntax used in these lecture notes. We have the standard grammar of predicate logic, with *scope, binding, free and bound occurrence, substitution, substitutability, alphabetic variants, positive and negative occurrence*. A useful measure of semantic expressive power over patterns of objects is the *quantifier depth* of a formula: i.e., the maximum length of a nest of quantifiers occurring in it. Recursively,

(a) $qd(\varphi) = 0$, for atomic formulas φ,

(b) $qd(\neg\varphi) = qd(\varphi)$,

(c) $qd(\varphi \# \psi) = \max(qd(\varphi), qd(\psi))$, for all connectives $\#$, and

(d) $qd(Qx\varphi) = qd(\varphi) + 1$, for both quantifiers Q.

Semantics Evaluation uses structures $\mathcal{D} = (D, \mathcal{O}, \mathcal{P})$, with D a non-empty domain of objects, $\mathcal{O}$ a set of distinguished objects, and $\mathcal{P}$ a set of predicates. (Many texts use ad-hoc notation for structures of special interest – like we did for modal logic.) An *interpretation function* I maps individual constants c to objects $I(c) \in \mathcal{O}$, and k-ary predicate symbols Q to k-place predicates $I(Q) \in \mathcal{P}$. Finally, auxiliary (but nevertheless, important) functions a called *assignments* map individual variables x to objects $a(x) \in D$. By contrast, the interpretation function I is a more permanent linkage between language and model and a a more local "dynamic" one. Next we define *term values*:

$$value(x, \mathcal{D}, I, a) = a(x), \qquad value(c, \mathcal{D}, I, a) = I(c)$$

The truth definition defines the notion "φ is true in $\mathcal{D}$ under I and a":

$$\mathcal{D}, I, a \models \varphi$$

through inductive clauses (the atomic case is done here by example):

$\mathcal{D}, I, a \models Rt_1t_2$ iff $I(R)(value(t_1, D, I, a), value(t_2, D, I, a))$
$\mathcal{D}, I, a \models t_1 = t_2$ iff $value(t_1, D, I, a)$ equals $value(t_2, D, I, a)$
$\mathcal{D}, I, a \models \neg\varphi$ iff   not $\mathcal{D}, I, a \models \varphi$
$\mathcal{D}, I, a \models \varphi \lor \psi$ iff $\mathcal{D}, I, a \models \varphi$ or $\mathcal{D}, I, a \models \psi$
and likewise for the other Boolean propositional connectives,
$\mathcal{D}, I, a \models \exists x\varphi$ iff   there exists some $d \in D$ with $\mathcal{D}, I, a_d^x \models \varphi$
and likewise for the universal quantifier.

Here a_d^x (sometimes written $a[x := d]$) is the assignment b that is a except for the possible difference of assigning object d to variable x. (The resulting relation is also written as $a =_x b$).

Usually, the interpretation function I is taken for granted, and "hard-wired". We then write $M, a \models \varphi$, where a model M is a pair $(\mathcal{D}, I)$ of a structure and an interpretation function.

Basic semantic properties Here are some useful basic features:

Lemma (Finiteness Lemma). Given a fixed domain $\mathcal{D}$ and interpretation function I, if two assignments agree on all free variables of a formula, then they give the same truth value to that formula.

Hence, for truth of "sentences" without free variables in a model, assignments may be disregarded.

Lemma (Substitution Lemma). Assume that term t is freely substitutable for x in formula φ. Then we have the equivalence

$$M, a \models [t/x]\varphi \quad \text{iff} \quad M, a^x_{value(t,M,a)} \models \varphi$$

Finally, here is one more elementary syntax-semantics connection. The formula $(\varphi)^A$ arises from φ by replacing every quantifier $\exists x, \forall x$ by relativized $\exists x(Ax \wedge \cdots, \forall x(Ax \rightarrow \cdots$. $M|A$ arises from M by taking domain $I^M(A)$ and restricting predicate interpretations to it:

Lemma (Relativization Lemma). For all variable assignments a taking their values in $I(A)$,

$$M, a \models (\varphi)^A \quad \text{iff} \quad M|A, a \models \varphi$$

Extended logics These notions set a pattern for other formal languages that surface in these lectures. *Infinitary first-order logic* allows conjunctions and disjunctions over arbitrary sets of formulas. For more information, see Keisler (1971), Barwise (1975), Ebbinghaus and Flum (1995). *Second-order languages* add quantification over sets, standing for properties and predicates. See van Benthem and Doets (1983) for such systems, including connections to type theories. A still wider array of logical systems, including generalized quantifiers and other expressive extensions, is studied in "Abstract Model Theory".

A.2 Expressive power, invariance and games

Isomorphism Independently from any language, structures have mathematical relations. Most basically, two models $M = (D, \mathcal{O}, \mathcal{P}, I)$, $M' = (D', \mathcal{O}', \mathcal{P}', I')$ are *isomorphic* if there exists an *isomorphism* between them, i.e., a bijection F between D and D' that respects distinguished objects in $\mathcal{O}, \mathcal{O}'$ (and operations, if any) and also respects matching predicates in $\mathcal{P}, \mathcal{P}'$:

$F(I(c)) = I'(c)$, for all individual constants c,

$I(Q)(d)$ iff $I'(Q)(F(d))$, for all tuples of objects d in D.

Invariance A fundamental measure of the expressive power of a language are its characteristic invariances across models, via such structural relations. Here is a typical illustration:

Lemma (Isomorphism Lemma). Tuples related by an isomorphism satisfy the same first-order formulas:

$$M, a \models \varphi \text{ iff } M', F \circ a \models \varphi$$

Thus isomorphic models are *elementarily equivalent*: they verify the same first-order sentences. The converse fails, though on *finite* models, isomorphism and elementary equivalence coincide.

Potential isomorphism Closer to elementary equivalence, models M, M' are *potentially isomorphic* if there is a non-empty family PI of finite *partial isomorphisms* (isomorphisms between finite sub-models of M, M') satisfying two back-and-forth clauses:

(a) for any partial isomorphism $F \in PI$ and any d in the domain of M, there is an object e in the domain of M' with $F \cup \{(d, e)\} \in PI$,
(b) analogously in the opposite direction.

The Isomorphism Lemma generalizes to partial isomorphisms in such families PI. Sill, no converse holds for first-order logic – but we do have the following important equivalence with the earlier-mentioned *infinitary* language allowing arbitrary set conjunctions and disjunctions, for tuples of objects in any two models M, M':

M, d and M', e satisfy the same formulas of infinitary first-order logic iff there is a potential isomorphism PI between M, M' with some F sending d (in that order) to e.

Comparison games To add fine-structure to structural comparisons, one uses *Ehrenfeucht-Fraïssé Games*. The "n-round comparison game" between two models M, N has two players A and E in n successive rounds, each consisting of (a) selection of a model and an object in its domain by player A, (b) selection of an object in the other model by player E that gets matched to the one chosen by A. After n rounds, the partial map between M, N created by all matches is inspected. If it is a partial isomorphism for all predicates, then E has won – otherwise, the win is for A. Here is an illustration.

Example (Integer versus rational order). The integers $\mathbb{Z}$ and the rationals $\mathbb{Q}$ have different first-order properties: the latter is dense, the former discrete. Here is how soon this will surface in the game:

By choosing objects well, player E has a winning strategy in the game over two rounds. But A can always win the game in three rounds:

Round 1 A chooses 0 in $\mathbb{Z}$ E chooses 0 in $\mathbb{Q}$
Round 2 A chooses 1 in $\mathbb{Z}$ E chooses $\frac{1}{3}$ in $\mathbb{Q}$
Round 3 A chooses $\frac{1}{5}$ in $\shortparallel$ any response for E is losing.

Write $WIN(\boldsymbol{M}, \boldsymbol{N}, n, \boldsymbol{E})$ if player E has a *winning strategy* in the game. The following basic result links this to our first-order language:

Theorem 78 (Adequacy Theorem). The following are equivalent:

(a) $WIN(\boldsymbol{M}, \boldsymbol{N}, n, \boldsymbol{E})$,
(b) $\boldsymbol{M}, \boldsymbol{N}$ verify the same sentences up to quantifier depth n.

This rests on a more general version with assignments, proved by induction on formulas. (Cf. Doets (1996), an excellent game-based course in mathematical logic.) Equivalently, one can state an equivalence between the existence of a first-order "difference formula" up to depth n distinguishing the models and the existence of a winning strategy for the opposite player A. That one player must always have a winning strategy in a game like this follows from a general result about finite depth two-player zero-sum games called "Zermelo's Theorem".

There is more to the link. Consider again Integers versus Rationals.

Example (Definable differences and winning strategies). Player A can use the syntactic definition of density: $\forall x \forall y(x < y \rightarrow \exists z(x < z \wedge z < y))$ to win the game, by maintaining a difference between the models of stepwise decreasing syntactic depth. A starts by noting that $\exists x \exists y(x < y \wedge \neg \exists z(x < z \wedge z < y))$ is true in $\mathbb{Z}$, but false in $\mathbb{Q}$ (#). He then chooses an integer witness d for $\exists x$, making $\exists y(d < y \wedge \neg \exists z(d < z \wedge z < y))$ true in $\mathbb{Z}$. Player E can take any d' in $\mathbb{Q}$: $\exists y(d' < y \wedge \neg \exists z(d' < z \wedge z < y))$ is always false for it, by #: $\mathbb{Z} \models \exists y(d < y \wedge \neg \exists z(d < z \wedge z < y))$, and *not* $\mathbb{Q} \models \exists y(d' < y \wedge \neg \exists z(d' < z \wedge z < y))$. In the second round, A continues with a witness e for the new outermost quantifier $\exists y$ in the true existential formula in $\mathbb{Z}$: making $d < e \wedge \neg \exists z(d < z \wedge z < e)$ true there. Again, whatever object e' E now picks in $\mathbb{Q}$, $d' < e' \wedge \neg \exists z(d' < z \wedge z < e')$ is false there. In the third round, A analyses the mismatch in truth value. If E kept $d' < e'$ true in $\mathbb{Q}$, then, as $\neg \exists z(d < z \wedge z < e)$ held in $\mathbb{Z}$, $\exists z(d' < z \wedge z < e')$ holds in $\mathbb{Q}$. A then switches to $\mathbb{Q}$, chooses a witness for the existential formula, and wins.

Thus, even model switches for A are encoded in the difference formulas. These are mandatory when there is a syntactic switch in "polarity" from one outermost quantifier to a lower one. The following result makes the match between logical language and strategies explicit:

Theorem 79. There is an *explicit correspondence* between

(a) winning strategies for A in the n-round game for M, N

(b) sentences φ of quantifier depth n with $M \models \varphi$, *not* $N \models \varphi$

For player E, winning strategies in infinite comparison games match the potential isomorphisms between the given models.

Comparison games exist for many logical languages, including fragments of first-order logic. The analysis can be refined by measuring the number of variables used in the formulas (free or bound) in terms of some finite set $\{x_1, \ldots, x_k\}$. Comparison games then use sets of *pebbles* to select objects for inspection.

Other logic games There are logic games for many other tasks, including semantic evaluation, where a Verifier and a Falsifier dispute the truth of a formula in some model, drawing objects from the domain that can be tested for atomic facts. Logic games also exist for finding proofs (after all, argumentation is a game), or constructing models. van Benthem (1999), van Benthem (2007b) are broad surveys of the area.

Other invariances: ultraproducts There are also other structural characterizations of first-order predicate logic, mathematically deeper than the game analysis. *Keisler's Theorem* says that a class of models is *elementary*: definable as $\{M \mid M \models \varphi\}$ for some first-order sentence φ, iff it is closed under the formation of ultraproducts and potential isomorphisms. Here, *ultraproducts* are a sophisticated construction of new models out of given families $\{M_i\}_{i \in I}$ of models plus some *ultrafilter* on the index set I. We refer to the literature for details.

A.3 Model Constructions

Key meta-properties Here are two central results:

Theorem 80 (Compactness Theorem). If each finite subset of a set of first-order formulas Σ has a model plus assignment verifying it, then so does the whole Σ *simultaneously*.

Theorem 81 (Löwenheim-Skolem Theorem). If a set of formulas Σ is verified in some model plus assignment, then it is already verified in some *countable* model.

Applications These theorems are often used to show undefinability of mathematical properties in first-order logic: a standard example is *finiteness* of the domain. They also have positive applications in finding new models with "transfer" of first-order properties. By way of illustration, here is a typical compactness technique, involving the following ubiquitous model relation:

N is an *elementary extension* of M if (a) M is a sub-model of N, and (b) M, N agree on the truth value of all first-order formulas (whether atomic or complex) over objects in M.

Now call a model M ω-*saturated* if, for each set Σ of first-order formulas in a finite set of free variables $x_1, \ldots, x_k$ and involving only finitely many objects from M's domain as fixed parameters (named by individual constants), the following holds: "if each finite subset of Σ has some k-tuple of objects satisfying it in M, then there exists some k-tuple of objects satisfying the whole set Σ in M".

Fact. Each model has an ω-saturated elementary extension.

For a proof, cf. Chang and Keisler (1973), Doets (1996).

Abstract model theory The two stated properties are characteristic of first-order logic. The following important result says how:

Theorem 82 (Lindström's Theorem). First-order predicate logic is maximal with respect to containing the first-order language and satisfying both the Compactness and Löwenheim-Skolem properties.

Other model constructions Other important model relations and constructions need not preserve the whole first-order language. Two typical example are *sub*-models and *direct products* of models. Such constructions may still capture useful *fragments*, as stated in so-called "preservation theorems". Here are two classical examples:

Theorem 83 (Los-Tarski Theorem). A first-order sentence is truth-preserved under going to sub-models iff it is logically equivalent to a syntactically *universal* formula, constructed from a quantifier-free formula by prefixing universal quantifiers.

Theorem 84 (Lyndon's Theorem). A first-order sentence is semantically *monotone in* Q (i.e., its truth in a model is preserved whenever the extension of the predicate Q is enlarged) iff it is logically equivalent to a formula with only *positive* syntactic occurrences of Q.

Intertwined semantic behaviour and syntactic form is typical in logic. **Interpolation** There are more deep properties of first-order logic:

Theorem 85 (Interpolation Theorem). For all first-order formulas φ, ψ, if $\varphi \models \psi$, then there is a first-order formula α with $Voc(\alpha) \subseteq (Voc(\varphi) \cap Voc(\psi))$ and $\varphi \models \alpha \models \psi$.

This implies, for instance, Beth's Theorem that two natural notions of "definability" coincide for first-order logic: semantic implicit definability as "fixing denotations" and explicit syntactic definability. Barwise and van Benthem (1999) use interpolation to analyze entailment along any model relation R: If $M \models \varphi$ and MRN, then $N \models \psi$.

Theorem 86. The following are equivalent for first-order φ, ψ:

(a) φ entails ψ along *sub-models*,
(b) there is a universal formula α such that $\varphi \models \alpha \models \psi$.

Mason (1985) shows that the full meta-theory of first-order logic is as complex as true first-order Arithmetic, and so, by Gödel's Theorem it is undecidable, non-axiomatizable, and very complex. We may therefore reasonably hope for the discovery of exciting new meta-theorems.

A.4 Validity and syntactic axiomatization

Semantic consequence Consequence in predicate logic is defined as "transmission of truth":

$\Sigma \models \psi$ if for all models M and assignments a, if $M, a \models \varphi$ for all $\varphi \in \Sigma$, then $M, a \models \psi$.

On this notion, statements in the following pairs are mutual consequences, and hence logical synonyms: $\varphi \lor \psi / \neg(\neg\varphi \land \neg\psi)$, $\varphi \to \psi / \neg\varphi \lor \psi$, $\forall x\varphi / \neg\exists x\neg\varphi$. Thus, attention may be restricted to subsets of logical constants, whenever convenient. (This is different with other notions of validity for a first-order language, like that of intuitionistic logic, which we do not discuss here.) The quantification over the totality of all models makes validity a quite abstract notion. But, there exist more concrete methods of testing it, such as Beth's *semantic tableaux*.

Inference and derivation More concrete is the *deductive* approach, with a long historical pedigree in the field, proceeding from combinatorial systems of inferential steps forming proofs:

$\Sigma \vdash \psi$ if there exists a *derivation* for ψ from assumptions in Σ using only permissible rules of some logical proof calculus.

A good example is the axiom system for predicate logic in Enderton (1971). It consists of all universal closures of arbitrary Boolean propositional laws plus the three quantifier axioms

$\forall x(\varphi \to \psi) \to (\forall x\varphi \to \forall x\psi)$

$\varphi \to \forall x\varphi$ *provided that x does not occur free in φ*

$\forall x\varphi \to [t/x]\varphi$ *provided that t is free for x in φ*

Pragmatic validity in argumentation Some authors revive the origins of logic as a debating game, and propose a third notion:

> $\Sigma \models \psi$ if a defender of claim ψ has a guaranteed *winning strategy* against an opponent granting Σ in a logical game of argumentation.

Completeness theorem While semantic validity serves as a touchstone of adequacy, proof-theoretic or game-theoretic views embody vivid ideas about structuring arguments and procedures for reasoning. Arguably the main meta-result in modern logic (for suitable axiom systems and languages) is this result of Gödel's

Theorem 87 (Completeness Theorem). $\Sigma \models \psi$ iff $\Sigma \vdash \psi$, for all Σ, ψ in first-order logic.

A well-known proof method uses "Henkin models". This result is so influential, that it has set standards for getting a logic paper published.

A.5   Decidability and undecidability

Undecidability Expressive power always comes at a price. First-order logic is much less expressive than, say, second-order logic, but in contrast, its validities are axiomatizable. However, some complexity remains: there is no effective machine algorithm that can infallibly test validity of given input formulas.

Theorem 88 (Church's Theorem). First-order validity is undecidable.

This can be proved in many ways (cf. Chapter 24). One quick road is to first show the undecidability of some natural computational problem, such as the Halting Problem for Turing Machines, or geometrical Tiling Problems. Then one shows how to reduce such problems effectively to satisfiability or validity problems for first-order formulas describing them. Then validity must be undecidable, too.

Fragments and complexity Undecidability says something about first-order logic as a whole. But there is fine-structure inside. In these lectures, we have emphasized how modal logic is a weak decidable fragment of first-order logic. Many such fragments exist Börger et al. (1997), including *monadic* first-order logic (only one-place predicates), the *two-variable* fragment of first-order logic (its *three-variable* fragment is undecidable), the Guarded Fragment in Chapter 7 of these notes, and more may yet be discovered.

Decidability calls for analysis of the precise computational *complexity* of satisfiability or validity problems. In Chapter 6, we have looked at complexity of other basic tasks associated with a logic, such as model-checking or model comparison. Papadimitriou (1994) is an excellent introduction to Complexity Theory with a lucid explanation of the many links to logic.

B

Modal algebra

B.1 Universal algebra

An *algebra* is a tuple $\boldsymbol{A} = (A, \boldsymbol{F})$ with A a set of objects, and $\boldsymbol{F}$ a set of operations on A, with the $f \in \boldsymbol{F}$ taking specified finite numbers of arguments. Here the 0-ary operations are the "distinguished objects" of the algebra. For instance, a "Boolean algebra" has two distinguished objects $0, 1$, one unary operation $-$, and two binary operations $+, \bullet$. Logicians can think of general algebras as structures for a first-order language that has function symbols for building complex terms and just one atomic identity predicate $=$ for building formulas.[281] Such an *equational language* has object variables and function symbols with arities indicated, and terms are created from variables and 0-place function symbols (names for distinguished objects) by the rule

"if $t_1, \ldots, t_k$ are terms, then so is $f^k\, t_1 \ldots t_k$"

Formulas of the language are equations $t = t'$ for all terms t, t' (no Boolean operators or first-order quantifiers are used). The *semantics* works recursively for terms t and algebras $\boldsymbol{A}$. More precisely, we need an interpretation I of function symbols as operations in $\boldsymbol{A}$ of the matching arity, and an assignment a of objects to variables. Usually, the map I is absorbed into the structure $\boldsymbol{A}$, and one just deals with the variable assignment a. Then, the denotation $t_a^{\boldsymbol{A}}$ of terms t in $\boldsymbol{A}$ under I, a has the key recursive clause

$$f^k\, t_{1a}{}^{\boldsymbol{A}}, \ldots, t_{ka}{}^{\boldsymbol{A}} = I(f)(t_{1a}{}^{\boldsymbol{A}}, t_{ka}{}^{\boldsymbol{A}})$$

An equation $t = t'$ is true in $\boldsymbol{A}$ under a if its two terms t, t' denote the same object. An equation is "globally true" in an algebra if it is true under all assignments: this is the "schematic" universal sense in which one usually takes algebraic axioms of a mathematical theory.

---

[281] But one can also reformulate all of first-order logic in an algebraic manner, including Booleans and quantifiers (cf. the "cylindric algebra" of Henkin et al. (1985)).

A set of equations X *implies* an equation $t = t'$ (or, $t = t'$ *follows from* X) if each A, a that makes each equation in X true, also makes $t = t'$ true. The *equational calculus* is the proof system consisting of reflexivity, symmetry, and transitivity for terms, plus the rule of substitution of identicals: "$t_1 = t'_1, \ldots, t_k = t'_k$ implies $f^k\, t_1 \ldots t_k = f^k\, t'_1 \ldots t'_k$. *Completeness theorem*: an equation follows from a set of equations X if it is derivable using equations from X with only principles of the equational calculus. There are simple modifications when we take the equations of a theory X as *schemata*, allowing for arbitrary instances via an additional *substitution* rule. The completeness proof is via a simple "term algebra" whose objects are the equivalence classes of terms under the relation of provable identity given the equations in X as additional axioms.[282] In this algebra, under the obvious assignment sending syntactic variables to their equivalence classes under provability viewed as objects in the algebra, the semantic object denoted by any term t is just the equivalence class of t under provability.[283]

Model-theoretically, algebras support three major operations. A *sub-algebra* is a sub-model in the usual sense, closed under the operations. A *homomorphic image* of an algebra is the range of a *homomorphism*, a structure-preserving map h from an algebra A to an algebra B satisfying the commutation law $h(f^A(a_1, \ldots, a_k)) = f^B(h(a_1), \ldots, h(a_k))$. Finally, the *direct product* $\Pi_{i \in I} A_i$ of a family of algebras $\{ A_i \mid i \in I \}$ consists of all objects in the Cartesian product $\Pi_{i \in I} A_i$ with operations defined component-wise: e.g., $f^{\Pi_{i \in I} A_i}((a_i)_{i \in I}) = (f^{A_i}(a_i))_{i \in I}$. It is easy to prove that all these operations preserve global truth of algebraic equations – for instance, if an equation holds in all components of a direct product, it holds in the whole product. Moreover, this preservation behaviour captures definability in equational logic precisely in the sense of *Birkhoff's Theorem*: A class K of algebras is definable in the form $Alg(X)$ for some set of equations X [284] iff K is closed under taking sub-algebras, homomorphic images, and direct products. [285] There are algebraic proofs, but the result can also be derived purely model-theoretically. Other model-theoretic themes concern the existence of special algebras with nice properties that sometimes have no counter-

---

[282] This is the origin of the syntactic "Lindenbaum algebra's" in algebraic logic.

[283] In terms of our main text, this is a simple but elegant "Truth Lemma".

[284] $Alg(X)$ consists of all algebras satisfying all of the equations in X in the sense of global truth; such classes of algebras are called "equational varieties".

[285] More precisely, one can show that, for any class K, an algebra A satisfies the equational theory of K (all equations true globally in all algebras of K) iff $A \in \mathrm{HSP}(K)$, the class of algebras that are homomorphic images of some sub-algebra of some direct product of algebras from K.

part in first-order logic. An example are algebras $\boldsymbol{A}$ that are *freely generated* from some set of objects C, in the sense that any map from C into any algebra $\boldsymbol{B}$ can be extended uniquely to a homomorphism from all of $\boldsymbol{A}$ to $\boldsymbol{B}$. The earlier syntax algebra in the completeness proof is an example, with the objects corresponding to the variables serving as the generating set.

B.2   Boolean algebra

Many further issues become visible with special classes of algebras. In particular, *Boolean algebras* are tuples $(A, 0, 1, -, +, \bullet)$, where the following equations have to be true:

$$
\begin{aligned}
x + (y + z) &= (x + y) + z & x \bullet (y \bullet z) &= (x \bullet y) \bullet z \\
x + y &= y + x & x \bullet y &= y \bullet x \\
x + x &= x & x \bullet x &= x \\
x + (y \bullet z) &= (x + y) \bullet (x + z) & x \bullet (y + z) &= (x \bullet y) + (x \bullet z) \\
x + (x \bullet y) &= x & x \bullet (x + y) &= x \\
-(x + y) &= -x \bullet -y & -(x \bullet y) &= -x + -y \\
x + 0 &= x & x \bullet 0 &= 0 \\
x + 1 &= 1 & x \bullet 1 &= x \\
x + -x &= 1 & x \bullet -x &= 0 \\
& & - - x &= x
\end{aligned}
$$

This is a selection of principles that are valid when you read them in an obvious way as equivalences in propositional logic. The term language of Boolean algebra is still close to formulas of propositional logic: each term becomes a formula by reading variables as proposition letters, and Boolean algebraic operations as logical $\neg$, $\vee$ and $\wedge$.[286] The same principles are valid as laws of binary arithmetic, computed in the usual truth tables: or stated differently, the truth value algebra 2 with just two objects, $-$ as flipping 0 and 1, $+$ as maximum, and $\bullet$ as minimum, is a concrete Boolean algebra. But there are many other Boolean algebras, more abstract and more concrete. Typical concrete examples are families of subsets of some domain X, containing both $\emptyset$ and X, and closed under set-theoretic complement, unions, and intersections.

In this setting, the point of the ordinary completeness theorem for propositional logic is this – where we use the form that the syntactically consistent formulas are the ones having a satisfying semantic valuation. By general equational logic, each consistent formula can be made true for some assignment in an abstract Boolean term algebra, but we can

---

[286]There is also a converse translation, that forms the basis for the wellknown "algebraization" of propositional logic.

even take that satisfying algebra to be the *truth value algebra* **2**. This fact is related to two general algebraic results. The first is the *Stone Representation Theorem*: each Boolean algebra is isomorphic with a family of sets over some domain with the usual set-theoretic operations. The proof introduces the set of all *ultrafilters* U on the algebra A, families of sets containing the distinguished object 1 and not the 0, and satisfying the properties $a + b \in U$ iff $a \in U$ or $b \in U$, and $a \bullet b \in U$ iff $a \in U$ and $b \in U$.[287] The ultrafilters are the domain of the set algebra, and objects a in the algebra A are mapped to the set $\{\, U \mid a \in U \,\}$. Representation results are important in algebra, since they tie abstract algebras to "concrete" ones that may be easier to grasp.

The further fact that equations satisfied by objects in some Boolean set algebra are also satisfiable in the special algebra **2** can be seen by an ad-hoc argument. But it is also related to another general theorem of Birkhoff. First, a *sub-direct product* is a sub-algebra of some direct product of algebras A_i all of whose set-theoretic projections to factors A_i are onto. Now, each algebra is isomorphic to a sub-direct product of *subdirectly irreducible* algebras satisfying the same equations. Subdirectly irreducible algebras are defined to be "minimal" in the following sense: if they are a sub-direct product of a family of algebras, they are already isomorphic to one of the factors. **2** is the only sub-directly irreducible Boolean algebra. Knowing the sub-directly irreducible algebras in a class often tells us all about it. A famous tool for this is *Jónsson's Lemma*: In an equational variety K where the lattice of congruence relations on the algebras is distributive,[288] each algebra is isomorphic to a homomorphic image of a sub-algebra of some *ultraproduct* of sub-directly irreducible algebras in K. Jónsson's Lemma improves the Birkhoff characterization of equational varieties from direct products to ultraproducts, a construction that does not just preserve true algebraic equations, but sentences of the full first-order language (cf. our Appendix on first-order logic).

B.3 Modal algebra

A *modal algebra* is a Boolean algebra with an added unary operation m (for the existential modality) satisfying the two equations (i) $m0 = 0$, (ii) $m(x+y) = mx+my$.[289] Again the connection with basic modal logic is a simple "Gestalt switch", with algebraic identities corresponding to equivalence formulas, and conversely, modal formulas denoting terms.

---

[287]Alternatively, these areo homomorphisms from A to the algebra **2**.

[288]We do not explain this special condition, but it is often satisfied in modal logics.

[289]These assumptions correspond to the postulates of the minimal modal logic.

A particular concrete type of modal algebras arises by taking a Boolean algebra of subsets of some relational frame (W, R), that is also closed under the set-theoretic operation $m(X) = \{\, y \in W | \exists x \in X : Ryx \,\}$. The whole structure consisting of the frame plus this algebra is called a *general frame*, that can be thought of as a frame plus some prescribed range of "admissible propositions". Most earlier definitions apply as is to modal algebras, though it may be harder to determine basic items such as the sub-directly irreducible algebras in a modal variety. In particular, the Stone representation extends, as observed by Jónsson and Tarski (1951): every modal algebra is isomorphic to an algebra on the frame whose worlds are the ultrafilters, with the relation RUV defined by $\forall a \in V : ma \in U$.[290] We can view this as a general operation *Frame* taking modal algebras A to isomorphic algebras on a general frame $Frame(A)$, while under a converse operation, general frames G directly induce algebras $Alg(G)$. What is more, under this duality, structure-preserving operations in the two areas correspond precisely. For instance, any homomorphism from an algebra A onto an algebra B induces a map from $Frame(B)$ into $Frame(A)$ that is a bijection onto a generated sub-frame. We omit details, but these links can be worked into a complete duality in the sense of mathematical category theory.

Many results in modal logic have been proved through this link with algebraic methods. General frames were discovered in this way, and they were important in the study of deductive "frame-incompleteness" for simple modal logics, as explained in Chapter 26.[291] Another famous example is the *Goldblatt & Thomason Theorem* saying that a first-order definable class of frames K is definable by a set of modal formulas iff K is closed under *generated subframes, disjoint unions, p-morphic images*, while the complement class $-K$ is closed under *ultrafilter extensions*. We do not define these operations on (general) frames here, but the first three have to do with sub-algebras, homomorphic images and direct products within the realm of algebras, while the fourth notion comes from the above map *Frame* that took modal algebras to general frames. Goldblatt and Thomason's model-theoretic result was first proved by translating from frames to modal algebras, then applying the Birkhoff characterization of equational varieties, and finally moving back using the Jónsson-Tarski version of the Stone representation.

Digression. We sketch the proof, for a glimpse of how algebraic and modal methods interact. First, the four stated closure properties hold by known preservation properties of modal formulas. E.g., for ultrafilter

---

[290] This is like accessibility in basic modal completeness proofs; cf. Chapter 5.

[291] An extensive algebraic study of modal incompleteness was made in Blok (1980).

extensions, if $ue(\boldsymbol{F}) \models \varphi$, then $\boldsymbol{F} \models \varphi$. Conversely, start with any frame $\boldsymbol{F}$ satisfying the modal theory $Th_{mod}(\boldsymbol{K})$ of the class $\boldsymbol{K}$ (all modal formulas true in every frame in $\boldsymbol{K}$): this will be our desired modal definition. Equivalently, this can be written in algebraic terms as follows: $Alg(\boldsymbol{F}) \models Th_{identities}(Alg(\boldsymbol{K}))$. By the earlier-mentioned HSP version of the Birkhoff Theorem, this gives us a line

$Alg(\boldsymbol{F})$ homomorphic image of $\boldsymbol{A}$ sub-algebra of product $\Pi_{i \in I} Alg(\boldsymbol{F}_i)$ with all the frames $\boldsymbol{F}_i \in \boldsymbol{K}$

Using the above-mentioned duality connecting algebras and (general) frames under the Stone representation $Frame$, we see successively that

$\Pi_{i \in I} Alg(\boldsymbol{F}_i)$ is isomorphic with $Alg(+_{i \in I} \boldsymbol{F}_i)$ (+ is disjoint union)

$Frame(Alg(+_{i \in I} \boldsymbol{F}_i))$ maps p-morphically onto $Frame(\boldsymbol{A})$

$Frame(Alg(\boldsymbol{F}))$ is isomorphic to a generated sub-frame of $Frame(\boldsymbol{A})$

with $Frame(Alg(\boldsymbol{F}))$just the ultrafilter extension $ue(\boldsymbol{F})$. In a picture:

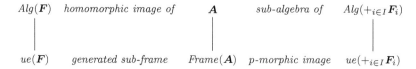

To walk from right to left in the diagram, all the way to the initial frame $\boldsymbol{F}$, we use all four closure conditions on $\boldsymbol{K}$ and its complement. But we must close one gap. We need the ultrafilter extension $ue(+_{i \in I} \boldsymbol{F}_i)$ in $\boldsymbol{K}$. This requires one separate model-theoretic observation:

> For every frame $\boldsymbol{F}$, $ue(\boldsymbol{F})$ is a p-morphic image of some frame $\boldsymbol{F}'$ that is elementarily equivalent to $\boldsymbol{F}$.[292]

Now, since the class $\boldsymbol{K}$ is first-order definable, it is clearly closed under elementarily equivalent models, and by closure under p-morphic images, it is closed under ultrafilter extensions.

B.4   Algebra and logic in general

Algebraic methods are used in many areas related to modal logic. Cf. the *Handbook of Process Algebra* (Bergstra et al., 2007) for one impressive example in computer science. Also, there are many further entanglements between algebraic and logical methods. Németi

---

[292] *Proof.* Expand $\boldsymbol{F}$ to a model for a first-order language with new unary predicates P_X for each $X \subseteq W$. Take an ω-saturated elementary extension $\boldsymbol{F}'$ of the expanded $\boldsymbol{F}$ (see Appendix A for this notion), and map its objects w to the ultrafilter of all sets X for which w satisfies P_X. This is a p-morphism onto $ue(\boldsymbol{F})$.

(1991) is an wide and deep survey of algebraic logics and their connections with other systems. The interplay, or rivalry, between algebraic and model-theoretic methods has proved highly useful to modal
logic, and far beyond. For instance, some of the key algebraic results
mentioned above extend to larger universal fragments of the first-order
language.[293] Indeed, basic algebraic results may sometimes be proved
in model-theoretic terms: cf. the proof of Jónsson's Lemma in van
Benthem (1988b). Also, concrete algebraic proofs may suggest new
model-theoretic ones (and also vice versa): an example is the purely
model-theoretic proof of the Goldblatt-Thomason theorem in van Benthem (1993). On the other hand, right now, there is a surge in algebraic theory about non-Boolean algebras such as distributive lattices, or
just lattices with monotone operations, where standard model-theoretic
methods seem to be lagging behind (Venema, 2006). This is the usual
interplay of natural stances in mathematics.

---

[293] E.g., a class of models K is definable by a set of universal first-order formulas
iff K is closed under forming *isomorphic images*, *sub-models* and *ultraproducts*.

Answers and hints to selected exercises

Chapter 2

1(a) The most remarkable point in the model is 3: an end-point, that satisfies $\Box\bot$. Points 1, 2 and 4 differ in their access to it: 2 uniquely satisfies $\Diamond\top \wedge \Box\Box\bot$. The "dirty solution" for world 1: it is the only world to see world 2: $\Diamond(\Diamond\top \wedge \Box\Box\bot)$. The still dirtier solution for world 4: conjoin the negations of the definitions for 1, 2 and 3.

1(b) You can still define the points 3 and 1 uniquely, using $\Box\bot$, $\Diamond\Diamond\top$ respectively. You can prove by induction that 2, 4 satisfy the same modal formulas. The other option is to see that interchanging 2, 4 is a bisimulation (see Chapter 3) for this model with itself, and then use the Invariance Lemma that is proved there.

2(a) Compute a table for truth of all sub-formulas in all worlds:

p:	1, 2		$\Diamond p$:	2, 3
$\Box\Diamond p$:	3, 4		$\Diamond\Box\Diamond p$:	1, 3, 4

Such tabulations will be the basis for a fast model-checking algorithm in Chapter 6.

2(b) This is more physical than mental labour, and never gives students problems.

2(c) In this game, V has a winning strategy. She should stick to true formulas as follows: she could choose world 3 in the first step making $\Box\Diamond p$ true. Then, F can choose either world 3 or 2, in both of which $\Diamond p$ is true, and so V has a final winning move.

Chapter 3

1(a) The indicated dotted lines between the given models do the job:

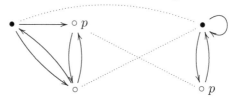

1(b) In this situation, only the black dot to the left satisfies the formula $\Box(\Box\bot \vee \Diamond\Box\bot)$.

1(c) Spoiler starts with a world where $\Box(\Box\bot \vee \Diamond\Box\bot)$ is false (i.e., on the right), as this gives him a successor to keep a false formula $\Box\bot \vee \Diamond\Box\bot$: i.e., the left-most dot. Duplicator must respond on the left, and can take either the black dot, or the white one: in either case, $\Box\bot \vee \Diamond\Box\bot$ is true, so Spoiler has "maintained" a difference: either $\Box\bot$ or $\Diamond\Box\bot$. Depending on which one, he picks his next successor, still in the model on the right, and arrives at a situation where an endpoint is matched with a non-endpoint, allowing him to win against Duplicator in one more move.

The general rule: (a) *maintain a modal difference formula of depth k in the game with k rounds to go at the current link (w, v)*, (b) *always select the model where the leading $\Diamond$-formula is true (or, the $\Box$-formula is false) – and pick an appropriate successor there*, (c) *use Boolean decomposition to find the new difference formula*.

2 Here is the contracted model for the modified Treasure Island:

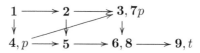

No further bisimulation contractions are possible, as worlds for these different cases satisfied different modal formulas in the original model.

3 The proof of the Adequacy Lemma is by induction on the depth of modal formulas, both ways. Here are some highlights.

Depth 0: we are talking about a 0-length game, that just consists in inspection of the initial link (s, t): if s, t satisfy the same atoms, then D wins, otherwise S. Note that two worlds satisfy the same atoms iff they satisfy the same formulas without modal operators, i.e., all modal formulas of depth 0.

Depth $k + 1$: each modal formula of this depth can be viewed as a Boolean combination of formulas of depth $\leq k$ and (at worst) formulas $\Diamond\psi$ – where ψ has depth k. So we can concentrate on the latter. Suppose that D has a winning strategy over $k+1$ rounds. Let $\boldsymbol{M}, s \models \Diamond\psi$. Then there exists some u with Rsu and $\boldsymbol{M}, u \models \psi$. *Consider a game where S starts with this choice of u.* Since D has a winning strategy, it must cope with this eventuality, and produce a corresponding choice Rtv in the other model $\boldsymbol{N}$ such that, playing from the new link (u, v) according to the remainder of the strategy, D can win the remaining k-round game. *Inductive hypothesis*: u, v satisfy the same modal formulas up to depth k. In particular, then, $\boldsymbol{N}, v \models \psi$ – and so $\boldsymbol{N}, t \models \Diamond\psi$: which is what we needed to show.

Now consider the opposite direction, where s, t satisfy the same modal formulas up to depth $k+1$. How to produce a winning strategy for D? The first move requires the

Lemma (Finiteness Lemma). There are only finitely many non-equivalent modal formulas up to any fixed finite depth.

This is a simple induction, presupposing that our set of atoms $p, q, \ldots$ is *finite*. Take any opening move by S: say, Rsu in $\boldsymbol{M}$. How should D respond? We take a finite (!) conjunction α of all formulas of depth k true in $\boldsymbol{M}, u$, which implies that $\boldsymbol{M}, s \models \Diamond\alpha$ – and so $\boldsymbol{N}, t \models \Diamond\alpha$, because this formula is of depth $k+1$. But then let player D take any Rtv with $\boldsymbol{N}, v \models \alpha$. Clearly, u, v agree on all modal formulas of depth $\leq k$, and hence, by the *inductive hypothesis*, D has a winning strategy in the k-round game starting from (u, v). What we have described altogether then is a winning strategy over $k + 1$ rounds for D, starting from the initial mach (s, t).

Chapter 4

1(a) Here is one example of a rule. Consider the implication going from $\Sigma, A \Rightarrow B$ to $\Sigma \Rightarrow A \rightarrow B$. The consequent says that $\Sigma \Rightarrow \neg(A \wedge \neg B)$, which follows from $\Sigma, A \wedge \neg B \Rightarrow$, which follows from $\Sigma, A, \neg B \Rightarrow$, which indeed follows from $\Sigma, A \Rightarrow B$.

1(b) Only the first stated principle is valid. Take any successor t of the current world s where p holds. By the antecedent $\Box(p \rightarrow q)$, the implication $p \rightarrow q$ also holds at t, and then so does q, making t a witness for the truth of $\Diamond q$ in s.

The second implication is invalid, and one concrete counter-example is the left-most world of the following model, where the formula $\Diamond p \rightarrow \Diamond q$ holds, but $\Box(p \rightarrow q)$ does not:

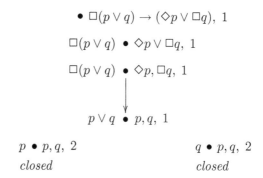

2(a) Here is the crux. In the joint rooting construction, we need to make sure that truth of modal formulas does not change when computed in those models by themselves, or when lying *as sub-models* in the new tree model. Intuition: no new successors are added in the construction. Precise reason: the identity relation is a *bisimulation* between the separate models and their counterparts in the rooted tree model.

2(b) A modal sequent of the form $\boldsymbol{p}, \Box\varphi_1, \ldots, \Box\varphi_k \Rightarrow \Box\psi_1, \ldots \Box\psi_m, \boldsymbol{q}$ holds iff either (a) $\boldsymbol{p}, \boldsymbol{q}$ overlap, or (b) for some i ($1 \leq i \leq m$) the sequent $\varphi_1, \ldots \varphi_k \Rightarrow \psi_i$ is valid.

You can see this is equivalent by unpacking $\Diamond$ as $\neg\Box\neg$ and referring to the special "conjunction to disjunction" definition of validity of modal sequents.

2(c) Here is a closed tableau refuting existence of a counter-example:

- $\Box(p \vee q) \to (\Diamond p \vee \Box q)$, 1

$\Box(p \vee q) \bullet \Diamond p \vee \Box q$, 1

$\Box(p \vee q) \bullet \Diamond p, \Box q$, 1

$p \vee q \bullet p, q$, 1

$p \bullet p, q$, 2 $q \bullet p, q$, 2
closed   *closed*

3 We prove by induction that for all sub-formulas α of φ:

$$M, s \models \alpha \text{ iff } \alpha \text{ holds at } s^\sim \text{ in the filtrated model } M^\sim.$$

Here is the salient case. (a) Suppose $M, s \models \Diamond\beta$. By the truth definition, there is a world t with sRt and $M, t \models \beta$. By the definition of $R^\sim$ it follows that $s^\sim R^\sim t^\sim$. And so by the inductive hypothesis, $M^\sim, t^\sim \models \beta$. By the truth definition again, $M^\sim, s^\sim \models \Diamond\beta$.

(b) Next, suppose that $M^\sim, s^\sim \models \Diamond\beta$. There is some $t^\sim$ with $s^\sim R^\sim t^\sim$ and $M^\sim, t^\sim \models \beta$. By the inductive hypothesis then $M, t \models \beta$. This time, we have no direct information about s, t: in particular, we do not know if sRt. What we do know by definition of $R^\sim$: there are $u \sim s, v \sim t$ with uRv. But then $M, v \models \beta$ (as v, t agree on all relevant formulas), so $M, u \models \Diamond\beta$ (by the truth definition), and $M, s \models \Diamond\beta$ (because s, u agree).

4 This is a simple modification of the standard translation, dropping the syntactic restriction with the R-atom. There is also a converse translation, by first bringing monadic first-order formulas into an equivalent normal form where they only say the following: "some specified exhaustive combinations of (negated) atomic properties $(\neg)Px \wedge (\neg)Qx \wedge \cdots$ occur in the model, while all others do not".

Chapter 5

1 The trick in modal deduction is usually finding an underlying propositional tautology, and then modalizing this. From left to right, use: $(\varphi \wedge \psi) \rightarrow \varphi$, $(\varphi \wedge \psi) \rightarrow \psi$. From right to left, modalize $\varphi \rightarrow (\psi \rightarrow (\varphi \wedge \psi))$ and use Distribution twice.

2 In finding formal modal deductions, it often helps to first do a semantic argument. In this particular case, you will repeatedly need transitivity of the model plus the existence of successors at any reachable point. To match this syntactically, use the $K4$ axiom to extend modal □-sequences – while the minimal modal logic K allows you auxiliary implications like $\square\square\varphi \wedge \square\Diamond\top \rightarrow \square\Diamond\varphi$.

3 Suppose that neither $\vdash \alpha$ nor $\vdash \beta$. By the completeness theorem, there are models plus worlds verifying $\neg\alpha$ and $\neg\beta$. Put these models together disjointly under a joint new root connected only to the two refuting worlds, and observe that at that root, $\square\alpha \vee \square\beta$ is false. Therefore, this formula cannot have been provable.

4 These are standard facts from logic textbooks.

5 See the *Manual of Intensional Logic* (van Benthem, 1988a) for this simple argument, and a reference to a paper by Tore Langholm, who attended an early version of this course, where this logic is developed in more detail.

Chapter 6

1(a) Each round of checking can take $|M|$ steps, and we have a number of nested rounds equal to the modal operator depth of φ: so in total, order of $|M|^{|\varphi|}$ steps.

1(b) The algorithm in the text finds the truth values of sub-formulas once and for all at each world in a round, and need not "re-compute" them in nested settings. This is because the modal language has no deeper polyadic dependencies between choices.

1(c) For first-order logic, what would correspond to worlds are *variable assignments*. But the number of these is exponential, if we give arbitrary formulas as input. By taking a bit more care, though, reusing memory locations when cycling through assignments, this problem may be seen to be *PSPACE*. The general observation: if we *fix a finite number of variables*, and only feed formulas of that fragment to the model, then the modal-style algorithm works, and it runs again in *PTIME*.

2(b) Counting very roughly, with n the maximum of the sizes of the two models, each stage of the bisimulation algorithm requires comparing all still available pairs of worlds, looking at all their successors: $n^2 * n^2 = n^4$ steps. There are n^2 rounds, since one pair disappears in each round: total order n^6. Actually, this hugely over-counts!

3 Being a celebrity is definable by the first-order formula $\forall y \neq x(\neg Kxy \land Kyx)$. Existence of a celebrity is then $\exists x \forall y \neq x(\neg Kxy \land Kyx)$, of quantifier depth 2. So you would expect a quadratic-time algorithm for testing this, but in fact it can be done in linear time! Give each person a red ball. Now repeat the following until no longer possible: Take any two persons x, y from the group you have not eliminated yet, and check if Kxy. If *YES*, then take away the red ball from x; if *NO*, then take it away from y. It is easy to prove that the last person whose still has a red ball is a celebrity. The moral: *general complexity is sometimes circumvented by clever special programs*.

Chapter 7

1(a) $\exists y(R_b xy \land (\exists x(R_a yx \land Px) \land \forall x(R_b yx \to \exists y(R_a xy \land Qy))))$.

1(b) The formula *SINCE pq* is not invariant for bisimulation. It is true in the black world in the model to the left, but not in that of the bisimilar model to the right:

1(c) This simple translation goes again into monadic first-order logic.

1(d) This dependence formalism translates into the Guarded Fragment in an obvious way using a family of atomic predicates for the independence relations of each arity.

2(a) The 2-variable translation for the basic modal language in our main text does not need additional variables to deal with the two new inductive cases for E and U.

2(b) In the following diagram, the dotted line is a standard modal bisimulation: but Ep holds to the left, and not to the right.

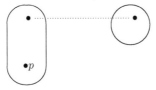

2(c) To match modal logic with the universal modality, take ordinary modal bisimulations, and add a further condition of "totality": each point in each model must be connected to a point in the other model.

2(d) By the same reasoning as with the algorithm for the basic modal language, model-checking stays *PTIME*.

2(e) The total $\{\Diamond, E\}$-bisimulation between a 2-cycle and a reflexive 1-cycle refutes this.

3(a) We already saw how to define this property: $\exists y(y < x \land Py \land \forall z((y < z \land z < x) \to Qz))$.

3(b) The solution favoured by most students uses the following principle. If I have a translation of φ with a free variable x using (possibly) bound variables x, y, z only, then there is an equivalent formula (in a suitable sense) with y as its only free variable, again using x, y, z as bound variables. Better: do a simultaneous version: show that every formula has three analogous $\{x, y, z\}$ 3-variable translations, with free variables x, y, z respectively. Then the induction will work smoothly.

4(a) The translation takes any hybrid formula φ and variable x, and writes an equivalent first-order formula $ST_x(\varphi)$ with the free variable x. The clauses for proposition letters and Booleans are as in the standard translation. Here are the rest:

$$ST_x(\Diamond \varphi) \quad := \quad \exists y(Rxy \land ST_y(\varphi)) \quad \text{for some fresh variable } y$$
$$ST_x(@_y\varphi) \quad := \quad ST_y(\varphi)$$
$$ST_x(\downarrow y \cdot \varphi) \quad := \quad [y/x]ST_x(\varphi)$$

5(b) First find a suitable notion of "guarded bisimulation" (or look this up in Andréka et al. (1998)). Then use two very simple finite models with a guarded bisimulation between them to establish the non-invariance of the formula $Ex \neg Px$.

6 The most relevant properties are linear order for both relations, their discreteness (if a point has a successor, it has an immediate successor), and the existence of a beginning, but no end point. To relate the two orders, the crucial property is "confluence": going *"North East"* leads to the same spot as going *"East North"*. You can try to write this up for yourself now, or look at Chapter 24 for more hints.

Chapter 8

1 One can prove this Depth One feature semantically, or via the earlier translation into monadic first-order logic, which has the same Quantifier Depth One property. An explicit syntactic algorithm uses a bunch of valid equivalences, where the *S4*-laws compress sequences $\Box\Box$ and $\Diamond\Diamond$. Next, modalities $\Box$ can be distributed over conjunctions and $\Diamond$ over disjunctions, moving ever further inside. To overcome the remaining barriers, one uses the following principles, valid and provable in *S5*:

$$\Box(A \wedge \Box B) \leftrightarrow (\Box A \vee \Box B), \qquad \Box(A \wedge \Diamond B) \leftrightarrow (\Box A \vee \Diamond B)$$

Another method (actually, a bit nicer) works by observing that, over *S5*-models, inside occurrences of modalities can be removed by the following valid schema:

$$\varphi(\ldots \Diamond B \ldots) \leftrightarrow (\Diamond B \wedge \varphi(\ldots \top \ldots)) \vee (\neg \Diamond B \vee \varphi(\ldots \bot \ldots))$$

4 Along the finite "spines", we show that *GL holds on each finite strict linear order*, by induction on the length. Let $\Box(\Box p \to p)$ hold anywhere along the spine. Then $\Box p \to p$ holds everywhere to the right. Look at the endpoint: $\Box p$ holds there.

$$
\begin{array}{ccccc}
\Box(\Box p \to p) & \Box p \to p & \Box p \to p & \Box p \to p & \\
\bullet & \bullet & \bullet & \bullet & \Box p \\
\Box p & p & p & p &
\end{array}
$$

But then we have p there, which makes $\Box p$ true at the one-but last point: which makes p true there, which makes $\Box p$ true at ... etcetera, until you get a "round-trip" ending in the conclusion that $\Box p$ was true at the original point.

For the root, show that if Löb's Axiom fails there, it would also fail on one of the spines. If $\Box(\Box p \to p)$ is true in the root, and $\Box p$ is not, then there is a successor (on a spine!) where $\neg p$ holds, as well as $\Box p \to p$, and hence $\neg \Box p$. Moreover, $\Box(\Box p \to p)$ still holds in this point (since, by transitivity, $\Box\Box(\Box p \to p)$ holds in the root).

5 This is a standard argument in completeness theorems for special modal logics. For instance, to prove reflexivity, assume that $\Box\varphi$ belongs to a maximally consistent set Σ. Since we have the T-axiom, and maximally consistent sets are closed under deductive consequences, we must also have φ in Σ. By definition of the order in Henkin models, this means that $R\Sigma\Sigma$. (Arguments are not always as easy as this!)

6 No: the modal logic becomes richer. On finite trees the McKinsey Axiom $\Box\Diamond\varphi \to \Diamond\Box\varphi$ is valid, due to the existence of end-points. But this principle is not derivable in $S4$, and it fails, for instance, on the infinite reflexive and transitive frame of the natural numbers $(\mathbb{N}, \leq)$, setting $V(p)$ equal to the even numbers.

Chapter 9

1 To practice, you should do a few examples in detail, and then acquire the facility of reading off the correspondents directly from the modal forms. This is easy – but many professional modal logicians are bad at it! Here are the two correspondents:

$$\forall y(Rxy \to \exists z(Rxz \land \forall u(Rzu \to u = y))),$$
$$\forall y(R_bxy \to \forall z(R_ayz \to \exists u(R_axu \land R_buz))).$$

2 The axioms give precisely the two inclusions for the relation R_P to be the *converse* of R_F.

3 Here are the key points in the proof of the Sahlqvist Theorem for frame correspondence, ignoring manipulations up to logical equivalence in the method. First, any universal second-order formula implies all its (first-order) substitution instances, and so the second-order frame form of the modal axiom implies the computed first-order correspondent. Conversely, let that correspondent hold in a frame. Consider any valuation V making the antecedent of the modal axiom true. V contains a first-order definable minimal valuation V_{min} still making the antecedent true. By construction, this means that the antecedent of the computed correspondent holds, and hence also its consequent. But since that consequent is syntactically positive, it will continue to hold for the valuation V extending V_{min}.

4 This is a tricky correspondence. In one direction, it is easy to see that atomic pre-orders validate the McKinsey Axiom. But the converse is a non-routine argument involving the Axiom of Choice to find a subset $V(p)$ in a non-atomic preorder with $\Box\Diamond p$, $\Box\Diamond\neg p$ both true.

Chapter 10

1(a) $\Diamond pq$ translates into $\exists yz(Rxyz \land Py \land Qz)$; 3 variables suffice for the fragment. Incidentally, it is of some interest to determine what you take to be the move for this dyadic modality in a natural *evaluation game* for the language.

1(b) Bisimulation arguments for polyadic modal logic are simple once you have the right zigzag clauses. Here is one direction: if xEx' and Rx, yz, then there exist y', z' with $Rx', y'z'$ and yEy', zEz'.

1(c) The correspondence for Associativity is a simple Sahlqvist substitution case, and it yields (draw a picture to see what happens) the first-order "re-composition" principle

$$\forall yzus((Rx, yz \wedge Ry, us) \to \exists t(Rx, ut \wedge Rt, sz)).$$

2 The triangle to the right has all points uniquely definable. E.g., the two p-points differ since only one satisfies $\Diamond qr$. The three q-points can be distinguished likewise by their environments. The left-hand triangle contracts to one with just one r-point. *Comment*: if you picture the result, you will find that (betweenness-) bisimulation contractions of figures in the plane need not themselves be planar figures!

3(a) It is easy to draw counter-examples to both distribution laws, but the reason behind them should be clear: the neighbourhood semantics treats modalities as quantifier combinations $\exists \forall$, and this blocks both forms of distribution holding for the separate quantifiers.

3(b) The notion of bisimulation here is basically the "topo-bisimulation" of Chapter 19. The converse result for finite models is like the basic modal argument in Chapter 3, but you need some more "bookkeeping" for two reasons: (a) we are relating worlds to sets of worlds, and (b) the zigzag clause involves a 2-quantifier combination.

3(c) This is a patent (though surprisingly widespread) fallacy. For instance, intuitionistic propositional logic (*PSPACE*-complete) is weaker than classical logic (*NP*-complete)! Or even better: classical logic is weaker than the *inconsistent logic* (with all formulas "valid"), but the complexity of membership for the latter is trivial.

3(d) Here is an example of the semantic construction behind the decomposition fact. Suppose that formula A_1 does not imply either B_1 or B_2. Take neighbourhood models M_{11}, s_{11} for $A_1 \wedge \neg B_1$ and M_{21}, s_{12} for $A_1 \wedge \neg B_2$. Do the same for A_2: this gives 4 models in total. Now *put all these models together disjointly* with one new world s that has only two neighbourhoods $\{s_{11}, s_{12}\}$ and $\{s_{21}, s_{22}\}$. These suffice for making $\Box A_1, \Box A_2$ true at s, without making $\Box B_1$ or $\Box B_2$ true. *Note*: this "glueing" of models is simpler than the earlier joint-rooting construction in relational models, since neighbourhood models are so "loose". The complexity of deciding validity is simpler now, as the next rounds of attempts at validity with the outer □ "peeled off" do not repeat subformulas across cases. We leave it to the reader to see why the resulting process can be done in NP-time.

Chapter 11

1 To refute the modal Distribution Axiom on these general models, take a world 1 with domain $\{d\}$ which has an accessible world 2 with domain $\{e\}$. Let $P(d)$ hold in 1, and nowhere else. Consider a variable assignment sending x to d and y to e. Then $\Box Px$ and $\Box(Px \to Py)$ are both true in world 1 (note that *no world* has both the objects needed for the second formula), but $\Box Py$ is false.

2 This is a simple exercise. We give an explicit answer for the more complex next question.

3 The key step in the correspondence proof is this. Suppose that wRv, but D_v has an object d that is not in D_w. Now make the predicate P true for all objects from D_w in any world where they occur. This valuation makes the formula $\forall x \Box Px$ true at w, but $\Box \forall x Px$ fails, since the domain of the accessible world v has an object d which lacks P.

Actually, this correspondence can also be found "automatically" by an easy extension of the substitution method of Chapter 9 to models with domains at worlds: syntactically, the Barcan Axiom then has "generalized Sahlqvist form".

4 This is somewhat tricky, though you can see some special cases: for instance, the principle will hold in a frame if all worlds have just one object. Computing frame correspondences for non-first-order modal predicate-logical axioms is a nice sport!

5 Here is a sketch of the undefinability proof (you will agree that this is really too hard for an exercise). Take a family of frames F_n having a root w plus n successors $v_1, \ldots, v_n$. The domain of w is the natural numbers, and each v_i only has two objects: v_1 has $\{1, 2\}$, v_2 $\{2, 3\}$, $\ldots$, v_n $\{n, n+1\}$. On each such frame, $\Diamond \exists x Px \to \exists x \Diamond Px$ is true. It is clearly true in all v_i, as these have no successors. Next, suppose $\Diamond \exists x Px$ holds at w, under any valuation. Either object 1 has P in v_1, and we get $\Box P1$, since v_1 is the only world where 1 occurs, or it does not. Then 2 has the property P in v_1, and either it also has P in v_2, and w has

$\Box P2$, or we go on. If we never get $\exists x \Diamond Px$ in this way, the final point $n+1$ in v_n is a witness for $\Box P(n+1)$ at w.

Next, assume that our modal $\Diamond \exists x Px \rightarrow \exists x \Diamond Px$ has a first-order frame equivalent α in L_{corr}: we shall derive a contradiction. First, using Compactness for first-order logic, we can describe the union of $\{\alpha\}$ and the theory of these models in such a way that there exists a model M for them of the following form. M consist of a root w, and an infinite set of successor worlds v lying in a discrete linear order with a unique beginning and endpoint and no "limit points". Thus, the ordering of the v's is like the natural numbers followed by copies of the integers, and ending in a copy of the negative integers. Here each successor world v has two objects, while each object occurs in exactly two worlds, except for the endpoints, at each of which an isolated object occurs. But then, we can refute our modal predicate-logical principle $\Diamond \exists x Px \rightarrow \exists x \Diamond Px$:

> Let P be false of the isolated objects at the beginning and end world v, and, using the special ordering of the v's described, make P true for just one object in each world so as to avoid ever making the same object P across worlds.

As a result, the antecedent $\Diamond \exists x Px$ holds in model M at the initial world w, but the consequent $\exists x \Diamond Px$ does not. But the first-order sentence α was true in M by construction, and it was to be equivalent to our modal axiom: a contradiction.

6 Instead of a prove, note that the key to this modified translation is a binary "existence" predicate Ewx saying that object x exists in world w. The clauses for the quantifiers use E-restricted quantification, and those for the modalities may use E to restrict attention to worlds containing the relevant objects.

Chapter 12

Note: Models are always supposed to have equivalence relations, but just the minimal set of their "uncertainty lines" is displayed in the pictures that follow.

1(a) Only one p-world has $\langle 1 \rangle \neg p$, only one has $K_1 p \wedge \langle 2 \rangle \langle 1 \rangle \neg p$.

1(b) The bisimulation contraction has only two worlds:

2 The first is valid, just using reflexivity. Counter-example for the second: take the following two worlds indistinguishable for 1 but distinguishable for 2:

$$p \xrightarrow{\quad 1 \quad} \neg p$$

3(b) The main point of the fixed-point axiom is that having φ true at the end of every finite sequence of accessibility links means the same as (a) having φ true right now, and (b) at the end of every single link, having φ true at the end of every finite sequence of accessibility links. The induction axiom follows from an application of standard induction on the natural numbers, though abstractly, it expresses that common knowledge is a *greatest fixed-point* in the sense of Chapter 22.

3(c) Consider an infinite alternation $1 \sim_A 2 \sim_E 3 \sim_A 4 \sim_E \cdots$. Common knowledge of p in the group $\{A, E\}$ says that each world in this sequence satisfies p. But it is easy to prove that each formula φ of operator depth k without common knowledge has its truth value at world n determined by the worlds reachable from n in at most k steps. Therefore, outside of that, we can make p false without any change in truth value for φ.

3(d) The implication from left to right fails: just think of groups 1, 2: knowledge of the single agents does not guarantee common knowledge. The converse is valid: by the semantic definition of common knowledge, it is inherited by subgroups.

Chapter 13

1 To check the axiom, consider any closest $A \vee B$ world. This is either A or B. Without loss of generality, suppose the former. Then it is also a closest A-world: for, if there were still closer A-worlds, then there would also be closer $A \vee B$-worlds. But our premise $A \Rightarrow C$ says that it is then also a C-world, and we are done.

2 This argument is a bit technical, though it becomes easy once you analyze just why this axiom is valid on connected orders. The exercise is useful to see that frame correspondence techniques work just as well for more complex modal operators.

3 If my most plausible worlds do not satisfy p, then any conditional $p \to q$ is true there, and by our truth definition, I believe it. But this says nothing whatsoever about my conditional beliefs $B^p q$ were I to move to the area of the p-worlds.

4 Assume the defining modal formula $U(A \to \langle\le\rangle(A \wedge [\le](A \to B)))$. Consider a minimal A-world x. Given the condition, there is an A-world y at least as close (so, equally close as x) such that all A-worlds at least as close as that satisfy B. This implies that x satisfies B. Conversely, suppose that all minimal A-worlds satisfy B. Consider any A-world: it must have some minimal A-world s below it, since the model is *finite* (and given the other conditions on our ordering). But that s satisfies $A \wedge [\le](A \to B)$: any still lower A-world is equally close, and hence it is minimal, too, and hence it satisfies B by assumption.

5 The intuitive reason for the failure of weakening of knowledge is this. Suppose that I Nozick-know that A: then (a) A is true, (b) I believe that A, and (c) I would have believed that $\neg A$, had $\neg A$ been true: which refers to the closest worlds to the actual one where $\neg A$ holds. Now consider knowledge of $A \vee B$. In particular, were this to be false, that is, $\neg A \wedge \neg B$ holds, I would have to believe that. But the closest worlds where $\neg A \wedge \neg B$ holds need not be closest worlds where $\neg A$ holds, so our premise of knowledge about A gives us no information about what holds in $\neg A \wedge \neg B$-worlds. It is easy to turn this into a concrete model as a counter-example. The more technical reason is that the *logical form* of Nozick's epistemic explanation has both positive and negative occurrences of the proposition B, blocking either upward or downward semantic monotonicity.

Chapter 14

1 The first principle is valid, the second is not: for obvious reasons.

2 For instance, semantically, the second principle says that arbitrary finite sequences of a and b transitions can also be viewed as arbitrary sequences of segments arising from first taking zero or more a transitions and then zero or more b transitions. Formal proofs are complicated: you have to use the Induction Axiom repeatedly.

3 A successful execution of the program *WHILE E DO S*, or $(?E; S)^*$ $;(\neg E)?$, is a finite sequence of states satisfying the condition E with completed S-transitions between them, and ending with an S-transition to a state where $\neg E$ holds. We start with a state where I holds, and thanks to the global truth of $\{I\}S\{I\}$, we know that each S-transition in the given sequence leads to an I-state. Therefore, the final state reached has both I and $\neg E$. We can also proceed formally, with a *PDL*-proof for the valid formula $I \to [(?E; S)^*; (\neg E)?](I \wedge \neg E)$. This is equivalent to the formula $I \to [(?E; S)^*](\neg E \to (I \wedge \neg E))$, that follows in the minimal modal logic from $I \to [(?E; S)^*]I$. The latter can be proved with the Induction Axiom, using a globally given implication $I \to [S]I$ to which the Necessitation Rule can be applied.

4(a) Valid: items 2, 3, 5 only. The answers are simple modal logic.

4(b)

$$\{A\}S\{B\}, \{B\}S\{C\} \Rightarrow \{A\}S; S\{C\}$$
$$\{A\}S\{B\} \Rightarrow \{\neg B\}\textbf{converse}(S)\{\neg A\}$$

5 The first axiom is a Sahlqvist form, both ways. The two directions say that (a) $R_b \subseteq Id \cup (R_a; R_b)$, and (b) $Id \subseteq R_b, (R_a; R_b) \subseteq R_b$. The Induction Axiom is not a Sahlqvist form, but given the other principles, we do get that $R_b \subseteq (R_a)^*$.

6 In the inductive step of invariance for formulas $\langle \pi \rangle \varphi$, we want to proceed as in the modal case $\langle a \rangle \varphi$ in Chapter 2, but this step requires the same zigzag behaviour for *complex defined transition relations* R_π as for the given atomic relations R_a.

8(a) $\langle \neg (R) \rangle \varphi \leftrightarrow (\varphi \wedge \neg \langle R \rangle \top)$

8(b)

$$\begin{aligned}
\langle \neg (R; \neg \neg S) \rangle p &\leftrightarrow p \wedge \neg \langle R; \neg \neg S \rangle \top \\
&\leftrightarrow p \wedge \neg \langle R \rangle \langle \neg \neg S \rangle \top \\
&\leftrightarrow p \wedge \neg \langle R \rangle (\top \wedge \neg \langle \neg S \rangle \top) \\
&\leftrightarrow p \wedge \neg \langle R \rangle (\top \wedge \neg (\top \wedge \neg \langle S \rangle \top)) \\
&\leftrightarrow p \wedge \neg \langle R \rangle \neg \neg \langle S \rangle \top \\
&\leftrightarrow p \wedge \neg \langle R \rangle \langle S \rangle \top \\
&\leftrightarrow p \wedge \neg \langle R; S \rangle \top \\
&\leftrightarrow \langle \neg (R; S) \rangle p
\end{aligned}$$

Chapter 15

1 The question does not change the diagram. The answer goes to

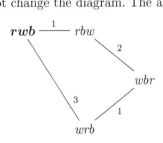

Here only 2 knows the cards, the others do not, but for instance, agent 3 knows that 2 knows.

2(a) The point is that the sequence does not terminate in common knowledge any more. Referring to the diagram in the text: When the first dirty child says she does not know her status, only world DCC is ruled out. So 2 now knows her status, and can say so. This rules out all worlds except CDC and DDC. 3 also knows her status now, and can say that next, but this was already common knowledge by this stage, and the model does not change. But in this model, 1 still does not know his status, and repeating the procedure gets stuck at this model, instead of just the actual DDC.

3(a) The information model is as follows:

$$\boldsymbol{wrw} \overset{3}{\rule{2cm}{0.4pt}} wwr$$

with $2,3$ on the left edge and 3 on the right edge, and

$$rww \underset{1,2,3}{\rule{2cm}{0.4pt}} www$$

3(b) True, and the update goes to

$$\boldsymbol{wrw} \overset{3}{\rule{2cm}{0.4pt}} wwr$$

3(c) The man in the middle knows his colour now, but announcing that fact does not help the man at the bottom.

4(a) Here is one example of a valid diamond conversion: $\langle !P\rangle\langle i\rangle\varphi \leftrightarrow P \wedge \langle i\rangle\langle !P\rangle\varphi$.

4(b) In removing dynamic modalities from *PAL*-formulas in the completeness proof, it suffices to start from their *innermost* occurrences. The given axioms deal with that, and make the innermost dynamic modality eventually disappear when it hits atomic formulas. After that, the formula is less complex, and we repeat this procedure.

5 This Sahlqvist form has a first-order meaning describing a "commuting diagram" between action and indistinguishability:

$$\forall y(R_a xy \rightarrow \forall z(R_i yz \rightarrow \exists u(R_i xu \wedge R_a uz))).$$

6(a) The first event is just announcement via world elimination.

6(b) The second event requires, not world elimination but "link cutting" (cf. Chapter 23): all of 2's uncertainties between worlds where 1 has different cards disappear.

6(c) This cuts the uncertainty links between 1's card positions for the other players.

8(a) In a model with just a p-world and a $\neg p$-world, mutually epistemically accessible and equiplausible, $[!p]Kp$ holds, and hence, in our semantics, also $[!p]BKp$. But the conditional belief formula B^pKp is not true, since even in just the p-world, I do not know that p, because I still have epistemic access to the $\neg p$-world outside.

8(b) Here are the most striking laws of belief change to be checked. First consider changes in conditional belief under hard information: $[!P]B^\psi\varphi \leftrightarrow (P \rightarrow B^{P\wedge[!P]\psi}[!P]\varphi)$. On the left hand side, this says that in the new model $M|P, s$, φ is true in the most plausible ψ-worlds. With the usual precondition for true announcement, the right-hand side says that in M, s, the most plausible worlds that are P now and will become ψ after announcing P, will also become φ after announcing P. This is indeed equivalent. Next consider belief change after soft information changing the plausibility order:

$$[\Uparrow P]B^\psi\varphi \leftrightarrow$$
$$(\Diamond(P \wedge [\Uparrow P]\psi) \wedge B^{P\wedge[\Uparrow P]\psi}[\Uparrow P]\varphi) \vee$$
$$(\neg\Diamond(P \wedge [\Uparrow P]\psi) \wedge B^{[\Uparrow P]\psi}[\Uparrow P]\varphi)$$

The left-hand side says that, after the P-upgrade, all most plausible ψ-worlds satisfy φ. On the right-hand side, there is a case distinction. Case (1): there are accessible P-worlds in the original model M that become ψ after the upgrade. Then lexicographic reordering $\Uparrow P$ makes the "best" of these worlds in M the best ones over-all in $M\Uparrow P$ to satisfy ψ. Now, in the original model M – viz. its epistemic component visible from the current world s – the worlds of Case 1 are just those satisfying the formula $P \wedge [\Uparrow P]\psi$. Therefore, the formula $B^{P\wedge[\Uparrow P]\psi}[\Uparrow P]\varphi$ says that the best among these in M will indeed satisfy φ after the upgrade. And these best worlds are the same as those described earlier, as lexicographic reordering does not change the ordering of worlds inside the P-area. Case (2): no P-worlds in the original M become ψ after upgrade. Then the lexicographic reordering $\Uparrow P$ makes the best worlds satisfying ψ after the upgrade just the same best worlds over-all as before that satisfied $[\Uparrow P]\psi$. Here, the relevant formula $B^{[\Uparrow P]\psi}[\Uparrow P]\varphi$ in the reduction axiom says that the best worlds become φ after upgrade.

8(e)

$$[\Uparrow P]B^+\varphi \leftrightarrow$$
$$(P \wedge B^+(P \to [\Uparrow P]\varphi)) \vee$$
$$(\neg P \wedge B^+(\neg P \to [\Uparrow P]\varphi) \wedge K(P \to [\Uparrow P]\varphi))$$

Chapter 16

1 Here is perhaps the most striking axiom linking $\langle \leq \rangle$ and $\langle < \rangle$:

$$\varphi \wedge \langle \leq \rangle \psi \to \langle < \rangle \psi \vee \langle \leq \rangle (\psi \wedge \langle \leq \rangle \varphi)$$

To see that this is valid, suppose that $\varphi \wedge \langle \leq \rangle \psi$ is true in a world x. So we have a $\leq$-successor y of x where ψ holds. Now either $y \leq x$, and so we have $\langle \leq \rangle \varphi$ true in y, and hence $\langle \leq \rangle (\psi \wedge \langle \leq \rangle \varphi)$ true at x, or *not* $y \leq x$, so $x < y$, and then $\langle < \rangle \psi$ is true at x.

2 The antecedent talks about a successor world that agrees with the current world on the truth value of the formula α. But then we can just as well include α in the set Γ of formulas for which there was no difference in truth value.

3 The equivalence

$$[\#\varphi]\langle \leq \rangle \psi \leftrightarrow (\neg\varphi \wedge \langle \leq \rangle [\#\varphi]\psi) \vee (\varphi \wedge \langle \leq \rangle (\varphi \wedge [\#\varphi]\psi))$$

closely follows the three options in the definition of the preference relation following our "taking" of the suggestion $\#\varphi$ The only old preference arrows that do *not* pass are those running from φ-world to a "better" $\neg\varphi$-world. For the latter worlds, this leaves all preference arrows in the new model, for the former, only those toward φ-worlds.

4 The lifted set order is easily seen to be reflexive and transitive on *non-empty* sets. It is also linear, if the underlying order was: for, if some object in X has no preferred object in Y, then each object in Y will be majorized by that X-object. Moreover, the set order will have new properties, such as *downward monotonicity* in its first argument: If $P\,XY$ and $Z \subseteq X$, then $P\,ZY$. Likewise there is upward monotonicity in the second argument, etcetera.

5(a) These properties of the induced object ordering follow directly from those of linear priority sequences. E.g., consider the connectedness of object ordering: the smallest index where the objects differ in a property determines which one is "better". Conversely, every finite connected order can be obtained from some P in this way. Take the "properties" to be the equivalence classes of the relation $x \leq y \leq x$ ("mutually connected"), and order these properties in the order of proper precedence. It is easy to show that $x \leq y$ holds iff the objects x, y satisfy the above criterion.

5(b) Associate each property P in the priority sequence with an object ordering $x \leq^P y$ iff $Px \rightarrow Py$. Then, on finite sequences, the "compensation criterion" given for the graphs reduces to the one given earlier by an easy argument. In this manner also, the induced ordering for the disjoint union of two priority graphs will be the *intersection* of the induced orders for the separate graphs.

Chapter 17

1 Let $move_{II}$ be the union of all moves for player II. The formula describing final outcomes is $[((turn_{II}; move_{II}) \cup (turn_I; \sigma))^*](end \rightarrow p)$.

2 In finite game models of this "distinguishing" kind, by a simple argument, each state s has a unique defining formula DEF_s. Then we can define every pair (s, t) in the given strategy σ as the program $?DEF_s; T; ?DEF_t$, where T is the universal relation. A finite union of such pairs then defines the strategy relation σ.

3 This game law is like earlier Perfect Recall principles in Chapter 15, expressing commuting diagrams between moves and epistemic indistinguishability – now specialized to specific players at specific turns. Uncertainties that a player has after playing move a must come from uncertainties she had before playing that move: no new uncertainties are created by her own actions. In such games, uncertainty can only grow through actions of other players, owing to defective observation.

4 The formula $[bi^*](end \rightarrow \varphi) \rightarrow [move]\langle bi^*\rangle(end \wedge \langle\leq\rangle\varphi)$ says the following. Let playing the Backward Induction move a lead to final outcomes that all satisfy φ. No other available move b can have all its outcomes better than all those of a, since then we should not have chosen a. Therefore, there is at least one outcome from b through further Backward Induction play for which some a-outcome is at least as good, and this verifies the formula $\langle\leq\rangle\varphi$. The method of "minimal substitution" of Chapter 9 turns this into a real correspondence argument.

5 For instance, the axiom $[!P]\{\sigma\}\varphi \leftrightarrow (P \rightarrow \{\sigma|P\}[!P]\varphi)$ says that the effect of playing strategy σ in the game having only its former P-nodes remaining is φ in that pruned game iff the totally P-restricted strategy $\sigma|P$ arising from σ by making sure that only moves are played inside the P-area, and tests are made relativized to A leads to states that will become after the update, i.e., satisfying not φ, but $[!P]\varphi$.

6 From each node in the game tree, there can be only finite upward sequences in the *move* relation that is the union of all moves for all players. This is a case of well-foundedness on a transitive relation, and therefore, Löb's Axiom holds for the corresponding modality.

7 Here is an illustration. Consider a sequence of Backward Induction steps as creating expectations, changing plausibility among branches of game trees viewed as worlds:

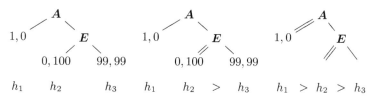

$$h_1 \quad h_2 \qquad h_3 \qquad h_1 \quad h_2 \; > \; h_3 \qquad h_1 \; > \; h_2 \; > \; h_3$$

Start with the empty plausibility relation. At a turn for player i, successor node x "strictly dominates" node y for i if all currently most plausible end nodes following x are worse for i than all currently most plausible end nodes following y. The *BI* procedure then essentially consists in iterated soft updates using the rationality assertion that "No player plays a strictly dominated move at her turns".

Chapter 18

1 $(Hp \wedge Pq) \rightarrow P(p \wedge q)$ is valid, and so is its mirror image $(Gp \wedge Fq) \rightarrow F(p \wedge q)$. Also, $p \rightarrow GPp$ is valid, and so is its mirror image $p \rightarrow HFp$. The idea should be clear.

2 This is standard: the corresponding first-order formula of this tense-logical axiom is so-called "forward discreteness" of temporal order: $\forall x \exists y (x < y \wedge \forall z (z < y \rightarrow (z = x \vee z < x)))$.

3 Visualize this on a line. For instance, the complement of the finite union of convex intervals $(0, 1] \cup (2, + \inf)$ is the finite union $(- \inf, 0] \cup (1, 2]$. And the operation $F(X) = \{ s \mid \exists x \in X : s < x \}$ takes any non-empty set to a downward-closed infinite convex one.

5 A typical connection in an interval setting is that $i < j$ iff $p(i) < p(j)$ where a set interval X precedes Y if all members of X precede all members of Y. The following observations are crucial here: (a) $i \in F$ for each filter F in $p(i)$, (b) $p(i) < p(j)$ implies that $F_i < F_j$ for the special filters F_i of the form $\{ j \mid i \le j \}$, and (c) $F_i < F_j$ implies that $i' < j'$ for some extensions of i, j, respectively, and this implies $i < j$ by Monotonicity for intervals.

6(a) The only valid modal-temporal principle here is $F\Diamond\varphi \to \Diamond F\varphi$: if a branch forks off from the actual history later, then it is a possible history right here already. Simple counter-examples may be drawn for all other stated principles in branching trees. For instance, $\Diamond F\varphi \to F\Diamond\varphi$ is refuted to the left in the following tree with 3 nodes, where the double line marks the actual history:

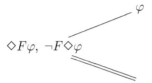

6(b) The previous answer does part of this, but we can make the matching principle more agent- and action-specific in the following form: $F_a\langle i\rangle\varphi \leftrightarrow (F_a\top \wedge \langle i\rangle F_a\varphi)$. The meaning of this is that branches that are epistemically accessible for an agent at some later stage t than the present s are also accessible right now, since their course from s to t was like the current history. Similar extensions may be given for our dynamic-doxastic principles concerning belief change after updates, again along histories in trees.

Chapter 19

1(a) The main inductive clause in the proof of the Locality Lemma is for the modality $M, s \models \Box\varphi$. If φ is true in some open neighbourhood of s, then it is also true in the intersection of that neighbourhood with the given open set U, which is open again. If φ is true in some open set inside the model $M|U$, then the latter is also an open neighbourhood in the whole model.

1(b) A topo-bisimulation leaves modal formulas invariant. Here is the crucial case. Suppose that sEt, while $M, s \models \Box\varphi$. That is, in M, all points in some open set O containing s satisfy φ. The topo-bisimulation E then gives us an open set U in N containing t all of whose members are E-linked to some point in O. So, take any point u in U: by the inductive hypothesis, it will satisfy φ, and thus t satisfies $\Box\varphi$. Finally, the *identity relation* from the sub-model $M|U$ is a topo-bisimulation with the full model M: this derives the Locality Lemma.

2(a) The "two-fork" model indeed satisfies the axiom displayed. Consider the implication $(\neg\varphi \wedge \Diamond\varphi) \to \Diamond\Box\varphi$, where φ denotes a finite union of convex sets. $\Diamond\varphi$ says that the current point s is infinitely approached by points in φ, i.e., by representatives of intervals (different from s because of the $\neg\varphi$) from the finite union denoted by φ. Therefore, one of these intervals must occur *infinitely often* converging toward s. But that can only happen when s has that interval all the way toward its left or right, making the apparently stronger statement $\Diamond \Box \varphi$ true.

3(a) For "filling" a tetrahedron, you might think you get the edges with Cp, the faces with CCp, and the complete interior only with $CCCp$. But once you have all edges, each point in the interior is on a segment between points on two "cross edges".

3(b) The real numbers satisfy $C\varphi \leftrightarrow CC\varphi$ since the C-operator already turns a set into its convex closure on this linear ordering.

4(a) In addition to the triangle inequality stated for *distance xy < distance xz*, the list also includes valid principles for *distance xy ≥ distance xz* and *distance xy = distance xz*. In the plane, you can even find further valid principles of this sort, expressing its low dimensionality. For instance, it is easy to define *equidistance* from our comparative distance order $Nxyz$. Then you can state the fact that any circle has precisely 6 points equidistant with the origin and themselves.

4(b) It is actually an interesting open problem what further valid principles we would get here.

5 In mathematical morphology, we defined $X \circ S$ as $(S \to X) + S$, or in vector notation for sets, as: $(X - S) + S$. Now consider the stated equation $(X \circ S) \circ S = X \circ S$. The corresponding logical law is $(S \to X) + S \Leftrightarrow (S \to ((S \to X) + S) + S)$, and this can be proved from the valid laws for "resource implication" (both in linear logic and in arrow logic) that (both ways:) $S \to X \Leftrightarrow S \to ((S \to X) + S)$.

Chapter 20

1 The only intuitionistically invalid De Morgan law is $\neg(\varphi \wedge \psi) \to (\neg\varphi \vee \neg\psi)$. You can give a simple and illuminating counter-example in a 3-world model with two incomparable successors from the root, one verifying φ only and the other verifying ψ only. The converse implication is intuitionistically valid. A proof of the disjunction $\neg\varphi \vee \neg\psi$ is a proof of one disjunct, say of $\neg\varphi$. But then from any proof of the conjunction $\varphi \wedge \psi$, I can manufacture a contradiction by first deriving φ, and then feeding this into the proof for $\neg\varphi$, which will produce a proof for an absurdity.

2 Intuitionistic propositional logic has the Disjunction Property. This works by "joint rooting" of counter-examples like the similar splitting of valid disjunctions of necessity formulas that held for the minimal modal logic (cf. Chapter 5).

6(a) There is a winning strategy in a dialogue game for the Proponent in defending the two formulas $p \wedge \neg(p \wedge q) \to \neg q$, $((p \to q) \wedge r) \to (p \to (q \wedge r))$. Here is a typical play for the second law (A stands for "attack", D for "defense"):

1	**P**	$((p \to q) \wedge r) \to (p \to (q \wedge r))$	
2	**O**	$(p \to q) \wedge r$	[A,1]
3	**P**	$p \to (q \wedge r)$	[D,2]
4	**O**	p	[A,3]
5	**P**	$q \wedge r$	[D,4]
6	**O**	?L	[A,5]
7	**P**	?L	[A,2]
8	**O**	$p \to q$	[D,7]
9	**P**	p	[A,8]
10	**O**	q	[D,9]
11	**P**	q	[D,6]
12	**O**	?R	[A,5]
13	**P**	?R	[A,2]
14	**O**	r	[D,13]
15	**P**	r	[D,14]

O has nothing legitimate left to say, and loses.

6(b) For Proponent, winning strategies in a dialogue game are *proofs* for the implication from premises to conclusion. For Opponent, winning strategies are *intuitionistic counter-models* verifying the premises but not the conclusion.

7 Intuitionistic predicate logic also has the Heredity property. To make sure that this holds, the existential quantifier gets the same reading as the one in modal predicate logic (Chapter 11), stating existence of a witness in the domain of the current world. The universal quantifier needs stronger force since object domains may grow – and it now says that each object in each domain of an accessible world has the property.

Chapter 21

1(a) Analyzing the Löb variant $\Box(\Box p \leftrightarrow p) \to \Box p$ semantically, you get exactly the same properties as for Löb's Axiom: transitivity and upward well-foundedness. This is surprising, and this variant provability logic axiomatizes a deductively weaker logic with the same frames, a case of "frame incompleteness" (cf. Chapter 26).

1(b) The modal formula $[1]([2]p \rightarrow p) \rightarrow [3]p$ is equivalent on trimodal frames $F = (W, R_1, R_2, R_3)$ to the conjunction of the following two relational conditions: (a) $R_3; (R_2)^* \subseteq R_1$ (with $(R_2)^*$ the reflexive-transitive closure of R_2), (b) "prefix upward well-foundedness" in the following sense: no world x starts an infinite upward sequence of worlds $x R_3 y_1 R_2 y_2 R_2 y_3 \cdots$.

2 Hint: use a finite universe of relevant formulas for the whole construction, and in that setting, show that maximally consistent successor sets that witness existential modalities can be chosen so that the number of relevant true universal modalities increases. The reason is the following equivalent form of the Löb's Axiom: $\Diamond \varphi \rightarrow \Diamond (\varphi \wedge \Box \neg \varphi)$. This special witnessing procedure enforces finite depth.

3 First use the transitive closure modality $[*]$ instead of the regular $\Box$ (this gives the same effect as requiring transitivity of the models for the basic $\Box$ language). Then restrict attention to well-founded models inside the modal μ-calculus by noting that the latter property is defined by the smallest fixed-point formula $\mu p \cdot \Box p$.

Chapter 22

1 To understand the meaning of the μ-calculus formula $\mu p \cdot \Box p$, consider first what the successive approximations do in the well-founded structure $(\mathbb{N}, >)$: you get the empty set, $\{0\}$, $\{0, 1\}$, etcetera. In general, any ordinal α will only be "admitted" in α stages. In general, the sub-model defined here is its "well-founded part": the set of worlds from which there are no infinite downward R-sequences.

2 The soundness of the laws for reasoning with the μ-operator arises as follows. The equation immediately expresses the fixed-point character. The rule say that, as in the proof of the Tarski-Knaster Theorem, the smallest fixed-point is a smallest "prefixed point": i.e., a set closed under applying the approximation map F_φ.

3 The operator $[\pi]\varphi$ of *PDL* is definable as a greatest fixed point by using the definition $[\pi]\varphi = \neg \langle \pi \rangle \neg \varphi$, plus the definition of formulas $\nu q \cdot \varphi(q)$. Or argue directly about the approximation sequence for a greatest fixed-point. This starts allowing all points, and then stepwise removes all points with some obvious "defect". This leaves the largest set of points satisfying the fixed-point equation, and in the case of the universal modality, it removes all points that can reach some $\neg\varphi$-point via the program transition relation (which takes finitely many steps).

4 All formulas of the μ-calculus are invariant for bisimulation. For any model M, its cardinality is an upper bound to the length of "unfolding" any fixed-point in the language. Each step of the approximation procedure for, say, $\mu q \cdot \varphi(q)$ leads to a definable set: $\bot, \varphi(\bot/q), \varphi(\varphi(\bot/q)/q), \ldots$ taking infinite disjunctions at limit steps. Thus, we can write any μ-calculus formula in infinitary modal logic, replacing (working inside out) fixed-point formulas by infinitary counterparts. So, given two models M, N with a bisimulation between them, all formulas are equivalent to their unfolded counterparts up to the maximum of the model sizes, and we can use the known invariance for bisimulation of the infinitary modal language.

5 Deriving $(\Box\varphi \wedge [^*](\varphi \rightarrow \Box\varphi)) \rightarrow [^*]\varphi$ from Löb's Axiom plus the Fixed-Point Axiom $[^*]\varphi \leftrightarrow (\Box\varphi \wedge \Box[^*]\varphi)$ requires a relatively routine unpacking of definitions.

6 Programs are what makes *PDL* so versatile and attractive. But they seem to fit best with an emphasis on finite reachability via some transition relation π. Can we also add programs to the π-calculus after all? Suggestively, a non-*PDL* μ-calculus formula like $\nu q \cdot \langle a \rangle q$, which says that there exists some infinite sequence of a-transitions from the current point ("the program never breaks down") is also naturally associated with a non-terminating program like *WHILE* $\top$ *DO a*. The proper formulation of this broader view seems an open problem.

7 The existence of a smallest fixed-point really depends on the existence of sequences of approximations where each next stage includes the preceding one(s). For, given the fixed cardinality of the specific model that we are computing on, such a sequence cannot keep increasing forever. Monotonicity of the approximation maps F_φ. guarantees this cumulation property, but it is not necessary. The format $F_\varphi(X) = \{ s \in W \mid M, p := X, s \models \varphi \} \cup X$ of the inflationary μ-calculus also guarantees it, and moreover, for monotonic maps, it produces the same results as before.

8 You must show that simultaneous fixed-point equations of the form $\mu pqr \cdots \cdot \vec{\varphi}(p, q, r, \ldots)$ in the μ-calculus yield unique minimal solutions for all predicates $p, q, r, \ldots$ that can be defined explicitly with standard formulas using only iterated single μ-operators. This is not difficult per se, but the combinatorial details are hard, unless you really study some hands-on computations with fixed-points from a textbook.

Chapter 23

1 If player 2 shows his card only to player 1, the resulting model is

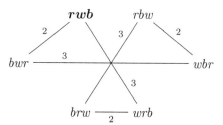

In terms of event models, player 3 remains uncertain between two events: "showing white" and "showing red". This results in the link-cutting outcome displayed here.

2 The successive levels of the tree look as follows. Start with the following epistemic model:

$$\left(P \bullet \xrightarrow{\quad 1 \quad} \circ \, \neg P \right) \qquad M$$

The event model for the given scenario is this:

$$\boxed{P! \text{ (precondition: } P) \xrightarrow{\quad 2 \quad} Id \text{ (precondition: } \top)} \qquad E$$

The next two product levels of $Tree(M, E)$ then become as follows:

$$\left((P, P!) \xrightarrow{\quad 2 \quad} (P, Id) \xrightarrow{\quad 1 \quad} (\neg P, Id) \right) \qquad M \times E$$

$$\left((P, P!, P!) \xrightarrow{2} (P, P, Id) \xrightarrow{2} (P, Id, P!) \xrightarrow{2} (P, Id, Id) \xrightarrow{1} (\neg P, Id, Id) \right)$$

$$M \times E \times E$$

There is an epistemic *bisimulation* between these two levels, connecting the lower three worlds to the left with the single world $(P, P!)$ in $M \times E$. Thus, $M \times E \times E$ is bisimilar with $M \times E$, and the tree iteration is finite modulo bisimulation.

3 If M and E are both transitive, then so is the product model $M \times E$. For, if $(s, e) \sim (t, f) \sim (u, g)$, then by the definition of product update, we have $s \sim t \sim u$, and hence $s \sim u$ by transitivity in M, and also $e \sim f \sim g$, which implies $e \sim g$ by transitivity in E. By product update once more, $(s, e) \sim (u, g)$. This argument fails with linear order. Say, to have that $(s, e) \leq (t, f)$ we need that both $s \leq f$ and $e \leq f$, but even when M and E are both linear, why would the ordering in both cases go the same way? It is easy to also draw concrete counter-examples. One general principle is this: at least those relational conditions on models are preserved that are definable by so-called *universal Horn clauses* $\forall x_1 \cdots \forall x_k (A \to B)$, where A, B are conjunctions of atoms.

5 Perfect Recall implies Synchronicity by a simple induction. First, it immediately rules out that the empty sequence could be $\sim$-related to any longer sequence. Next, if two non-empty histories X, Y are $\sim$-related, then so are the sub-sequences X^-, Y^- of length one less. But by the inductive hypothesis, these already had the same length.

6 A simple principle in the epistemic-temporal language that corresponds to the *DEL* recursion axiom for knowledge is $F_a \Diamond \varphi \leftrightarrow (F_a \top \wedge \Diamond F_a \varphi)$. You can also try to find more sophisticated ones.

7 For *TPAL* on protocol models, the axiom $\langle !P \rangle q \leftrightarrow (\langle !P \rangle \top \wedge q)$ always holds from left to right. And from right to left, if $!P$ is executable according to the protocol, then it will not change truth values of atomic statements. As for the key knowledge axiom $\langle !P \rangle K_i \varphi \leftrightarrow (\langle !P \rangle \top \wedge K_i (\langle !P \rangle \top \wedge \langle !P \rangle \varphi))$, it is a similar adaptation of the *PAL* knowledge axiom, putting executability assertions in the right places.

8 In particular, to formalize the Muddy Children, we need a *common knowledge* modality C_G, and as it stands, we have no *TPAL* analysis for this. More ambitiously, Muddy Children involves a process where implicit distributed knowledge D_G of agents eventually gets turned into common knowledge, so we would need extensions of our temporal languages that can deal with distributed knowledge.

Chapter 24

1 If we can tile the whole plane, then we can obviously tile each finite quadrant. Conversely, given some finite set of tiles, consider a tree whose nodes are tilings for quadrants of successive increasing sizes. Note that this tree is finitely branching, as there are only finitely possible tilings for a quadrant. Note also that the tree has infinitely many nodes. By

Koenig's Lemma, there must be some *infinite branch* through the tree. But such a branch is a tiling of the whole plane!

2 We have discussed this issue in Chapter 7 already: the crucial point in the proof for the *first-order* case is the assertion that the models of the first-order formula *Grid* start with a copy of $\mathbb{N} \times \mathbb{N}$. This requires close scrutiny of the ordering properties that you have written down. In the *modal* version of the result, the tricky step is this. Suppose that the modal formula describing the tiling holds in some abstract grid model M, whose precise nature we do not know. How do we read off a correct tiling from M for the concrete structure $\mathbb{N} \times \mathbb{N}$ in a consistent manner? This requires some care with the function matching worlds in M and pairs (m, n). You may want to check Blackburn et al. (2001).

3(a) We can indeed write in the first-order language that for each position, there is one to the *East* where the given tile occurs, and this makes sure that there are infinitely many occurrences of that tile on the horizontal row in any model for our formula. However, this does not enforce that this infinite repetition already occurs *on the initial segment N* of that row (#). And the latter is what we need to solve the real Recurrent Tiling problem. In fact, given that the high complexity of the latter does not occur with first-order logic, we may conclude that # is not first-order definable!

3(b) Modal logics can have this high complexity, for instance, when we give them non-first-order operators like the *PDL*-modality [*] that run over just the reachable row positions that correspond to standard natural numbers.

4 The temporal logic of the natural numbers with the relations of immediate successor and $\leq$ is decidable using Rabin's Theorem. To see this, observe that (a) that order can be viewed as a very simple tree in the Rabin sense, and (b) the temporal language can be defined in that of the monadic second-order logic with the relevant relations of subsequence and immediate successor.

5 Memory-free epistemic agents only remember the last-observed event. At least if there are only finitely many events, their knowledge modality $K\varphi$ is then definable as $\bigvee_e (P_e\top \wedge U(P_e\top \to \varphi))$, where P_e is the past modality saying that the last event was e, and U is the universal modality. But this means that the epistemic-temporal logic of such agents can be embedded in the pure temporal logic of the tree models, which is usually of much lower complexity.

6(a) Rabin's Theorem fails when trees also have a *simultaneity* relation. We can now describe a grid pattern inside these models using first-order formulas in much the same way as suggested by our "rhomboid" pictures for epistemic temporal logics on tree models with complex *DEL*-style agents. (With more coding acumen, much more unlikely countable structures can be seen to be embedded in the Rabin tree.)

6(b) Against this background, epistemic-temporal logics on trees that might still have low complexity are those that lack modal operators referring to the mixed transitions $(\sim_i; e)^*$ mentioned in the text. A good example of the latter: our standard epistemic-temporal language itself, with common knowledge and future modalities.

Chapter 25

1 We need the "total bisimulations" of Chapter 7 whose domain and range are the whole relevant models. Then the Invariance Theorem has essentially the same formulation as before. In the whole proof, there is only one change (except for checking the invariance): when two ω-saturated models satisfy the same formulas in this extended language, they also have a bisimulation of this stronger sort.

2(a) If φ, ψ are first-order formulas, and α a modal "interpolant" with $\varphi \models \alpha \models \psi$, then, if $M, s \models \varphi$, and there is a bisimulation between M, s and N, t, then $N, t \models \psi$. This looks impressive, but it follows immediately from the definition of valid consequence plus invariance of modal formulas for bisimulation.

2(b) The converse is this: if a first-order formula φ entails a first-order formula ψ along bisimulation, then there exists a modal interpolant α with $\varphi \models \alpha \models \psi$. This can be proved with essentially the same argument as that given for the Modal Invariance Theorem. Now, if a first-order φ is invariant for bisimulation, this says that φ *entails φ itself along bisimulation*. So, there is a modal interpolant α, and that is immediately the required modal equivalent.

3 There is no modal Lindström theorem when we replace invariance for bisimulation by the Löwenheim-Skolem property. For, first-order logic itself is a proper extension of the basic modal language that has both Compactness and the Löwenheim-Skolem property. So, we need to be careful about traditional characterization results for weaker languages. But the observation also suggests new types of theorems, talking about strongest proper extensions of logics satisfying certain properties: see the cited paper by van Benthem, ten Cate & Väänänen.

4 To derive the Modal Invariance Theorem from the Modal Lindström Theorem, start with any first-order formula φ that is invariant for bisimulation. *Add* φ as a new sentence to the basic modal language, and then close up under Boolean operations and relativizations to unary proposition letters. It is easy to show that the result is an abstract modal logic L extending the basic language, satisfying (a) Compactness (since L is a fragment of first-order logic), and (b) Bisimulation Invariance (φ has this property by assumption, Boolean operations and relativizations preserve it). Therefore, by the modal Lindström Theorem, L is contained in the basic modal logic, and in particular, φ was modally definable.

5 The proof of the Modal Lindström Theorem to the modal language with an added universal modality breaks down, because the Finite Depth Lemma fails. For instance, in a tree, the modal formula $U \Diamond \top$ says that each node has successors, and this cannot be enforced at any fixed finite depth. This failure seems significant, and no alternative proof is known for this language, since it is also too weak to mimic the original proof of the Lindström Theorem for first-order logic.

Guide to further literature

The literature on modal logic is vast, and it comes in various forms. We mention a few relevant items, with no attempt at completeness:

Handbooks While handbooks may not be an ideal medium for learning details, they do provide a good sense of a field, as well as credits and extensive strategic references. We have mentioned the *Handbook of Modal Logic* (Blackburn et al., 2006) several times, and its chapters cover much of what has been introduced in these lectures. In addition, much valuable material can be found in the *Handbook of Philosophical Logic* (Gabbay and Günthner, 1983-1989), the *Handbook of Logic in Artificial Intelligence and Logic Programming* (Gabbay et al., 1994), the *Handbook of Spatial Logics* (Aiello et al., 2007), and other handbooks that include modal logic in areas like philosophy, computer science, and game theory. Many of these resources are now available on-line.

Textbooks There are many textbooks in modal logic, with many different slants. You can find them geared to just about every audience, from philosophers to computer scientists, and also, emphasizing different methods, such as formal proof, or algebraic techniques. Of the textbooks congenial to these lectures, Goldblatt (1987) and especially, Blackburn et al. (2001) provide more technical detail, especially on methods for proving completeness. Other attractive textbooks on more specialized topics include Meyer and van Der Hoek (1995), Fagin et al. (1995) (epistemic logic), Huth and Ryan (2000) (logic and computation), and Boolos (1993) (provability logic).

In addition, separate chapters of this book presuppose knowledge of further areas of logic and mathematics. *First-order logic* is well-explained in many textbooks, with Enderton (1971) as an evergreen, and Doets (1996) as a neat model-theoretic version including games. Higher-order logic is explained in the chapter by van Benthem &

Doets in Gabbay and Günthner (1983-1989). For fixed-point logics, see Ebbinghaus and Flum (1995). Decidable fragments of first-order logic are found in Börger et al. (1997), and a logic-friendly introduction to complexity theory is Papadimitriou (1994). A good source on universal algebra is (Burris and Sankappanavar, 1981), and a classic on topology is Dugundji (1966). Osborne and Rubinstein (1994) is an excellent introduction to game theory.

Special monographs The next level is that of heavier-duty monographs with special mathematical perspectives, such as Chagrov and Zakharyaschev (1997), Kracht (1999), Marx and Venema (1997), or many publications from the "London School" of Gabbay and others: cf. Gabbay et al. (2003), Gabbay et al. (2009).

Further sources There are also many internet resources for topics in these lectures, with home pages of special communities like Hybrid Logic, or conferences like

Advances in Modal Logic, http://www.aiml.net/

TARK, http://www.tark.org/

LOFT, http://www.econ.ucdavis.edu/faculty/bonanno/loft.html

The electronic Stanford Encyclopedia of Philosophy,

http://plato.stanford.edu/

has also been mentioned many times. The website supporting this book,

http://www.illc.uva.nl/lgc/MLoM/

will provide more systematic links.

References

Abramsky, Samson. 2008. Information, processes and games. In Adriaans and van Benthem (2008), pages 483–549.

Adriaans, Peter and Johan van Benthem, eds. 2008. *Handbook of the Philosophy of Information*, Amsterdam. Elsevier Science Publishers.

Aiello, Marco, Ian Pratt-Hartmann, and Johan van Benthem, eds. 2007. *Handbook of Spatial Logics*. Dordrecht: Springer. ISBN 978-1-4020-5586-7.

Andréka, Hajnal, István Németi, and Johan van Benthem. 1998. Modal languages and bounded fragments of predicate logic. *Journal of Philosophical Logic* 27(3):217–274.

Artemov, Sergei. 2008. Modal logic and mathematics. In Adriaans and van Benthem (2008), pages 927–969.

Aumann, Robert J. 1976. Agreeing to disagree. *The Annals of Statistics* 4(6):1236–1239.

Ballarin, Roberta. 2008. Modern origins of modal logic. http://plato.stanford.edu/entries/logic-modal/.

Baltag, Alexandru, Lawrence S. Moss, and Hans van Ditmarsch. 2008. Epistemic logic and information update. In Adriaans and van Benthem (2008), pages 361–455.

Barwise, Jon. 1975. *Admissible Sets and Structures*. Berlin: Springer Verlag.

Barwise, Jon and Lawrence S. Moss. 1996. *Vicious Circles: on the mathematics of non-wellfounded phenomena*. Stanford, USA: CSLI Publications.

Barwise, Jon and Johan van Benthem. 1999. Interpolation, preservation, and pebble games. *Journal of Symbolic Logic* 64(2):881–903.

Bergstra, Jan A., Alban Ponse, and Scott A. Smolka, eds. 2007. *Handbook of Process Algebra*. Amsterdam: North-Holland.

Blackburn, Patrick, Maarten de Rijke, and Yde Venema. 2001. *Modal logic*. No. 53 in Cambridge Tracts in Theoretical Computer Science. New York, USA: Cambridge University Press. ISBN 0-521-80200-8.

Blackburn, Patrick, Johan van Benthem, and Frank Wolter, eds. 2006. *Handbook of Modal Logic*. Amsterdam: Elsevier.

Blok, Wim. 1980. On the degree of incompleteness in modal logics and the covering relation in the lattice of modal logics. Tech. Rep. 78-07, Department of Mathematics, University of Amsterdam.

Boolos, George. 1993. *The Logic of Provability*. Cambridge University Press.

Börger, Egon, Erich Grädel, and Yuri Gurevich. 1997. *The Classical Decision Problem*. Perspectives of Mathematical Logic. Berlin: Springer-Verlag. Second printing (Universitext) 2001.

Borghuis, Tijn. 1994. *Coming to Terms with Modal Logic*. Ph.D. thesis, Informatics Department, University of Eindhoven, Eindhoven, The Netherlands.

Burris, Stanley and Hanamantagouda P. Sankappanavar. 1981. *A course in universal algebra*, vol. 78 of *Graduate Texts in Mathematics*. New York: Springer-Verlag. ISBN 0-387-90578-2.

Chagrov, Alexander V. and Michael Zakharyaschev. 1997. *Modal Logic*. Oxford: Clarendon Press.

Chang, Chen Chung and H. Jerome Keisler. 1973. *Model Theory*. Amsterdam: North-Holland.

Doets, Kees. 1996. *Basic Model Theory*. Studies In Logic, Language and Information. Stanford: CSLI Publications.

Dugundji, James. 1966. *Topology*. Allyn and Bacon Inc.

Ebbinghaus, Heinz-Dieter and Jörg Flum. 1995. *Finite Model Theory*. Berlin: Springer.

Enderton, Herbert. 1971. *A Mathematical Introduction to Logic*. New York: Academic Press.

Fagin, Ronald, Joseph Y. Halpern, Yoram Moses, and Moshe Y. Vardi. 1995. *Reasoning about knowledge*. Cambridge, Mass.: The MIT Press.

Freudenthal, Hans. 1960. *LINCOS: Design of a Language for Cosmic Intercourse*. Amsterdam: North-Holland.

Gabbay, Dov M. and Franz Günthner, eds. 1983-1989. *Handbook of Philosophical Logic*. Dordrecht: Kluwer.

Gabbay, Dov M., Christopher J. Hogger, John Alan Robinson, and Jörg H. Siekmann, eds. 1994. *Handbook of Logic in Artificial Intelligence and Logic Programming*. Oxford University Press.

Gabbay, Dov M., Agi Kurucz, Frank Wolter, and Michael Zakharyaschev. 2003. *Many-dimensional modal logics: theory and applications*. No. 148 in Studies in Logic and the Foundations of Mathematics. Elsevier.

Gabbay, Dov M., Valentin B. Shehtman, and Dimitrij Skvortsov. 2009. *Quantification in Nonclassical Logic, Volume I*. No. 153 in Studies in Logic and the Foundations of Mathematics. Amsterdam: Elsevier. ISBN 0-444-52012-0.

Geanakoplos, John D. 1992. Common knowledge. *The Journal of Economic Perspectives* 6(4):53–82.

Geanakoplos, John D. and Heraklis M. Polemarchakis. 1982. We can't disagree forever. *Journal of Economic Theory* 28(1):192–200.

Girard, Patrick. 2008. *Modal Logic for Belief and Preference Change*. Ph.D. thesis, Department of Philosophy, Stanford University, Stanford, CA, USA. ILLC Dissertation Series DS-2008-04.

Goldblatt, Robert. 1987. *Logics of Time and Computation*. Stanford: CSLI Publications. ISBN 0-937073-12-1.

Goldblatt, Robert and Edwin D. Mares. 2006. A general semantics for quantified modal logic. In G. Governatori, I. M. Hodkinson, and Y. Venema, eds., *Advances in Modal Logic*, pages 227–246. College Publications. ISBN 1-904987-20-6.

Halpern, Joseph Y. and Moshe Y. Vardi. 1989. The complexity of reasoning about knowledge and time, I: lower bounds. *Journal of Computer and System Sciences* 38(1):195–237.

Harel, David. 1987. *Algorithmics, the Spirit of Computing*. Reading MA: Addison-Wesley.

Harel, David, Dexter Kozen, and Jerzy Tiuryn. 2000. *Dynamic Logic*. Cambridge, MA: MIT Press. ISBN 0-262-08289-6.

Henkin, Leon, James Donald Monk, and Alfred Tarski. 1985. *Cylindric Algebras, Part II*. North Holland.

Hodges, Wilfrid. 1983. Elementary predicate logic. In D. M. Gabbay and F. Günthner, eds., *Handbook of Philosophical Logic: Volume I: Elements of Classical Logic*, pages 1–131. Dordrecht: Reidel. Reprint, Springer Science Publishers, 2001.

Hughes, George Edward and Max J. Cresswell. 1984. *A Companion to Modal Logic*. London: Methuen.

Huth, Michael and Mark Ryan. 2000. *Logic in Computer Science: Modelling and Reasoning about Systems*. Cambridge, United Kingdom: Cambridge University Press, 2nd edn.

Jacquette, Dale, ed. 2007. *Handbook of the Philosophy of Logic*. Amsterdam: Elsevier.

Jónsson, Bjarni and Alfred Tarski. 1951. Boolean algebras with operators, part I. *American Journal of Mathematics* 73:891–939.

Kaldeway, Anne. 1990. *Programming: the Derivation of Algorithms*. Englewood Cliffs NJ: Prentice Hall.

Keisler, H. Jerome. 1971. *Model Theory for Infinitary Logic*. Amsterdam: North-Holland.

Kracht, Marcus. 1999. *Tools and Techniques in Modal Logic*. No. 142 in Studies in Logic and the Foundations of Mathematics. Amsterdam: Elsevier.

Lenzen, Wolfgan. 1979. *Glauben, Wissen und Wahrscheinlichkeit*. Berlin: Springer.

Liu, Fenrong. 2008. *Changing for the Better. Preference Dynamics and Agent Diversity*. Ph.D. thesis, Institute for Logic, Language and Computation, Universiteit van Amsterdam, Amsterdam, The Netherlands. ILLC Dissertation series DS-2008-02.

Marx, Maarten and Yde Venema. 1997. *Multi-Dimensional Modal Logic*, vol. 4 of *Applied Logic Series*. Kluwer Academic Press.

Mason, Ian A. 1985. The metatheory of the classical propositional calculus is not axiomatizable. *Journal of Symbolic Logic* 50(2):451–457.

Meyer, John-Jules Ch. and Wiebe van Der Hoek. 1995. *Epistemic Logic for AI and Computer Science*. New York, NY, USA: Cambridge University Press. ISBN 0 521 46014 7.

Miller, Joseph S. and Lawrence S. Moss. 2005. The undecidability of iterated modal relativization. *Studia Logica* 79(3):373–407.

Monk, James Donald. 1976. *Mathematical Logic*. New York: Springer.

Németi, István. 1991. Algebraizations of quantifier logics: An introductory overview. *Studia Logica* 50(3-4):485–569. Later extended versions, Mathematical Institute, Hungarian Academy of Sciences, Budapest.

Ono, Hiroakira. 1999. Algebraic semantics for predicate logics and their completeness. In E. Orlowska, ed., *Logic at Work. To the Memory of Elena Rasiowa*. Heidelberg: Physica Verlag.

Osborne, Martin J. and Ariel Rubinstein. 1994. *A Course in Game Theory*. Cambridge, Massachusetts: The MIT Press. ISBN 0262650401.

Papadimitriou, Christos M. 1994. *Computational complexity*. Massachusetts: Addison-Wesley. ISBN 0201530821.

Parikh, Rohit and Ramaswamy Ramanujam. 2003. A knowledge based semantics of messages. *Journal of Logic, Language and Information* 12(4):453–467.

Plantinga, Alvin. 1978. *The Nature of Necessity*. Oxford: Clarendon.

Pratt, Vaughan R. 1976. Semantical considerations on floyd-hoare logic. In *17th Annual Symposium on Foundations of Computer Science, 25-27 October 1976, Houston, Texas, USA*, pages 109–121. IEEE.

Quine, Willard Van Orman. 1966. *Selected Logic Papers*. New York: Random House.

Roy, Olivier. 2008. *Thinking Before Acting. Intentions, Logic, Rational Choice*. Ph.D. thesis, Institute for Logic, Language and Computation, Universiteit van Amsterdam, Amsterdam, The Netherlands. ILLC Dissertation series DS-2008-03.

Steltzner, Werner. 1996. *Gottlob Frege. Jena und die Geburt der modernen Logik*. Verein zur Regional-förderung von Forschung, Innovation und Technologie.

ten Cate, Balder. 2005. *Model theory for extended modal languages*. Ph.D. thesis, Institute for Logic, Language and Computation, Universiteit van Amsterdam, Amsterdam, The Netherlands. ILLC Dissertation Series DS-2005-01.

Troelstra, Anne S. and Dirk van Dalen. 1988. *Constructivism in Mathematics*. Amsterdam: North-Holland Publishing.

Väänänen, Jouko. 2007. *Dependence Logic*. Cambridge: Cambridge University Press.

van Benthem, Johan. 1979. Syntactic aspects of modal incompleteness theorems. *Theoria* 45(2):63–77.

van Benthem, Johan. 1985. *Modal Logic and Classical Logic*. Napoli: Bibliopolis.

van Benthem, Johan. 1988a. *A Manual of Intensional Logic*. Stanford, CA: CSLI, 2nd edn.

van Benthem, Johan. 1988b. A note on jónsson's theorem. *Algebra Universalis* (25):391–393.

van Benthem, Johan. 1993. Modal frame classes revisited. *Fundamenta Informaticae* 18(2/3/4):307–317.

van Benthem, Johan. 1996. *Exploring Logical Dynamics*. Stanford: CSLI Publications.

van Benthem, Johan. 1999. Logic in games, lecture notes. ILLC Amsterdam & Department of Philosophy, Stanford University.

van Benthem, Johan. 2005. Guards, bounds, and generalized semantics. *Journal of Logic, Language and Information* 14(3):263–279.

van Benthem, Johan. 2007a. Computation as conversation. In B. Cooper, B. Löwe, and A. Sorbi, eds., *New Computational Paradigms: Changing Conceptions of What is Computable*, pages 35–58. New York: Springer.

van Benthem, Johan. 2007b. Logic games, from tools to models of interaction. In A. Gupta, R. Parikh, and J. van Benthem, eds., *Logic at the Crossroads*, pages 283–317. Mumbai: Allied Publishers.

van Benthem, Johan and Guram Bezhanishvili. 2007. Modal logics of space. In Aiello et al. (2007), pages 217–298. ISBN 978-1-4020-5586-7.

van Benthem, Johan and Denis Bonnay. 2008. Modal logic and invariance. *Journal of Applied Non-Classical Logics* 18(2-3):153–173.

van Benthem, Johan and Kees Doets. 1983. Higher-order logic. In D. M. Gabbay and F. Günthner, eds., *Handbook of Philosophical Logic: Volume I: Elements of Classical Logic*, pages 275–329. Dordrecht: Reidel. Reprint, Springer Science Publishers, 2001.

van Benthem, Johan and Daisuke Ikegami. 2008. Modal fixed-point logic and changing models. In A. Avron, N. Dershowitz, and A. Rabinovich, eds., *Pillars of Computer Science*, vol. 4800 of *Lecture Notes in Computer Science*, pages 146–165. Springer. ISBN 978-3-540-78126-4.

van Benthem, Johan and Eric Pacuit. 2006. The tree of knowledge in action. In G. Governatori, I. M. Hodkinson, and Y. Venema, eds., *Proceedings of Advances in Modal Logic, 2006 (AiML 2006)*. King's College Press.

van Benthem, Johan, Balder ten Cate, and Jouko Väänänen. 2007. Lindström theorems for fragments of first-order logic. In *LICS '07: Proceedings of the 22nd Annual IEEE Symposium on Logic in Computer Science*, pages 280–292. Washington, DC, USA: IEEE Computer Society. ISBN 0-7695-2908-9.

van Benthem, Johan, Jan van Eijck, and Barteld Kooi. 2006. Logics of communication and change. *Information and Computation* 204(11):1620–1662.

van Ditmarsch, Hans, Wiebe van der Hoek, and Barteld Kooi. 2007. *Dynamic Epistemic Logic*, vol. 337 of *Synthese Library Series*. Springer.

van Otterloo, Sieuwert. 2005. *A Strategic Analysis of Multi-agent Protocols*. Ph.D. thesis, Department of Computer Science, University of Liverpool, Liverpool, United Kingdom. ILLC Dissertation series DS-2005-05.

Venema, Yde. 2006. Algebras and coalgebras. In Blackburn et al. (2006), pages 331–426.

Index